Beginning jQuery 2 for ASP.NET Developers

Using jQuery 2 with ASP.NET Web Forms and ASP.NET MVC

Bipin Joshi

Apress®

Beginning jQuery 2 for ASP.NET Developers: Using jQuery 2 with ASP.NET Web Forms and ASP.NET MVC

ISBN-13 (pbk): 978-1-4302-6304-3

ISBN-13 (electronic): 978-1-4302-6305-0

President and Publisher: Paul Manning
Lead Editor: Gwenan Spearing
Technical Reviewer: Alex Thissen
Editorial Board: Steve Anglin, Mark Beckner, Ewan Buckingham, Gary Cornell, Louise Corrigan,
    James DeWolf Jonathan Gennick, Jonathan Hassell, Robert Hutchinson, Michelle Lowman, James Markham,
    Matthew Moodie, Jeff Olson, Jeffrey Pepper, Douglas Pundick, Ben Renow-Clarke, Dominic Shakeshaft,
    Gwenan Spearing, Matt Wade, Steve Weiss
Coordinating Editor: Anamika Panchoo
Copy Editor: Nancy Sixsmith
Compositor: SPi Global
Indexer: SPi Global
Artist: SPi Global
Cover Designer: Anna Ishchenko

Distributed to the book trade worldwide by Springer Science+Business Media New York, 233 Spring Street, 6th Floor, New York, NY 10013. Phone 1-800-SPRINGER, fax (201) 348-4505, e-mail orders-ny@springer-sbm.com, or visit www.springeronline.com. Apress Media, LLC is a California LLC and the sole member (owner) is Springer Science + Business Media Finance Inc (SSBM Finance Inc). SSBM Finance Inc is a Delaware corporation.

For information on translations, please e-mail rights@apress.com, or visit www.apress.com.

Apress and friends of ED books may be purchased in bulk for academic, corporate, or promotional use. eBook versions and licenses are also available for most titles. For more information, reference our Special Bulk Sales–eBook Licensing web page at www.apress.com/bulk-sales.

Any source code or other supplementary materials referenced by the author in this text is available to readers at www.apress.com. For detailed information about how to locate your book's source code, go to www.apress.com/source-code/.

At the holy feet of Lord Shiva.

—Bipin Joshi

Contents at a Glance

Contents

About the Author

Bipin Joshi is an author, blogger, and IT trainer who writes about seemingly unrelated topics: yoga and technology! He conducts professional training programs to help developers learn .NET and web technologies better and faster. Bipin has been programming since 1995 and has worked with the .NET framework since its inception. He is a published author and has authored or co-authored more than a half-dozen books and numerous articles on .NET technologies. He runs `http://www.binaryintellect.net`, a web site dedicated to articles, tutorials, and code samples on ASP.NET and other cutting-edge web technologies. Bipin was a Microsoft Most Valuable Professional (MVP) and a Microsoft Certified Trainer (MCT) during 2002–2008. Bipin has also penned a few books on yoga. Having embraced the yoga way of life, he enjoys the intoxicating presence of God and writes about yoga on his blog. He can be reached at `http://www.bipinjoshi.com`.

About the Technical Reviewer

Alex Thissen has spent several years working as a Microsoft Certified Trainer and trained and coached many developers in small and large development teams. Currently, he is principal architect for the largest insurance company in The Netherlands. He started working with the .NET Framework in 2001 during the early betas. Alex has written various articles for a number of magazines such as the Dutch .NET Magazine, SDN Magazine, Office Magazine and Visual Basic Group and is a book reviewer for Apress.

He is a frequent speaker at events from community groups like Software Developer Network, VBCentral, and DotNed. He also makes a regular appearance at Microsoft events and is an international speaker for INETA. He likes just about anything related to .NET, but tries to focus on web application development with a mix of architecture, technology and security.

Alex is Microsoft Regional Director for The Netherlands and has received the Microsoft MVP award for Visual C# since 2007.

Acknowledgments

Although the name of an author alone appears on the book, many contribute to the process directly or indirectly. I must express my deep feeling of devotion toward Lord Shiva. Without His blessings and yogic teachings, this would not have been possible.

Writing a book is about teamwork. Input from the technical reviewer, Alex Thissen, was very useful in rendering the book accurate. The whole team at Apress was very helpful. Thank you, team, for playing your part wonderfully.

Introduction

Welcome to the exciting world of jQuery! If you're an ASP.NET developer looking to turbocharge your ASP.NET applications with jQuery, you picked the right book. Modern web applications leverage browsers' resources through client-side scripting. Although JavaScript is a *de facto* standard as far as client-side scripting is concerned, there are several libraries built on top of JavaScript that help developers accomplish their job quickly and easily. jQuery is one of the most popular JavaScript libraries available today. If you want to develop Ajax-driven, dynamic, and cross-browser web applications using ASP.NET, understanding jQuery is an invaluable skill.

While using jQuery in ASP.NET Web Forms and ASP.NET MVC projects, you need to combine the power of jQuery with server controls, controllers, services, and APIs. It is crucial to understand how jQuery can be used effectively in combination with ASP.NET features and technologies.

To that end, this book teaches you how to harness the power of the jQuery library in your ASP.NET Web Forms and MVC applications. It helps you understand the foundations of jQuery from the perspective of an ASP.NET developer in a clear, step-by-step way, so that you can quickly ensure you have this invaluable skill under your belt.

Who This Book Is For

This book is for ASP.NET web developers who want to tap the power of jQuery in their existing or new web applications. This book doesn't teach you ASP.NET features. I assume that you're already comfortable working with ASP.NET and doing web application development in general.

All the code samples discussed in this book use C# as the server-side programming language, so you should also know C#. Although no prior knowledge of jQuery is expected, I assume that you're familiar with the basics of JavaScript.

The examples illustrated throughout the book use SQL Server and Entity Framework. Although you need not have a detailed understanding of these technologies, you should at least be familiar with them.

The book uses Visual Studio as the development tool. You should know how to work with Visual Studio to perform basic tasks such as creating projects and debugging code.

Software Required

To work through the examples in this book, you need the following software:

- Visual Studio 2013
- SQL Server 2012
- jQuery, jQuery UI, and jQuery Mobile library files
- Web browsers: Internet Explorer 9+, Firefox, Chrome, Opera, and Safari

Although I used Visual Studio Ultimate 2013 to develop the book's examples, most of the examples can also be developed using Visual Studio Express 2013 for Web.

All the data-driven examples were developed using SQL Server 2012 Express Edition. I use the Northwind sample database in many examples, and I suggest you install it. You can download the Northwind database and its script from the MSDN downloads web site.

I used jQuery 2.0.3 to write the examples presented in this book. You should consider downloading the latest versions of jQuery, jQuery UI, and jQuery Mobile from their official web sites.

It's always a good idea to test the client scripts you write in all the major browsers. So you might consider installing the latest versions of Internet Explorer, Firefox, Chrome, Opera, and Safari.

How This Book Is Structured

This book is organized into 11 chapters and one appendix. Here's a quick overview:

- *Chapter 1* gives you a quick recap of JavaScript programming. You can brush up on your JavaScript skills before taking on jQuery.

- *Chapter 2* gives you a peek into jQuery. You learn the basics, such as downloading and installing jQuery on your machine. You also develop a simple application in ASP.NET Web Forms and MVC.

- *Chapter 3* gives you a detailed understanding of jQuery selectors. You learn to match DOM elements using powerful and flexible selectors. This chapter also details techniques to deal with server controls while selecting them in the jQuery code.

- *Chapter 4* teaches you one of the most commonly used features: event handling. It covers commonly used events such as window, keyboard, and mouse events. Some advanced concepts relating to event handling, such as passing custom data to the event handler, are also covered.

- *Chapter 5* is about DOM manipulation using jQuery. Topics covered include applying CSS styles, working with attributes, and manipulating DOM elements.

- *Chapter 6* covers DOM navigation and filtering techniques, including tree traversal, iterating, searching, working with custom data attributes, and more.

- *Chapter 7* teaches you how to apply jQuery effects and animations to Web Form controls and page elements. You learn to apply fancy effects such as fade-in, fade-out, slide-up and slide-down. You also learn to apply custom animation effects to page elements.

- *Chapter 8* covers an important topic: Ajax techniques offered by jQuery. This chapter discusses how ASMX web services, WCF services, MVC action methods, and the Web API can be called from the jQuery code. It also discusses the JSON format and its use in Ajax communication.

- *Chapter 9* discusses plugins—a technique to extend the jQuery core. You can develop plugins to enhance and extend the core functionality offered by jQuery. The chapter discusses the steps involved in building a plugin and gives you some recommendations to be followed during the process.

- *Chapter 10* gives you an overview of jQuery UI and jQuery Mobile. jQuery UI provides various widgets that you can add to ASP.NET web applications to provide professional user interface elements such as dialogs, menus, accordions, and sliders. jQuery Mobile helps you develop web applications targeted at mobile devices.

- *Chapter 11* presents a few recipes that you will find useful in real-world applications. The recipes covered include implementing Ajax-based paging, client-side sorting, file upload, autocomplete text box, and cascading drop-down lists.

- The Appendix lists some jQuery learning resources.

Downloading the Source Code

The complete source code for the book is available for download at the book's companion web site. Visit http://www.apress.com and go to the book's information page at http://www.apress.com/9781430263043. You can then download the source code from the Source Code/Downloads section.

Contacting the Author

You can reach me via my web site: http://www.binaryintellect.net. You can also follow me on popular social-networking web sites such as Facebook and Twitter (visit my web site for details).

CHAPTER 1

■ ■ ■

The JavaScript You Need to Know

JavaScript is a programming language that adds interactivity and dynamic content to otherwise static HTML pages. Behind most fancy frills such as mouseover effects, animations, drop-down menus, and form validations, you will usually find JavaScript being used in some way or another. jQuery is a JavaScript library that simplifies your client-side programming tasks and uses the same programming constructs as JavaScript for variables, branching, and looping. While writing jQuery code, you often need to use these JavaScript programming constructs. Therefore, before you delve into jQuery programming, you must refresh your JavaScript skills. This chapter is intended to give you a quick overview of commonly used JavaScript features so that you can use the knowledge gained in this chapter in the remainder of the book. If you are already familiar with JavaScript, you can skip this chapter, or glance over its content and jump to the next chapter.

Specifically, you will learn how to do the following:

- Understand basic programming constructs used in JavaScript for branching and looping

- Work with JavaScript variables and data types

- Use built-in string, number, and date functions

- Create and use your own functions

■ **Note** Although this chapter is intended to give you an overview of the JavaScript language, it does not cover all JavaScript features. For more information on JavaScript programming, see https://developer.mozilla.org/en-US/docs/Web/JavaScript.

Your First JavaScript Program

In this section, you will develop a simple ASP.NET Web Form that makes use of JavaScript to seek a confirmation from the end user. Although the application is not very sophisticated, it does throw light on some basics of JavaScript. Figure 1-1 shows the Web Form you will develop.

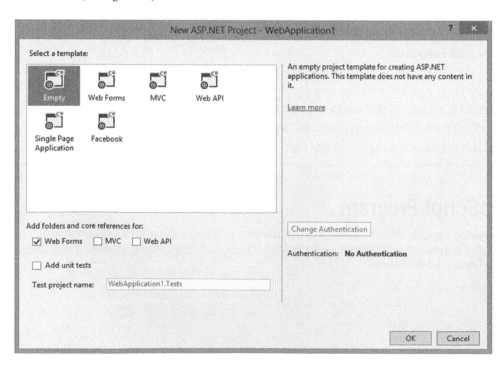

Figure 1-1. *Your first JavaScript program*

As shown in Figure 1-1, the Web Form consists of a couple of Label controls, a TextBox, and a Button server control. Once you enter a name and hit the Submit button, a confirmation dialog is shown that seeks your consent to submit the form. Depending on your choice, either the form submission is canceled or the form is submitted to the server. Upon postback, the entered name is displayed in a Label control.

To begin developing this application, create a new ASP.NET Web Application based on the Empty project template using Visual Studio (see Figure 1-2).

Figure 1-2. *Creating a new ASP.NET Empty Web Application using Visual Studio*

Add a new Web Form to the project and name it **FirstJS.aspx**. Design the Web Form as shown in Figure 1-1 by dragging and dropping the respective server controls from the toolbox. The HTML and server control markup of the Web Form is shown in Listing 1-1.

Listing 1-1. Markup of FirstJS.aspx

```
<%@ Page Language="C#" AutoEventWireup="true" CodeBehind="FirstJS.aspx.cs" Inherits="Chapter_01.
FirstJS" %>
...

<body>
    <form id="form1" runat="server">
        <h1>First JavaScript Program</h1>
        <asp:Label ID="Label1" runat="server" Text="Enter your name :"></asp:Label>
        <br />
        <br />
        <asp:TextBox ID="TextBox1" runat="server"></asp:TextBox>
        <br />
        <br />
        <asp:Button ID="Button1" runat="server" Text="Submit" OnClick="Button1_Click" />
        <br /><br />
        <asp:Label ID="Label2" runat="server" Font-Bold="True" ForeColor="Red"></asp:Label>
    </form>
</body>
</html>
```

The markup contains two Label controls: one that acts as the prompt for the name text box, and the other that is placed below the Submit button. The server-side click event handler of Button1 simply outputs the name entered by the user in Label2. Listing 1-2 shows this event handler.

Listing 1-2. Submit Button Server-Side Click Event Handler

```
protected void Button1_Click(object sender, EventArgs e)
{
  Label2.Text = "Hello " + TextBox1.Text;
}
```

So far, the application doesn't use any JavaScript. In the next step, you add some JavaScript code that is invoked when the user clicks the Submit button. To do so, modify the markup of the Submit button as shown here:

```
<asp:Button ID="Button1" runat="server" Text="Submit" OnClientClick="return confirmName();" ... />
```

You can add the OnClientClick attribute in two ways: you can either switch to the source view of Visual Studio IDE and key in the markup shown in bold letters, or set the OnClientClick property of Button1 in the Properties window. The OnClientClick property is used to specify the client-side (JavaScript) code that is to be executed when the button is clicked. In this case, you set the OnClientClick property to return confirmName(). confirmName() is a custom JavaScript function that you will write next.

Go into the <head> section of the Web Form and add a <script> block, as shown in Listing 1-3.

Listing 1-3. confirmName() Function

```
<script type="text/javascript">
  function confirmName() {
    var textbox = document.getElementById("TextBox1");
    var flag = window.confirm("You entered : " + textbox.value + "\n\nDo you wish to continue?");
    if (flag) {
      return true;
    }
    else {
      return false;
    }
  }
</script>
```

The `<script>` block shown in Listing 1-3 contains a custom JavaScript function named `confirmName()`. The `confirmName()` function is intended to seek confirmation from the end user and accordingly cancel or continue with the form submission. First, it grabs a reference to the text box using the `getElementById()` method of the document object. The `document` object represents the current web page loaded in the browser window. The `getElementById()` method accepts an ID of an HTML element and returns a Document Object Model (DOM) object representing the element. The return object is stored in a JavaScript variable named `textbox`. Notice the use of the `var` keyword to declare a variable.

■ **Note**   The Document Object Model, or DOM, is a tree structure of the entire HTML page loaded in the browser window. Each HTML element from the page has a corresponding object in the DOM tree that can be used to manipulate the underlying HTML element.

The next line declares a JavaScript variable named `flag` to store the return value of a built-in function: `window.confirm()`. The `confirm()` function belongs to the `window` object and allows you to display a dialog to the user with a developer-defined message. The dialog has OK and Cancel buttons. If the user selects OK, `confirm()` returns a Boolean value of true; otherwise, it returns false. The `window` object represents the container of the document being displayed (the browser window or a tab in which the page is loaded).

In this example, you display the name entered by the user. Notice the use of the escape sequence \n\n in the message string to add new lines in the message. The `value` property of the text box DOM element returns the text entered in the text box. An if-else block checks the `flag` variable. If `flag` is true, the `if` block returns true; otherwise, the `else` block returns false. Depending on the value returned by the `confirmName()` function, the form is submitted (true) or the form submission is canceled (false).

■ **Note**   Although `confirm()` is a method of the `window` object, in most of the browsers you can simply call it as if it were a stand-alone function. So, `window.confirm()` and `confirm()` mean the same thing in your JavaScript code.

Refer to Figure 1-1 again. Can you see the timestamp printed in the footer of the Web Form? That's the job of another `<script>` block that you place just above the `</body>` (the end body tag). Listing 1-4 shows this `<script>` block.

Listing 1-4. Outputting the Timestamp in the Page Footer

```
...
...
  </form>
  <script type="text/javascript">
    document.write("<hr />");
    document.write("Page rendered on " + new Date().toString());
  </script>
</body>
```

This time, you use another method of the document object: `write()`. The `write()` method accepts a string and writes it in the document at the place where the call to `write()` is placed. In this case, the first call to `write()` outputs a horizontal rule; the second call outputs the timestamp. Notice how the timestamp is obtained: you use the JavaScript Date object and invoke its `toString()` method to get a string representation of the current date and time.

This completes your code. Run the Web Form in the browser, enter a name in the text box, and click the Submit button. Figure 1-3 shows a sample run of the Web Form.

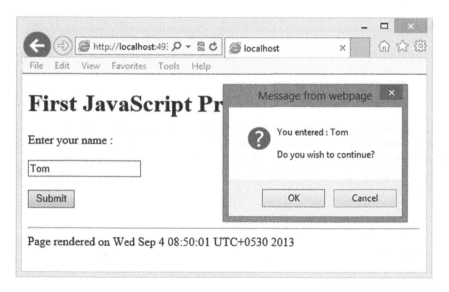

Figure 1-3. *Sample run of the Web Form*

Notice that the name entered by the user is displayed, followed by new lines and then the message seeking confirmation.

Basic Programming Constructs

Like most other programming languages such as C# and Visual Basic, JavaScript has its own language constructs. These constructs form the building blocks for writing simple to complex programs. By using these constructs, you accomplish programming tasks such as conditional execution of your code and looping. This section discusses some constructs you will use every day while working with JavaScript.

Statements

A JavaScript program consists of one or more statements. Simply put, a *statement* is an instruction to the JavaScript engine to do something. Every statement ends with a semicolon (;). For example, here are a couple of statements:

```
document.write("Hello World!");
var textbox = document.getElementById("TextBox1");
```

The first statement uses the `write()` method of the `document` object to output a string: `Hello World!` The second statement declares a variable named `textbox` and stores a reference to the `TextBox1` DOM element in it.

Comments

Comments are used to add explanatory text to your program. As a good developer, you should place comments in your code so that you and fellow developers can understand the code at some later stage. JavaScript has two types of comments: single line comments and block comments. The syntax for both of them is exactly the same as C# commenting syntax. The following example makes it clear:

```
// this is a single line comment

/*
This is a block comment
That can span multiple lines
*/
```

Keep in mind that JavaScript code gets downloaded from the web server to the client browser. Every line of comment that you add to the code also adds to the overall network bandwidth, so you should use ASP.NET's "minification" feature to strip away comments to make the resulting code compact and tidy. Of course, during development you can place comments as required to ease the overall debugging experience and apply minification to the release version of the JavaScript code.

■ **Note** *Minification* of JavaScript involves many steps, including removal of white spaces, new line characters, comments, and so on. Of course, the minification process preserves the original functionality of the code.

Built-in Functions

Earlier in this chapter, you created a function called `confirmName()`. This was a developer defined function. JavaScript also has several built-in functions that you can use in your code. Just like any .NET Framework method, a JavaScript function encapsulates certain functionality so you need not rewrite it. For example, the `confirmName()` function that you created earlier uses a built-in function, `confirm()`, which displays a developer defined message to the end user and seeks confirmation in the form of OK and Cancel. Two more JavaScript functions that you will find yourself using often are `alert()` and `prompt()`.

Let's modify the `confirmName()` function to use these two functions. Listing 1-5 shows the modified `confirmName()` function that makes use of `alert()` and `prompt()`.

Listing 1-5. Using alert() and prompt()

```javascript
function confirmName() {
  var textbox = document.getElementById("TextBox1");
  alert("You will now be asked to enter your name.");
  var enteredName = prompt("Please enter your name below:", "name goes here...");
  var flag = confirm("You entered : " + enteredName + "\n\nDo you wish to continue?");
  if (flag) {
      textbox.value = enteredName;
   return true;
  }
  else {
    return false;
  }
}
```

Notice the lines marked in bold. The first line uses alert() to display a message box to the user with a specified text. The alert dialog has an OK button. The second line uses the prompt() function to prompt the user to enter a name. The prompt() function displays a dialog with a text box and has OK and Cancel buttons. The two parameters supplied to prompt() are the prompt text and a default value for the text box. Figure 1-4 shows how these two dialogs are displayed in Chrome.

Figure 1-4. *The alert() and prompt() functions displayed in Chrome*

Notice that the prompt dialog displays a default value in the text box. Once the user clicks OK, the prompt() function returns the entered value (or the default value if the user didn't make any changes). If the user clicks Cancel, prompt() returns null. In the previous example, after the user clicks the OK button of the prompt dialog, you seek a confirmation from the user about the form submission. If a user wants to submit the form, you assign the enteredName to the text box's value property. This way, the server-side code still finds the value entered by the user in the prompt dialog.

■ **Tip**   JavaScript contains many built-in objects and functions. This section merely touches on a few of them. As you continue through the book, you will come across other built-in functions that will be discussed.

Data Types

Unlike .NET languages such as C# and Visual Basic, JavaScript doesn't offer a plethora of data types. Broadly speaking, data involved in JavaScript can be of the string, number, Boolean, and object data types.

String

The string data type is used often in JavaScript programs. JavaScript strings are enclosed in either double quotes ("...") or single quotes ('...'). This is unlike C#, in which strings are always enclosed in double quotes, and a character is enclosed in single quotes. A string enclosed in quotes can include quotes as part of the string data. However, you need to use the escape character (\) to embed quotes into a string. The following are a few examples of JavaScript strings:

```
"Hello World!"
'Hello Universe!'
"Hello 'Tom'"
'Hello "Jerry"'
"Hello \"Tom & Jerry\""
```

The first two examples are quite straightforward. The third string embeds single quotes inside a double quote, and the third string embeds double quotes inside single quotes. Although this process doesn't create any problem for the code, if you want to embed double quotes in a string that uses double quotes as the enclosure, you need to escape the embedded double-quote characters (as shown in the last example). The same principle applies to single-quote characters embedded in a string enclosed by single quotes.

Number

Just like C#, you can use numbers in JavaScript. Unlike C#, in which there are different data types such as int, float, decimal, and double to represent a number, JavaScript treats all types of numeric values as numbers. A number can be an integer or a floating point number, and it can be positive or negative. Unlike strings, numbers don't use enclosures. Following are a few examples of JavaScript numbers:

```
100
1.23
-200
```

Boolean

Boolean data types can hold one of the two values: true or false. Commonly Boolean values are used while conditionally checking something. They are also used as flags to indicate some state within a program. JavaScript Boolean values are quite similar to the C# bool data type.

Object

In addition to the string, number, and Boolean data types, JavaScript code often uses objects. An object can be built-in or developer defined. For example, while working with dates and times, you use the JavaScript Date object. While making Ajax calls to the server you often send and receive data as a custom object. These are developer defined objects and are often referred to as JavaScript Object Literals or plain objects.

Variables

In .NET languages such as C#, you normally declare a variable of a specific data type to store some value. For example, a variable of type int is declared in C# as follows:

```
int a = 100;
```

Unlike C#, JavaScript doesn't allow you to declare a variable with a specific data type; it has the keyword var for declaring any type of variable. Depending on whether you store a string, a number, or a Boolean value in the variable, it is treated as a string, a number, or a Boolean. Consider the following variables:

```
var name = "Tom";
var age = 25;
var flag = true;
```

In the preceding example, name is a string variable, age is a numeric variable, and flag is a Boolean variable. It is not necessary to assign a value to a variable at the time of declaring it. If no value is assigned to a variable, it is treated as undefined. Have a look at the following code fragment:

```
var myvariable;
alert(typeof myvariable);
myvariable = "Tom";
alert(typeof myvariable);
myvariable = 100;
alert(typeof myvariable);
```

The first line of the code block declares a variable named myvariable. It then uses alert() and the typeof operator to display the type of the variable. Because myvariable is not yet assigned, the first alert() displays 'undefined'. Then the code assigns a string "Tom" to myvariable, and the second alert() displays the type of myvariable as 'string'. Then a value of 100 is assigned to myvariable, and the third alert() displays the type of myvariable as 'number'. Notice that the same variable is treated first as a string and then as a number, depending on the value it holds.

■ **Caution** Although you can store different types of data in the same variable (string and number, for example), you should avoid doing so because it makes your code hard to understand and can introduce errors that are difficult to trace.

Although you can name your JavaScript variables anything you want, the names you choose must adhere to the following basic rules:

- Just like C#, JavaScript variable names are case sensitive (e.g., FNAME and fname are treated as different variables).

- Variable names can contain only letters, numbers, _, and $ (e.g., age, _fname, $age2),

- Variable names must begin with a letter, _, or $ (e.g., 123age is an invalid variable name).

■ **Caution**   It is important that you give readable and meaningful names to JavaScript variables; otherwise, your code may become difficult to understand. Also, use a consistent naming convention for your variables throughout the application.

Arrays

JavaScript arrays allow you to store multiple values together in the form of a list. An array consists of zero or more items called elements. Each element is capable of storing a value. An array element can be accessed by its sequence number, called the *array index*, which starts from 0 (the first element can be accessed at index 0, the second at index 1, and so on). The total number of elements in an array is referred to as its length or size. Although JavaScript arrays are similar to C# arrays in many ways, C# arrays are fixed in size, and you can't add or remove array elements dynamically. JavaScript allows you to add or remove elements even after an array is declared, dynamically changing its size.

Arrays come in handy when you are dealing with too many variables that are related. For example, suppose that you are dealing with a calendaring application that deals with month names. One option is to declare 12 independent variables to hold the month names (January, February, and so on). Although this is possible, doing so makes your code difficult because you need to track 12 different variables. Alternatively you can declare an array and store all 12 month names in it. Another example is when you don't know the number of variables in advance. In such cases, arrays can be useful because you can dynamically add data to them.

To understand how arrays are created and used, let's develop a simple Web Form (see Figure 1-5).

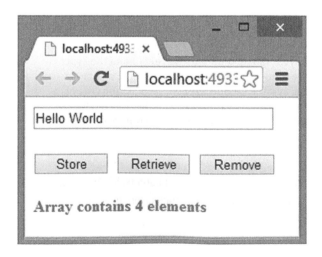

Figure 1-5. *Web Form dealing with arrays*

As shown in Figure 1-5, the Web Form consists of a text box and three button controls. Clicking the Store button stores the value specified in the text box into an array. The text box serves two purposes: it specifies a string that gets stored in the array and specifies an array index while retrieving an array element. Clicking the Remove button removes the last array element (the array gets truncated from the bottom, one element at a time). Clicking the Retrieve button retrieves an array element whose index is specified in the text box. At the bottom of the Web Form is a Label control that displays the total number of elements in the array at a given point in time. Listing 1-6 shows the relevant markup from the Web Form.

Listing 1-6. Markup of Web Form Dealing with Arrays

```
<form id="form1" runat="server">
  <asp:TextBox ID="TextBox1" runat="server" Width="235px"></asp:TextBox>
  <br />
  <br />
  <asp:Button ID="Button1" runat="server" OnClientClick="return storeData();" Text="Store" Width="75px" />
  <asp:Button ID="Button2" runat="server" OnClientClick="return retrieveData();" Text="Retrieve"
Width="75px" />
  <asp:Button ID="Button4" runat="server" OnClientClick="return removeData();" Text="Remove"
Width="75px" />
  <br />
  <br />
  <asp:Label ID="Label1" runat="server" Font-Bold="True" ForeColor="Red"></asp:Label>
</form>
```

Notice the OnClientClick property of the button controls. It is set to call the storeData(), retrieveData(), and removeData() JavaScript functions, respectively. These three functions go in a <script> block placed in the head section of the Web Form (see Listing 1-7).

Listing 1-7. Declaring and Manipulating an Array

```
var myData = ["This","is","Array"];

function storeData() {
  var data = document.getElementById("TextBox1").value;
  myData.push(data);
  document.getElementById("Label1").innerHTML = "Array contains " + myData.length + " elements";
  return false;
}

function retrieveData() {
  var index = document.getElementById("TextBox1").value;
  alert(myData[index]);
  return false;
}

function removeData() {
  myData.pop();
  document.getElementById("Label1").innerHTML = "Array contains " + myData.length + " elements";
  return false;
}
```

The code begins by declaring an array variable named myData. Notice how myData is initialized to some default values. You use [and] to enclose all the initial elements that go in the array. In this case, you store three string elements: This, is, and Array, respectively. If you want to create an empty array, you can use [] (square brackets without any default values). There is an alternative syntax for declaring an array:

```
var myData = new Array("This","is","Array");
```

This line does the same thing as before, but uses an Array object and its constructor to specify initial elements. The myData variable is declared globally because you need to access it in all three functions.

■ **Tip** For the sake of simplicity, this example doesn't perform any checks to see whether the array indexes are within permissible values. In a real-world application, of course, you will add such checks and associated error handling.

The storeData() function stores user-specified values in the myData array. It first grabs the value entered by the user into the text box using the getElementById() method and value property. It then calls the push() method on the array. The push() method accepts a new element and adds it at the bottom of the array. Notice how the number of elements in the array is displayed. The length property of myData returns the total number of elements in the array. You then display this count in the Label. To set the Label value, use the innerHTML property of the Label1 DOM element.

The retrieveData() function retrieves an array element based on an index entered in the text box. First, it grabs the index entered in the text box and stores it in a variable named index. It then retrieves an array element at that index using the myData[index] syntax. So, if a user enters 2 in the text box, myData[2] returns the third element from the array. The array element thus retrieved is displayed to the user using an alert().

The removeData() function calls the pop() method on myData. The pop() method removes the last element from the array. In other words, it truncates the array one element at a time. removeData() then displays the total number of array elements again.

All three functions—storeData(), retrieveData(), and removeData()—return false because you don't want to submit the form in this example.

■ **Tip** The unshift() and shift() methods are similar to push() and pop(). The unshift() method adds an array element at the beginning of the array, and the shift() method removes an element from the beginning.

Conditional Checking

One of the most frequently needed tasks in a JavaScript program is checking for some condition. For example, you may want to see whether values entered in various form controls have the appropriate format (valid e-mail, URLs, phone numbers, and so on) so you can proceed with or cancel the form submission. Just like C#, JavaScript has an if-else construct to check for conditions. The following code fragment shows a simple if-else block:

```
var textbox = document.getElementById("TextBox1");
if (textbox.value == "Blue")
{
  //display something in blue color
}
else
{
  //display something in default color
}
```

The code consists of an if-else block that checks a value entered in a text box for some condition. The `if` keyword is followed by a condition in brackets. In this case, the condition says "If the textbox value is equal to Blue, perform some developer defined task". You can have multiple conditions in the `if` block, as shown here:

```
if(textbox.value == "Blue" || textbox.value == "Red")
{
  //do something
}
```

This example uses the OR operator (||). Other operators are summarized in Table 1-1.

Table 1-1. *Comparison Operators*

Operator	Name	Description
==	Equal to	Compares two values for equality.
!=	Not equal to	Checks whether two values are not the same.
>	Greater than	Checks whether the value on the left side is greater than the value on the right side.
<	Less than	Checks whether the value on the left side is less than the value on the right side.
>=	Greater than or equal to	Checks whether the value on the left is greater than or equal to the value on the right side.
<=	Less than or equal to	Checks whether the value on the left side is less than or equal to the value on the right side.
===	Strict equal to	Checks the left side and right sides not only for equality of value but also for equality of data type. For example, if(3=="3") evaluates to true because the value is the same. However, if(3==="3") evaluates to false because although the values are the same, their data types aren't. The left side is a number; the right side is a string.
!==	Strict not equal to	Compares values as well as data types of the left and right sides for inequality. For example, if(3!= "3") evaluates to false, and if(3!== "3") evaluates to true because of different data types.

Notice the `Strict equal to` and `Strict not equal to` operators shown in Table 1-1. They don't have any direct equivalent in C#. Although the normal `Equal to` and `Not equal to` operators compare values, these operators compare data types as well as values.

The `else` block specifies a piece of code that you want to execute if the condition specified in the `if` block evaluates to false. You can have a series of conditions specified using if-else if-else blocks, as shown here:

```
if (textbox.value == "Blue")
{
  //some code here
}
```

```
else if (textbox.value == "Red")
{
  //some code here
}
else if (textbox.value == "Green")
{
  //some code here
}
else
{
  //some code here
}
```

In this case, you first check whether the textbox value is Blue; if not, you then check whether it is Red, and so on. If none of the conditions matches, the code in the else block is executed.

Although a series of if-else if-else blocks is a great way to check for multiple conditions in sequence, there is an alternative that you can use: the switch statement. It allows you to compare a source value against a series of target values and then a block of code is executed according to the matched value. You can use string, number, or Boolean types in switch statements, but they always check the values using the equality operator. The following example shows how the same if-else if-else block can be rewritten using a switch statement:

```
switch(textbox.value)
{
  case "Blue":
    // some code here
    break;
  case "Red":
    // some code here
    break;
  case "Green":
    // some code here
    break;
  default:
    // some code here
}
```

A switch statement has one or more case blocks and an optional default block. Each case block contains code for that specific value (Blue, Red, and so on). The previous code checks whether the value entered in the textbox equals Blue, Red, or Green. Accordingly, the appropriate code block is executed.

If the value is other than Blue, Red, or Green, code from the default block is executed. Notice the break statement at the end of each case block. If you forget to include the break statement, the execution runs through that block, but instead of halting before the next case, it continues with the following case until a break is found or until the end of the switch statement is reached.

Looping

JavaScript programs often need to perform repetitive tasks, which is where *looping* comes into the picture. JavaScript looping constructs allow you to execute the same set of instructions repeatedly until some condition evaluates to true. There are three looping constructs in JavaScript:

- while loop

- do-while loop

- for loop

A while loop executes a block of code as long as a certain condition evaluates to true. For example, consider the following while loop that iterates through all the array elements of an array named myData:

```
var i = 0;
while (i < myData.length) {
  //do something here
  i++;
}
```

Here, you declare a variable named i that holds an initial value of 0. You then run a while loop. The terminating condition for the while loop says, "Run this loop while i is less than the length of the myData array. Thus, if myData contains three elements, the code inside the while loop is executed three times. It is important to increment the value of i inside the while loop; otherwise, the while loop never terminates. Just like an if block, the while loop can also use multiple conditions and the same set of operators.

In the case of a while loop, the terminating condition is checked first, and depending on its outcome, the loop is entered. There is another flavor of looping (do-while) that checks for the terminating condition after executing the block of statements. So unlike the while loop, a do-while loop runs at least once. The following code shows how a do-while loop can be used:

```
do {
  //some code here
  i++;
} while (i < myData.length);
```

The block following the do keyword defines one or more code statements, and the while condition is placed at the end.

The third type of looping construct, the for loop, comes in handy for iterating through an array or collection where index is relevant in the code. It requires an iterator variable that increments or decrements from a start value to an end value. The statements enclosed within a for loop are executed that many times (the difference between the start and end values). The following example shows how a for loop can be used to iterate through a myData array:

```
for ( var i = 0 ; i < myData.length ; i ++)
{
  // do something
}
```

The for loop specifies three parts, separated by a semicolon (;). The first part declares an iterator variable i that has an initial value of 0. The second part specifies the terminating condition. In this case, as long as the value of i is less than the total number of elements in myData, the code is executed. The third part increments (or decrements) the iterator variable by a certain amount. In this case, it increments i by one after every iteration.

Working with Strings

String data types are often used in JavaScript code and they have many uses. For example, you may want to find out whether a string contains certain characters or you may want to convert a string from lowercase to uppercase characters. Luckily, JavaScript offers many functions that allow you to play with strings. This section explores some of JavaScript's most frequently used string functions.

Finding String Length

Sometimes you need to find out the length of a string. For example, you might have a user registration page and want to ensure that the first name, last name, username, and password all meet certain requirements of minimum and maximum length. In such cases, knowing how many characters a string contains becomes necessary. The length property of a String object allows you to do just that. The following example shows how the length property is used:

```
var firstName = document.getElementById("txtFirstName").value;
if ( firstName.length < 3 || firstName.length > 50 )
{
  alert("Invalid First Name! ");
}
```

This code retrieves the value entered in the txtFirstName text box and stores it in a variable: firstName. Because you store a string value in the firstName variable, you can call any of the String object methods and properties on it. In this case, an if statement is used to check the length property of firstName. If the length is fewer than 3 characters or more than 50 characters, an error message is shown using an alert dialog.

Finding a String within Another String

Sometimes you need to search for a string within another string. For example, you may want to find out whether an e-mail address contains an @ character or whether a URL contains www. JavaScript offers two methods that can be used in such situations: indexOf() and lastIndexOf(). The indexOf() method accepts a string to be searched within another string and then returns the start position of the first occurrence of that string. The position starts from 0. The lastIndexOf() method is similar to indexOf(), but it searches for the last occurrence of a given string. Both these methods return -1 if the specified string cannot be found. The following code shows how they are used:

```
var url="http://www.somewebsite.com";
var result=url.indexOf("www");
alert(result);
result = url.lastIndexOf(".");
alert(result);
```

The first line of the code creates a variable named url and stores a URL string in it. The indexOf() method is then called on the url variable for searching www. The return value of indexOf() is stored in the variable. An alert() displays the result to the user. In this example, indexOf() returns 7 because www begins at the seventh position (positioning starts from 0).

Next, the lastIndexOf() method is called on the url variable to find out the last occurrence of a dot. In this case, the result is 22 because the last dot is found just before com.

Extracting Part of a String

JavaScript provides two ways to extract a portion of a string: substr() and substring(). The substr() method accepts two parameters: the start index within the string where the extraction should begin (again, counting from 0 for the first character) and the total number of characters to be extracted. If the second parameter is omitted, the rest of the string is extracted. The substring() method is similar, but with a minor difference. The second parameter of substring() specifies the end index (not the length) before which the extraction should stop. The following code shows how these methods are used:

```
var data = "hello world";
var result = data.substr(1,3);
```

```
alert(result);
result = data.substring(1,7);
alert(result);
```

The first line of this code declares a data variable and stores a string (hello world) into it. It then calls the substr() method. The start index is specified as 1, and the number of characters to extract is mentioned as 3. Thus, the first alert() outputs ell.

The code then proceeds to call the substring() method on the data variable. The first parameter of substring() is the start index, and the second parameter is the end index. In this case, substring() returns hello w. Notice that at the seventh position is the letter o (from world) and it is excluded from the extraction.

Replacing Part of a String

Sometimes you need to look for a string within another string and then replace that string with something else. JavaScript provides the replace() method to do just that. The replace() method takes two parameters. The first parameter indicates a string that is to be searched, and the second parameter indicates a string that is to be substituted in place of the first string. If there are multiple occurrences of a search string, only the first occurrence is substituted. The following code shows how the replace() method can be used:

```
var data = "hello world";
var result = data.replace("world", "universe");
alert(result);
```

The first line of the code declares the data variable and stores hello world into it. It then calls the replace() method on the data variable with an intention to replace world with universe. The replace() method returns the substituted string as a new string that is displayed using alert(). In this example, the result is hello universe.

Getting an Array from a String

Sometimes you need to convert a comma or | delimited string into an array. You can, of course, use string manipulation functions discussed so far to devise such a mechanism, but that's too much work. Luckily, JavaScript offers the split() method that does this job for you. The split() method accepts a delimiter character or string as a parameter and then returns an array by splitting the string at all the occurrences of the delimiter. split() can also accept an optional second parameter that controls the maximum number of elements in the array. The following code shows how the split() method can be used:

```
var data = "blue,red,green,yellow";
var result = data.split(",");
for (var i = 0; i < result.length; i++) {
  alert(result[i]);
}
result = data.split(",", 3);
for (var i = 0; i < result.length; i++) {
  alert(result[i]);
}
```

The first line of the code declares the data variable and stores a comma separated list of colors into it. It then calls the split() method, specifying comma (,) as the separator. This results in an array with four elements, as confirmed by the first for loop. The second call to the split() method specifies 3 as the maximum number of elements in the array, so it now contains only three elements: blue, red, and green.

■ **Note** An array object has the `join()` method that does the reverse of `split()`: it returns a string after joining all the elements of the array with a specified separator.

Changing String Character Casing

The `toUpperCase()` and `toLowerCase()` String object methods allow you to convert character casing of a string to uppercase and lowercase, respectively. The following code fragment shows how they are used:

```
var data = "Hello World";
var result = data.toUpperCase();
alert(result);
result = data.toLowerCase();
alert(result);
```

The first line of the code creates a `data` variable and stores `Hello World` into it. Then the `toUpperCase()` method is called on `data`, and the uppercase string returned is stored in the `result` variable. The first `alert()` confirms that the string is indeed converted into uppercase and outputs `HELLO WORLD`. The `toLowerCase()` method is called on `data`, and the result is stored in the `result` variable. This time, the `alert()` displays `hello world`, which indicates that the string has been converted to lowercase characters.

Removing White Spaces from the Beginning and End of a String

Sometimes strings contain leading and trailing white spaces that are undesirable. For example, a user registration page might accept a first name from the end user, but that user might add leading or trailing white spaces to the name. While processing this data or sending it to the server, it is necessary to remove these white spaces, and the `trim()` method allows you to do just that. The following code shows how `trim()` can be used:

```
var data = "   Hello World   ";
var result = data.trim();
alert("'" + result + "'");
```

The `data` variable stores a string with leading and trailing white spaces. It then calls the `trim()` method on `data` and stores the returned string in the `result` variable. The `alert()` function confirms that leading and trailing white spaces are indeed removed by the `trim()` method.

Working with Numbers

While working with JavaScript, you may need to deal with numeric data. Unlike string data, which "just works" in almost all cases, dealing with numbers can be a bit tricky and prone to errors (for example, if you accept numeric data in a text box, and a user enters a string instead of a number). There can also be calculation-related errors such as dividing by zero. Additionally, you may want to convert numbers to some fixed format (currency, for example) for the sake of displaying it on the page.

Luckily, JavaScript provides many functions that can be useful while dealing with numbers. This functionality comes in two ways: standard JavaScript functions and Math object methods. This section doesn't cover all the methods, but a few frequently used methods for dealing with numbers are discussed.

Converting a String into a Number

You often accept numeric data as string values. For example, you may accept information such as a user's age and salary in text boxes. Any value entered in a text box is essentially a string, and you may want to convert it into a number before processing it any further. What happens if such a conversion is not done? Have a look at the following code that illustrates this:

```
var val1 = document.getElementById("TextBox1").value;
var val2 = document.getElementById("TextBox2").value;
alert(val1 + val2);
```

The first two lines of the code grab values entered in two text boxes—TextBox1 and TextBox2—and store them in variables val1 and val2 respectively. The alert() outputs the addition of val1 and val2. If you enter numbers, say 10 and 20, into the text boxes, you probably expect the alert() to show you 30. But because anything entered in a text box is a string, val1 and val2 are treated as string variables, and (val1 + val2) returns 1020!

To convert a string into a number, JavaScript offers three useful functions: Number(), parseInt(), and parseFloat(). The Number() function accepts a value and returns a number after converting the value into a number. If for some reason the Number() fails to convert the value into a number, it returns a special value NaN, which stands for "not a number." Number() deals with integers as well as floating point numbers. The following code shows how the Number() function can be used:

```
var val1 = Number(document.getElementById("TextBox1").value);
var val2 = Number(document.getElementById("TextBox2").value);
alert(val1 + val2);
```

In the code, the Number() function is used to convert the values entered in TextBox1 and TextBox2 into the corresponding numbers. Assuming that you entered 10 and 20 in these text boxes, this time the alert() correctly outputs 30.

The Number() function works great if the source value contains a string representation of only the number under consideration. Sometimes a number may accompany some text. For example, in a salary text box, the user may enter "5000 dollars per month" instead of just 5000. In this case, Number() will fail to convert the number because the numeric data has some text appended to it. That is where parseInt() and parseFloat() come into the picture. These functions parse a string and return an integer or floating point number, respectively. The following code shows how they are used:

```
var val1 = parseInt(document.getElementById("TextBox1").value);
var val2 = parseFloat(document.getElementById("TextBox2").value);
alert("Age : " + val1);
alert("Salary : " + val2);
```

The code assumes that TextBox1 is intended to specify age, and TextBox2 is used to specify salary. Age being an integer value, the first line calls the parseInt() method to parse the value entered in TextBox1. The second line uses parseFloat() because salary can be a floating point number. If you enter age as "25 years" and salary as "5000 dollars" in the text boxes, the alerts show 25 and 5000, respectively.

As mentioned earlier, if conversion from a string to a number fails for any reason, the result is NaN. To check whether a value is NaN, JavaScript provides the isNaN() function. The following code shows how isNaN() can be used:

```
if (!isNaN(val1) && !isNaN(val2)) {
  var result = val1 + val2;
  alert(result);
}
```

The code uses the isNaN() function to check whether val1 and val2 are valid numbers. If so, it adds val1 and val2 and displays the result.

Deciding the Number of Digits after the Decimal Point

When you work with currencies, a common task is to convert numbers into a string maintaining a specified number of digits after the decimal point. The resulting value is often used for onscreen display purposes. You can use the toFixed() method to accomplish this task. The toFixed() method accepts a number indicating the number of decimals and returns a string representation of the number. Consider the following piece of code that shows how toFixed() is used:

```
var salary = 20000.12345;
var amount = salary.toFixed(2);
alert(amount);
```

The code stores a floating point number with five decimal places in the salary variable. The toFixed() method is called on the salary variable by passing a value of 2. This indicates that you intend to convert the salary value to a two-decimal number. The alert() shows 20000.12 as its output.

Determining the Total Number of Digits in a Number

Although the toFixed() method deals with decimal places, there is another method, toPrecision(), that deals with the total number of digits in a number. The toPrecision() method accepts the total number of digits in a number and converts a number into a string with that much length. The following code shows how toPrecision() works:

```
var salary = 20000.12345;
var amount = salary.toPrecision(6);
alert(amount);
```

The first line of code stores 20000.12345 in the salary variable. The second line calls the toPrecision() method and specifies 6 as the total number of digits in the resulting value. In this case, the amount variable will be 20000.1, as outputted by alert().

■ **Note**   You can also use the toString() method on a number to convert it into a string. However, in most of the cases in which a number is concatenated with string data, calling toString() explicitly is not needed.

Working with Dates and Times

JavaScript offers the Date object to work with dates and times. JavaScript dates are counted as the number of milliseconds since midnight on January 1, 1970. The Date object has many methods that allow you to access various parts of a date such as year, month, day, and hour. You can create Date objects in several ways, as shown here:

```
var dt1 = new Date();
var dt2 = new Date(2013, 3, 15);
var dt3 = new Date(2013, 1, 20, 10, 29, 0, 0);
```

The first line creates a Date object that represents the current date and time. You can create a Date object that represents a specific date and time by passing parameters to the Date constructor, as shown in the next two lines. The second line creates a Date object by passing a year, month, and date. Month numbers start from 0 (January is 0, February is 1, and December is 11). Date values are between 1 and 31. So the second line of code represents April 15, 2013. On the same lines, hours take values between 0 and 23, minutes between 0 and 59, and seconds between 0 and 59. Thus, the third Date object represents February 20, 2013 at 10:29:00 a.m. Table 1-2 lists some of the most commonly used Date object methods.

Table 1-2. *Date Object Methods*

Method	Description
getFullYear()	Returns a full year from a Date object (e.g., 2013).
setFullYear(val)	Sets the year of a Date object.
getMonth()	Returns the month from a Date object. Month values are between 0 and 11 (January is 0, and December is 11).
setMonth(val)	Sets the month in a Date object.
getDate()	Returns the day of the month from a Date object. Date values are between 1 and 31.
setDate(val)	Sets the day of the month in a Date object.
getDay()	Returns the day of the week from a Date object. Weekday values are between 0 and 6, 0 being Sunday and 6 being Saturday.
setDay(val)	Sets the weekday of a Date object.
getHours()	Returns the number of hours from a Date object. Hour values are between 0 and 23.
setHours(val)	Sets the number of hours of a Date object.
getMinutes()	Returns the number of minutes from a Date object. Minute values are between 0 and 59.
setMinutes(val)	Sets the number of minutes of a Date object.
getSeconds()	Returns the number of seconds from a Date object. Second values are between 0 and 59.
setSeconds(val)	Sets the number of seconds of a Date object.
getTime()	Returns the total number of milliseconds since midnight on January 1, 1970.
toString()	Returns the string representation of a Date object that includes date, time, and time zone information (e.g., Mon Apr 15 2013 10:29:00 GMT+0530 [Indian Standard Time]).
toDateString()	Returns just the date part of a Date object as a string (e.g., Mon Apr 15 2013).
toTimeString()	Returns just the time part of a Date object as a string (e.g., 10:29:00 GMT+0530 [Indian Standard Time]).

The following code illustrates how some of the methods listed in Table 1-2 are used:

```
var dt = new Date();
alert(dt.getDate() + " - " + (dt.getMonth() + 1) + " - " + dt.getFullYear());
dt.setFullYear(2010);
dt.setMonth(3);
dt.setDate(10);
alert(dt.toDateString());
```

The first line of code creates a new Date object that holds the current date and time. The second line calls the getDate(), getMonth(), and getFullYear() methods and displays the date in the *dd-MM-yyyy* format using alert(). The getMonth() and getDate() methods return integers and can be single digit or two digits depending on the month and day number. The code then sets year, month, and date of the same Date object using the setFullYear(), setMonth(), and sctDatc() mcthods. The toDateString() method then outputs the new Date using an alert(). In this case, the new date is outputted as Sat Apr 10 2010.

Many times you need to convert a string into a Date object. For example, you might accept a date from the end user in *dd-MM-yyyy* format and then want to convert it into a Date object for further processing. Here's a simple way to do this:

```
var str = "30/12/2013";
var dtArray = str.split("/");
var dt = new Date(dtArray[2],dtArray[1]-1,dtArray[0]);
alert(dt.toDateString());
```

The first line of code stores a date in a *dd-MM-yyyy* format str variable. It then uses the split() method to split the date string and retrieve an array. It constructs a Date object by passing the appropriate elements of the array. Notice that the second parameter of the Date object is reduced by one because month values are between 0 and 11. Finally, toDateString() displays the string representation of the date as Mon Dec 30 2013.

Writing Functions

In the preceding sections, you created simple custom functions. A JavaScript program can consist of dozens of functions, which provide a way to reuse your code across the application. A JavaScript function is similar to a C# method in that it allows you to reuse your code easily. However, unlike C#, in which methods always belong to a class, a JavaScript function is just a stand-alone piece of code that you create for convenience and to promote reuse. The general syntax of a JavaScript function is as follows:

```
function function_name([parameter list])
{
  //code goes here
  //optionally return some value
  return <return_value>;
}
```

A function definition begins with the function keyword followed by a function name. A function may or may not have parameters. If a function takes some parameters, a comma separated list of parameters is placed inside the round brackets (and). Otherwise, an empty () is placed. A function may or may not return a value. If a function returns a value, the return value is passed from the function to the calling code using a return statement.

To illustrate what has been discussed so far, let's create a Web Form that allows users to enter a temperature value in Celsius and then convert it to the equivalent in Fahrenheit. Figure 1-6 shows what the Web Form looks like:

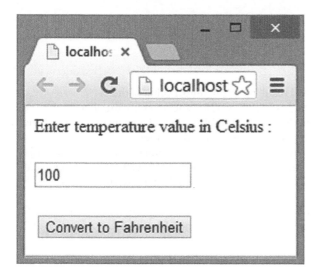

Figure 1-6. *Web Form to convert temperature values from Celsius to Fahrenheit*

The Web Form consists of a text box and a button. The user enters a temperature value in the text box and clicks the Convert to Fahrenheit button. Doing so displays the result of conversion in an alert box.

Begin by creating a new ASP.NET web site and add a Web Form to it. Drag and drop a TextBox server control and a button control on it, and design the Web Form as shown in Figure 1-6. Set the Text property of the button to Convert to Fahrenheit and the OnClientClick property of the button control to return calculate();. Listing 1-8 shows the relevant markup of the Web Form.

Listing 1-8. Markup of Web Form Converting Celsius to Fahrenheit

```
<form id="form1" runat="server">
  <asp:Label ID="Label1" runat="server" Text="Enter temperature value in Celsius :"></asp:Label>
  <br /><br />
  <asp:TextBox ID="TextBox1" runat="server" Width="136px"></asp:TextBox>
  <br /><br />
  <asp:Button ID="Button1" runat="server" OnClientClick="return calculate();" Text="Convert to
Fahrenheit" />
</form>
```

Once the Web Form is ready with the text box and the button, add a <script> block in the head section of the Web Form and write the two functions shown in Listing 1-9.

Listing 1-9. calculate() and celsiusToFahrenheit() Functions

```
<script type="text/javascript">
      function calculate() {
          var result = celsiusToFahrenheit();
          alert("Result = " + result + " degrees Fahrenheit");
          return false;
      }

      function celsiusToFahrenheit() {
          var textbox = document.getElementById("TextBox1");
          var celsius = textbox.value;
          var fahrenheit = (celsius * 1.8) + 32;
```

```
        return fahrenheit;
    }

</script>
```

The calculate() function declares a variable named result and stores the return value of the celsiusToFahrenheit() function in it. The celsiusToFahrenheit() function is another custom function that is shown below the calculate() function. The value returned in the result variable is then displayed to the user using alert(). The calculate() function returns false to cancel the form submission to the server.

The celsiusToFahrenheit() function gets a reference to the text box DOM object using the getElementById() method. It then stores the value entered in the text box in the celsius variable. It then converts this Celsius value into Fahrenheit using a formula. The result of the formula is stored in the fahrenheit variable. Finally, the value of the fahrenheit variable is returned to the caller.

Run the Web Form, enter a temperature value in the text box and click the Convert to Fahrenheit button. You should see an alert box with the converted value. Figure 1-7 shows a sample run of the Web Form.

Figure 1-7. *Temperature conversion in action*

As you can see, the text box has a value of 100. This value in Celsius is converted to 212 degrees Fahrenheit and displayed to the user.

Now let's try to improve the code written in the preceding example so that it becomes more independent and reusable. In the preceding example, the celsiusToFahrenheit() function grabbed the value entered in the text box. To make the celsiusToFahrenheit() function more independent of the Web Form and its controls, it is better if celsiusToFahrenheit() accepts the temperature value in Celsius as a parameter. This way, celsiusToFahrenheit()

need not include any code to extract the temperature values from the form controls; it can come from form controls, or you can supply it programmatically. To do this, modify the `calculate()` and `celsiusToFahrenheit()` functions as shown in Listing 1-10.

Listing 1-10. CelsiusToFahrenheit() Now Accepts a Parameter

```
function calculate() {
  var textbox = document.getElementById("TextBox1");
  var result = celsiusToFahrenheit(textbox.value);
  alert("Result = " + result + " degrees Fahrenheit");
  return false;
}

function celsiusToFahrenheit(celsius) {
  var fahrenheit = (celsius * 1.8) + 32;
  return fahrenheit;
}
```

The `calculate()` function now grabs a reference to the text box using the `getElementById()` method. It then passes `textbox.value` to the `celsiusToFahrenheit()` function. Notice the new signature of `celsiusToFahrenheit()`: it now accepts one parameter named `celsius`. Inside, it uses the parameter value to calculate the temperature in Fahrenheit.

In its current form, `celsiusToFahrenheit()` can be used only to convert temperatures from Celsius to Fahrenheit. What if you also need to convert Fahrenheit to Celsius? Wouldn't it be nice to have a function that does both types of conversion? Let's code such a function and use it in place of `celsiusToFahrenheit()`. Listing 1-11 shows such a function.

Listing 1-11. convertTemperature() Function

```
function convertTemperature(value, scale) {
  var convertedValue;
  if (scale == "C") {
    convertedValue = (value * 1.8) + 32;
  } else if (scale == "F") {
    convertedValue = (value - 32) / 1.8;
  }
  else {
    convertedValue = NaN;
  }
  return convertedValue;
}
```

The `convertTemperature()` function accepts two parameters: `value` and `scale`. The `value` parameter indicates the temperature value to be converted; the `scale` parameter indicates whether the value is in Celsius (`"C"`) or Fahrenheit (`"F"`). Inside, the function has an if-else if-else statement to check the scale of the value. If the scale is passed as `"C"`, it converts the value into Fahrenheit; if the scale is passed as `"F"`, it converts the value into Celsius. The converted value is stored in a variable named `convertedValue`. If anything else is passed as the `scale` parameter, it stores `NaN` in `convertedValue`, indicating an error. You can call the `convertTemperature()` function from the `calculate()` function or from any other part of the Web Form like this:

```
var result = convertTemperature(100, "C");
```

It is possible to invoke a JavaScript function that accepts parameters without supplying one or more parameter values. for example, you could have called convertTemperature(), as shown here:

```
var result = convertTemperature(100);
```

What happens in such cases? What value is assumed for the missing parameters? It is important to remember that such a call is perfectly valid and in the preceding example you would have received -1 as the result because the if-else if block would have been skipped.

Sometimes you want to find out from within the function body whether a particular parameter has been supplied. When you don't supply a parameter while calling a function, its value is undefined, and you can check the value of a parameter as shown in Listing 1-12.

Listing 1-12. Checking for Missing Parameters

```
function convertTemperature(value, scale) {
  if (typeof scale == "undefined") {
    scale = "C";
  }
  var convertedValue;
  if (scale == "C") {
   convertedValue = (value * 1.8) + 32;
  } else if (scale == "F") {
    convertedValue = (value - 32) / 1.8;
  }
  else {
    convertedValue = -1;
  }
  return convertedValue;
}
```

In its modified form, convertTemperature() checks the scale parameter against undefined using the typeof keyword. If a parameter is not supplied, it is undefined and you can set its value to be "C". This time, calling convertTemperature() with just the first parameter returns 212 because the scale is assumed to be Celsius.

■ **Tip**   There are several ways to determine whether all the function parameters have been supplied. The example shown here is one common approach.

Writing JavaScript Code in a Separate File

So far in this chapter, you wrote JavaScript code right into the Web Form .aspx file. Although this approach is common practice and serves the purpose, there are a few shortcomings, as follows:

- As your JavaScript code grows, placing a huge amount of JavaScript in a web page hampers the readability of the web page markup due to a lack of separation between page markup and JavaScript code.

- A piece of JavaScript code placed inside a web page can be used only by that web page, not by any other pages.

- If the web page and JavaScript code are being developed by two different developers, merging them in a single page and dealing with future modifications can be difficult.

- Putting JavaScript code in a separate file also enables the browser to cache the script file so that the same file need not be downloaded again for other pages that need it.

It is recommended to place your JavaScript code in a separate file if it grows to a considerable size. To do so, you can add a new JavaScript file to a project using the Add New Item dialog of Visual Studio (see Figure 1-8).

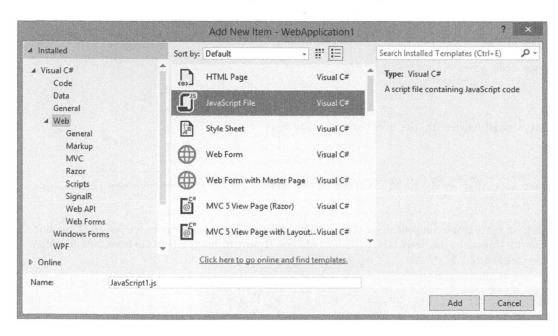

Figure 1-8. Adding a new JavaScript file to an ASP.NET project

The dialog shows a new file being added named JavaScript1.js. Once you add a JavaScript file, you can write all the code inside the file. Remember not to include the <script> blocks inside the file. How do you use the code from a JavaScript file into your web page? You need to use a <script> tag that points to the JavaScript file like this:

```
<script src = "JavaScript.js" type="text/javascript"></script>
```

In this example, a web page contains a <script> tag in the <head> section, and its src attribute is pointing to the JavaScript file. The type attribute is used to identify the scripting language used inside the script and is specified as the MIME type. Some possible values include text/javascript (JavaScript) and text/ecmascript (ECMA script). If you don't include the type attribute, by default script is assumed to be JavaScript. Just like a <script> block, a script reference usually appears in the <head> section. After referencing a JavaScript file, you can use any of the code inside the file as if it were in the same page.

■ **Tip**　Although not mandatory, it is common practice to store all the JavaScript files in a folder named Scripts. ASP.NET project templates, for example, follow this folder-naming convention.

Error Handling

As the complexity of your JavaScript code grows, the chances of runtime errors also increase. Many kinds of error can occur in your code—the ones you anticipated while writing the code as well as the ones that you never imagined. If an error condition is generated at runtime, either your code won't behave as expected or it can cause the browser to throw errors to the end users. Therefore, it is good programming practice to handle errors at the code level whenever possible. Just like C#, JavaScript has try-catch-finally keywords at your disposal. The general syntax of these blocks is shown below:

```
try
{
  //attempt some code here
}
catch (err)
{
  // write what should happen in the event of an error here
}
finally
{
  //execute some code that needs to be executed in any case
}
```

The try block contains JavaScript code that can potentially cause an exception. It can be a misspelled function name or even an error thrown by the developer. To understand how try-catch-finally blocks are used, let's develop a simple Web Form (see Figure 1-9).

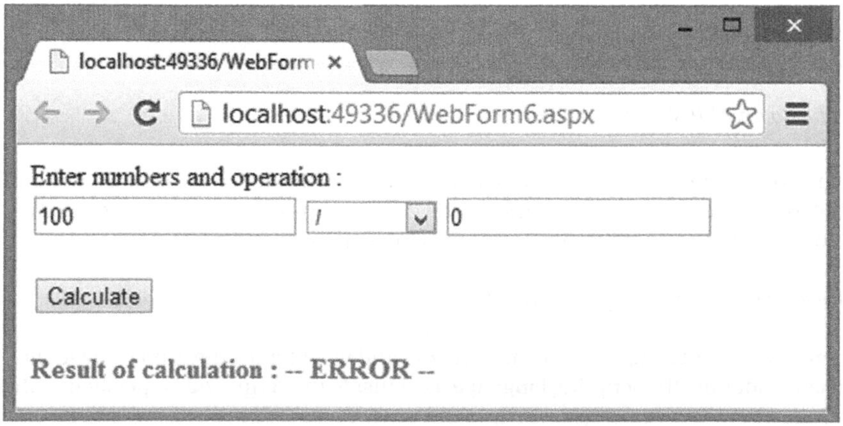

Figure 1-9. *Web Form illustrating error handling*

The Web Form consists of two text boxes for entering numbers. A drop-down list allows you to select a mathematical operation such as addition, subtraction, multiplication, or division. Clicking the Calculate button triggers the operation selected in the list. If any errors occur while the code executes, an alert() displays information about the error. Finally, a label displays the calculation result.

Listing 1-13 shows the relevant Web Form markup.

Listing 1-13. Web Form Markup

```
<form id="form1" runat="server">
  <asp:Label ID="Label2" runat="server" Text="Enter numbers and operation :"></asp:Label>
  <br />
  <asp:TextBox ID="TextBox1" runat="server"></asp:TextBox>
  <asp:DropDownList ID="DropDownList1" runat="server" Font-Bold="True" Font-Size="12px" Width="75px">
    <asp:ListItem>+</asp:ListItem>
    <asp:ListItem>-</asp:ListItem>
    <asp:ListItem>*</asp:ListItem>
    <asp:ListItem>/</asp:ListItem>
  </asp:DropDownList>
  <asp:TextBox ID="TextBox2" runat="server"></asp:TextBox>
  <br />
  <br />
  <asp:Button ID="Button1" runat="server" Text="Calculate" OnClientClick="return calculate();" />
  <br />
  <br />
  <asp:Label ID="lblMsg" runat="server" Font-Bold="True" ForeColor="Red"></asp:Label>
</form>
```

Most of the markup of the Web Form is trivial. Notice that the OnClientClick property of the button is set to return calculate();. The calculate() function is shown in Listing 1-14.

Listing 1-14. Handling and Throwing Errors

```
function calculate() {
  var result;
  try {
    var val1 = document.getElementById("TextBox1").value;
    var val2 = document.getElementById("TextBox2").value;
    var operator = document.getElementById("DropDownList1").value;
    switch (operator) {
      case "+":
        result = val1 + val2;
        break;
      case "-":
        result = val - val2;
        break;
      case "*":
        result = val1 * val2;
        break;
      case "/":
        result = val1 / val2;
        break;
    }
```

```
    if (isNaN(result)) {
      result = undefined;
      throw new Error("Result is not a number!");
    }
    if (!isFinite(result)) {
      result = undefined;
      throw new Error("Result is infinity!");
    }
  }
  catch (err) {
    alert(err.name + "\n" + err.message );
  }
  finally {
    var label = document.getElementById("lblMsg");
    var resultMsg = "Result of calculation : ";
    if (typeof result === "undefined") {
      resultMsg += " -- ERROR -- ";
    }
    else {
      resultMsg += result;
    }
    label.innerHTML = resultMsg;
  }
  return false;
}
```

The calculate() function begins by declaring a result variable for storing the result of the calculation. It then places a try block, followed by a catch block and a finally block. This usage of try-catch-finally closely matches C# error handling. The try block retrieves the values entered in the text boxes using the getElementById() method and value property. The values are stored in two local variables: val1 and val2. A switch statement checks for the required mathematical operation; and addition, subtraction, multiplication, or division is then carried out. JavaScript doesn't throw exceptions for operations such as divide by zero.

The code uses two built-in functions: isNan() and isFinite(). The isNaN() function accepts a value and returns true if the value is not a number. In this example, if you enter some text in the text boxes instead of a number, the resulting operation produces NaN. The isFinite() function returns true if the supplied number is a finite number. This function takes care of finding out whether there was any divide by zero attempt, in which case the result is Infinity. If a value is NaN or Infinity, the code sets the result variable to undefined and throws a developer defined error using the throw keyword. The throw keyword is followed by a new instance of the Error object, which is a built-in type provided by JavaScript. The constructor of the Error object accepts an error message that is passed along with the object. Throwing an error using the throw keyword is quite similar to throwing exceptions in C# using throw.

If any of the exceptions is generated by the code in the try block, the control shifts to the catch block, which receives the Error object associated with the exception. This example uses the name and message properties of the Error object to display an alert()to the end user. Thus, the catch block handles the exception raised from within the try block. Figure 1-10 shows a sample run of the Web Form that causes an error.

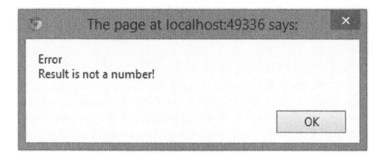

Figure 1-10. *Error message shown to the user*

The `finally` block is executed even if there was an error. In this case, the `finally` block does a good job displaying the result of the calculation to the end user. It checks whether the `result` variable is `undefined`. If so, it appends `ERROR` to a `resultMsg` variable; otherwise, it appends the result to the `resultMsg`. The `innerHTML` property of the `lblMsg` DOM element is set to the `resultMsg` variable.

Summary

jQuery is a JavaScript library that uses the same programming constructs as JavaScript. Any jQuery developer should master these JavaScript basics in order to effectively use jQuery in ASP.NET applications. These fundamentals include data types, variables, conditional statements, looping, and creating custom functions.

This chapter provided a quick overview of all these features. Although many of these features closely match C#, there are certain differences that you should keep in mind while programming in jQuery. With the knowledge gained from this chapter under your belt, you are ready to take your first peek at jQuery in the next chapter.

■ ■ ■

CHAPTER 2

A First Look at jQuery

In the first chapter, you learned that jQuery is a JavaScript library, so whatever you can do using jQuery can also be done using plain JavaScript code. What's the benefit of using jQuery? The biggest benefit is that it is easy to use and allows you to accomplish the same task in fewer lines of code. The official jQuery web site (`http://jquery.com`) rightly puts it: *write less, do more.* As you will see in the rest of this book, jQuery takes away the complexity of using JavaScript so that even seemingly hard to achieve tasks can be performed with ease.

This chapter is intended to give you a first peek inside the jQuery library. Specifically, you will learn about the following:

- What jQuery is and what it can do for you

- Installing jQuery using various options

- Visual Studio features that make working with jQuery easier

- Writing basic jQuery programs in ASP.NET Web Forms and MVC applications

What Is jQuery?

The official web site for jQuery (`http://jquery.com`) defines jQuery as follows:

> *jQuery is a fast, small, and feature-rich JavaScript library. It makes things like HTML document traversal and manipulation, event handling, animation, and Ajax much simpler with an easy-to-use API that works across a multitude of browsers. With a combination of versatility and extensibility, jQuery has changed the way that millions of people write JavaScript.*

Let's try to understand this definition of jQuery in a bit more detail.

jQuery Is a JavaScript Library

As an ASP.NET developer, you have probably used JavaScript in one way or another while developing ASP.NET web sites. Plain JavaScript helps you code rich, interactive, and more-responsive web pages, but the amount of code that you need to write is often too great. For example, if you want to write a client script that shows a fancy pop-up menu complete with animation effects using plain JavaScript, it will be a time-consuming task. To simplify your client-side scripting and make you more productive, several JavaScript libraries are available, and jQuery is one of them. (Others include Mootools, Prototype, and Dojo.) The fact that Microsoft is using jQuery extensively in ASP.NET projects clearly indicates its popularity. As you would expect, jQuery works across a multitude of browsers and supports all leading browsers, including Internet Explorer, Firefox, Chrome, Opera, and Safari.

■ **Note**   While learning about JavaScript libraries like jQuery, you may come across two terms: cross-browser and multi-browser. A script is said to be cross-browser when it works in all browsers. A multi-browser script, on the other hand, works only with a set of predefined browsers. Read http://en.wikipedia.org/wiki/Cross-browser, http://en.wikipedia.org/wiki/JQuery and http://jquery.com/browser-support for more details.

---

jQuery Is Fast, Small, and Feature-Rich

jQuery is a highly optimized library and quite small in size. This compactness means less data to be downloaded at the client side without compromising on UI effects. jQuery is not just a fast and compact library but it is also feature-rich, as explained in the next few sections of this chapter.

jQuery Simplifies HTML Document Traversing, Event Handling, Animating, and Ajax Interactions

jQuery simplifies HTML Document Object Model (DOM) navigation and manipulation considerably. It offers many ways to traverse DOM trees and parent-child elements. Most of the JavaScript functionality goes in client-side event handlers. jQuery is handy when it comes to event handling. jQuery also allows you to make Ajax calls to ASP.NET Web Services, Page Methods, WCF services, and MVC controller actions.

jQuery Is Designed to Change the Way You Write JavaScript

jQuery dramatically changes the way you write JavaScript code. If you have never used jQuery before, initially you may find its syntax bit odd, but once you get hang of it you will probably never use any other library (or at the very least, you won't want to go back to writing plain JavaScript code). For example, a common JavaScript file contains too many small to huge functions, and you have to keep calling them individually whenever required. With jQuery, the "chain" of operations makes your code compact and handy.

What Can jQuery Do for You?

Before using jQuery in ASP.NET applications, you should be aware of its capabilities. Knowing what jQuery can do for you helps you plan your script and client-side features well. Let's see some of the most important areas in which jQuery can be a huge help.

Selecting HTML DOM Elements

While writing client-side script, you often need to select one or more DOM elements. jQuery offers a very powerful mechanism to select DOM elements aptly named jQuery selectors. *jQuery selectors* allow you to select elements based on various criteria such as their IDs, CSS classes, tag names, parent-child relationships, and more. Once they're selected, you can process the DOM elements per your requirements.

Handling Events

Event handling is one of the most frequently used features in client script. What should happen when a user clicks the Submit button? How should the page respond when a user changes selections from a drop-down list? What kind of validation do you want to run when a user submits a form? These and many other tasks can be performed by handling events such as click, dblclick, mousedown, and keypress. Although plain JavaScript allows you to write and wire event handlers to their respective events, jQuery allows you to do so in a consistent and easy manner.

Manipulating DOM Elements and Their Content

Sometimes you need to render a dynamic layout in the browser. Adding or removing DOM elements on the fly becomes important in such cases. jQuery offers a rich set of functions to add or remove DOM elements to and from a page. Moreover, you can manipulate the content within DOM elements and modify, replace, or remove it as necessary.

Adding Fancy Effects and Animations to Web Pages

Adding fancy frills such as sliding effects, hiding and showing content, and eye-catching animations is quite easy in jQuery because jQuery has methods specifically designed for these requirements. Although not all web pages need them, you have the option to add them to your web site whenever required. Examples of practical uses of these effects include fancy accordions, pull-down and hover menus, and progress animations.

Making Ajax Calls to Server-Side Resources

For ASP.NET developers, the one feature that is invaluable is making Ajax calls to server-side resources. Modern web applications rely heavily on Ajax and use partial page postback to get the job done. In such cases, you need to call ASP.NET web services, page methods, generic handlers (`.ashx`), MVC action methods, and Web API from the client-side script. jQuery provides very rich and flexible ways to make Ajax calls to the server.

jQuery 1.x and 2.x

Currently, jQuery is available in two lines: 1.x and 2.x. Although most of the core application programming interface (API) remains the same across these two lines, there is an important change in the 2.x line that you should be aware of: jQuery 2.x doesn't support Internet Explorer (IE) 6, 7, and 8. If you expect your clients to use any of these versions of IE, it is recommended to stick with the 1.x line. Due to elimination of this support, jQuery can now avoid patches needed exclusively for IE 6, 7, and 8, resulting in a reduction in size compared to jQuery 1.9.

Throughout this book, you will use 2.x line of the jQuery library. However, remember that the API of 2.x is the same as 1.9, so merely changing the jQuery library script references from 2.x to 1.9 should work fine without needing any change in the code. Refer to the official jQuery web site (`http://jquery.com`) for more details.

Adding jQuery to ASP.NET Projects

Before you use any jQuery features, you need to add it to your ASP.NET Web Forms and MVC projects. You can add the jQuery library to your projects in three ways:

- Add a copy of the jQuery library to a local folder.
- Add the jQuery library using the jQuery NuGet package.
- Add a reference to the jQuery library from the Content Delivery Network (CDN).

Let's see how each of these types of installations can be performed.

Adding a Copy of the jQuery Library to a Local Folder

This is probably the most basic way to add the jQuery library to your project. In this approach, you first get a copy of the jQuery library from the official jQuery web site (`http://jquery.com`) and then place that copy in your ASP.NET project. Figure 2-1 shows the official jQuery web site and the download area.

Figure 2-1. *Downloading jQuery from the official web site*

When you click the Download jQuery button, you are taken to a page where you can select the version of jQuery to download. As of this writing, there are two branches of jQuery versions: 1.x and 2.x. As mentioned earlier, although jQuery versions from both of these branches support all the leading browsers such as Firefox, Chrome, Opera, Safari, and IE, the versions from the former branch support IE 6-10 and the versions from the later branch support only IE 9 and later. Although the API is largely the same across these two branches, this book uses 2.x for most of the examples.

All the jQuery downloads are available in two flavors:

- Compressed production version
- Uncompressed development version

The compressed version is smaller than the uncompressed one and is also referred to as a *minified version*. Minification techniques such as stripping comments and whitespaces are applied to the compressed version to produce a file with a smaller size. This version is suitable for production use where debugging is not needed.

The uncompressed version includes comments, white spaces, and line breaks, making it more readable than the compressed version. The uncompressed version is larger, but it is suitable to use during development phases.

While downloading the jQuery library, you can save the file with any name. However, it is strongly recommended that you follow the default naming conventions. For example, when you download jQuery version 2.0.3, its file name should be this:

```
jquery-2.0.3.js
jquery-2.0.3.min.js
```

The first file represents the uncompressed version and has the version number included in the file name, making it quite clear to developers. The compressed version adds .min to the end of version number, making it clear that it is a compressed version.

It is recommended that you create a subfolder named Scripts inside your project and place jQuery library files there instead of immediately inside the root folder or any other folder. ASP.NET project templates use this convention. For example, if you create a new ASP.NET Web Forms or MVC project, you will find a folder named Scripts that includes certain versions of the jQuery library. Figure 2-2 shows the Scripts folder from a Web Forms project.

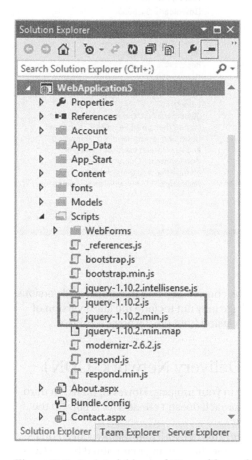

Figure 2-2. *Scripts folder and jQuery library files*

Notice that by default ASP.NET projects use jQuery version 1.10.2. You need to place your copy of the jQuery library in the same folder using the Add Existing Item dialog of Visual Studio. If you plan to use the newly added jQuery library file throughout a project, you can remove the other versions of jQuery from the Scripts folder; otherwise, you can leave the other versions as they are.

Adding the jQuery Library Using the jQuery NuGet Package

There is an alternative way of adding a local copy of jQuery: via a NuGet package. To do so, select the Manage NuGet Packages menu option from the PROJECTS menu. In the Manage NuGet Packages dialog, search for jQuery. Figure 2-3 shows the jQuery library NuGet package in the dialog.

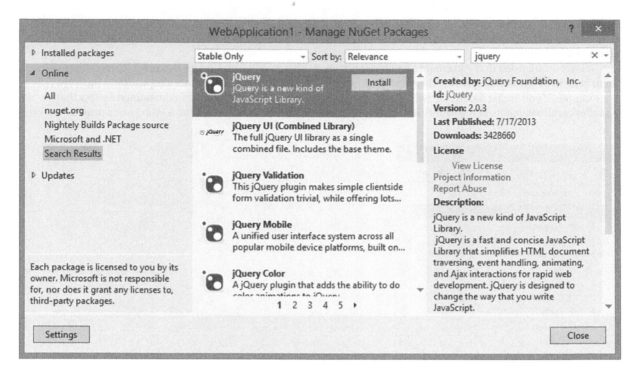

Figure 2-3. *Installing the jQuery NuGet package*

Once you click the Install button, the NuGet package manager adds the compressed and uncompressed versions of the jQuery library in the Scripts folder. Note that the jQuery NuGet package may not include the latest version of jQuery. For the sake of the examples illustrated in this book, however, any version from the 2.x branch suffices.

Referencing the jQuery Library from a Content Delivery Network (CDN)

The two ways described previously create a local copy of the jQuery library in your projects. However, there is a third way to access jQuery: using a CDN. Unlike the other methods, the CDN approach doesn't create a local copy of the jQuery library; instead, you refer to the jQuery library hosted on CDN servers.

A CDN is a network of servers situated at key locations across the globe. This network maintains cached copies of files that are to be delivered to the client. When a client tries to access any file that is being maintained by the CDN, the server nearest to the requesting client fulfills the request. This technique is known as *edge caching* because the servers toward the "edge" supply the content.

There are many CDNs available at your disposal, including these:

- jQuery CDN (http://code.jquery.com/)

- Microsoft Ajax CDN (http://www.asp.net/ajaxlibrary/cdn.ashx)

- Google CDN (https://developers.google.com/speed/libraries)

To use jQuery library files from these CDNs, you need to know the URLs to the respective jQuery files, which can be found on the web sites of the respective CDNs. For example, jQuery CDN URLs for jQuery 2.0.3 are as follows:

```
http://code.jquery.com/jquery-2.0.3.js
http://code.jquery.com/jquery-2.0.3.min.js
```

So instead of having a local copy of the jQuery library, you can refer to one hosted at `code.jquery.com`.

■ **Caution** As with the NuGet package, you should check the version numbers of the jQuery libraries available on the CDN you want to use. Because these CDNs are maintained by third parties, it is quite possible that they don't yet host the latest versions of jQuery.

Benefits of Using a CDN

Although it might seem like a deviation from the main subject of this chapter, you should know how using a CDN instead of local copies of jQuery can improve application performance. Beginners often overlook this aspect and prefer using local copies of jQuery, as explained in the earlier sections. Although local copies are great during development and for intranet applications in which machines are not connected to the Internet all the time, a CDN can be a good performance booster for public web sites.

To understand how using CDN can be beneficial to your web application, let's assume that you have a web server located in the United States. Your web site, developed in ASP.NET, is hosted on that server and is using the jQuery library. Now let's further assume that clients from India are trying to use your web site. Without any CDN in the picture, all requests for the jQuery library are served by the single web server located in the United States. The files needed by the clients from India will be downloaded all the way from the U.S.-based web server. Figure 2-4 shows a CDN at work.

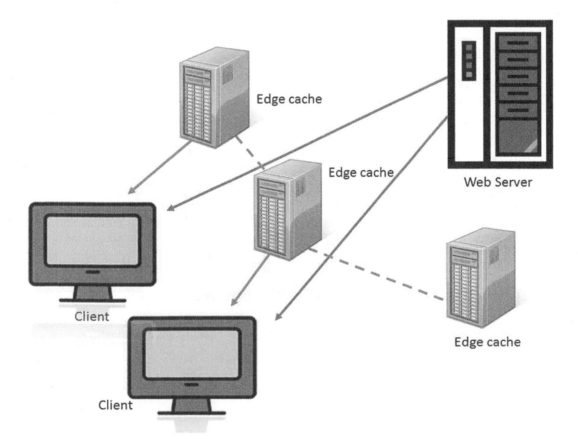

Figure 2-4. How a CDN works

Suppose that you have introduced CDN for jQuery files, and these libraries are now hosted in edge cache servers. Further assume that one of the edge cache servers is located in India. Now when a request originating from India is received, there is no need to fetch the files from the U.S.-based web server. Instead, they can be readily served by the nearest edge cache server located in India. This process will obviously improve the overall performance of your web site. If the edge cache server located in India is unavailable, the requests can be routed to other servers in the network, ensuring high availability.

Using a CDN also lessens the load on the web server. Let's say your Web Form is making use of five JavaScript files. In the absence of a CDN, each client sends at least six requests (one for the Web Form and five for the JavaScript files) to the web server software (IIS, as far as ASP.NET is concerned). However, with a CDN in place, only the Web Form request reaches the web server. The other five requests are served by the CDN. This process reduces the load on the web server considerably.

Consider a case in which you have developed two web sites, both making use of jQuery, and you are not using a CDN. If the same client tries to use both of the web sites, the client browser downloads the jQuery library files twice—once for each web site (see Figure 2-5).

```
          key:  http://localhost:49326/Scripts/jquery-2.0.3.min.js
   fetch count:  6
  last fetched:  2013-07-09 11:33:38
 last modified:  2013-07-09 11:33:35
       expires:  2013-07-09 11:34:04
     Data size:  83612


          key:  http://localhost:49382/Scripts/jquery-2.0.3.min.js
   fetch count:  7
  last fetched:  2013-07-09 11:35:42
 last modified:  2013-07-09 11:35:39
       expires:  2013-07-09 11:35:42
     Data size:  83612
```

***Figure 2-5.** Not using a CDN causes a performance penalty*

Figure 2-5 shows two web sites—localhost:49326 and localhost:49382—making use of the jquery-2.0.3.min.js file. Because the web sites are not using a CDN, the browser downloads the same file for each web site, as shown by the FireFox cache entries. With a CDN in place, both web sites reference the jquery-2.0.3.min.js file from the CDN. Now the browser downloads just one copy of jquery-2.0.3.min.js because both web sites are pointing to the same file (the same URL).

Referencing jQuery from Web Forms and Views

Once you decide how to consume the jQuery library, the next step is to reference it from your web pages. To reference the jQuery library in your web pages, use the <script> tag in the head section of a web page, as shown here:

```
<script src = "/scripts/jquery-2.0.3.min.js" type = "text/javascript"> </script>
```

The src attribute of the script element points to the jQuery library. In ASP.NET applications, you can place the <script> tag in any of the following:

- Web Form (.aspx) files
- MVC views

- Master page, view master page and layout page files

- User control, view user control and partial page files

In case your Web Forms use a master page, it is better to place the jQuery reference in the master page than the Web Forms. Whenever you add a reference to the jQuery library, you can make use of ASP.NET's built-in methods to generate a correct URL to the jQuery library. In Web Forms, you can use the `Page.ResolveUrl()` method that accepts a virtual URL and returns one relative to the web site root. The following line of code shows how this is done:

```
<script src='<%= Page.ResolveUrl(" ~/scripts/jquery-2.0.3.min.js") %>'></script>
```

The call to `ResolveUrl()` returns `/script/jquery-2.0.3.min.js`. This way, even if you move your pages from one folder to another, you need not make any adjustments to the jQuery path.

In ASP.NET MVC applications, you can use the `Url.Content()` method to accomplish the same thing. The following line of code shows how:

```
<script src='@Url.Content("~/scripts/jquery-2.0.3.min.js")'></script>
```

The `Content()` method of the `UrlHelper` class accepts a relative URL and returns a path relative to the root folder.

■ **Note**   Included in the ASP.NET project templates is another way of specifying URLs: `Scripts.Render()`. The `Scripts` class comes from the `System.Web.Optimization` namespace and is often used with the bundling and minification features of ASP.NET.

In Web Forms applications, you can add a `<script>` tag programmatically in of the following ways:

- Use the `RegisterClientScriptInclude()` method

- Add a `HtmlGenericControl` to the head section

Let's see how the first technique is used. See Listing 2-1, which shows how `RegisterClientScriptInclude()` can be used to emit a `<script>` block referencing jQuery.

Listing 2-1. Adding a <script> Reference Using RegisterClientScriptInclude()

```
protected void Page_Load(object sender, EventArgs e)
{
    Page.ClientScript.RegisterClientScriptInclude(this.GetType(),
    "jquery", Page.ResolveUrl("~/scripts/jquery-2.0.3.min.js"));
}
```

The Page_Load event handler has a call to the `Page.ClientScript.RegisterClientScriptInclude()` method. The `RegisterClientScriptInclude()` method registers a script with the Page object using a key and a URL. The key is a developer-defined unique identifier for the script. The URL can be obtained with `ResolveUrl()`, as discussed earlier.

The `RegisterClientScriptInclude()` method emits a `<script>` tag inside the `<form>` section of the Web Form. In most cases, this doesn't create any problems, but if you want to add the `<script>` section in the head section instead of `<form>`, you can resort to the second technique. Listing 2-2 shows how the second approach works.

Listing 2-2. Adding a <script> Tag to the Head Section Programmatically

```
protected void Page_Load(object sender, EventArgs e)
{
    HtmlGenericControl control = new HtmlGenericControl("script");
    control.Attributes.Add("src", Page.ResolveUrl("~/scripts/jquery-2.0.3.min.js"));
    control.Attributes.Add("type", "text/javascript");
    Page.Header.Controls.Add(control);
}
```

The code begins by creating an instance of HtmlGenericControl, which represents a generic HTML markup; in this case, a <script> tag name is passed in its constructor. Then two attributes, src and type, are added to the Attributes collection of HtmlGenericControl. The src attribute points to the jQuery library, whereas the type attribute specifies the MIME type of the script. The control is finally added to the header of the Page object using the Add() method of the Controls collection, which adds a <script> tag in the head section.

There is yet another way to reference the jQuery library: you can use the ScriptManager control and add a ScriptReference to the jQuery library. To do so, you can add ScriptResourceMapping for jQuery:

```
void Application_Start(object sender, EventArgs e) {
    ScriptManager.ScriptResourceMapping.AddDefinition("jquery", new ScriptResourceDefinition {
        Path = "~/scripts/jquery-2.0.3.min.js",
        DebugPath = "~/scripts/jquery-2.0.3.js",
        CdnPath = "http://ajax.microsoft.com/ajax/jQuery/jquery-2.0.3.min.js",
        CdnDebugPath = "http://ajax.microsoft.com/ajax/jQuery/jquery-2.0.3.js"
    });
}
```

This code from the Application_Start event adds a definition named jquery that uses the Path, DebugPath, CdnPath, and CdnDebugPath properties to point to jQuery files. The Path and CdnPath properties are used during release mode and point to the minified versions of jQuery. The DebugPath and CdnDebugPath properties point to development versions of jQuery.

Once ScriptResourceMapping is ready, you can use the ScriptManager control on an ASP.NET Web Form or master page like this:

```
<asp:ScriptManager ID="ScriptManager1" runat="server">
  <Scripts>
    <asp:ScriptReference Name="jquery" />
  </Scripts>
</asp:ScriptManager>
```

The ScriptManager control has a ScriptReference that uses the jQuery ScriptResourceMapping you added earlier.

Visual Studio IDE and jQuery Code

Although jQuery code can be written in any text editor, when you work with ASP.NET projects, you generally use the Visual Studio IDE for writing jQuery code. The Visual Studio IDE provides help for writing jQuery code in the following ways:

- Code formatting and navigation
- IntelliSense

- Reference directives

- Debugging jQuery code

Let's examine these features in detail. Note that many of these features are applicable to any JavaScript code; they are not specific to the jQuery library.

Code Formatting and Navigation

While writing jQuery code, you need to pay attention to proper formatting for the sake of better readability. Formatting includes things such as code indentation and curly bracket matching. The Visual Studio IDE automatically indents and arranges curly brackets, as shown in Figure 2-6.

```
<script type="text/javascript">
    function confirmName(evt) {
        var textbox = document.getElementById("TextBox1");
        var flag = window.confirm("You entered : " + textbox.value
        if (flag) {
            return true;
        }
        else {
            return false;
        }
    }
</script>
```

Figure 2-6. *Automatic code formatting in the Visual Studio IDE*

As shown in Figure 2-6, the statements of the `confirmName()` function are automatically indented as you type. Also notice that the start curly bracket and end curly bracket are automatically formatted. When you go to a start or end curly bracket, the matching end or start curly bracket is highlighted, making it easy for you to know the code block enclosed by that pair of curly brackets. You can also expand and collapse a block of code using the left side collapse and expand nodes of the editor.

If your script consists of several functions, you may need to jump from one function definition to another function definition. You can easily do this by using the Go To Definition shortcut menu option (see Figure 2-7).

Figure 2-7. *Go To Definition menu option*

Suppose that you have two functions—`Function1()` and `Function2()`—and inside `Function1()` you are calling `Function2()`. If you right-click the `Function2()` call and select Go To Definition, you will land on the function definition of `Function2()`, which makes code navigation easier.

IntelliSense

One of the most useful features of the Visual Studio IDE to jQuery developers is IntelliSense, which shows a list of properties and methods of an object, function signatures, function overloads, and more as you start coding in the IDE. IntelliSense also makes you more productive because you can select various code items from the autocomplete window rather than keying them in. Figure 2-8 shows how IntelliSense lists members of a document object.

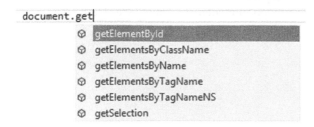

Figure 2-8. *IntelliSense window for a document object*

The IntelliSense window lists the members of the document object, and you can easily select one from the list to incorporate it in the code. The beauty of the IntelliSense feature is that it not only works for built-in JavaScript objects but also for the jQuery library without any special configuration. For example, Figure 2-9 shows IntelliSense for jQuery code.

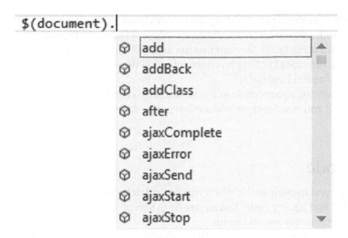

```
$(document).|
    ⊕  add
    ⊕  addBack
    ⊕  addClass
    ⊕  after
    ⊕  ajaxComplete
    ⊕  ajaxError
    ⊕  ajaxSend
    ⊕  ajaxStart
    ⊕  ajaxStop
```

Figure 2-9. *IntelliSense for jQuery code*

To get IntelliSense for jQuery code, you don't need to do anything other than add a `<script>` reference for the jQuery library.

Reference Directives

Sometimes your script is large enough to go in multiple script files. Suppose that you have a script in two files: `JavaScript1.js` and `JavaScript2.js`. While coding in `JavaScript2.js`, IntelliSense shows all the functions contained in `JavaScript2.js` only, by default. If you want to get functions contained in `JavaScript1.js` in IntelliSense, you need to add a *reference directive*, which is an XML comment (`///`) followed by a `<reference>` tag. The `path` attribute of the `<reference>` tag points to the other JavaScript file (`JavaScript1.js`) that you want to refer to in the current file. The `<reference>` tag must appear before any other code statements (this process is quite similar to using C# statements). You can place more than one reference directive in a file.

Have a look at Figure 2-10, which shows how a reference directive is used.

```
///<reference path="JavaScript1.js" />


function HelloWorld2() {
    hello|
}
    ⊕  Function
    ●  Geolocation
    ⊕  getComputedStyle
    ⊕  getSelection
    ⊕  HelloWorld
    ⊕  HelloWorld2
    ●  history
    ●  History
    ●  HTMLAnchorElement
```

Figure 2-10. *Using a reference directive*

Figure 2-10 shows the HelloWorld2() function from JavaScript2.js being written in Visual Studio. At the top of the file, a reference directive is placed using the XML comment syntax (///). Notice that the <reference> tag points to the JavaScript1.js file via the path attribute. The JavaScript1.js file contains the definition of the HelloWorld() function (not shown in the figure). Because a reference to JavaScript1.js has been added in the JavaScript2.js file, the IntelliSense window shows HelloWorld() as well as HelloWorld2().

Reference directives are quite useful when you are writing jQuery code in a separate JavaScript file (.js) and want to get IntelliSense for jQuery code. In such cases, all you need to do is add a reference to the jQuery library file using a <reference> tag.

Debugging JavaScript and jQuery Code

Visual Studio offers a very powerful debugger that helps you tremendously while writing and debugging code. This powerful debugger can also be used to debug JavaScript and jQuery code. Just as you do in server-side C# code, you can set breakpoints, use a Watch window to add watch variables, and so on.

However, there is a catch: Visual Studio JavaScript debugging works only with IE. It's still a great help because of the ease of debugging and ability to use most of the features the debugger offers to managed code. Figure 2-11 shows the confirmName() function that you developed in Chapter 1 being debugged in the Visual Studio IDE. You can set a breakpoint, see a variable value in the Watch window, step through the code, and more.

Figure 2-11. *Debugging JavaScript code in Visual Studio*

A breakpoint has been set at the first line of the confirmName() function. By pressing the F10 and F11 keys, you can step over and step into the code. The Watch window shows the flag and textbox variables being observed.

■ **Tip**   If you want to run client-side script in browsers other than IE, you can use external tools for debugging your JavaScript and jQuery code. Browsers such as Chrome and IE9/10 come with developer tools that allow you to examine and debug your client script in addition to many other aspects of the page being viewed. Popular add-ons such as Firebug can be used for debugging client script in Firefox.

Writing Your First jQuery Program in ASP.NET Web Forms

Now that you have a basic understanding of what jQuery is and what it can do for you, it's time to dive into the code-level details of using jQuery. In this section, you will develop a simple Web Forms application that makes use of jQuery to set the CSS properties of DOM elements. The main Web Form of the application is shown in Figure 2-12.

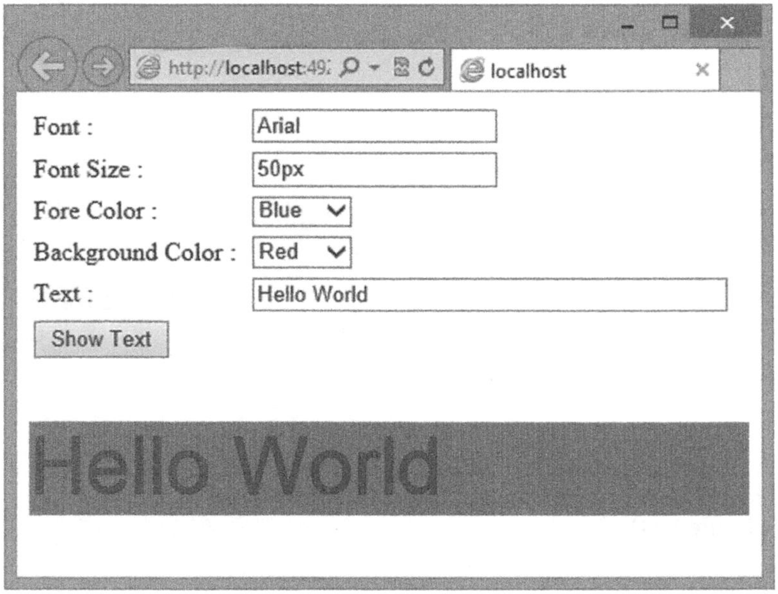

Figure 2-12. *Setting the CSS properties of a DOM element using jQuery*

The application allows you to specify values of font, font size, text color, and background color. It then displays the specified text in a `<div>` element. CSS properties such as font and color are applied to the `<div>` so the text is displayed with those properties.

Because this is your first jQuery program, you will develop it in a step-by-step manner to understand what's happening at each step. You'll then test the application.

1. Download the latest uncompressed version of the jQuery library from the official jQuery web site at http://jquery.com and save it in a local folder on your machine. The rest of this example assumes that you have downloaded version 2.0.3 of jQuery and saved it as jQuery-2.0.3.js on your local machine.

2. Start Visual Studio and select the New Project menu option from the FILE menu. This will open the New Project dialog shown in Figure 2-13.

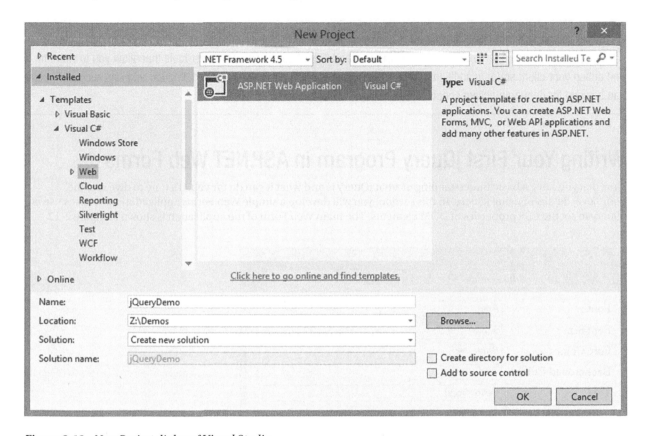

Figure 2-13. *New Project dialog of Visual Studio*

3. In the New Project dialog, select Web under Visual C# templates and then select ASP.NET Web Application template. Name the project **jQueryDemo** and click OK. You will be asked to select a project template (see Figure 2-14).

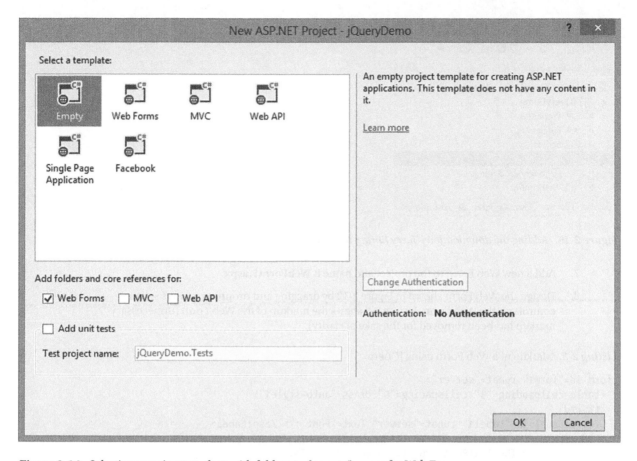

Figure 2-14. *Selecting a project template with folders and core references for Web Forms*

4. Select Empty project template and also check the Web Forms check box under the Add folders and core references for section.

■ **Note** In the remainder of the book, whenever you are asked to create an ASP.NET Web Forms application, follow the previous procedure to create the project.

---

5. Right-click the project in Solution Explorer and add a new folder to the project named **Scripts** using the Add ➤ New Folder shortcut menu option.

6. Right-click the Scripts folder and select the Add ➤ Existing Item shortcut menu option. In the Add Existing Item dialog, select the jQuery-2.0.3.js file you downloaded earlier to add it to the project. Figure 2-15 shows the Scripts folder after the jQuery library is added.

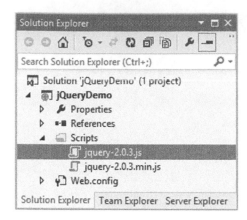

Figure 2-15. *Adding the downloaded jQuery library to an ASP.NET project*

7. Add a new Web Form to the project and name it **WebForm1.aspx**.

8. Design the Web Form shown in Figure 2-12 by dragging and dropping various server controls on the Web Form. Listing 2-3 shows the markup of the Web Form (unnecessary markup has been removed for the sake of clarity).

Listing 2-3. Markup of a Web Form using jQuery

```
<form id="form1" runat="server">
  <table cellpadding="3" cellspacing="0" class="auto-style1">
  <tr><td>
    <asp:Label ID="Label1" runat="server" Text="Font :"></asp:Label>
  </td><td>
    <asp:TextBox ID="TextBox1" runat="server"></asp:TextBox>
  </td></tr><tr><td>
    <asp:Label ID="Label2" runat="server" Text="Font Size :"></asp:Label>
  </td><td>
    <asp:TextBox ID="TextBox2" runat="server"></asp:TextBox>
  </td></tr><tr><td>
    <asp:Label ID="Label3" runat="server" Text="Fore Color :"></asp:Label>
  </td><td>
    <asp:DropDownList ID="DropDownList1" runat="server">
      <asp:ListItem>Blue</asp:ListItem>
      <asp:ListItem>Red</asp:ListItem>
      <asp:ListItem>Green</asp:ListItem>
    </asp:DropDownList>
  </td></tr><tr><td>
    <asp:Label ID="Label4" runat="server" Text="Background Color :"></asp:Label>
  </td><td>
    <asp:DropDownList ID="DropDownList2" runat="server">
      <asp:ListItem>Blue</asp:ListItem>
      <asp:ListItem>Red</asp:ListItem>
      <asp:ListItem>Green</asp:ListItem>
    </asp:DropDownList>
  </td></tr><tr><td>
```

```
    <asp:Label ID="Label5" runat="server" Text="Text :"></asp:Label>
  </td><td>
    <asp:TextBox ID="TextBox3" runat="server" Width="296px"></asp:TextBox>
  </td></tr><tr><td>
    <asp:Button ID="Button1" runat="server" Text="Show Text" />
  </td><td> </td></tr>
</table>
<div id="container"></div>
</form>
```

The Web Form consists of three TextBox controls for entering font, font size, and text. The two DropDownList controls allow users to pick text color and background color, respectively. Clicking the Show Text button displays the text specified in TextBox3 in a <div> element with the container ID. The CSS properties such as font, font size, and color are applied to the container <div> element.

9. In the <head> section of the Web Form, add a <script> reference to the jQuery library, as shown here:

    ```
    <script src="Scripts/jquery-2.0.3.js"></script>
    ```

10. Just below the <script> reference, add an empty <script> block for writing your jQuery code:

    ```
    <script type="text/javascript">
    </script>
    ```

11. Add the following line inside the <script> block:

    ```
     $(document).ready(OnReady);
    ```

    Notice that the previous line of code begins with a $ symbol. The jQuery library is actually implemented as a JavaScript function. In the context of jQuery, $ refers to the base jQuery function. You can also use the literal word jQuery in place of $. So, the line of code can also be written as follows:

    ```
    jQuery(document).ready(OnReady);
    ```

    Most developers prefer $ over jQuery because it saves them some typing. What goes in the brackets following the $ symbol is called a *selector* (you will learn more about selectors in Chapter 3). As its same suggests, a *selector* selects zero or more DOM elements. In this case, the code selects the document element of the page being displayed. The jQuery ready() method is then invoked, and a function is passed to it as a parameter. The ready() method is called by the jQuery library when the page being accessed is loaded in the browser and is ready for accessing and manipulation. OnReady() is a developer-defined function that you will write in the next step.

12. Add the OnReady() function definition at the end of the previous line of code. It looks like this:

    ```
    function OnReady() {
      $("#Button1").click(OnButtonClick);
    }
    ```

The OnReady() function contains just one line of code. This time, it uses $, followed by the ID selector to get a reference to the Show Text button. Notice the jQuery way of referring to DOM element IDs. The actual ID—Button1—is prefixed with the # symbol. This selector is similar to the document object's getElementById() method and instructs the jQuery library to retrieve a DOM element whose ID attribute is specified. Once the element is retrieved, you can perform some action on it. In this case, you call a click() method on the button element and pass the OnButtonClick function as its parameter. Just like ready(), click() is a built-in jQuery method that wires the supplied function as the click event handler of the underlying DOM element. So after the Show Text button is clicked, the OnButtonClick() function is called. You will write the OnButtonClick() function next.

13. Now add the OnButtonClick() function below the OnReady() function. The OnButtonClick() function is shown in Listing 2-4.

Listing 2-4. OnButtonClick Function

```
function OnButtonClick(evt) {
    var font = $("#TextBox1").val();
    var fontSize = $("#TextBox2").val();
    var foreColor = $("#DropDownList1").val();
    var backColor = $("#DropDownList2").val();
    var text = $("#TextBox3").val();
    $("#container").css("font-family", font);
    $("#container").css("font-size", fontSize);
    $("#container").css("color", foreColor);
    $("#container").css("background-color", backColor);
    $("#container").html(text);
    evt.preventDefault();
}
```

The OnButtonClick() function accepts an evt parameter that represents an event object passed to the event handler. The event object gives more information about the event. Inside, five local variables are declared: font, fontSize, foreColor, backColor and text. The code retrieves values entered or selected in the text boxes and the drop-down lists by selecting the corresponding element with the ID selector and then calling the val() method. The val() method is another jQuery method that returns the value entered or selected in form elements such as a text box or drop-down list.

Once all the values are retrieved and stored in the local variables, the code assigns the CSS properties of the container <div> element. This is done by selecting the container <div> element using its ID and then calling the css() method on it. jQuery's css() method accepts two parameters: the first parameter indicates the CSS property that you want to assign, such as font-family and color; the second parameter indicates the value of the CSS property. In this case, values are picked from the local variables.

Once the CSS properties are set, the code invokes the html() method on the <div> element. The html() method accepts a string and sets the inside content of the selected element to that string. In this case, whatever has been entered in TextBox3 is assigned as the content of the container <div> element.

The last line of code—evt.preventDefault()—cancels the default action of the button. In this case, because the Show Button is a submit button, the default action is to cause a postback. Calling preventDefault() cancels the form submission. The form submission needs to be canceled for correct functioning of the application.

14. Save the Web Form file and set breakpoints at the ready() method call, OnReady() function, and OnButtonClick() function.

15. Set the browser to Internet Explorer in Visual Studio and press F5 to start debugging the application.

    Visual Studio now runs the Web Form in an instance of Internet Explorer and halts the execution at the first breakpoint. You can now use F10 and F11 to step over and step into the code.

16. After checking the debugging feature, press F5 to continue the execution and load the page in the browser.

Enter some valid values in various text boxes, select color values from the drop-down lists, and click the Show Text button to display the text with the specified CSS property values.

Anonymous Functions

In the preceding example, you used named functions such as OnReady() and OnButtonClick(). Although doing so is technically correct, there is a more compact and popular way of doing the same thing: using anonymous functions. An *anonymous function* is a function that doesn't have any name and can be passed directly wherever a function is expected or can be assigned to a variable. Thus, instead of creating separate named functions such as OnReady() and OnButtonClick(), you can create an anonymous function and pass it in as the respective method parameter. The code in Listing 2-5 shows how anonymous functions can be used.

Listing 2-5. Using Anonymous Functions

```
$(document).ready(function () {

  $("#Button1").click(function (evt) {

    var font = $("#TextBox1").val();
    var fontSize = $("#TextBox2").val();
    var foreColor = $("#DropDownList1").val();
    var backColor = $("#DropDownList2").val();
    var text = $("#TextBox3").val();

    $("#container").css("font-family", font);
    $("#container").css("font-size", fontSize);
    $("#container").css("color", foreColor);
    $("#container").css("background-color", backColor);
    $("#container").html(text);

    evt.preventDefault();
  });
});
```

Now the code doesn't have any named functions. Instead, anonymous functions are directly passed at their respective places. If you've never used them before, they may look a bit strange to you. But make sure you understand them thoroughly because you will find them used everywhere in jQuery—from event handlers to method parameters to Ajax calls.

Chaining jQuery Methods

Another interesting feature of jQuery is *method chaining*. Listing 2-5 used the css() and html() methods against the container element on five separate lines. Each line selected the container <div> element using the same selector; the corresponding method was then invoked on the element. Instead of selecting an element and calling a method on it separately on each line, you can chain multiple method calls one after the other. For example, the css() and html() method calls from Listing 2-5 can also be written like this:

```
$("#container").css("font-family", font)
               .css("font-size", fontSize)
               .css("color", foreColor)
               .css("background-color", backColor)
               .html(text);
```

Now four calls to the css() method and one call to the html() method are made in the same code statement. (The entire statement is broken on multiple lines only for the sake of readability; you could have written everything as one long line of code.) In jQuery, when you append a method call to another method call, the latter call is invoked against the base selector (#container in this case), not against the outcome of the previous method call. Method chaining helps you write compact and tidy code.

Server Control IDs and the jQuery ID Selector

The preceding example used the jQuery ID selector to select ASP.NET server controls such as Button, TextBox, and DropDownlist. This was quite easy because the controls were placed directly in the Web Form. At runtime, ASP.NET converts your server controls to a set of HTML markup and assigns the element the same ID as the server-side control. For example, if you set the ID property of the Button server control to Button1, ASP.NET creates an <input> element of type Submit and sets its ID attribute to Button1. The following lines of code make this conversion clear:

```
<asp:Button ID="Button1" runat="server" Text="Show Text" />
<input  type="submit"  name="Button1" value="Show Text" ID="Button1" />
```

The Button control has an ID of Button1, and the HTML markup rendered in the browser has the same ID. Therefore, you can safely use the ID of the server controls in your jQuery code. This arrangement works well as long as the client-side ID generated by ASP.NET is exactly same as the server control ID. However, suppose that server controls are placed inside a Web User control, or a master page has been attached to the Web Form. In such cases, the client-side ID isn't be the same as the server-side ID of the control because ASP.NET automatically generates the client-side IDs for such server controls to ensure that there are no duplicate IDs across the whole page. Consider the following example:

```
<asp:Button ID="Button1" runat="server" Text="Show Text" />
<input  type="submit"  name="WebUserControl11$Button1" value="Show Text" ID="WebUserControl11_Button1" />
```

The code example assumes that a Button server control is placed inside a Web User control named WebUserControl1.ascx. The server-side ID of the Button control is Button1. When this button gets rendered in the browser, its ID becomes WebUserControl11_Button1. This ID autogeneration can create problems if you use server-side IDs in the jQuery code because jQuery can't find any control matching the given ID. To deal with such situations, you can either use jQuery attribute selectors (discussed in the next chapter) or assign static IDs to the server controls housed inside the Web User control.

To assign a static ID to a server control, you use the ClientIDMode property of the control. Figure 2-16 shows how this property can be set in the Visual Studio Properties window.

Figure 2-16. *Setting ClientIDMode property server controls*

Setting ClientIDMode to Static ensures that the ID is not autogenerated at runtime. So if you set the ClientIDMode property of the Button server control to Static, the client-side markup will look like this:

```
<input  type="submit" name="WebUserControl11$Button1" value="Show Text" ID=" Button1" />
```

The ID of the submit button is now Button1. Now you can use the same server-side ID in your jQuery code because ASP.NET no longer autogenerates it.

There is another way to grab the client-side IDs of server controls inside the jQuery code. You can use the <%= %> code block to emit the ClientID property value of a server control. The following code shows how this is done:

```
<asp:Button ID="Button1" runat="server" Text="Show Text" />
$("#<%=  Button1.ClientID %>").click(...);
```

The first line of code shows the server control markup for a Button server control with an ID of Button1. If this button is part of a Web User control, the client-side ID will be different, as explained earlier. You can get the client-side ID of the button inside jQuery code by using the <%= Button1.ClientID %> code block. The ClientID property of a server control returns its client-side ID, and that ID is then emitted in the jQuery code. The click() method then wires a click event handler to the button's client-side click event.

Writing Your First jQuery Program in ASP.NET MVC

Now that you have some knowledge about jQuery under your belt, let's see how jQuery can be used with ASP.NET MVC projects. The process remains basically the same; the main difference is that you don't have server controls to deal with. Instead you work with plain HTML elements.

In this section, you will develop the ASP.NET MVC application shown in Figure 2-17.

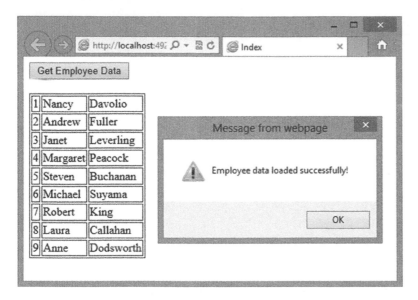

Figure 2-17. *ASP.NET MVC application that loads server-side data using jQuery*

The application consists of an Index view that has a button on it. Clicking the button fetches an HTML table with employee details such as EmployeeID, FirstName, and LastName; and displays the table in a <div>. An alert() notifies the user about the success of the operation.

Let's begin the step-by-step development of this application:

1. Open Visual Studio and select New Project from the FILE menu.

2. In the New Project dialog, select ASP.NET Web Application, as in the previous example, and name the project **FirstjQueryAppMVC**. Click OK.

3. In the Project Template dialog, select the Empty project template, check the MVC check box under Add folders and core references for section, and click OK (see Figure 2-18).

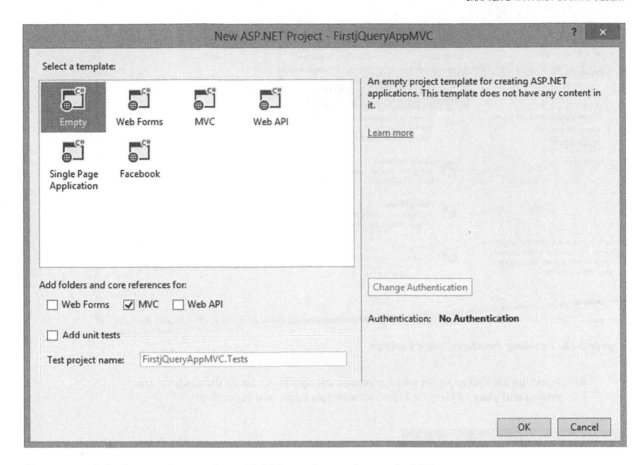

Figure 2-18. Selecting a project template with folders and core references for MVC

■ **Note** In the remainder of the book, whenever you are asked to create an ASP.NET MVC application, you need to follow this procedure.

---

4. Once the project is created, select Manage NuGet Packages from the PROJECT menu.

5. In the resulting dialog, search for jQuery and install the jQuery NuGet Package (see Figure 2-19).

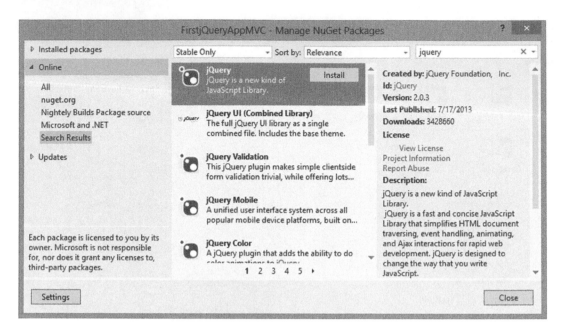

Figure 2-19. *Installing the jQuery NuGet Package*

6. Installing the jQuery NuGet package creates a Scripts folder inside the newly created project and places jQuery 2.0.3 files in the Scripts folder (see Figure 2-20).

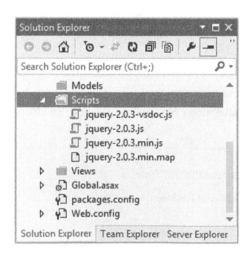

Figure 2-20. *The jQuery NuGet package adds the Scripts folder and jQuery files*

7. Right-click the Models folder and select Add ➤ New Item. Select ADO.NET Entity Data Model in the Add New Item dialog. In the dialog, name the model Northwind.edmx and click OK.

8. A wizard guides you through the creation of the Entity Framework data model for the Northwind database. Select the Employees table. Your data model should resemble Figure 2-21.

Figure 2-21. *Data model class for the Employees table*

9. Right-click the Controllers folder and add a new empty controller class named HomeController (see Figure 2-22).

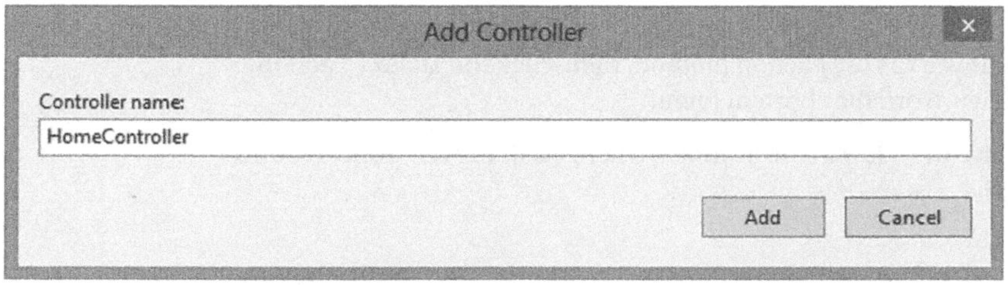

Figure 2-22. *Adding the HomeController class*

10. The HomeController contains the Index() action method by default. Add another action below it called GetEmployeeTable(), which returns an HTML table in the form of a string to the caller. The HTML table contains three employee details: EmployeeID, FirstName, and LastName. Listing 2-6 shows the complete code of the GetEmployeeTable() action method.

Listing 2-6. GetEmployeeTable() Action Method

```
public string GetEmployeeTable()
{
  NorthwindEntities db = new NorthwindEntities();
  var data = from e in db.Employees
                 orderby e.EmployeeID
                 select e;

  StringBuilder sb = new StringBuilder();
  sb.Append("<table border='1'>");
  foreach (Employee e in data)
  {
    sb.Append("<tr><td>");
    sb.Append(e.EmployeeID);
    sb.Append("</td><td>");
    sb.Append(e.FirstName);
    sb.Append("</td><td>");
    sb.Append(e.LastName);
    sb.Append("</td></tr>");
  }
  sb.Append("</table>");
  return sb.ToString();
}
```

The GetEmployeeTable() action method begins by creating an instance of the NorthwindEntities data context class. It then runs a LINQ to Entities query that fetches all the records from the Employees table. The data variable holds the LINQ to Entities query. A foreach loop iterates through the Employee collection and generates an HTML table. The HTML markup is stored in a StringBuilder for efficiency. The code inside the foreach loop adds three columns to the table: EmployeeID, FirstName, and LastName. Finally, the ToString() method of the StringBuilder is called, and the HTML markup is returned to the caller.

11. After creating the GetEmployeeTable() action method, right-click the Index() action method and select Add View from the shortcut menu.

12. In the Add View dialog, give the View name as Index. Uncheck all the check boxes, and click OK (see Figure 2-23).

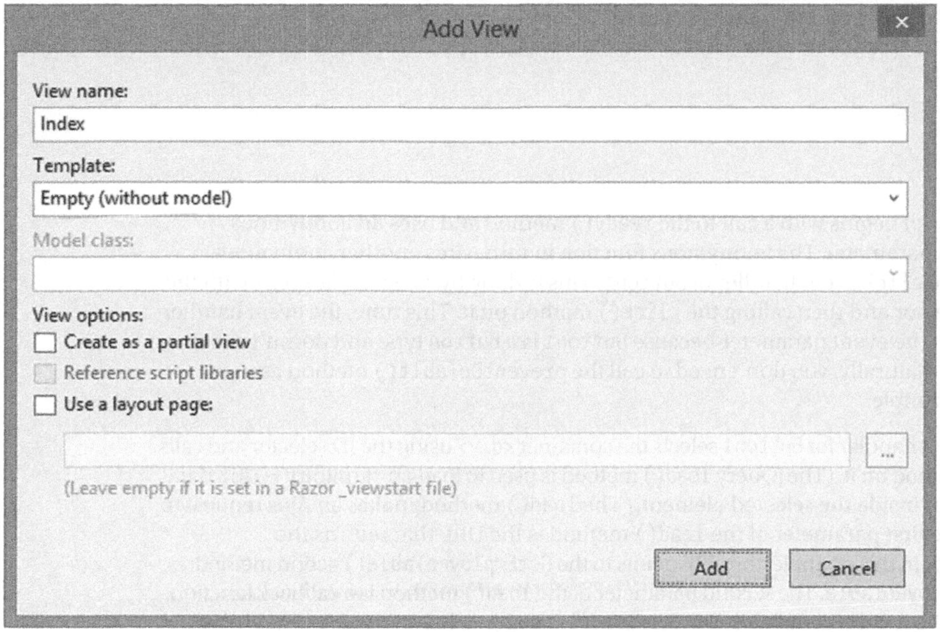

Add View

View name:

Index

Template:

Empty (without model)

Model class:

View options:
☐ Create as a partial view
☐ Reference script libraries
☐ Use a layout page:

(Leave empty if it is set in a Razor _viewstart file)

Add   Cancel

Figure 2-23. *Adding the Index view*

13. Open the view file and add the following HTML markup to it:

```
<body>
    <input type="button" id="Button1" value="Get Employee Data" />
    <br /><br />
    <div id="container"></div>
</body>
```

The HTML markup consists of an <input> element of type button. The id of the button is Button1 and its value is Get Employee Data. There is also a <div> element with the id container, which is intended to display the HTML table returned by the GetEmployeeTable() action method.

14. Add a <script> reference to the jQuery library in the head section, as shown here:

```
<script src='@Url.Content("~/Scripts/jquery-2.0.3.js")'></script>
```

The Content() method of UrlHelper is used to get the full URL of the jQuery library.

15. Add a <script> block below the jQuery script reference you just added and key in the code shown in Listing 2-7.

Listing 2-7. Using the jQuery load() Method

```
<script type="text/javascript">
  $(document).ready(function () {
    $("#Button1").click(function () {
      $("#container").load("/home/getemployeetable", function () {
        $("#container").css("font-family", "Arial");
        $("#container").css("font-size", "20px");
```

```
            $("#container td").css("padding", "6px");
            alert("Employee data loaded successfully!");
        });
    });
});
</script>
```

The jQuery script begins with a call to the ready() method and uses an anonymous function as its parameter. The anonymous function in turn wires another anonymous function as the click event handler of Button1. This is done by selecting Button1 with the jQuery ID selector and then calling the click() method on it. This time, the event handler doesn't accept the event parameter because Button1 is a button type and doesn't cause any postback. Naturally, you don't need to call the preventDefault() method as in the Web Forms example.

The click event handler for Button1 selects the container <div> using the ID selector and calls the load() method on it. (The jQuery load() method is used to load any arbitrary HTML data from the server inside the selected element.) The load() method makes an Ajax request to the server. The first parameter of the load() method is the URL that returns the HTML markup. In this example, the URL points to the GetEmployeeTable() action method: /home/getemployeetable. The second parameter of the load() method is a callback function invoked after the request completes. Because load() is being called on the container <div> element, the markup returned from the URL is loaded in the container <div> element.

The callback function passed in the load() method sets the font-family and font-size CSS properties using the css() method. It also sets the padding of all the <td> elements using the css() method. Notice that the selector is specified for the line that sets padding CSS property. The selector is $("#container td"), which is the ID selector followed by a white space and then followed by td. This selector indicates that all the <td> elements that are children to the container element are to be selected. Once the CSS properties are assigned, an alert() is displayed that informs the user that the load() operation is complete.

16. Save the Index view and run the application by pressing F5. Test the application by clicking the Get Employee Data button to see whether the HTML table is displayed inside the container <div> element.

Summary

jQuery is a flexible and feature-rich JavaScript library. This chapter gave you a glimpse at what jQuery is and how it can be used in Web Forms and MVC projects. You can reference the jQuery library in an ASP.NET project in three ways: by manually downloading it from the official jQuery web site, via a NuGet package, and through a CDN. You may find the CDN approach appealing because it can improve application performance.

Once the jQuery library is referenced, you are all set to use its functionality. Most commonly, the jQuery ready() method is called to perform some initialization work as the page loads. You will also use the ready() function to wire event handlers to various controls such as buttons and drop-down lists.

The Visual Studio IDE offers many features that enhance your programming experience with jQuery, including IntelliSense, code formatting, navigation, reference directives, and client-side script debugging.

This chapter concluded with two ASP.NET projects (an ASP.NET Web Forms project and an MVC project) that showed you what jQuery code looks like and how jQuery is used alongside ASP.NET.

In this chapter, you used jQuery's ID selector, but plenty of other selectors are available. When you use jQuery selectors, you can precisely control which elements are selected for further processing. The next chapter will discuss jQuery selectors in detail.

■ ■ ■

CHAPTER 3

ASP.NET Controls and jQuery Selectors

To perform operations such as event handling, changing CSS properties, or getting or setting the element content of any DOM element, you first need to get that element. In situations where only one element is involved, things are quite easy because JavaScript and the HTML DOM allow you to access elements by their IDs. However, life is not always that simple. Often you need to select elements from a web page based on some complex criteria.

That is where jQuery selectors come into the picture. jQuery selectors are the jQuery constructs that allow you to select DOM elements based on variety of criteria. Many of the jQuery selectors are based on CSS (versions 1–3) selectors, and jQuery adds more to the list. jQuery selectors are so rich that they are grouped in eight main categories. This chapter discusses all these selectors in detail. Specifically, you will learn the following:

- What selectors are and how to use them in ASP.NET applications

- How to use basic jQuery selectors

- How to use advanced jQuery selectors

- How to use jQuery selectors while working with ASP.NET controls such as DropDownList, Button, and GridView

Overview of jQuery Selectors

jQuery selectors allow you to select DOM elements based on certain criteria. Once selected, you can manipulate the selected elements according to your needs. For example, you might want to select a text box with the ID TextBox1 and retrieve the text entered in it for the sake of performing validation or you might want to select all the <input> elements from a web page that are of type Submit and disable them unless a certain condition is fulfilled. The kind of operation you perform on DOM elements depends on the nature of the application you are developing and can vary a lot from one application to another, but they all have one task in common: selecting the necessary DOM elements for further processing. This is where jQuery selectors come in handy.

jQuery selectors are extremely powerful in that they allow you to select DOM elements based on complex conditions. jQuery offers a plethora of selectors; due to their richness, they are often categorized as shown in Table 3-1.

Table 3-1. *Types of jQuery Selectors*

Selector Type	Description
Basic selector	Allows you to select DOM elements based on certain basic conditions. Some of these basic conditions include selecting based on element ID, selecting based on element tag name, and selecting based on presence of a CSS class.
Basic filter	Allows you to filter a set of DOM elements by applying predefined filters. These filters make it possible for you to select odd or even DOM elements as well as DOM elements greater than, less than, or equal to a certain index and more.
Attribute selector	Allows you to select elements based on their attribute values. You can select elements not just on "equal to" conditions but also conditions such as "starts with," "ends with," and "contains."
Child filter	Allows you to filter elements from a set of elements based on their position with respect to a parent element. For example, you can select an element that is the first or last child of its parent.
Content filter	Allows you to filter elements from a set of elements based on their content. For example, you may select elements that contain a specific text or a specific element.
Form filter	Allows you to filter elements from an HTML form. For example, you may filter `<input>` elements that are of type `Submit` or `Password`.
Hierarchy filter	Allows you to filter elements from a set of elements that meet a certain hierarchy criterion. The hierarchy criterion could be parent-child relationship, ancestor-descendant relationship, or sibling relationship.
Visibility filter	Allows you to select elements based on their visibility status (i.e., visible or hidden).

The jQuery selectors listed in Table 3-1 can be used against any HTML elements. While working with ASP.NET Web Forms, you mainly work with ASP.NET server controls such as `TextBox`, `Button`, and `GridView`. It is important to know what HTML markup these controls render in the browser because in your jQuery code you need to specify the details of the HTML elements, not the server controls. For example, the ASP.NET `GridView` control is represented by the following markup in the server-side code:

```
<asp:GridView ID="GridView1" runat="server"></asp:GridView>
```

The server-side tag that represents a `GridView` is `<asp:GridView>`. However, when the `GridView` is rendered in the browser, it is rendered as an HTML table. So if you want to select a `GridView` or any of its constituent elements using jQuery selectors, you should use the `<table>` tag in your jQuery code, not the `<asp:GridView>` tag. The same is applicable to other ASP.NET server controls.

Table 3-2 lists a few commonly used ASP.NET server controls, their server-side markup tags, and their HTML tags as rendered in the browser.

Table 3-2. *ASP.NET Server Controls and HTML Elements*

Server Control	Server-side Tag	HTML Tag
TextBox	`<asp:TextBox>`	`<input type="text" />`
DropDownList, ListBox	`<asp:DropDownList>` `<asp:ListBox>`	`<select>` `<option>` `</select>`
Button	`<asp:Button>`	`<input type="submit">`
Label	`<asp:Label>`	`<span>`
RadioButton	`<asp:RadioButton>`	`<input type="radio" />`
RadioButtonList	`<asp:RadioButtonList>`	`<table>` `<input type="radio" name="radio1" />` `<input type="radio" name="radio1" />` `</table>`
GridView, DetailsView, FormView	`<asp:GridView>` `<asp:DetailsView>` `<asp:FormView>`	`<table>`
HyperLink	`<asp:HyperLink>`	`<a>`
Image	`<asp:Image>`	`<img>`

ASP.NET MVC applications use raw HTML markup in many places. Additionally, developers use HTML helpers to render form elements such as text boxes and drop-down lists. The previous discussion is applicable to HTML helpers, too. As a developer, you should be aware which HTML tags an HTML helper is emitting. This is relatively straightforward because most of the HTML helpers map directly to the corresponding form element types (`Html.TextBox()` and `Html.DropDownList()`, for example). This is the reason why this chapter presents most of the examples using ASP.NET Web Forms. (The concluding example in this chapter illustrates how jQuery selectors are used with HTML helpers in an MVC application.)

Now that you know what selectors are, let's discuss each category of the selectors listed in Table 3-1.

Basic Selectors

Basic selectors allow you to select DOM elements based on certain basic conditions. Some of these basic conditions include selecting based on element ID, element tag name, and presence of a CSS class. In all, there are five selectors in this category (see Table 3-3).

Table 3-3. *Basic Selectors*

Selector	Description	Example
All selector	Selects all the DOM elements from a web page.	$("*")
Element selector	Selects all the DOM elements matching a specified tag name.	$("p")
ID selector	Selects a DOM element matching a specific ID.	$("#TextBox1")
Class selector	Selects all the DOM elements that have a specified CSS class applied to them.	$(".Class1")
Multiple selector	Allows you to specify a comma-separated list of any other selectors and then returns a result that is a combination of the result of the individual selectors in the list.	$("p,span,td")

To understand many of the basic selectors listed in Table 3-3, you will develop the ASP.NET application shown in Figure 3-1.

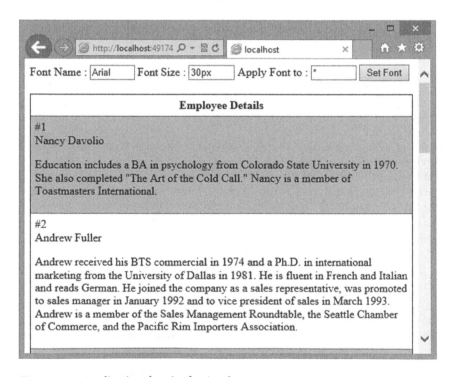

Figure 3-1. *Application showing basic selector use*

The application consists of a Web Form that houses several server controls. At the top are three TextBox server controls that accept font name, font size, and target elements, respectively. Notice the Apply Font To text box. This text box accepts one of the basic selectors such as *, a tag name, an ID, or a CSS class name. Clicking the Set Font button applies the specified font to the specified target elements.

The main area of the Web Form is occupied by a GridView control that displays data from the Employees table of the Northwind database. The `GridView` contains a single `TemplateField` and displays the `EmployeeID`, `FirstName`, `LastName`, and `Notes` columns of the Employees table.

To begin developing this application, create an empty ASP.NET Web Forms application. Add a new ADO.NET Entity Data Model to the web application and configure it to generate the Employee data model class (refer to Chapter 2 for more details about generating the data model). Figure 3-2 shows what the Employee data model class looks like.

Figure 3-2. Employee data model class

Then add a new Web Form to the project and design it as shown in Figure 3-1. The arrangement of labels and text boxes is quite straightforward and is shown in Listing 3-1.

Listing 3-1. Markup of Labels and Text Boxes

```
<asp:Label ID="lblFontName" runat="server" Text="Font Name : "></asp:Label>
<asp:TextBox ID="txtFontName" runat="server" Columns="5"></asp:TextBox>
<asp:Label ID="lblFontSize" runat="server" Text="Font Size : "></asp:Label>
<asp:TextBox ID="txtFontSize" runat="server" Columns="5"></asp:TextBox>
<asp:Label ID="lblTarget" runat="server" Text="Apply Font to : "></asp:Label>
<asp:TextBox ID="txtTarget" runat="server" Columns="5"></asp:TextBox>
<asp:Button ID="btnSetFont" runat="server" Text="Set Font" />
```

The markup consists of three Label controls, three TextBox controls and a Button control. The text boxes txtFontName, txtFontSize, and txtTarget allow the end user to enter a font name, font size, and target, respectively. Clicking the Set Font button changes the font of the target elements to the specified values.

Designing the GridView requires some explanation. To design the GridView, drag and drop one on the Web Form. Using the Edit Columns option from the smart tag, add a TemplateField to the GridView. Figure 3-3 shows what the GridView Fields dialog looks like.

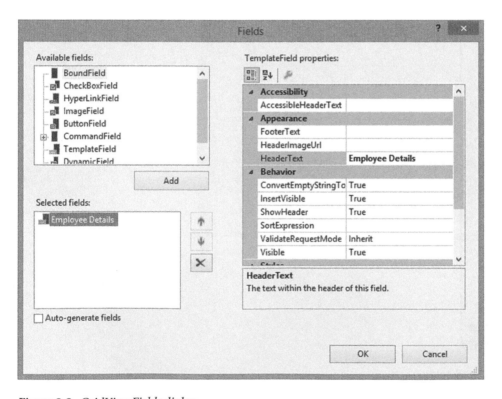

Figure 3-3. *GridView Fields dialog*

Set the HeaderText property to Employee Details and design the ItemTemplate of the GridView as shown in Listing 3-2.

Listing 3-2. GridView ItemTemplate

```
<asp:GridView ID="GridView1" runat="server" SelectMethod="SelectEmployees"
ItemType="BasicSelectors.Employee">
  <Columns>
    <asp:TemplateField HeaderText="Employee Details">
      <ItemTemplate>
        <div>#<%# Item.EmployeeID %></div>
        <asp:Label ID="Label1" runat="server" Text="<%# Item.FirstName %>"></asp:Label>
        <asp:Label ID="Label2" runat="server" Text="<%# Item.LastName %>"></asp:Label>
        <p>
            <%# Item.Notes %>
        </p>
      </ItemTemplate>
    </asp:TemplateField>
  </Columns>
  <RowStyle CssClass="Row" />
  <AlternatingRowStyle CssClass="AlternateRow" />
</asp:GridView>
```

The GridView SelectMethod property is set to SelectEmployees, which is a custom method that you will write shortly. The ItemType property is set to the fully qualified name of the Employee data model class. Make sure to change the ItemType depending on your project namespace. The ItemTemplate uses HTML tags such as <div> and <p> as well as Label server controls to render Employee details such as EmployeeID, FirstName, LastName, and Notes. Notice the use of the Item object inside <%# and %>.

Based on the ItemType specified for the GridView, the Item object shows the corresponding properties in the IntelliSense. The RowStyle and AlternatingRowStyle elements set the CssClass of rows and alternating rows to Row and AlternateRow, respectively. You will create these CSS classes shortly.

Next, go in the code behind of the Web Form and add the SelectEmployees() method as shown in Listing 3-3.

Listing 3-3. SelectEmployees() Method

```
public List<Employee> SelectEmployees()
{
  NorthwindEntities db=new NorthwindEntities();
  var data = from e in db.Employees
                 orderby e.EmployeeID ascending
                 select e;
  return data.ToList();
}
```

The SelectEmployees() method returns a generic List of Employee objects. Inside, it creates an instance of the NorthwindEntities data context class. A LINQ to Entities query is then used to select all the employees from the database. The ToList() method of the data dynamic variable returns a generic List of Employee objects that are then returned to the caller. Calling the ToList() method executes the LINQ to Entities query you wrote earlier and fetches the required data. This way, GridView gets all the Employee objects for the sake of displaying in the browser.

Add a new CSS file in the root folder of the project and name it StyleSheet1.css. Define two CSS classes, Row and AlternateRow, in StyleSheet1.css, as shown here:

```
.Row {
    background-color:silver;
}

.AlternateRow {
    background-color:white;
}
```

The Row CSS class sets the background color of GridView rows to silver, whereas the AlternateRow CSS class sets the background to white. Make sure to link StyleSheet1.css in the head section of the Web Form.

Next, add a Scripts folder to the project and place the jQuery library in it. Then add a <script> reference to the jQuery library in the head section of the Web Form. Further, add a <script> block and key-in the jQuery code, as shown in Listing 3-4.

Listing 3-4. jQuery Code Using Basic Selectors

```
$(document).ready(function () {
  $("#btnSetFont").click(function (evt) {
    var target = $("#txtTarget").val();
    var fontName=$("#txtFontName").val();
    var fontSize=$("#txtFontSize").val();
    $(target).css("font-family", fontName).css("font-size", fontSize);
    evt.preventDefault();
  });
});
```

The jQuery code shown in Listing 3-4 attaches a click event handler function to the Set Font button. The first line of code inside the click event handler uses the ID selector to retrieve the txtTarget text box. The ID selector is formed by prefixing the ID of an element with #. The val() method returns the value entered in a text box. Along the same lines, values entered in txtFontName and txtFontSize are obtained in local variables fontName and fontSize, respectively.

Then the code uses the value of the target variable as a jQuery selector and applies the font-family and font-size CSS properties using the css() method. In this case, the value of the target variable depends on a value entered in the txtTarget text box. Depending on this value, one of the basic selectors (the all selector, element selector, ID selector, or class selector) will be used to select the DOM elements. The css() method will then change the font-family and font-size of the selected DOM elements.

Table 3-4 shows some sample values that you can enter in txtTarget while testing.

Table 3-4. *Basic Selector Examples*

Value	Description
*	Causes the all selector to be used.
td	Causes the element selector to be used.
#GridView1	Causes the ID selector to be used.
.Row / .AlternateRow	Causes the class selector to be used.
p,span	Causes the multiple selector to be used.

The last line of code calls the preventDefault() method on the event object so that the form submission is prevented. Figure 3-4 shows what the Web Form looks like when an element selector is used.

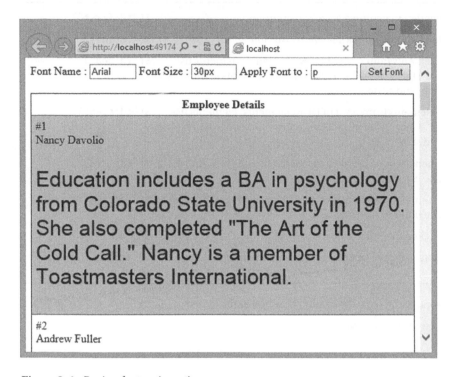

Figure 3-4. *Basic selectors in action*

Notice that only the notes are displayed in Arial 30px because the target text box specified p (an element selector) as the selector.

■ **Note** This example and the examples that follow don't perform any validation on the data being entered in various controls. This is done purely to keep the code simple and clutter-free.

Basic Filters

Basic filters allow you to filter the results of other selectors. In the process, they enhance selectors by providing additional selection logic. For example, an element selector can select all the <td> elements from a table. But to work with the first or last <td> element, additional filtering is necessary, which is provided by basic filters. Table 3-5 lists some of the most commonly used jQuery basic filters.

Table 3-5. Basic Filters

Basic Filter	Description	Example
First selector	Selects the first element matching a selection criterion.	$("td:first")
Last selector	Selects the last element matching a selection criterion.	$("td:last")
Odd selector	Selects only odd elements from a set of DOM elements. Elements use a zero-based index. Thus, the odd selector returns elements at indexes second, fourth, sixth, and so on.	$("td:odd")
Even selector	Selects only even elements from a set of DOM elements. Elements use a zero-based index. Thus, the even selector returns elements at indexes first, third, fifth, and so on.	$("td:even")
Lt selector	Selects all the elements whose index in the matched set is less than a specified value. The index is zero based.	$("td:lt(3)")
Gt selector	Selects all the elements whose index in the matched set is greater than a specified value. The index is zero based.	$("td:gt(5)")
Eq selector	Selects the element at a specified index.	$("td:eq(3)")
Not selector	Selects all the elements from a matched set that do not match the specified selector.	$("td:not(.Class1)")

To understand how basic selectors can be used, let's build the application shown in Figure 3-5.

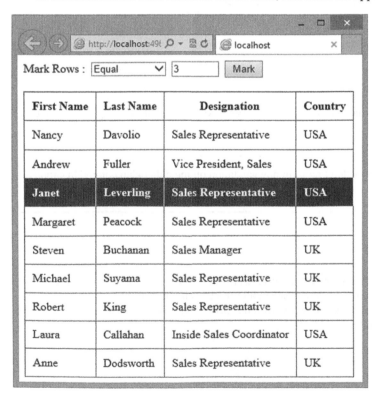

Figure 3-5. Web Form making use of basic filters

The application consists of a Web Form that has a DropDownList, a TextBox and a Button at the top. Below is a GridView that displays records from the Employees table. The DropDownList allows the user to select one of the options: First, Last, Odd, Even, Less Than, Greater Than, or Equal. A value entered in the text box is relevant only if the DropDownList selection is Less Than, Greater Than, or Equal. Clicking the Mark button marks one or more GridView rows with highlighting.

To develop this application, create an empty ASP.NET Web Forms project and add a Web Form to it. Design the Web Form as shown in Figure 3-5 and add a Scripts folder to the project as in the previous example. Add a CSS file to the project with the following CSS class:

```css
.Highlight {
    background-color:navy;
    color:white;
    font-weight:bold;
}
```

Add a <script> reference to the jQuery library followed by a <script> block. Listing 3-5 shows the jQuery code that goes inside this <script> block.

Listing 3-5. Using jQuery Basic Filters

```javascript
$(document).ready(function () {
  $("#Button1").click(function (evt) {
    var target = $("#DropDownList1").val();
    var index = $("#TextBox1").val();
    $(".Highlight").removeClass("Highlight");
    switch (target) {
      case "FR":
        $("tr:first").addClass("Highlight");
        break;
      case "LR":
        $("tr:last").addClass("Highlight");
        break;
      case "OD":
        $("tr:odd").addClass("Highlight");
        break;
      case "EV":
        $("tr:even").addClass("Highlight");
        break;
      case "LT":
        $("tr:lt(" + index + ")").addClass("Highlight");
        break;
      case "GT":
        $("tr:gt(" + index + ")").addClass("Highlight");
        break;
      case "EQ":
        $("tr:eq(" + index + ")").addClass("Highlight");
        break;
    }
    evt.preventDefault();
  });
});
```

The code in Listing 3-5 wires an event handler function to the `click` event of the Mark button (`Button1`). Inside the `click` event handler, the selection from the `DropDownList` is retrieved using the ID selector and `val()` method. The selection is stored in a local variable: `target`. Similarly, the value entered in the `TextBox1` is stored in an `index` variable.

The code then selects all the DOM elements that have the `Highlight` CSS class applied. Once selected, the `Highlight` class is removed from those elements using the jQuery `removeClass()` method. The `removeClass()` method removes a specified CSS class from the selected DOM elements. This way, the `GridView` is cleared of any highlighted rows from the previous run of the code.

A switch statement then tests the target variable against various possible values such as `FR` (First Row), `LR` (Last Row), `OD` (Odd), `EV` (Even), `LT` (Less Than), `GT` (Greater Than), and `EQ` (Equal). In each of the case blocks, a jQuery basic selector is used to select the corresponding `<tr>` elements. Remember that `GridView` is rendered as an HTML table in the browser, so to access any `GridView` row from jQuery, you need to filter elements on the basis of the `<tr>` element. For example, consider the `OD` block. It uses the odd selector to select odd GridView rows: `$("tr:odd")`. (Remember that the index starts from zero, so the odd rows such as second, fourth, sixth, and so on are selected.) Once the odd rows are selected, the code applies a CSS class to those rows using the jQuery `addClass()` method. The `addClass()` method accepts the name of a CSS class and applies that class to the selected elements.

Notice that the `:lt()`, `:gt()`, and `:eq()` selectors use the `index` variable to specify a zero-based index number. Note that the `GridView` header row is also a `<tr>` element and will count toward all the operations performed by the basic filters. So if you specify `3` as an index for the `:eq()` selector, the code will highlight the record for Janet Leverling.

Attribute Selectors

Attribute selectors allow you to match attributes of HTML elements with certain criteria. It is not just an "equal-to" kind of matching; several other options are available as outlined in Table 3-6.

Table 3-6. *Attribute Selectors*

Attribute Selector	Description	Example
Attribute Equals selector	Selects the element whose specified attribute value exactly equals a specific string value.	`$('img[src="foo.png"]')`
Attribute Not Equal selector	Selects the element whose specified attribute value doesn't match a specific string value, or if the specified attribute is missing.	`$('img[src!="foo.png"]')`
Attribute Starts With selector	Selects the element whose specified attribute value begins with a specific value.	`$('img[src^="foo"]')`
Attribute Ends With selector	Selects the element whose specified attribute value ends with a certain string value.	`$('img[src$="png"]')`
Attribute Contains selector	Selects the element whose specified attribute value contains a specific string.	`$('img[src*="foo"]')`
Attribute Contains Word selector	Selects the element whose specified attribute value contains a specific string as a whole word (i.e., the value is separated by whitespace).	`$('img[src~="foo"]')`
Attribute Contains Prefix selector	Selects the element whose specified attribute value is exactly equal to the specified value, or that starts with the specified value followed by a - (hyphen).	`$('img[src|="foo"]')`
Has Attribute selector	Selects the element if a specified attribute is present.	`$('img[src]')`
Multiple Attribute selector	Is a combination of multiple attribute selectors.	`$('img[id][src$="png"]')`

To understand how attribute selectors can be used, let's develop the ASP.NET Web Forms application shown in Figure 3-6.

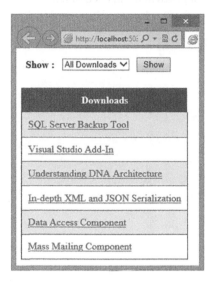

Figure 3-6. *Application using attribute selectors*

The Web Form contains a GridView with a list of download links, which include products, white papers, and software components. At the top of the Web Form is a drop-down list that allows you to filter the download links based on the category (product, white paper, component, and so on). You can select a download category from the drop-down list and click the Show button to filter the available downloads in that category. Listing 3-6 shows the relevant markup from the Web Form.

Listing 3-6. Markup of the Download Web Form

```
<form id="form1" runat="server">
...
  <asp:DropDownList ID="DropDownList1" runat="server">
    <asp:ListItem Value="A">All Downloads</asp:ListItem>
    <asp:ListItem Value="P">Products</asp:ListItem>
    <asp:ListItem Value="WP">White Papers</asp:ListItem>
    <asp:ListItem Value="C">Components</asp:ListItem>
  </asp:DropDownList>
...
  <asp:Button ID="Button1" runat="server" Text="Show" />
...
  <asp:GridView ID="GridView1" runat="server" CellPadding="10"
...
    <Columns>
      <asp:HyperLinkField DataNavigateUrlFields="URL" DataTextField="Title" HeaderText="Downloads" />
    </Columns>
...
  </asp:GridView>
</form>
```

Notice the Value property of the <asp:ListItem> elements. The values for all downloads, products, white papers, and components are "A", "P", "WP", and "C", respectively. The GridView consists of a single HyperLinkField that is bound with Title and URL properties. Figure 3-7 shows the properties of HyperLinkField that you need to set.

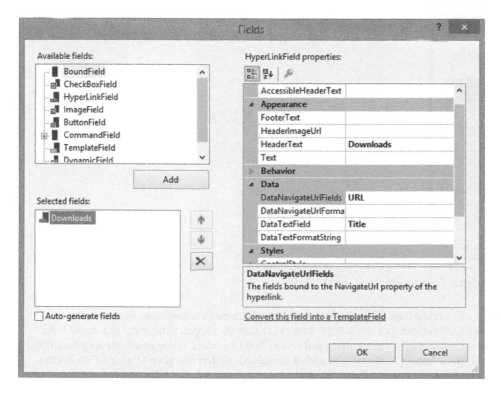

Figure 3-7. *Setting HyperLinkField properties*

The HeaderText property of the HyperLinkField is set to Downloads. More importantly, its DataNavigateUrlFields property is set to URL, and the DataTextField property is set to Title. The hyperlinks will display the Title property value of the Download object, and they will point to a URL as indicated by the URL property of the Download object.

The data displayed in the grid is not coming from any database; it is coming from an object collection. To represent a download, you need to define a Download class, as shown in Listing 3-7.

Listing 3-7. Download Class Stored as Download.cs

```
public class Download
{
  public Download()
  {
  }

  public Download(string title, string url)
  {
    this.Title = title;
    this.URL = url;
  }
```

```
  public string Title { get; set; }
  public string URL { get; set; }
}
```

The Download class consists of two properties, Title and URL, which represent the title of the file being downloaded and the URL to the file. The overloaded constructor of the Download class accepts title and url parameters and sets the corresponding properties.

Sample data needed to run the application is created in the Page_Load event handler, and the data is then bound with the GridView. Listing 3-8 shows how this is done.

Listing 3-8. Binding Sample Data with the GridView

```
protected void Page_Load(object sender, EventArgs e)
{
  List<Download> items = new List<Download>();
  items.Add(new Download("SQL Server Backup Tool", "products/Product1.aspx"));
  items.Add(new Download("Visual Studio Add-In", "products/Product2.aspx"));
  items.Add(new Download("Understanding DNA Architecture", "Paper-Topic1.aspx"));
  items.Add(new Download("In-depth XML and JSON Serialization", "Paper-Topic2.aspx"));
  items.Add(new Download("Data Access Component", "Component1-comp.aspx"));
  items.Add(new Download("Mass Mailing Component", "Component2-comp.aspx"));
  GridView1.DataSource = items;
  GridView1.DataBind();
}
```

The code inside the Page_Load event handler creates a generic List of Download objects. It then adds a few sample Download objects to the items generic List. Notice the URLs of the files being added. The product downloads are stored in the Products folder. The white paper URLs begin with a prefix of Paper and the software-component-related download URLs end with –comp. These URLs allow you to use and test many of the attribute selectors discussed earlier in this section.

Now add the jQuery code shown in Listing 3-9 that hides or shows GridView rows.

Listing 3-9. Using jQuery Attribute Selectors

```
$(document).ready(function () {
  $("#Button1").click(function (evt) {
    switch ($("#DropDownList1").val()) {
      case "A":
        $("#GridView1 tr a").parent().css("display", "block");
        break;
      case "P":
        $("#GridView1 tr a[href *= 'products/']").parent().css("display", "block");
        $("#GridView1 tr a[href |= 'Paper']").parent().css("display", "none");
        $("#GridView1 tr a[href $= '-comp.aspx']").parent().css("display", "none");
        break;
      case "WP":
        $("#GridView1 tr a[href *= 'products/']").parent().css("display", "none");
        $("#GridView1 tr a[href |= 'Paper']").parent().css("display", "block");
        $("#GridView1 tr a[href $= '-comp.aspx']").parent().css("display", "none");
        break;
```

```
        case "C":
          $("#GridView1 tr a[href *= 'products/']").parent().css("display", "none");
          $("#GridView1 tr a[href |= 'Paper']").parent().css("display", "none");
          $("#GridView1 tr a[href $= '-comp.aspx']").parent().css("display", "block");
          break;
      }
      evt.preventDefault();
    })
})
```

The main jQuery code goes inside the click event handler of the Show button (Button1). The switch statement checks for the value of the item selected in the drop-down list. So far, you used only one selector while working with elements. In this example, you will use multiple selectors. For example, consider the selector $("#GridView1 tr a"). This selector consists of an ID selector that filters elements for an ID equal to GridView1. It also uses a descendant selector to select the <tr> elements that are descendants of GridView1. The descendant selector (you'll learn more later in this chapter) is represented by #GridView1 followed by a white space and then followed by <tr>. All the <a> elements that are descendants of the <tr> element are filtered. Using a descendant selector ensures that only the links housed inside the GridView rows are selected for further manipulation.

If the selected value is "A", set the display CSS property of all the table rows containing the anchor elements to block using the css() method. The hyperlinks are housed inside table rows; for proper functioning of the application, you should hide the entire table row by using the parent() method on the selected anchor elements. Doing so will return table rows that are parents of the anchor elements. In this case, you simply use a combination of an ID selector and element selector to select all anchor elements. The code ensures that all types of downloads (products, white papers, and components) are shown in the grid.

If the selected value is "P", use the Attribute Contains selector (*=) to match all the anchor elements with an href attribute that contains the string "products/". In the download URLs, only two entries match this criterion. You then set the display of those table rows to block.

Use the Attribute Contains Prefix selector (|=) to select white paper downloads. Notice that URLs for white papers begin with "Paper-", but you specified only "Paper" in the selector because the Attribute Contains Prefix selector selects values that are equal to or begin with the specified value plus a hyphen (-). The relevant table rows are kept hidden by setting their display CSS property to none.

Finally, filter the component-related links using the Attribute Ends With selector ($=) and hide their parent table rows just like the white paper links. Recall that the component links end with –comp, so the Attribute Ends With selector uses –comp in the selection criteria.

The other cases of the switch block ("WP" and "C") are similar to the "P" case block discussed previously. The only difference is that they show the white paper and component links and hide the others.

■ **Note**   You will learn more about the parent() method in Chapter 6. For the sake of this example, it is enough to know that parent() method refers to the parent DOM element of an element under consideration.

Child Filters

Child filters allow you to work with child elements of their respective parents. Using child filters, you can get specific child elements such as first child, last child, and a child at a specific position. Table 3-7 shows the jQuery child filters.

Table 3-7. *jQuery Child Filters*

Child Filter	Description	Example
First child selector	Selects elements that are first child elements of their parent.	$("td:first-child")
Last child selector	Selects elements that are last child elements of their parent.	$("td:last-child")
Nth-child selector	Selects elements that are n-th child elements of their parent where *n* is a 1-based index number.	$("td:nth-child(3)")
Nth-last-child selector	Selects elements that are n-th child elements of their parent, counting back from the last element.	$("td:nth-last-child(3)")
Only child selector	Selects elements that are the only child elements of their parent.	$("div:only-child")
First-of-type selector	Selects elements that are the first among siblings of the same element type.	$("div:first-of-type")
Last-of-type selector	Selects elements that are the last among siblings of the same element type.	$("div:last-of-type")
Nth-of-type selector	Selects elements that are the n-th child of their parent with respect to other siblings of the same element type.	$("div:nth-of-type(3)")
Nth-last-of-type selector	Selects elements that are the n-th child, counting from the last element, of their parent, with respect to other siblings of the same element type.	$("div:nth-last-of-type(3)")

Remember that child filters use a 1-based index to specify element positions. Child filters can be grouped as "child" selectors and "type" selectors. The former selectors return any element type (here *element type* refers to the tag name of the element such as p, span, and td) that meets the child selector criteria. The later selectors, on the other hand, return an element that meets the child selector criteria, additionally ensuring that the element is of a specific type.

To understand how child filters are used, let's develop the ASP.NET Web Forms application shown in Figure 3-8.

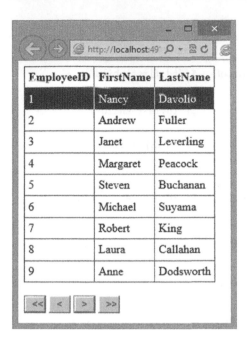

Figure 3-8. *Application using child filters*

The application consists of a Web Form that displays records from the Employee table in a GridView control. At the bottom of the Web Form are four buttons—First, Previous, Next, and Last—that provide VCR navigation to the grid. Depending on the current navigation position, that record is rendered with a highlight.

To develop this application, create an empty ASP.NET Web Forms project and add a Web Form to it. Place a GridView control and a SQL Data Source control on the Web Form. Configure the SQL Data Source control to fetch the EmployeeID, FirstName, and LastName columns from the Employees table of the Northwind database (see Figure 3-9).

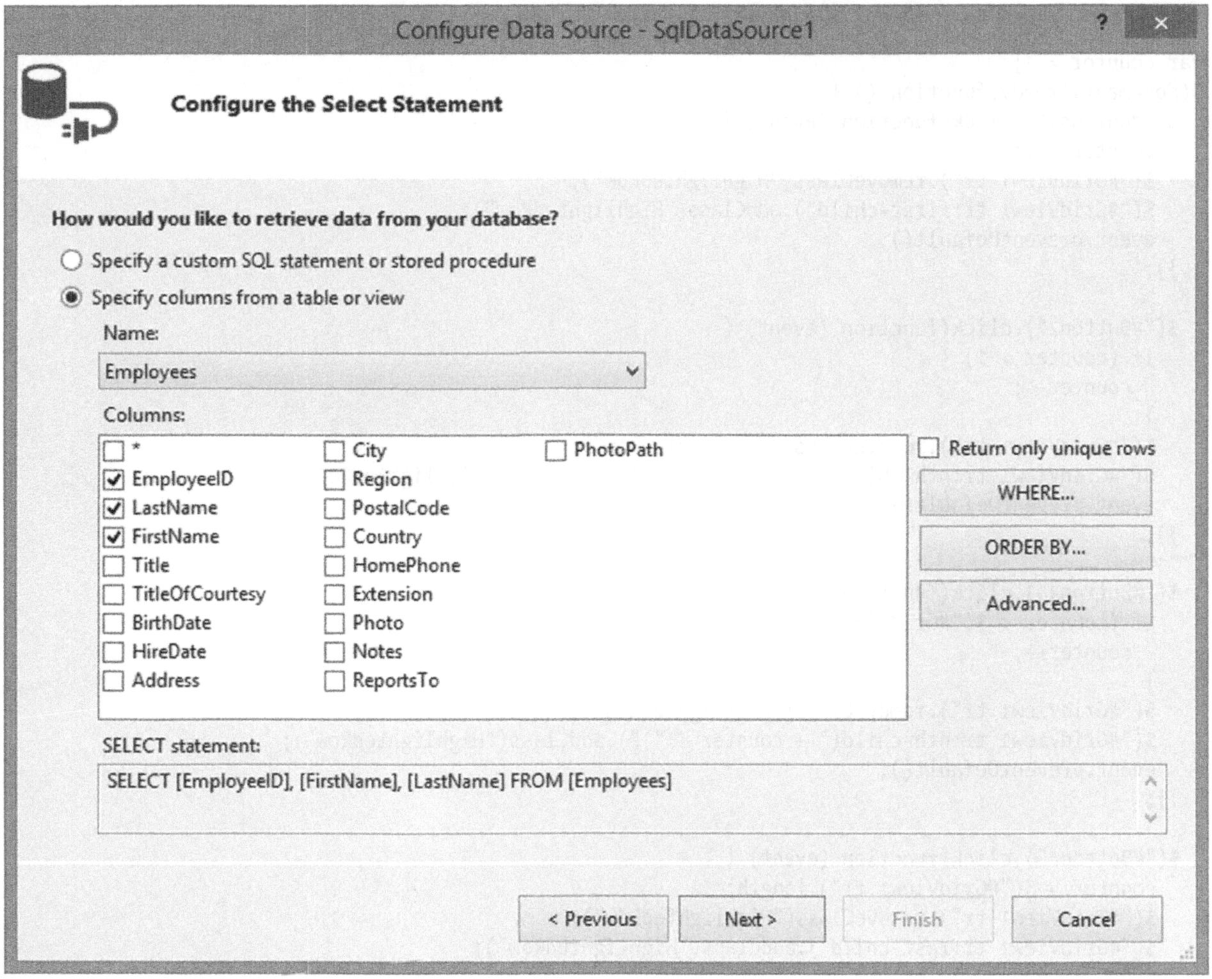

Figure 3-9. *Configuring SQL Data Source to fetch data from Employees table*

Drag and drop four buttons (Button1, Button2, Button3, and Button4) at the bottom of the Web Form, as shown in Figure 3-8. Then add a CSS file to the project and define the following CSS class in it:

```
.HighlightedRow
{
  background-color:navy;
  color:White;
}
```

The HighlightedRow CSS class defines the look and feel of the row being highlighted. Add a reference to this CSS file as well as to the jQuery library in the head section of the Web Form. Then add a <script> block and key in the code shown in Listing 3-10.

Listing 3-10. jQuery Code Using Child Filters

```
var counter = 1;
$(document).ready(function () {
  $("#Button1").click(function (event) {
    counter = 1;
    $("#GridView1 tr").removeClass("HighlightedRow");
    $("#GridView1 tr:first-child").addClass("HighlightedRow");
    event.preventDefault();
  });

  $("#Button2").click(function (event) {
    if (counter > 1) {
      counter--;
    }
    $("#GridView1 tr").removeClass("HighlightedRow");
    $("#GridView1 tr:nth-child(" + counter + ")").addClass("HighlightedRow");
    event.preventDefault();
  });

  $("#Button3").click(function (event) {
    if (counter < $("#GridView1 tr").length) {
      counter++;
    }
    $("#GridView1 tr").removeClass("HighlightedRow");
    $("#GridView1 tr:nth-child(" + counter + ")").addClass("HighlightedRow");
    event.preventDefault();
  });

  $("#Button4").click(function (event) {
    counter = $("#GridView1 tr").length;
    $("#GridView1 tr").removeClass("HighlightedRow");
    $("#GridView1 tr:last-child").addClass("HighlightedRow");
    event.preventDefault();
  });
})
```

The code shown in Listing 3-10 begins by declaring a global variable (counter) to keep track of the current record being highlighted. The ready() method handler wires event handlers for the click events of Button1, Button2, Button3, and Button4, respectively.

When the First button is clicked (Button1), the counter variable is set to 1. The counter is set to 1 because you don't want the table header to be included during the navigation. All the table rows of the grid are selected using the $("#GridView1 tr") selector and then the HighlightedRow CSS class is removed from them using the removeClass() method. This way, if any row was highlighted previously it will lose its highlight. Then the first child selector is used to select the first row of the table (the header row) and HighlightedRow class is applied to it using the addClass() method.

In the click event handler of the Previous button (Button2), the counter variable is decremented. This time, the nth child selector is used to select a table row at index equal to the counter value. The code in the click event handler of Button3 is quite similar to that of Button2 except that the counter variable is incremented because it is the Next button.

In the click event of the Last button, the counter variable is set to the total number of rows in the grid. The Last child selector is then used to select the last table row. The last table row is highlighted by applying the HighlightedRow class to the row using the addClass() method.

Content Filters

Content filters allow you to filter elements based on their content. For example, you can select elements that contain certain text or you can select elements that contain some other elements. Table 3-8 lists all the content filters.

Table 3-8. *Content Filters*

Content Filter	Description	Example
Contains selector	Selects all elements that contain the specified text.	`$("p:contains('ASP.NET')")`
Empty selector	Selects all the elements that are empty (i.e., the elements that don't have any child elements).	`$("div:empty")`
Has selector	Selects all the elements that contain elements matching a given selector.	`$("div:has(span)")`
Parent selector	Selects all the elements that are parents (i.e., contain one or more child elements).	`$("div:parent")`

To use some of the content filters, you will develop an example Web Form (see Figure 3-10).

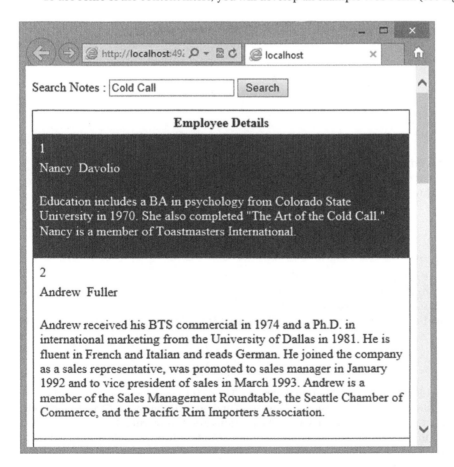

Figure 3-10. *Application using content filters*

The application consists of a Web Form that has a Label, TextBox, and a Button at the top and a GridView below. The text box allows you to enter some search phrase. When the Search button is clicked, notes for all the Employee records are searched for the specified text. The table row of those Employee records that contains the search phrase is highlighted to indicate the successful search.

To develop this application, create an empty Web Forms project and add a Web Form in it. Place a Label, a TextBox, and a Button at the top of the Web Form as shown in Figure 3-10. Drag and drop a SQL Data Source control and configure it to select the EmployeeID, FirstName, LastName, and Notes columns from the Employees table. Then place a GridView below the SQL Data Source and set its data source to the SQL Data Source control you just configured. Add a single TemplateField to the GridView and design the template as shown in Listing 3-11.

Listing 3-11. GridView TemplateField

```
<asp:TemplateField HeaderText="Employee Details">
  <ItemTemplate>
    <table cellpadding="3" cellspacing="0">
      <tr><td>
        <asp:Label ID="Label1" runat="server" Text='<%# Eval("EmployeeID") %>'></asp:Label>
      </td></tr>
      <tr><td>
        <asp:Label ID="Label2" runat="server" Text='<%# Eval("FirstName") %>'></asp:Label>
         
        <asp:Label ID="Label3" runat="server" Text='<%# Eval("LastName") %>'></asp:Label>
      </td> </tr><tr><td>
        <p><%# Eval("Notes") %></p>
      </td>
    </tr>
  </table>
  </ItemTemplate>
</asp:TemplateField>
```

Although the template markup is simple, notice that the Notes column is being displayed in a paragraph (<p>) element. The other columns are displayed using <asp:Label>. Next, add a <script> reference to the jQuery library and also add a <script> block for writing your jQuery code. Then key in the code shown in Listing 3-12 inside the <script> block.

Listing 3-12. Using Content Filters

```
$(document).ready(function () {
  $("#Button1").click(function (evt) {
    var searchString = $("#TextBox1").val();
    $("#GridView1 tr").removeClass("HighlightedRow");
    $("#GridView1 tr:has(p:contains('" + searchString + "'))").addClass("HighlightedRow");
    evt.preventDefault();
  });
});
```

The code wires a click event handler for the Search button (Button1). The click event handler retrieves the value entered in the search text box using the ID selector and val() method. It then calls the removeClass() method on all the table rows inside GridView1 to remove any highlight from the previous application run. Remember that the searching should happen only within the Notes column. The code, therefore, selects only those table rows that have a paragraph element containing the specified text.

Notice that the :has() and :contains() content filters are used in nested fashion to select the desired rows. The searchString is passed to the :contains() filter so that all the <p> elements containing the searchString are selected. Further, the result of :contains() is fed to :has() filter. This way, the <tr> elements that have <p> elements containing the searchString get filtered. The HighlightedRow CSS class is applied to the selected table rows using the addClass() method.

Form Filters

Form selectors allow you to select <form> elements based on their type (such as text box, check box, and radio button) or their status (such as selected, checked, and disabled). Form selectors are widely used when developing data-driven web applications and also when data-bound ASP.NET controls, such as GridView and DetailsView, are being used. Table 3-9 lists all the available Form selectors.

Table 3-9. *Form Selectors*

Form selector	Description	Example
Button selector	Selects all <button> elements as well as <input> elements of the type button.	$("input:button")
Checkbox selector	Selects all <input> elements that are of type checkbox.	$("input:checkbox")
Checked selector	Selects all checkboxes, radio buttons, and select elements that are selected.	$("input:checked")
Disabled selector	Selects all the form elements that are disabled.	$("input:disabled")
Enabled selector	Selects all the form elements that are enabled.	$("input:enabled")
File selector	Selects all <input> elements that are of type file.	$("input:file")
Focus selector	Selects an element if it is having focus.	$(":focus")
Image selector	Selects all <input> elements that are of type image.	$("input:image")
Input selector	Selects all the <input> elements.	$(":input")
Password selector	Selects all the <input> elements that are of type password.	$("input:password")
Radio selector	Selects all the <input> elements that are of type radio.	$("input:radio")
Reset selector	Selects all the <input> elements that are of type reset.	$("input:reset")
Selected selector	Selects all the <option> elements that are selected.	$(":selected")
Submit selector	Select all the <input> elements that are of type submit.	$("input:submit")
Text selector	Selects all the <input> elements whose type attribute is text.	$("input:text")

To understand how form selectors can be used, you will develop a web application as shown in Figure 3-11.

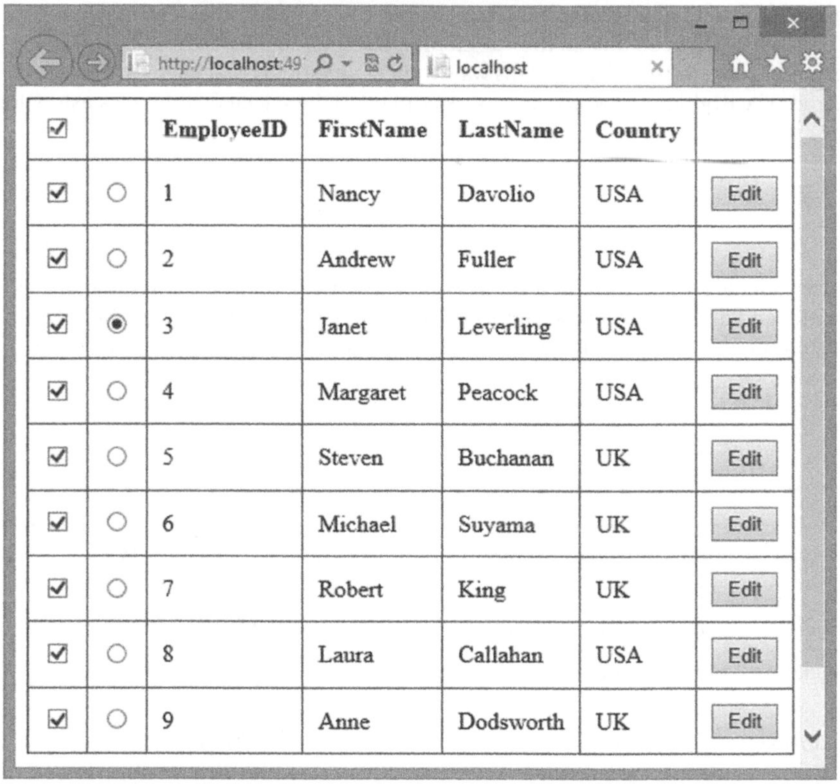

Figure 3-11. *Application using form selectors*

The application consists of a Web Form that has a GridView on it. The GridView is bound with the Employees table of the Northwind database. In all, the GridView has seven columns and exhibits the following features:

- The first column is a TemplateField that has a CheckBox placed in its ItemTemplate and HeaderTemplate. You can select multiple rows of the GridView by checking the respective check box.

- Clicking the header check box toggles the checked status of all the check boxes.

- The second column is a TemplateField with a RadioButton control placed in its ItemTemplate. Because ASP.NET generates a unique ID and name for all the constituent controls of a GridView, all the radio buttons behave in an independent manner, and you can select multiple radio buttons from the GridView. By using jQuery code, however, you ensure that only one radio button is selected at a time.

- Columns three through six are TemplateField columns and display the EmployeeID, FirstName, LastName and Country columns.

- The Country column has a DropDownList in its EditItemTemplate that is bound with distinct country names from the Employees table. The DropDownList also has a default item, Please Select, and actual countries get appended to it.

- The last column is a CommandField of type Edit, Update, Cancel.

- When a grid row is in edit mode, jQuery code ensures that some value is entered in the FirstName and LastName text boxes, and a country other than the default value is selected in the DropDownList. If no data is entered in the text boxes, an error message is displayed to the user in an alert dialog.

- At the bottom of the Web Form is an ImageButton (not shown in the figure) that simply displays how many check boxes and radio buttons are selected.

Although this example doesn't do anything special with the rows selected, by using a check box or radio button, you can access them from the server-side code for further processing.

To develop this application, begin by creating an empty ASP.NET Web Forms application. Add a Web Form to it and place two SQL Data Source controls on it. Configure the first SQL Data Source control (SqlDataSource1) to select EmployeeID, FirstName, LastName, and Country columns from the Employees table. Configure the other SQL Data Source control (SqlDataSource2) to select distinct Country rows from the Employees table. Then place a GridView on the Web Form and bind it with SqlDataSource1. Add TemplateField columns to the GridView, as shown in Figure 3-11, and data bind them with the respective columns of the Employees table.

While designing the first column, set the ID of the CheckBox in the ItemTemplate to chkRow and ID of the CheckBox in the HeaderTemplate to chkHeader. Similarly, set the ID of the RadioButton control placed inside the ItemTemplate of the second column to radRow. Also, set the ID property of the FirstName text box, LastName text box, and Country drop-down list to TextBox1, TextBox2, and DropDownList1, respectively. Listing 3-13 shows the complete markup for the GridView templates.

Listing 3-13. GridView Markup

```
<asp:GridView ID="GridView1" runat="server" AutoGenerateColumns="False" CellPadding="10"
DataKeyNames="EmployeeID" DataSourceID="SqlDataSource1">
  <Columns>
    <asp:TemplateField>
      <HeaderTemplate>
        <asp:CheckBox ID="chkHeader" runat="server" />
      </HeaderTemplate>
      <ItemTemplate>
        <asp:CheckBox ID="chkRow" runat="server" />
      </ItemTemplate>
    </asp:TemplateField>
    <asp:TemplateField>
      <ItemTemplate>
        <asp:RadioButton ID="radRow" runat="server" />
      </ItemTemplate>
    </asp:TemplateField>
    <asp:BoundField DataField="EmployeeID" HeaderText="EmployeeID" InsertVisible="False"
ReadOnly="True" SortExpression="EmployeeID" />
    <asp:TemplateField HeaderText="FirstName" SortExpression="FirstName">
      <EditItemTemplate>
        <asp:TextBox ID="TextBox1" runat="server" Text='<%# Bind("FirstName") %>'></asp:TextBox>
      </EditItemTemplate>
      <ItemTemplate>
        <asp:Label ID="Label2" runat="server" Text='<%# Bind("FirstName") %>'></asp:Label>
      </ItemTemplate>
    </asp:TemplateField>
```

```
    <asp:TemplateField HeaderText="LastName" SortExpression="LastName">
      <EditItemTemplate>
        <asp:TextBox ID="TextBox2" runat="server" Text='<%# Bind("LastName") %>'></asp:TextBox>
      </EditItemTemplate>
      <ItemTemplate>
        <asp:Label ID="Label3" runat="server" Text='<%# Bind("LastName") %>'></asp:Label>
      </ItemTemplate>
    </asp:TemplateField>
    <asp:TemplateField HeaderText="Country" SortExpression="Country">
      <EditItemTemplate>
        <asp:DropDownList ID="DropDownList1" runat="server" DataSourceID="SqlDataSource2"
DataTextField="Country" DataValueField="Country" SelectedValue='<%# Bind("Country") %>'
AppendDataBoundItems="True">
<asp:ListItem>Please select</asp:ListItem>
        </asp:DropDownList>
      </EditItemTemplate>
      <ItemTemplate>
        <asp:Label ID="Label1" runat="server" Text='<%# Bind("Country") %>'></asp:Label>
      </ItemTemplate>
    </asp:TemplateField>
    <asp:CommandField ButtonType="Button" ShowEditButton="True" />
  </Columns>
</asp:GridView>
```

Notice that the Edit, Update, and Cancel CommandField has ButtonType property set to Button. This way, the GridView will emit <input> tags with type set to submit.

Once the GridView is designed, add an ImageButton at the bottom of the Web Form and set its ImageUrl property to some image. Now add a <script> reference to jQuery library and also add a <script> block. Key in the jQuery code shown in Listing 3-14 in the <script> block.

Listing 3-14. jQuery Form Selectors for Check Box and Radio Button Functionality

```
$(document).ready(function () {
  $("#GridView1 input:checkbox[name$='chkHeader']").click(function () {
    if ($("#GridView1 input:checkbox[name$='chkHeader']").is(":checked")) {
      $("#GridView1 input:checkbox").prop("checked", true);
    }
    else {
      $("#GridView1 input:checkbox").prop("checked",false);
    }
  });
  $("#GridView1 input:radio").click(function (evt) {
    var currentRadioId = this.id;
    $("#GridView1 input:radio").each(function () {
      if (this.id != currentRadioId) {
        $(this).prop("checked",false);
      }
    });
  });
});
```

```
$("#form1 input:image").click(function (evt) {
    var chkCount = $("#GridView1 input:checkbox:checked").length;
    var radCount = $("#GridView1 input:radio:checked").length;
    alert(chkCount +  " checkboxes and " + radCount + " radio buttons are selected!");
    evt.preventDefault();
  });
});
```

The code shown in Listing 3-14 consists of three important pieces: the click event handler of the header check box, the click event handler of the radio buttons, and the click event handler of the image button. The click event handler of the header check box toggles the checked state of all the check boxes to checked or unchecked, depending on the state of chkHeader check box. Notice that a check box selector is used along with an Attribute Ends With selector to get the chkHeader check box. Once the reference to chkHeader is obtained a click event handler is wired to its click event using the click() method.

Inside the click event handler, you see whether chkHeader is checked by using the is() method. The is() method accepts a selector (:checked in this case) and returns true if any of the elements from the current matched set match with the specified selector. In this case, if chkHeader is checked, all check boxes from the grid are selected using the :checkbox selector. Once selected, their checked DOM property is set to true using the prop() method. The prop() method accepts the name of the DOM element property that you want to set (checked in this case) and its value (true in this case). If chkHeader is not checked, the checked property of all the check boxes is set to false.

■ **Note**　You will learn more about the prop()and is() methods in Chapter 5 and Chapter 6, respectively.

The click event handler of the radio button is attached using the :radio selector. Inside the click event handler, the ID of the radio button being clicked is retrieved using the this.id property and is stored in the currentRadioId variable. Because you need to ensure that only one radio button is selected, you iterate through all the radio buttons using the each() method and :radio selector. The each() method accepts a function that gets executed for every matched element. Inside the each() function, this refers to the element being iterated. If a radio button is not the one that is being clicked, its checked property is set to false using the prop() method. This way, only the radio button that is being clicked is checked; others are unchecked.

The image button is selected using the :image selector and a click event handler is wired to its click event. Inside the click event handler, you find out how many check boxes and radio buttons are checked using the :checkbox:checked and :radio:checked selectors. The former selector returns all the check boxes that are checked and the latter returns all the radio buttons that are checked. The length property returns the number of matched elements in each of the cases. An alert() is then displayed informing the user about the number of check boxes and radio buttons selected.

This completes the check box and radio button–related functionality of the Web Form. Let's add the validation logic inside the ready() handler to ensure that text boxes and drop-down lists contain valid values. Listing 3-15 shows the jQuery code responsible for this validation.

Listing 3-15. Validating Text Box Values and Drop-down List Selection

```
$("#form1").submit(function (evt) {
  if ($("#GridView1 input:text").length > 0) {
    if ($("#form1 :input[name$='TextBox1']").val() == "") {
      alert("Please enter first name!");
      evt.preventDefault();
    }
```

```
    if ($("#GridView1 :input[name$='TextBox2']").val() == "") {
      alert("Please enter last name!");
      evt.preventDefault();
    }
    if ($("#GridView1 :selected").val() == "Please select") {
      alert("Please select a country!");
      evt.preventDefault();
    }
  }
});
```

The code shown in Listing 3-15 begins by wiring an event handler function to the submit event of the form. This is done by using the ID selector and submit() method. The submit event is raised when a form is submitted to the server. Inside, the event handler first check whether any text box is being displayed. This is necessary because GridView renders text boxes and drop-down lists only in edit mode. If the :text selector returns more than zero elements, the grid is in edit mode.

You can then use the :input selector in combination with the Attribute Ends With selector to get TextBox1. You use the Attribute Ends With selector because at runtime GridView generates names of the GridView1$ctl02$TextBox1 form. Using the Attribute Ends With selector allows you to pick the text box by its name because the text box name gets added at the end.

Once you get a reference to TextBox1 (the FirstName text box), you can check whether it's empty by using the val() method. If the text box is empty, you display an alert() to the user and call preventDefault() on the evt object to cancel the form submission. Similarly, you ensure that the LastName text box also contains some value.

Finally, the :selected selector is used to select the <option> element that is selected in the drop-down list. If the option is Please Select, an error message is displayed asking the user to select a valid country and the form submission is cancelled by calling the preventDefault() method on the evt object.

Figure 3-12 shows how validation error messages are displayed.

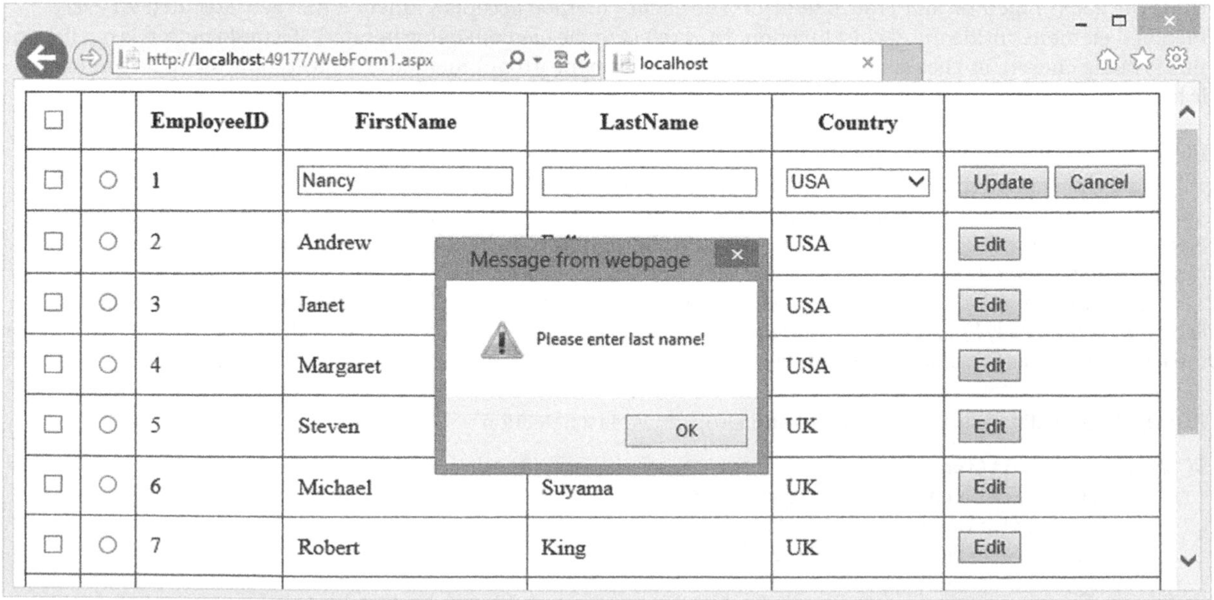

Figure 3-12. *Validation of text boxes and drop-down list in action*

Hierarchy Filters

As the name suggests, hierarchy selectors allow you to work with child and sibling elements. You might be surprised to know that you already used one of the hierarchy selectors in the preceding example. Whenever you used `$("#GridView1 tr")`, you were actually using one of the hierarchy selectors: the Descendant selector. Table 3-10 lists all the hierarchy selectors available to you.

Table 3-10. *List of Hierarchy Selectors*

Hierarchy Selector	Description	Example
Child selector	Selects all the child elements of a parent that are direct children.	`$("#GridView1 > tr")` will select all `<tr>` elements that are direct children of #GridView1
Descendant selector	Selects all the elements that are descendants of an ancestor element.	`$("#GridView td")` will select all the `<td>` elements that are descendants of #GridView1
Next Adjacent selector	Selects all the elements matching a selector that immediately follow a given sibling.	`$("div + span")` will select a `<span>` that is immediately next to a `<div>`.
Next Siblings selector	Selects all the elements matching a selector that follow a given sibling.	`$("div ~ span")` will select all the `<span>` elements that are after a `<div>`.

To understand how hierarchy selectors are used, let's develop the web application shown in Figure 3-13.

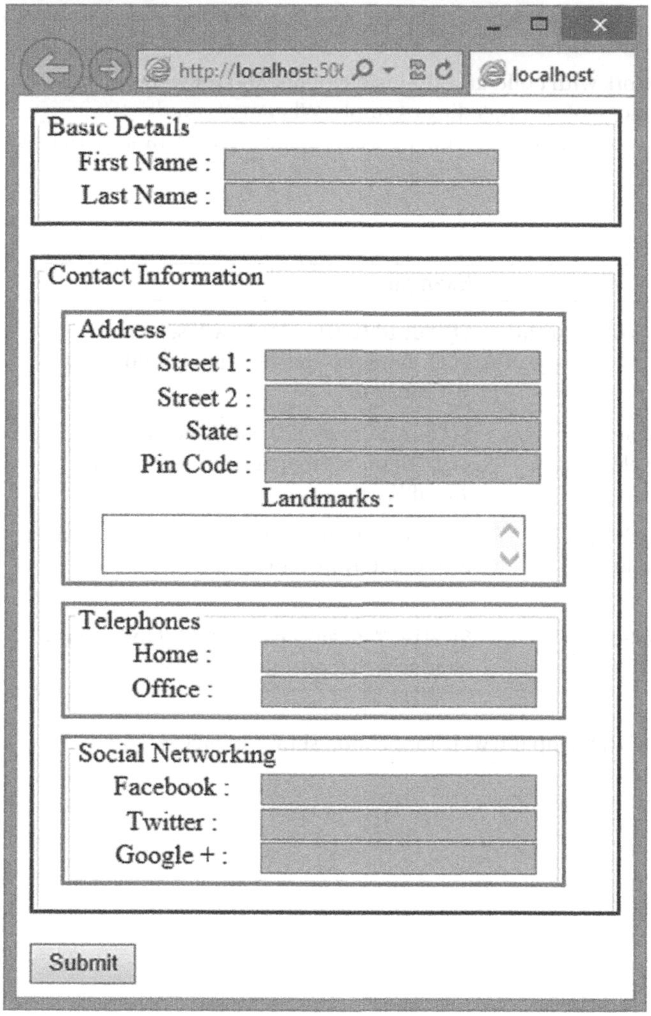

Figure 3-13. Application using hierarchy selectors

The application consists of a Web Form that represents a data entry screen for a hypothetical table. Various data entry controls are grouped using Panel server controls. When the page loads, hierarchy selectors are used to access various form elements, and some CSS properties (such as border and background color) are applied to them. The markup of the Web Form relevant to this example is shown in Listing 3-16.

Listing 3-16. Web Form Markup

```
<form id="form1" runat="server">
<asp:Panel ID="Container" runat="server">
<asp:Panel ID="Panel1" runat="server" GroupingText="Basic Details">
<asp:Label ID="Label5" runat="server" Text="First Name : " Width="100px"
style="text-align:right"></asp:Label> 
<asp:TextBox ID="TextBox6" runat="server"></asp:TextBox>
<br />
```

```
<asp:Label ID="Label6" runat="server" Text="Last Name : " Width="100px"
style="text-align:right"></asp:Label> 
<asp:TextBox ID="TextBox7" runat="server"></asp:TextBox>
</asp:Panel>
<br />
<asp:Panel ID="Panel2" runat="server" GroupingText="Contact Information" style="text-align:center">
<asp:Panel ID="Panel3" runat="server" GroupingText="Address" Width="300px">
<asp:Label ID="Label1" runat="server" Text="Street 1 : " Width="100px"
style="text-align:right"></asp:Label> 
<asp:TextBox ID="TextBox1" runat="server"></asp:TextBox>
<br />
<asp:Label ID="Label2" runat="server" Text="Street 2 : " Width="100px"
style="text-align:right"></asp:Label> 
<asp:TextBox ID="TextBox2" runat="server"></asp:TextBox>
<br />
<asp:Label ID="State" runat="server" Text="State : " Width="100px"
style="text-align:right"></asp:Label> 
<asp:TextBox ID="TextBox3" runat="server"></asp:TextBox>
<br />
<asp:Label ID="Label3" runat="server" Text="Pin Code : " Width="100px"
style="text-align:right"></asp:Label> 
<asp:TextBox ID="TextBox4" runat="server"></asp:TextBox>
<br />
<asp:Label ID="Label4" runat="server" Text="Landmarks : " Width="100px"
style="text-align:right"></asp:Label>
<br />
<asp:TextBox ID="TextBox5" runat="server" TextMode="MultiLine" Width="250px"></asp:TextBox>
</asp:Panel>
<asp:Panel ID="Panel4" runat="server" GroupingText="Telephones" Width="300px">
<asp:Label ID="Label7" runat="server" Text="Home :" Width="100px"></asp:Label>
<asp:TextBox ID="TextBox8" runat="server"></asp:TextBox>
<br />
<asp:Label ID="Label8" runat="server" Text="Office :" Width="100px"></asp:Label>
<asp:TextBox ID="TextBox9" runat="server"></asp:TextBox>
</asp:Panel>
<asp:Panel ID="Panel5" runat="server" GroupingText="Social Networking" Width="300px">
<asp:Label ID="Label9" runat="server" Text="Facebook :" Width="100px"></asp:Label>
<asp:TextBox ID="TextBox10" runat="server"></asp:TextBox>
<br />
<asp:Label ID="Label10" runat="server" Text="Twitter :" Width="100px"></asp:Label>
<asp:TextBox ID="TextBox11" runat="server"></asp:TextBox>
<br />
<asp:Label ID="Label11" runat="server" Text="Google + :" Width="100px"></asp:Label>
<asp:TextBox ID="TextBox12" runat="server"></asp:TextBox>
</asp:Panel>
</asp:Panel>
<br />
</asp:Panel>
<asp:Button ID="Button1" runat="server" Text="Submit" />
</form>
```

There are six Panel controls in all. The outermost panel houses two sibling Panel controls: Basic Details and Contact Information. The Basic Details panel contains Label and TextBox controls for entering basic details such as First Name and Last Name. The Contact Information panel houses three child Panel controls: Address, Telephones, and Social Networking. Notice that the GroupingText property of the Panel control governs the caption of the respective panel.

The jQuery code that makes the application functional is shown in Listing 3-17.

Listing 3-17. jQuery Code Using Hierarchy Selectors

```
$(document).ready(function () {
  $("#Container > div").css("border", "solid navy 2px");
  $("#Panel2 fieldset > div").css("border", "solid red 2px").css("margin", "10px");
  $("span + :text").css("background-color", "silver").css("border", "solid gray 1px");
  $("span ~ :text").css("font-family", "courier");
})
```

The Container panel has an ID set to Container. The second line of code selects all the direct child <div> elements of this Container panel. Remember that the ASP.NET Panel control is rendered as a <div> element in the browser. Because you want direct child <div> container elements, use the Child selector, which furnishes two panels (Panel1, Basic Details and Panel2, Contact Information); then set their border color to navy.

To get the panels that are inside the Contact information panel (Panel2), you again use the Child selector in combination with the Descendant selector. You have set the GroupingText property of all the panels to some meaningful text (Basic Details, Contact Information, and so on). When you set the GroupingText property, ASP.NET emits the <fieldset> and <legend> elements, as shown here:

```
<div id="Panel2" style="text-align:center">
 <fieldset>
  <legend>
    Contact Information
  </legend>
  <div id="Panel3" style="width:300px;">
...
```

So Panel3, Panel4, and Panel5 are not direct child elements of Panel2. They are child elements of the <fieldset> element. Hence, you need to use the <fieldset> element in the selector. Once selected, their border is set to red.

The Next Adjacent selector is now used to select all the text boxes. In this Web Form, Label controls and TextBox controls are placed side by side. If you want to select all the text boxes that are immediately next to labels, "span + :text" will do the job. The "span + :text" selector simply grabs all the text boxes that are placed immediately after span elements. Notice that because you used the Next Adjacent selector, the textarea won't get selected because there is a line brake (<br />) between the Landmarks label and the textarea (they are not adjacent. So the "span + :text" selector returns 11 text boxes (2 from Panel1, 4 from Panel3, 2 from Panel4, and 3 from Panel5). You then set the background color for these text boxes to silver and the border color to gray.

Finally, you used the Next Siblings selector "span ~ :text". This selector simply grabs all the text boxes that are anywhere after the span elements. Because the Next Siblings selector selects all the next siblings of an element, this time even the textarea will be selected. You then set the font-family of all the text boxes to courier.

Visibility Filters

Visibility filters allow you to select either hidden or visible elements. An element is considered hidden if it has the CSS `display` property set to none, it is an `<input>` element with type hidden, or its height and width are both 0. The setting of the CSS `visibility` property is not taken into account when deciding whether an element is visible or hidden. The selectors included in this category are given in Table 3-11.

Table 3-11. *Visibility Filters*

Visibility selector	Description	Example
Hidden selector	Selects all the elements that are hidden.	`$("tr:hidden")`
Visible selector	Selects all the elements that are visible.	`$("tr:visible")`

To understand how visibility filters can be used, you'll develop the web application shown in Figure 3-14.

Figure 3-14. *Application using visibility filters*

The application consists of a Web Form that houses a `Button`, a `Label` and a `GridView` control. The `GridView` control displays all the records from the `Employees` table by default. Clicking a table cell (`<td>` element) hides that complete row. The `Label` at the top shows the number of table rows that are visible and hidden. Clicking the Show All button makes all the table rows visible.

To develop this application, create an empty ASP.NET Web Forms application. Add a Web Form to it and design it as shown in Figure 3-14. The GridView is bound with SQL Data Source control, so add one to your Web Form and configure it to select the EmployeeID, FirstName, LastName and Country columns from the Employees table.

Add a <script> reference and a <script> block to the jQuery library. Key in the code shown in Listing 3-18 in the <script> block.

Listing 3-18. jQuery Code Using Visibility Filters

```
$(document).ready(function () {
  $("td").click(function (evt) {
    $(evt.target).parent().css("display", "none");
    var visibleCount = $("tr:visible").length;
    var hiddenCount = $("tr:hidden").length;
    $("#Label1").html( visibleCount + " rows are visible.<br/>" + hiddenCount + " rows are
hidden.");
  });
  $("#Button1").click(function (evt) {
    $("tr").css("display", "block");
    var visibleCount = $("tr:visible").length;
    var hiddenCount = $("tr:hidden").length;
    $("#Label1").html( visibleCount + " rows are visible.<br/>" + hiddenCount + " rows are
hidden.");
    evt.preventDefault();
  });
});
```

The code wires a click event handler for all the table cells by selecting the element selector for <td> elements and then attaching an event handler function using the click() method. Even if a user is clicking a table cell, you want to hide that entire row. Inside the click event handler, you grab the parent row of the table cell being clicked using the parent() method and then set its display CSS property to none. This way, the entire row will be hidden. You then use the :visible selector and :hidden selector to find out the total number of visible and hidden table rows. A message is displayed in the Label1 span element, informing the user about the hidden and visible rows.

The click event handler of the Show All button (Button1) simply sets the display CSS property of all the <tr> elements to block. This way all the table rows are made visible again. Details about the visible and hidden rows are again shown in Label1.

Using Selectors in ASP.NET MVC

So far in this chapter, you used various jQuery selectors in ASP.NET Web Forms applications. Let's conclude this chapter with an example that illustrates how they are used in ASP.NET MVC applications. Before you actually develop this example, take a look at some of the commonly used HTML helpers and the HTML tags emitted by them (see Table 3-12).

Table 3-12. *ASP.NET MVC HTML Helpers and HTML Elements*

HTML Helper	Server-side Tag	HTML Tag
ActionLink	Html.ActionLink()	`<a>`
Form	Html.BeginForm() Html.EndForm()	`<form>` `</form>`
Checkbox	Html.CheckBox() Html.CheckBoxFor()	`<input type="checkbox" />`
DropDownList	Html.DropDownList() Html.DropDownListFor()	`<select>`
ListBox	Html.ListBox() Html.ListBoxFor()	`<select multiple="multiple">`
Password	Html.Password() Html.PasswordFor()	`<input type="password" />`
RadioButton	Html.RadioButton() Html.RadioButtonFor()	`<input type="radio" />`
TextArea	Html.TextArea() Html.TextAreaFor()	`<textarea>`
TextBox	Html.TextBox() Html.TextBoxFor()	`<input type="text" />`

As in the case of server controls, keep in mind the HTML tags outputted by these helpers while accessing them in jQuery code.

In this section, you develop an MVC view like the one shown in Figure 3-15.

Figure 3-15. *Contact Us view showing validation errors*

The view represents a typical contact us form that allows the user to enter a first name, last name, e-mail address, subject, message, and a reason for the contact. Clicking the Send button sends the contact form details to a web site administrator through an email. When a user clicks the Send button, jQuery code ensures that the FirstName, LastName, Email, and Subject text boxes have some value entered and the Reason drop-down list has a reason selected.

To begin developing this application, create a new ASP.NET MVC application based on the empty project template. Then add HomeController to the Controllers folder and key in the action methods as shown in Listing 3-19.

Listing 3-19. Index( ) and ProcessForm( ) Action Methods

```
public ActionResult Index()
{
  List<string> reasons = new List<string>();
  reasons.Add("Please select");
  reasons.Add("General Feedback");
  reasons.Add("Billing related");
  reasons.Add("Technical query");
  SelectList list = new SelectList(reasons);
  ViewData["Reason"] = list;
  return View();
}
```

```
public ActionResult ProcessForm(ContactForm data)
{
  string msg = "";
  msg += data.Message + "\n\n";
  msg += "-" + data.FirstName + " " + data.LastName + "\n\n";
  SmtpClient client = new SmtpClient();
  client.Send(data.Email, "admin@somewebsite.com", data.Subject, msg);
  return View();
}
```

The Index() action method creates a generic list of strings for storing the options for the Reason drop-down list. It then forms a SelectList object based on this generic List. The SelectList object is stored in a ViewData key named Reason. It then returns the Index view.

The Contact Us form is submitted to the ProcessForm() action method, and the method accepts a parameter of type ContactForm. The ContactForm class is a simple class with six public properties corresponding to the form fields. It is added to the Models folder:

```
public class ContactForm
{
  public string FirstName { get; set; }
  public string LastName { get; set; }
  public string Email { get; set; }
  public string Subject { get; set; }
  public string Message { get; set; }
  public string Reason { get; set; }
}
```

Inside the ProcessForm() method, an e-mail message is formed using various properties of the ContactForm class. Although not shown in the code above, in a real world application you should perform validations on ContactForm properties to ensure that the data is in correct format. Then an instance of the SmtpClient class is created to send an e-mail. The Send() method of SmtpClient accepts four parameters—sender, recipient, subject, and message—and sends an e-mail to the recipient. Of course, you should change the recipient parameter according to your e-mail setup. The ProcessForm() method then returns the ProcessForm view informing the user about the successful form submission.

Add the Index view to the project and key in the markup shown in Listing 3-20.

Listing 3-20. Index view Markup

```
<h1>Contact Us</h1>
  @using(Html.BeginForm("ProcessForm","Home",FormMethod.Post)){
  <table>
    <tr>
      <td>@Html.Label("FirstName")</td>
      <td>@Html.TextBox("FirstName")</td>
    </tr>
    <tr>
      <td>@Html.Label("LastName")</td>
      <td>@Html.TextBox("LastName")</td>
    </tr>
```

```
  <tr>
    <td>@Html.Label("Email")</td>
    <td>@Html.TextBox("Email")</td>
  </tr>
  <tr>
    <td>@Html.Label("Subject")</td>
    <td>@Html.TextBox("Subject")</td>
  </tr>
  <tr>
    <td>@Html.Label("Message")</td>
    <td>@Html.TextArea("Message")</td>
  </tr>
  <tr>
    <td>@Html.Label("Reason")</td>
    <td>@Html.DropDownList("Reason")</td>
  </tr>
  <tr>
    <td colspan="2">
      <input type="submit" value="Send" />
      <ul id="message"></ul>
    </td>
  </tr>
</table>
}
```

The Index view uses HTML helpers such as Label(), BeginForm(), TextBox(), TextArea(), and DropDownList(). The BeginForm() helper specifies the action method name as ProcessForm, the controller name as Home, and the form method as Post. Usage of most of the HTML helpers is straightforward. The name parameter provided in all the HTML helpers indicates the name of the resultant HTML element. Notice that names of various HTML elements match the various properties of the ContactForm class. This way, MVC model binding can map field values with the ContactForm properties. Also notice that the DropDownList() helper automatically uses the Reason ViewData object you added earlier as the source of data to generate <option> elements. The message <ul> element is intended to display validation error messages, if any.

Now add a <script> reference to jQuery and a <script> block in the head section. Add the code shown in Listing 3-21 to the <script> block.

Listing 3-21. Validating form using jQuery

```
$(document).ready(function () {
  $("#message").css("color", "red");
  $("input:submit").click(function (evt) {
    $("input:text").each(function () {
    if ($(this).val() == "") {
      $(this).css("border", "1px solid red");
      $("#message").append("<li>Please fill in " + $(this).attr("name") + "  field.</li>");
      evt.preventDefault();
    }
    else
    {
      $(this).css("border-width", "0px");
    }
  });
```

```
  if ($(":selected").val() == "Please select") {
    $("select").css("border", "1px solid red");
    $("#message").append("<li>Please select a reason for contacting us.</li>");
    evt.preventDefault();
  }
  else
  {
    $("select").css("border-width", "0px");
  }
 });
});
```

The ready() handler function selects the message <ul> element using the ID selector and sets its color CSS property to red. It then selects the submit button using the input:submit selector and wires its click event handler. The click event handler of the submit button selects all the <input> elements with type text using the input:text selector. The each() method then iterates through the selected text boxes to find out whether a value has been entered by using the val() method. If a text box doesn't contain a value, its border is set to red and an <li> element is added to the <ul> using the append() method. The preventDefault() method of the event object is called to prevent the form submission. If a text box contains a value, its border is removed by setting the border-style CSS property to 0px.

The :selected selector is used to retrieve the <option> element selected in the drop-down list. The val() method then returns the value of this element. If the value of the selected element is Please Select, the user has not made a valid selection from the drop-down list. The <select> element is then displayed with a red border. An error message is also added in the message <ul> using the append() method. As before, the form submission is canceled by calling the preventDefault() method of the evt object. If the drop-down list contains a valid selection, its border is removed by setting the border-style CSS property to 0px.

Now run the application and test whether the jQuery code performs the necessary validations.

Summary

jQuery selectors provide a powerful and flexible way to select DOM elements that match certain criteria. They can be categorized in eight main groups: basic selectors, basic filters, child filters, content filters, attribute selectors, form selectors, hierarchy selectors, and visibility filters. Out of all the available selectors, the basic selectors and form selectors are the ones widely used in ASP.NET web applications. Working with selectors in a Web Forms application requires understanding how server controls are mapped to HTML elements.

Once the controls are selected, you often want to process them in some manner. One of the most common tasks is to handle the events of the selected elements. Although this chapter gave you a peek into jQuery's event handling capabilities, there are many more aspects to consider. To that end, the next chapter will take you straight to the heart of event handling in jQuery.

CHAPTER 4

■ ■ ■

Event Handling

One of the most common uses of jQuery in web applications is event handling. As an ASP.NET developer, you are already familiar with the concepts of events and event handling. Events raised by ASP.NET server controls, however, are server-side events. They are raised on the server after postback takes place. Events that you handle using jQuery are client-side events. JavaScript (and hence jQuery) offers a much richer set of events to developers than ASP.NET offers on the server side. These events are raised in the client browser and are also handled in the client browser. Events such as clicking a button, changing a selection from a drop-down list, or entering text into a text box are some of the examples of client-side events—and there are many more.

Because event handling is one of the most commonly performed tasks in client-side script, jQuery tries to offer a simplified mechanism to handle events. This chapter discusses several aspects of jQuery event handling in detail. Specifically, you will learn the following:

- What the commonly used JavaScript events are

- How to wire event handlers to events

- How to obtain information about an event

- How to perform advanced operations such as stopping event propagation, passing custom data to an event handler, and unwiring event handlers

Overview of Event Handling

An *event* is some action, usually performed by the end user, on a web page as a whole or on a Document Object Model (DOM) element contained within the web page. For example, when a web page finishes loading in the browser, this is an event applicable to the web page as a whole; whereas a user clicking a submit button is an example of an event being raised on a particular DOM element. Whenever any event is raised, there are a couple of possibilities:

- The web page developer might have written some code that deals with that event.

- The event might not have been dealt with by the web page developer.

The code that deals with an event is referred as an *event handler*. In the former case, a developer attaches an event handler to an event through code. This process is also referred to as *registering* an event handler or *wiring* an event handler. If an event has an event handler attached to it, the handler code gets executed whenever that event is raised. An event can also have more than one event handler; although you may not use this feature frequently, it can be useful when multiple independent pieces of code are to be conditionally wired to the same event.

If the event doesn't have an event handler attached with it, it is bubbled up to the parent element to see whether any other handlers are available. If so, they are executed and the bubbling process continues. Figure 4-1 shows this event bubbling pictorially.

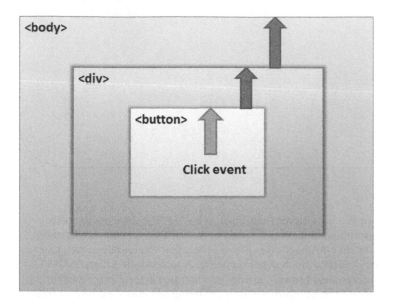

Figure 4-1. *JavaScript event bubbling*

Figure 4-1 shows a <button> element housed inside a <div> element that is, in turn, placed inside the <body> of the HTML page. If you click the button, the click event is raised on the <button> element. Once the click event handler of the button is executed (if one is found), the event is bubbled to the <div> element. If the <div> element has any click event handler, it gets executed and the event is bubbled up to the <body> element. If the <body> has wired any click event handler, that also gets executed. Thus, the click event gets bubbled up from the innermost element (<button>) to the outermost element (<body>).

■ **Note** Event bubbling can also be canceled from your code (you'll learn about it in later sections of the chapter). Here it is enough to know that some events can potentially be handled at more than one level depending on the DOM tree structure and nesting.

The events discussed in the remainder of this chapter are grouped into the following categories:

- Window and document events
- Mouse events
- Keyboard events
- Form events
- Miscellaneous events

The window and document events are raised by a browser's window and document object, respectively. For example, when a user scrolls the web page in the browser window, the scroll event is raised by the window object. Along the same lines, when a web page finishes loading in the browser, a load event is raised.

Mouse events are raised when a mouse button is pressed, released or clicked. For example, clicking a mouse button once raises a click event. Other mouse events include dblclick, mouseup and mousedown. Events related to drag-and-drop operations are also mouse events, in a way. Drag-and-drop events include events such as dragstart, drag, dragenter, and drop.

Keyboard events are raised when a key is pushed down, released, or pressed. Events such as keypress, keydown, and keyup belong to this category.

Form events are related to HTML form and form fields. For example, the submit event is raised when a form is submitted from the browser. Events such as submit, input, change, focus, and blur belong to this category.

Miscellaneous events are the events that do not fit into any of the other categories. For example, HTML5 audio and video elements offer many events, such as play and pause, which notify you when a media file is played or paused in the browser.

Now that you have a basic understanding of client-side events, let's go on to the jQuery way of handling events in the next couple of sections.

Handling and Raising Events

Handling an event involves attaching an event handler code to the event. Traditionally, web developers used HTML event attributes to attach event handler functions to their respective events. For example, consider the following piece of HTML markup:

```
<input id="button1" type="button" onclick ="OnClick()" value="Click Me" />
```

This markup represents an input element of the button type. Notice that the onclick attribute of the element is attaching the OnClick() JavaScript function as an event handler for the click event. This way, when the button is clicked, the OnClick() function gets invoked. The same task can be accomplished using plain JavaScript code, as follows:

```
document.getElementById('button1').onclick = OnClick;
```

Here, you first get a reference to the button using the getElementById() method and then set the onclick property to a function named OnClick.

jQuery has a more elegant and easy way of attaching event handlers to events. For most of the common events, such as click, dblclick, and keypress, jQuery offers built-in methods for registering event handlers. For example, the click() method allows you to wire a click event handler to the click event. In Chapters 2 and 3, you already used some of these methods. The general syntax of these built-in methods is as follows:

```
$(<jquery_selector>).event_method(event_handler)
```

Events are attached to DOM elements. So, the jQuery event methods are called on some DOM elements. These DOM elements are selected using some jQuery selector such as the ID selector or element selector. For most of the standard events, jQuery has event methods. Some of the event methods are click(), dblclick(), and keypress(). These methods are discussed in detail later in this chapter. Each event method accepts an event handler as its parameter. Consider the following code:

```
$("#button1").click(function () {
  alert('Inside OnClick event handler');
});
```

The previous code uses an ID selector to select button1. The click() method is then called to register an anonymous function as a handler for the click event. One immediate advantage of jQuery's way of attaching event handlers is that you can attach event handlers to more than one DOM element by selecting them with jQuery selectors.

Most of the time, an event is raised by some user action and your job is to handle it in your jQuery code using the technique you just learned. However, sometimes you need to programmatically call registered event handlers. For example, you may want to toggle the state of check boxes in the form when a button is clicked. One easy way to accomplish this task is to trigger the click event handler of all those check boxes programmatically. That way, all the check boxes toggle their checked state. To trigger an event handler programmatically rather than as a result of user action, you use the same event methods without any parameters. The following line of code makes this clear:

```
$("#button1").click();
```

This line of code triggers the button1 click event handler through code.

Obtaining Event Information

Sometimes you need more information about the event being handled inside an event handler. For example, suppose that you are developing a custom blog engine that has a web page for entering a blog post. For the sake of ease of use, you want to provide certain shortcuts to the users; for example, Ctrl+S for saving the draft, Ctrl+B to mark the selected text in bold letters, and so on. In this case, you need to figure out whether the user is holding down the Ctrl key. Luckily, the event handling mechanism of jQuery passes an event object to all the event handlers that simplify your job. The Event object exposes several properties and methods that can be used in your code.

Table 4-1 lists some of the commonly used properties of the Event object.

Table 4-1. *Properties of the Event Object*

Property	Description
currentTarget	A reference to the current DOM element that is receiving the event within the event bubbling chain.
data	An object passed to the event handler while attaching an event handler. Passing the data object is optional.
pageX	The x coordinate of the mouse pointer relative to the left edge of the document.
pageY	The y coordinate of the mouse pointer relative to the top edge of the document.
target	A reference to the DOM element that initiated the event.
type	The type of event; for example, click, keypress, and so on.
which	For mouse events, returns the mouse button that was clicked (1—left button, 2—middle button, and 3—right button). For keyboard events, indicates the key code of the key that was pressed.
altKey	Boolean property, returns true if the Alt key is pressed during mouse or keyboard events; false otherwise.
ctrlKey	Boolean property, returns true if the Ctrl key is pressed during mouse or keyboard events; false otherwise.
shiftKey	Boolean property, returns true if the Shift key is pressed during mouse or keyboard events; false otherwise.

Out of all the properties listed in Table 4-1, the keyboard-related properties such as which, altKey, ctrlKey, and shiftKey come in handy to detect the key pressed and the status of the Alt, Ctrl, and Shift keys. For example, in a keydown event handler, you may detect the key being pressed by checking the which property. You can also determine whether any of the special keys (Alt, Ctrl and Shift) are being pressed if the altKey, ctrlKey, or shiftKey properties return true.

The event object also has a few useful methods that allow you to alter the default behavior of an element as well as event bubbling. These methods are listed in Table 4-2.

Table 4-2. *Event Object Methods*

Method	Description
preventDefault()	Cancels the default action of an element. For example, the default action for a submit button is to submit a form and that of an anchor element is to navigate to the specified link. Calling preventDefault() on these elements cancels the respective default actions.
stopPropagation()	Stops an event from bubbling up in the DOM tree so that the parent event handlers are not invoked.
isDefaultPrevented()	Returns true if preventDefault() was ever called on the instance of the event object under consideration; false otherwise.
isPropagationStopped()	Returns true if the stopPropagation() method was ever called on the instance of the event object under consideration; false otherwise.

Specifying an event object in the event handler function signature is optional, but if you need any of the pieces of information mentioned in Table 4-1, you must include the event object in the event handler signature. For example, consider this code:

```
$("#button1").click(function (evt) {
  alert(' DOM element with ID ' + evt.target.id + ' was clicked.');
});
```

The code wires an event handler function to the click event of a button. Notice that the event handler function specifies evt as the parameter (this parameter name can be any valid JavaScript variable name). Inside, the event handler uses the evt.target property to find out the id of the DOM element being clicked. In this case, evt.target.id returns "button1". You will use many other properties of the event object while learning mouse and keyboard events later in this chapter.

Working with Common Events

Now that you are familiar with jQuery event handling, let's delve into more details. In the following sections, you will investigate each of the categories of the events listed earlier. You will also develop a working example of each category that makes use of the knowledge you learned in each section.

Window and Document Events

Window events are related to the browser window and are raised on the window object. The document events, on the other hand, are related to the web page being displayed in a browser window and are raised on the document object. To handle window and document events, jQuery offers the event methods listed in Table 4-3.

Table 4-3. *Window and Document Events*

Method	Window/Document	Description
scroll()	window	Binds an event handler to the scroll JavaScript event. The scroll event is raised when a browser window is scrolled. scroll() is also used to trigger the scroll event handler programmatically. This event is primarily applicable to the window object. Additionally, DOM elements with the overflow CSS property set to scroll cause this event to be raised.
resize()	window	Binds an event handler to the resize JavaScript event, which is raised when a browser window is resized. It is also used to trigger the resize event handler programmatically.
ready()	document	Doesn't have any direct equivalent in JavaScript, but is similar to the JavaScript load event. Unlike load event, which is raised when all the DOM elements are fully loaded, the ready() method invokes the supplied function when the DOM tree is fully constructed, the tree may or may not be fully loaded. ready() is commonly used to wire event handlers to various events and to perform web page initialization.

To understand how scroll(), resize(), and ready() are used, you will develop an application as shown in Figure 4-2.

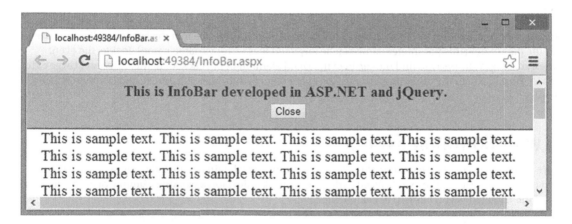

Figure 4-2. *InfoBar application using the scroll(), resize(), and ready() methods*

As you can see from Figure 4-2, the application consists of a Web Form that displays a notification bar at the top (it is referred to as *InfoBar* in this example. Widgets such as the InfoBar are commonly used on web sites to display notifications or alerts to users. A peculiar feature of InfoBar is that it always remains docked to the top edge of the browser window, even if the page is scrolled up or down. If a user clicks the Close button, the InfoBar is closed.

To remember the user's choice of closing the InfoBar, a cookie is issued with a flag that will be read during future runs of the page, so the InfoBar remains visible or hidden. Although this example uses a plain text message on the InfoBar, you can substitute anything there: Twitter or Facebook "follow us" buttons, custom graphics, or advertisements.

> ■ **Note** Browsers use their own infobars to display notifications. The jQuery InfoBar developed in this example is not related to the browser infobars except that the jQuery InfoBar also docks at the top of the document being shown.

To begin developing the InfoBar application, create an empty ASP.NET Web Forms application. Add a Scripts folder to the project and place the jQuery library into it. Then add a new Web Form to the project and add the markup shown in Listing 4-1 to it.

Listing 4-1. InfoBar HTML Markup

```
<form id="form1" runat="server">
  <asp:Panel ID="infobarDiv" runat="server" CssClass="InfoBar">
          This is InfoBar developed in ASP.NET and jQuery.
          <br />
          <asp:Button ID="closeBtn" runat="server" Text="Close" />
  </asp:Panel>
  ...
  ...
</form>
```

The infobar is made of an `<asp:Panel>` control with the ID of infobarDiv. The InfoBar CssClass controls the look and feel of the infobar and is stored in a style sheet file. The infobar panel contains a text message: This is InfoBar developed in ASP.NET and jQuery. It also includes a Close button in the form of a Button server control. The InfoBar CSS class that is applied to the CssClass property of the infobarDiv panel is shown here:

```
.InfoBar
{
    background-color: silver;
    color: #333333;
    font-weight: bold;
    position: absolute;
    width: 100%;
    top: 0px;
    left: 0px;
    text-align: center;
    border-bottom-width: 2px;
    border-bottom-color: #666666;
    border-bottom-style: solid;
    text-align:center;
    padding:10px;
}
```

Remember that at runtime `<asp:Panel>` will be rendered as a `<div>` element whereas `<asp:Button>` will be rendered as an `<input>` element of type submit. Now add a `<script>` reference to the jQuery library and also add a `<script>` block. Write the code shown in Listing 4-2 in the `<script>` block.

Listing 4-2. InfoBar jQuery Code

```
$(document).ready(function () {
  $(window).scroll(function () {
    if (GetCookieValue("ShowInfoBar") == null) {
      $("#infobarDiv").css("marginTop", $(window).scrollTop());
    }
  });

  $(window).resize(function () {
    if ($(window).width() < 300) {
      $("#infobarDiv").css('display', 'none');
    }
    else {
        $("#infobarDiv").css('display', 'block');
    }
  });

  $("#closeBtn").click(function (evt) {
    $("#infobarDiv").slideUp('slow');
    document.cookie = "ShowInfoBar=false;path=/";
    evt.preventDefault();
  });

  if (GetCookieValue("ShowInfoBar") == null) {
    $("#infobarDiv").css('display', 'block');
  }
  else {
      $("#infobarDiv").css('display', 'none');
  }
});
```

The code in Listing 4-2 consists of five important parts: the ready() method, scroll() method, resize() method, click() method, and cookie checking code. Let's discuss each part in detail.

The code begins by a call to the jQuery ready() method. As discussed earlier, the ready() method gets called when the DOM tree is fully constructed. The ready() method accepts a handler function that gets invoked when the DOM is fully constructed. (Notice that the ready() method is called on the document element). The handler function binds event handlers for scroll and resize events of the window object. A handler for the click event of the Close button is also wired. The handler function then checks whether a cookie called ShowInfoBar exists on the client machine with the GetCookieValue() helper function. The GetCookieValue() function looks like this:

```
var GetCookieValue = function (name) {
  var cookieName = name + "=";
  var cookieArray = document.cookie.split(';');
  for (var i = 0; i < cookieArray.length; i++) {
    var c = cookieArray[i];
    while (c.charAt(0) == ' ')
      c = c.substring(1, c.length);
    if (c.indexOf(cookieName) == 0)
      return c.substring(cookieName.length, c.length);
  }
  return null;
}
```

The GetCookieValue() function accepts the cookie name as its parameter. Inside, it creates an array of cookies using the document.cookie property and split() method. A for loop iterates through all the cookies from the array. If a cookie with the specified name is found (ShowInfoBar, in this case), its value is returned to the caller. The GetCookieValue() function returns null if a cookie with the specified name doesn't exist.

If the ShowInfoBar cookie is not found on the client machine, the infobarDiv element is displayed by setting its display CSS property to block. If the ShowInfoBar cookie is found, it indicates that the user previously opted to close the InfoBar, so the infobarDiv element is kept hidden by setting its display CSS property to none.

The scroll() method is used to bind a scroll event handler to the scroll event of the window object. The scroll event is raised whenever the browser window is scrolled in any direction. The scroll handler function first checks whether ShowInfoBar cookie is present on the client machine. If the cookie doesn't exist, the infobar should be displayed to the user. The marginTop CSS property of the infobarDiv element is set to a value returned by the scrollTop() method called on the window object. The marginTop CSS property indicates the top margin of an element. The scrollTop() method returns the current vertical scroll position of the scrollbar. The vertical scroll position is the number of pixels that are currently hidden from view and above the scrollable area. This way, the infobar always docks at the top edge of the document window.

The resize() method is used to bind a resize event handler to the resize event of the window object. The resize event is raised whenever the browser window is resized. The resize handler function uses the width() method on the window object to find the height of the window. If the window height is less than 300 pixels, the infobarDiv is kept hidden by setting its display CSS property to none; otherwise, infobarDiv is displayed by setting its display CSS property to block.

The click() method is used to bind a click event handler to the Close button click event. Unlike the scroll and resize event handler functions, the click event handler accepts an event parameter: evt. Inside, the click handler function calls the jQuery slideUp() method that rolls up the infobarDiv element with slow speed. slideUp() has been used here just to add a fancy effect while hiding the infobar. (You could have set the display CSS property to none to hide it.)

A cookie called ShowInfoBar is set with a value of false. Notice how this cookie is issued. The cookie property of the document object is set to a string containing a cookie name and value pair. The path of the cookie is set to the root folder (/). The click event handler needs to cancel the form submission by calling the preventDefault() method of the Event object. If you don't call preventDefault(), the form will be submitted to the server because the ASP.NET Button server control causes a postback.

Now run the Web Form and see what the infobar looks like. Try scrolling down and verify that the infobar indeed remains docked to the top edge of the document. Also check whether clicking the Close button hides the infobar. Finally, check whether the infobar becomes invisible when the browser width is reduced to a value that has fewer than 300 pixels.

Mouse Events

The mouse is possibly the most commonly used device for making selections and actions in a web page. Many of the fancy effects provided by the client-side script make use of mouse movements and actions performed by the user on a web page and its elements. Naturally, there are many events that deal with mouse operations. jQuery offers event methods for all these events and additionally adds a few more to simplify certain operations. The jQuery event methods that deal with mouse operations are listed in Table 4-4.

Table 4-4. jQuery Mouse Event Methods

Event Method	Description
click()	Binds an event handler for the JavaScript click event. It can also be used to trigger the click event handler programmatically. A click event is raised when the mouse button is pressed and released on an element.
dblclick()	Binds an event handler for the JavaScript dblclick event. It can also be used to trigger the dblclick event handler programmatically. The dblclick event is raised when the same element is clicked twice in succession.
mousedown()	Binds an event handler for the JavaScript mousedown event. It can also be used to trigger the mousedown event handler programmatically. The mousedown event is raised when any of the mouse buttons are pressed on an element. You can use the event object's which property to find out which button was pressed.
mouseup()	Binds an event handler for the JavaScript mouseup event. It can also be used to trigger the mouseup event handler programmatically. The mouseup event is raised when any of the mouse buttons that were pressed on an element are released.
mouseenter()	Binds a handler function that gets executed when the mouse pointer enters an element. It can also be used to trigger the mouseenter handler programmatically. The mouseenter event handler is executed only when the mouse pointer enters an element it is bound to, not when the mouse pointer enters any of its child elements.
mouseleave()	Binds a handler function that gets executed when the mouse pointer leaves an element. It can also be used to trigger the mouseleave event handler programmatically. The mouseleave event handler is executed only when the mouse pointer leaves an element it is bound to, not when the mouse pointer leaves any of its child elements.
mouseover()	Binds an event handler for the JavaScript mouseover event. It can also be used to trigger the mouseover event handler programmatically. The mouseover event is raised when the mouse pointer enters an element. The mouseover event differs from mouseenter in that the former is raised when the mouse pointer enters the element as well as any of its child elements.
mouseout()	Binds an event handler for the JavaScript mouseout event. It can also be used to trigger the mouseout event handler programmatically. The mouseout event is raised when the mouse pointer leaves an element. The mouseout event differs from mouseleave in that the former is raised when the mouse pointer leaves the element as well as any of its child elements.
mousemove()	Binds an event handler for the JavaScript mousemove event. It can also be used to trigger the mousemove event handler programmatically. The mousemove event is raised when the mouse pointer moves inside an element.
hover()	Binds event handlers for the mouseenter and mouseleave events in one go.

Besides the events discussed in Table 4-4, JavaScript also has a few more events related to mouse operations. In particular, HTML5 drag-and-drop events such as dragstart, dragenter, dragover, dragleave, drag, drop, and dragend are dependent on mouse operations. Although jQuery doesn't have event methods that wrap these events, you can attach event handlers for these events using another technique, which is discussed later in this chapter.

Now that you know the mouse event methods, let's develop an application that illustrates how many of them can be used. The main Web Form of the application is shown in Figure 4-3.

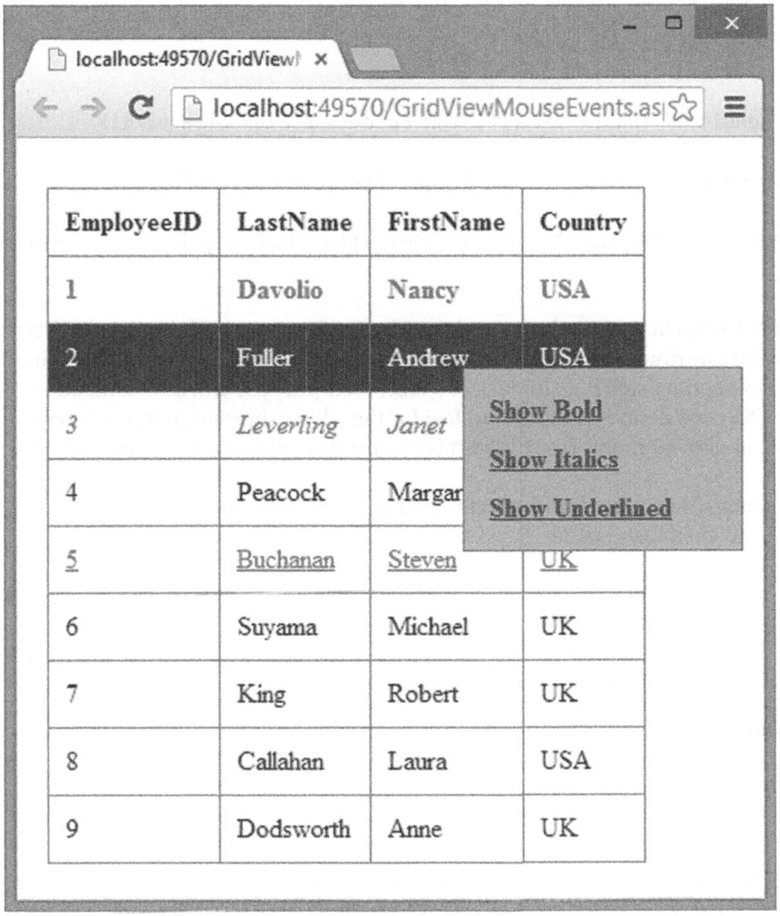

Figure 4-3. *Application showing mouse event methods*

The application consists of a Web Form that has a GridView control on it. If you hover your mouse pointer over any row of the GridView except the header row, that row is highlighted. Taking the mouse pointer away from that row removes the highlight. You can right-click the GridView to reveal a shortcut menu that contains three anchor elements. These elements represent the three actions that can be performed on the GridView row: Show Bold, Show Italics, and Show Underlined. Clicking any of the three anchor elements displays the text from that GridView row per the selected effect. When you move your mouse pointer over an anchor element, that element is highlighted to indicate the active selection. Clicking anywhere on the GridView or document removes the shortcut menu.

To begin developing this application, create an empty ASP.NET Web Forms application and add a new Web Form to it. Then place an SQL data source control and a GridView control on the Web Form. Configure the SQL data source control to select the EmployeeID, FirstName, LastName, and Country columns from the Employees table.

Set the DataSourceID property of the GridView to the ID of the SQL data source control you just configured. Then add a bulleted list below the GridView and add three LinkButton controls as the bulleted list items. The bulleted list markup is shown in Listing 4-3. (Because GridView markup doesn't include anything specific to jQuery, it's not shown here.)

Listing 4-3. Menu Items Bulleted List

```
<ul class="menu">
<li>
<asp:LinkButton ID="bold" CssClass="menuItem" runat="server">Show Bold</asp:LinkButton></li>
<li>
<asp:LinkButton ID="italic" CssClass="menuItem" runat="server">Show Italics</asp:LinkButton></li>
<li>
<asp:LinkButton ID="underline" CssClass="menuItem" runat="server">Show Underlined</asp:LinkButton></li>
</ul>
```

Notice that the `<ul>` element has the menu CSS class applied to it, and the LinkButton controls have the menuItem CSS class applied to them through the CssClass attribute. The menu, menuItem, and a few more CSS classes are defined in a style sheet. Although the actual CSS rules are not listed here for lack of space, their purpose will be discussed as and when they are encountered. The menu CSS class defines the look and feel for the whole shortcut menu, whereas the menuItem CSS class defines styles for the anchor elements (the LinkButton control is rendered as an anchor tag in the browser).

Now add a `<script>` reference to the jQuery library and link the style sheet to the Web Form. Add a `<script>` block and the ready() handler function, as shown in Listing 4-4.

Listing 4-4. ready() Handler Function

```
var currentRow=null;
$(document).ready(function () {
  $(".menu").css("display", "none");
  $("#GridView1").contextmenu(function () { return false; });
...
...
});
```

The code from Listing 4-4 declares a global variable (currentRow) to store a reference to a row in which the user clicks the right mouse button. (This variable is used later in the mousedown event.) The ready() handler function uses a CSS selector to select all the elements that have the menu CSS class attached to them. In this example, the selector returns the `<ul>` element representing the shortcut menu. Initially when the page loads, the shortcut menu is kept hidden by setting its display CSS property to none. Additionally, the contextmenu() method is called on GridView1 (GridView is rendered as a table in the browser), which is used to specify a handler function that cancels the browser's built-in shortcut menu. This is done by returning false from the handler method.

The shortcut menu is displayed to the user in the mousedown event handler, which is wired in the ready() method. The complete code of the mousedown event handler function is shown in Listing 4-5.

Listing 4-5. Handling the mousedown Event

```
$("#GridView1").mousedown(function (evt) {
  if (evt.which == 3) {
    $(".menu").css("left", evt.pageX)
              .css("top", evt.pageY);
    $(".menu").css("display", "block");
    currentRow = $(evt.target).parent();
  }
});
```

The mousedown() method is called on the GridView1 table. The event handler function accepts the event object (evt) as a parameter. Inside, it checks whether the right mouse button has been pressed with the help of the evt.which property. The value of 3 indicates that the right mouse button was pressed. If so, the code selects the shortcut menu <ul> element by its class (menu) and then sets the left and top CSS properties to evt.pageX and evt.pageY by using the css() method. So when the shortcut menu is displayed, it is positioned at the coordinates at which the mouse button was clicked. The shortcut menu is then displayed by setting its display CSS property to block. When a user presses the right mouse button, the underlying table cell (<td> element) becomes the target of the event. For highlighting, you need the table row that contains this target cell. A reference to the table row is obtained by calling the parent() method on the evt.target selector. The reference is stored in the currentRow variable declared earlier.

Now you add code that highlights a GridView row and the menu items. This code also goes inside the ready() handler (see Listing 4-6).

Listing 4-6. Highlighting GridView Row and Menu Items

```
$("#GridView1 tr:gt(0)").hover(function () {
  $(this).addClass("highlightedRow");
    }, function () {
    $(this).removeClass("highlightedRow");
});

$(".menuItem").mouseenter(function (evt) {
    $(evt.target).addClass("highlightedMenuItem");
});

$(".menuItem").mousemove(function (evt) {
    $(evt.target).addClass("highlightedMenuItem");
});

$(".menuItem").mouseleave(function (evt) {
    $(evt.target).removeClass("highlightedMenuItem");
});
```

To highlight a GridView row, you can use the hover() method. Because the GridView header need not participate in the process, the selector selects the table rows whose index is greater than 0. This is done using the :gt selector with an index of 0. The hover() method accepts two handler functions: the first one is called when the mouse enters a row; the second one gets called when the mouse leaves a row. Inside the former function, the addClass() method is used to add the highlightedRow CSS class to the row. Inside the function, this keyword points to the table row. Inside the second function, the highlightedRow CSS class is removed by calling the removeClass() method on that row.

For menu item anchor elements, highlight is added and removed using an alternative technique. Instead of using the hover() method, as discussed previously, the code uses the mouseenter(), mousemove(), and mouseleave() methods. The handler functions specified in the mouseenter() and mousemove() methods add the highlightedMenuItem CSS class to evt.target (the anchor element under consideration) using the addClass() method. The mouseleave() handler removes the highlightedMenuItem CSS class by using the removeClass() method.

In the final installment, you will add code that actually performs the action on the GridView row based on the menu item selected by a user. The relevant code goes in the click() method handler and is placed inside the ready() handler, as is shown in Listing 4-7.

Listing 4-7. Taking Action Based on Menu Item Selection

```
$(".menuItem").click(function (evt) {
  if (evt.currentTarget.id == "bold") {
    $(currentRow).removeClass("italicRow")
                 .removeClass("underlineRow")
                 .addClass("boldRow");
  }
  if (evt.currentTarget.id == "italic") {
    $(currentRow).removeClass("boldRow")
                 .removeClass("underlineRow")
                 .addClass("italicRow");
  }
  if (evt.currentTarget.id == "underline") {
    $(currentRow).removeClass("boldRow")
                 .removeClass("italicRow")
                 .addClass("underlineRow");
  }
  $(".menu").css("display", "none");
  evt.preventDefault();
});

$(document).click(function () {
  $(".menu").css("display", "none");
});
```

A jQuery class selector is used to select all the elements that have the menuItem CSS class. In this case, the selector returns all the anchor elements acting as menu items. The click() method handler checks the ID of the anchor element being clicked. If the ID of the element is bold, it indicates that the text from that GridView row is to be displayed in bold letters. To achieve this styling, the italicRow and underlineRow CSS classes are removed from the currentRow element, and the boldRow CSS class is added to currentRow. The boldRow CSS class displays text from the GridView row in bold letters. The italicRow CSS class displays the text in italics, whereas underlineRow CSS class displays the text as underlined. The other two if blocks do something similar. The only exception is that they remove and add corresponding CSS classes.

Once CSS classes are added and removed from currentRow, the shortcut menu is discarded. It is done by setting the display CSS property of the <ul> element to none. The LinkButton control is a postback causing control, so calling evt.preventDefault() is necessary. This prevents the form submission.

■ **Note** To save some space, the CSS classes used in this example are not given here. You can find the complete CSS file in the source code download for this chapter.

If a user clicks anywhere else on the document, the shortcut menu should be discarded, which ensures that the menu is hidden if a user opens it and then does some other action without making any selection. To accomplish this, the click() method is called on the document object that wires a click handler function. The click handler function simply sets the display CSS property of the <ul> element to none.

You can now run the Web Form and test whether various mouse events are dealt with correctly.

Keyboard Events

Keyboard events are raised whenever any keyboard key is pressed. Keyboard is the most common means to input text into HTML elements, especially form fields. Keyboard events allow you to trap the keyboard–related user actions such as a key being pressed down, a key being pressed, and a key being released. jQuery offers event methods that allow you to wire event handlers to these events. Table 4-5 lists these jQuery event methods.

Table 4-5. *Keyboard Event Methods*

Event Method	Description
keydown()	The keydown() method binds an event handler for a JavaScript keydown event. It can also be used to trigger the keydown event handler programmatically. The keydown event is raised when any keyboard key is first pressed.
keypress()	The keypress() method binds an event handler for a JavaScript keypress event. It can also be used to trigger a keypress event handler programmatically. The keypress event is raised when any keyboard key is pressed. The keypress event is not raised for modifier and nonprinting keys such as Shift, Alt, Ctrl and Backspace.
keyup()	The keyup() method binds an event handler for a JavaScript keyup event. It can also be used to trigger a keyup event handler programmatically. The keyup event is raised when any keyboard key is released.

Now that you know what keyboard events are and what jQuery methods can be used to handle them, let's create an application that puts these methods to use. Figure 4-4 shows a character counter application that displays a character counter as you enter text in a <textarea> element.

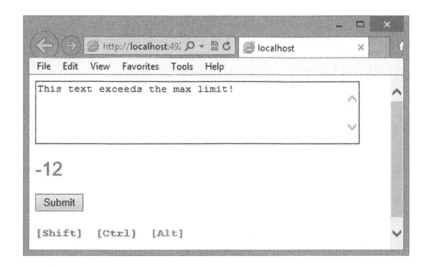

Figure 4-4. *Application that uses keyboard events to display a character counter*

You have seen character counters in blogging and social networking sites that allow you to post comments or short text messages. The Web Form that makes this application consists of a TextBox control, a few Label controls, and a Button control. As you start keying in text in the text box, a character counter below the text area displays the total number of characters that can be still entered in the text box. The character counter is displayed in a Label control.

Below the submit button are three Label controls that display whether the Shift, Ctrl and Alt keys are pressed. The figure shows the Shift and Ctrl keys being pressed, whereas the Alt key is not. Clicking the submit button causes a postback, and a message is displayed in another Label.

To begin developing this application, create an empty ASP.NET web application and add a Web Form to it. Then place a TextBox control on the Web Form and set its TextMode property to Multiline. Setting the TextMode property to Multiline renders the text box as a <textarea> element in the browser. Set the Rows and Columns properties to 5 and 50, respectively, to set the number of rows and columns that the text area contains. Then drag four Label controls and a Button control, and arrange them as shown in Figure 4-3: one Label for displaying character count, and the other three to display the status of the Shift, Ctrl, and Alt keys.

Listing 4-8 shows the relevant markup from the completed Web Form.

Listing 4-8. Markup of the Character Counter Web Form

```
<form id="form1" runat="server">
...
  <asp:TextBox ID="TextBox1" runat="server" Columns="50" Rows="5"
    TextMode="MultiLine"></asp:TextBox>
...
  <asp:Label ID="lblCounter" runat="server" CssClass="NormalCounter"></asp:Label>
...
  <asp:Button ID="Button1" runat="server" OnClick="Button1_Click" Text="Submit" />
...
  <asp:Label ID="lblShift" runat="server" CssClass="SpecialKeysOff" >[Shift]</asp:Label>
  <asp:Label ID="lblCtrl" runat="server" CssClass="SpecialKeysOff" >[Ctrl]</asp:Label>
  <asp:Label ID="lblAlt" runat="server" CssClass="SpecialKeysOff" >[Alt]</asp:Label>
...
  <asp:Label ID="Label2" runat="server" Font-Bold="True" ForeColor="Red"></asp:Label>
</form>
```

Notice that the CssClass property of lblCounter is set to NormalCounter; whereas that of lblShift, lblCtrl, and lblAlt are set to SpecialKeysOff. You will create these CSS classes shortly, along with a few more.

Now add a CSS style sheet to the project and the CSS rules to it, as shown in Listing 4-9.

Listing 4-9. CSS Rules for Label Controls

```
.NormalCounter
{
    font-family:Arial;
    font-size:25px;
    color:Navy;
}

.WarningCounter
{
    font-family:Arial;
    font-size:25px;
    color:Red;
}
```

```
.SpecialKeysOn
{
    font-family:'Courier New';
    font-size:15px;
    color:red;
    font-weight:bold;
}

.SpecialKeysOff
{
    font-family:'Courier New';
    font-size:15px;
    color:#808080;
    font-weight:bold;
}
```

Listing 4-9 shows four CSS classes: namely NormalCounter, WarningCounter, SpecialKeysOn, and SpecialKeysOff. The NormalCounter CSS class controls the styling of the lblCounter when the text area holds a number of characters fewer than the maximum permissible length. The WarningCounter CSS class controls the styling of the lblCounter when the text area exceeds the number of permissible characters. The SpecialKeysOn and SpecialKeysOff CSS classes govern the styling of the lblShift, lblCtrl, and lblAlt whenever the respective keys are pressed and released.

Next, add a <script> reference and a <script> block to the jQuery library. Listing 4-10 shows the ready() method handler and a few global variables.

Listing 4-10. The ready() Method Handler and Variable Declaration

```
var maxLength = 20;
var allowOverflow = true;
var counterType = 'Remaining';

$(document).ready(function () {
  $("#TextBox1").keydown(OnKeyDown);
  $("#TextBox1").keyup(OnKeyUp);
})
```

The code shown in Listing 4-10 declares three variables: maxLength, allowOverflow, and counterType. The maxLength variable holds the maximum number of characters that can be entered in the text box. In this example, maxLength is set to 20. The allowOverflow Boolean value indicates the behavior of the text box in case the character counter exceeds the permissible behavior. The value of true indicates that if the number of characters exceeds the maxLength value, the user can still enter text, but the counter label will be displayed using the WarningCounter CSS class in an attempt to grab the user's attention. If allowOverflow is set to false, you cannot enter any text beyond the limit set by the maxLength value. The counterType variable controls how the counter should be displayed. The value of Remaining means that the counter should display the remaining number of characters that can still be entered. The other possibility is Total, which means the counter will display the total number of characters that are entered in the text box.

The ready() handler function wires keydown and keyup event handlers of Textbox1. This is done using the corresponding event methods keydown() and keyup(), respectively. For the sake of easy readability, event handler functions of these event methods are written as functions: OnKeyDown() and OnKeyUp(). But you could also have written them as anonymous functions.

The main logic that displays the character counter as per the set configuration goes inside the keyup event handler function OnKeyUp(). This event handler is shown in Listing 4-11.

Listing 4-11. OnKeyUp() Event Handler Function

```
function OnKeyUp(evt) {
  var text = $("#TextBox1").val();
  if (text.length > maxLength) {
    if (!allowOverflow) {
      $("#TextBox1").val(text.substring(0, maxLength));
    }
  }
  var diff = 0;
  if (counterType == 'Remaining') {
    diff = maxLength - $("#TextBox1").val().length;
    if (diff < 0) {
      $("#lblCounter").removeClass("NormalCounter");
      $("#lblCounter").addClass("WarningCounter");
    }
    else {
      $("#lblCounter").removeClass("WarningCounter");
      $("#lblCounter").addClass("NormalCounter");
    }
  }
  if (counterType == 'Total') {
    diff = $("#TextBox1").val().length;
    if (diff > maxLength) {
      $("#lblCounter").removeClass("NormalCounter");
      $("#lblCounter").addClass("WarningCounter");
    }
    else {
      $("#lblCounter").removeClass("WarningCounter");
      $("#lblCounter").addClass("NormalCounter");
    }
  }
  $("#lblCounter").text(diff);
  ...
}
```

The OnKeyUp() function first grabs the text entered in TextBox1 using the ID selector of the jQuery and val() method. It then checks the length property of the TextBox to see whether it's greater than the maxLength value. If so, it further checks the allowOverflow setting to decide whether the text entry is to be accepted. If allowOverflow is set to false, the text is truncated to the size of maxLength using the substring() method. The truncated value is stored in the text box using the val() method.

The code then proceeds to declare a diff variable intended to hold the difference between the length of the entered text and the maxLength value. If the counterType is Remaining, an if-else block checks the value of the diff variable. If it is less than 0, it indicates that the length of the text entered in the text box has exceeded the maxLength value, and the counter Label is displayed with the WarningCounter CSS class applied to it. If the diff variable is greater than 0, the NormalCounter CSS class is applied to the Label. The CSS classes are added and removed using the addClass() and removeClass() methods, respectively. Both of these methods accept the name of a CSS class that is to be added or removed from the element under consideration.

If the counterType is Total, the diff variable simply holds the total number of characters entered in the text box. If this value is greater than maxLength, the counter Label is displayed with the WarningCounter CSS class applied; otherwise, the NormalCounter CSS class is applied to the counter Label. Finally, the value of the diff variable is displayed in the counter variable using the text() method, which accepts a string and sets the text content of an element to that string value.

To display the status of the Shift, Ctrl and Alt keys, you need to trap both the keydown and keyup events of the text box. In the keydown event handler, you check the which property of the evt parameter to determine which key was pressed. Listing 4-12 shows the OnKeyDown() function that acts as a keydown event handler.

Listing 4-12. OnKeyDown() Event Handler Function

```
function OnKeyDown(evt) {
  if (evt.which == 16) {
    $("#lblShift").addClass("SpecialKeysOn");
    $("#lblShift").removeClass("SpecialKeysOff");
  }
  if (evt.which == 17) {
    $("#lblCtrl").addClass("SpecialKeysOn");
    $("#lblCtrl").removeClass("SpecialKeysOff");
  }
  if (evt.which == 18) {
    $("#lblAlt").addClass("SpecialKeysOn");
    $("#lblAlt").removeClass("SpecialKeysOff");
  }
}
```

The OnKeyDown() event handler checks the value of the evt.which property. The which property returns the key code of a key being pressed. If the Shift key is pressed (key code 16), the SpecialKeysOn CSS class is added to the corresponding Label control and the SpecialKeysOff CSS class is removed. Similarly, the statuses of the Ctrl (key code 17) and Alt (key code 18) keys are checked, and CSS classes are added and removed from the Label controls accordingly.

■ **Tip** To find out the key codes of the UTF-8 character set, visit http://en.wikipedia.org/wiki/UTF-8.

To finish the Web Form, you need to place code similar to the OnKeyDown() at the end of the OnKeyUp() event handler. The only difference is that you will remove the SpecialKeyOn CSS class and add a SpecialKeysOff CSS class.

■ **Note** In this example, you didn't use a keypress event because you also need to display the counter when the Backspace and Delete keys are pressed. The keypress event is not raised for these keys. Also, note that for the sake of simplicity, this example doesn't check for other possibilities of entering data such as copy-paste or cut-paste operations. You can add that functionality by handling events such as cut, copy, and paste.

The server-side click event of the submit button simply displays a success in a Label as shown here:

```
protected void Button1_Click(object sender, EventArgs e)
{
  Label2.Text = "Data received successfully!";
}
```

The server-side click event handler sets the Text property of Label2 to "Data received successfully!"
You can now run the Web Form and test whether the character counter works as expected.

Form Events

As an ASP.NET developer, you need to deal with HTML forms day in and day out. Although ASP.NET validation
server controls perform a good job validating form fields, at times you need to take things into your own hands.
For example, consider a user registration page that allows a user to create an account with a web site. When the user
hits the submit button, you need to make an Ajax call to the server to figure out whether the user ID specified by
the user is still available or somebody has already grabbed it. You can't achieve this functionality using the built-in
validation controls.

Another example is when you want to display detailed help text or preview to users as they start entering data
in various controls. Because these features run on the client side, ASP.NET server controls aren't useful here. In such
cases, handling form events becomes necessary. Form events are primarily applicable to <form> element and form
controls such as <input> and <select>.

jQuery offers event methods that allow you to wire event handlers to form events. These event methods are listed
in Table 4-6.

Table 4-6. *Form Event Methods*

Event Method	Description
blur()	Binds an event handler for a JavaScript blur event. It can also be used to trigger a blur event handler programmatically. A blur event is raised when an element loses focus.
change()	Binds an event handler for a JavaScript change event. It can also be used to trigger a change event handler programmatically. A change event is raised when a value or selection in a control changes. For <select> elements, radio buttons, and check boxes, a change event is raised immediately upon change in the value; a change event is raised for text boxes and text areas when the element loses focus.
focus()	Binds an event handler for a JavaScript focus event. It can also be used to trigger a focus event handler programmatically. A focus event is raised when an element gets focus.
focusin()	Binds an event handler for a JavaScript focusin event. It can also be used to trigger a focusin event handler programmatically. A focusin event is raised when an element or any of its child elements get focus.
focusout()	Binds an event handler for a JavaScript focusout event. It can also be used to trigger a focusout event handler programmatically. A focusout event is raised when an element or any of its child elements loses focus.
select()	An event handler for a JavaScript select event. It can also be used to trigger a select event handler programmatically. A select event is raised when a user selects text inside of a text box or text area.
submit()	An event handler for a JavaScript submit event. It can also be used to trigger a submit event handler programmatically. A submit event is raised when a form is submitted.

Now that you have some idea about the form events and related jQuery event methods, let's put them to use by building an application. In this section, you will develop a Web Form as shown in Figure 4-5.

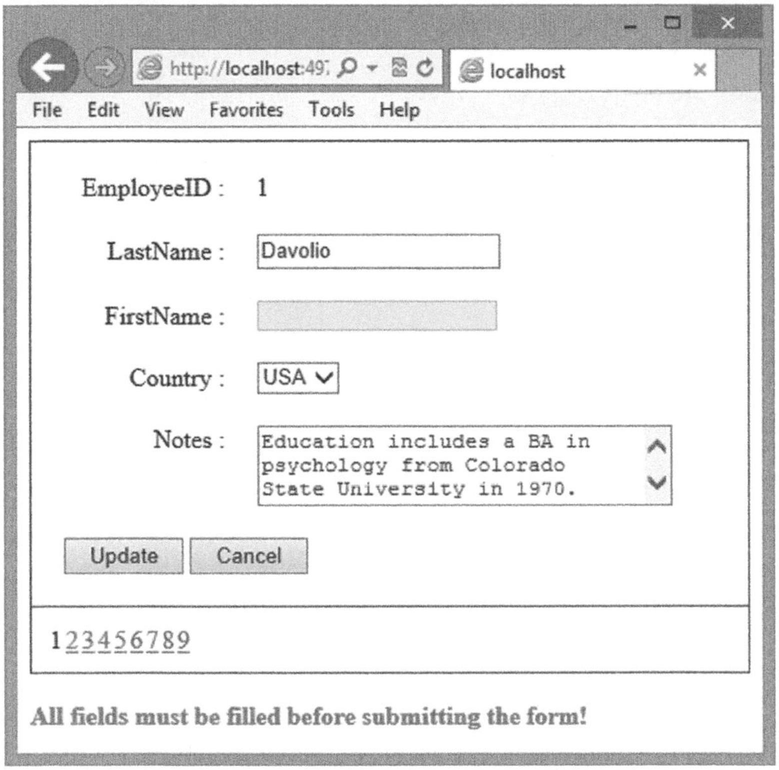

Figure 4-5. *Application making use of form event methods*

As shown in Figure 4-5, the application consists of a FormView control. The FormView displays records from the Employees table and also allows you to edit them. When a text box or text area gets the focus, it is highlighted by applying a CSS class to it. As soon the text box or text area loses focus, the highlight is also removed. If the user attempts to submit the form without entering any of the text boxes, an error message is displayed and the form submission is canceled. When the user changes the employee's country, a confirmation is sought about the change, and accordingly the data is changed or the changes are discarded. Clicking the cancel button doesn't trigger the text box validation described previously.

■ **Note**   The popular jQuery Validation Plugin can be used to perform many of form validations. You can read more about this plugin at http://jqueryvalidation.org.

To begin developing this Web Form, create an empty ASP.NET Web Forms application and add a Web Form to it. Then drag and drop a SQL Data Source Control on the Web Form and configure it to select the EmployeeID, LastName, FirstName, Country, and Notes columns from the Employees table of the Northwind database. Figure 4-6 shows the configuration wizard of the SQL Data Source control.

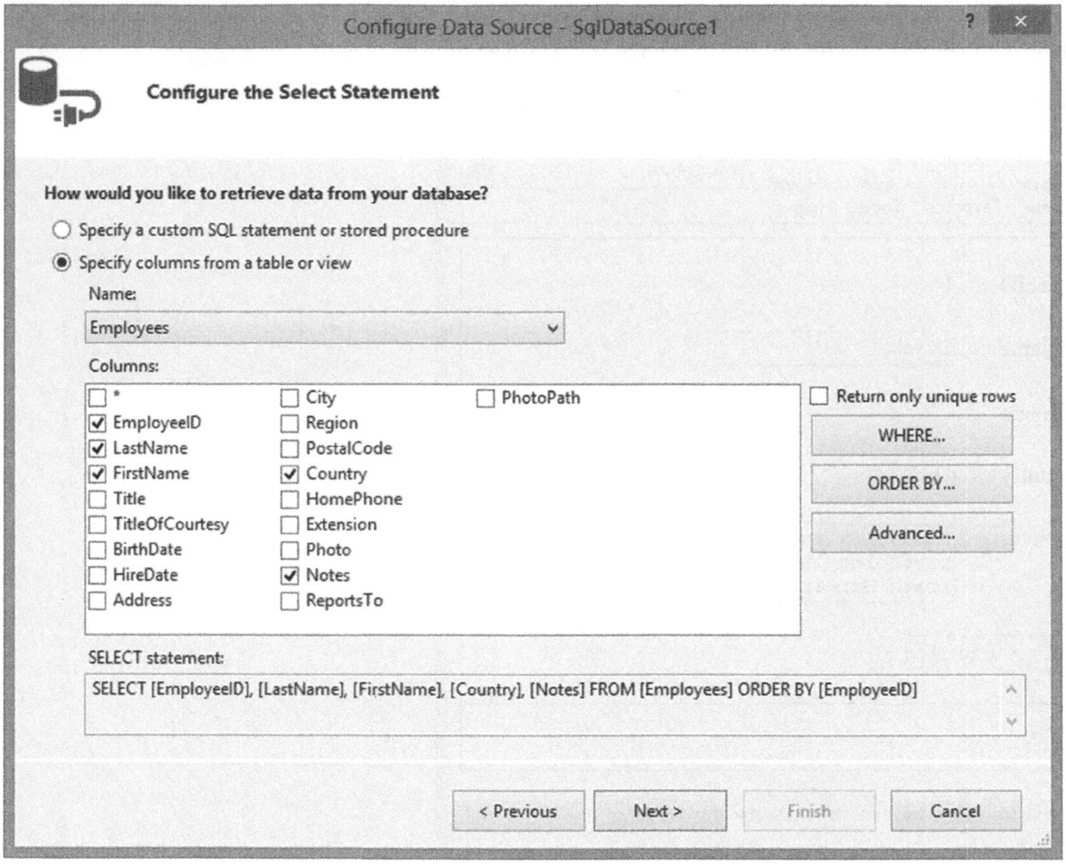

Figure 4-6. Configuring a SQL Data Source control to work with the Employees table

Make sure that the Generate INSERT, UPDATE, and DELETE Statements check box is selected under the Advanced options so that the SQL Data Source control can modify the employee data. Then add one more SQL Data Source control and configure it to select unique countries from the Employees table. The first SQL Data Source control will be data bound with the FormView, whereas the second SQL Data Source will be data bound with the country DropDownList. Next, place a FormView control on the Web Form and set its data source to the first SQL Data Source control. You need to design ItemTemplate and EditItemTemplate of FormView to resemble Figure 4-5. These templates are shown in Listing 4-13. (To improve readability, any unnecessary table markup has been deleted from the listing.)

Listing 4-13. FormView ItemTemplate and EditItemTemplate

```
<ItemTemplate>
...
<td align="right">EmployeeID : </td>
<td><asp:Label ID="EmployeeIDLabel" runat="server" Text='<%# Eval("EmployeeID") %>' />
...
<td align="right">LastName : </td>
<td><asp:Label ID="LastNameLabel" runat="server" Text='<%# Eval("LastName") %>' />
...
<td align="right">FirstName : </td>
<td><asp:Label ID="FirstNameLabel" runat="server" Text='<%# Eval("FirstName") %>' /></td>
```

124

```
...
<td align="right">Country : </td>
<td><asp:Label ID="CountryLabel" runat="server" Text='<%# Eval("Country") %>' /></td>
...
<td align="right" valign="top">Notes :</td>
<td><asp:Label ID="NotesLabel" runat="server" Text='<%# Eval("Notes") %>' /></td>
...
<asp:Button ID="Button1" runat="server" CommandName="Edit" Text="Edit" Width="75px" />
...
</ItemTemplate>
<EditItemTemplate>
...
<tr><td align="right">EmployeeID : </td>
<td><asp:Label ID="EmployeeIDLabel" runat="server" Text='<%# Eval("EmployeeID") %>' />
...
<td align="right">LastName : </td>
<td><asp:TextBox ID="TextBox1" runat="server" Text='<%# Bind("LastName") %>'></asp:TextBox>
...
<tr><td align="right">FirstName : </td>
<td><asp:TextBox ID="TextBox2" runat="server" Text='<%# Bind("FirstName") %>'></asp:TextBox>
...
<tr><td align="right">Country : </td>
<td><asp:DropDownList ID="DropDownList1" runat="server" DataSourceID="SqlDataSource2"
DataTextField="Country" DataValueField="Country" SelectedValue='<%# Bind("Country") %>'>
                          </asp:DropDownList>
...
<tr><td align="right" valign="top">Notes :</td>
<td><asp:TextBox ID="TextBox4" runat="server" Columns="30" Rows="3" Text='<%# Bind("Notes") %>'
TextMode="MultiLine"></asp:TextBox>
...
<tr><td colspan="2">
<asp:Button ID="Button1" runat="server" CommandName="Update" Text="Update" Width="75px" />
<asp:Button ID="Button2" runat="server" CommandName="Cancel" Text="Cancel" Width="75px"
CausesValidation="False" />
...
</EditItemTemplate>
```

The ItemTemplate displays the EmployeeID, LastName, FirstName, Country, and Notes columns in the Label controls. Observe the Button control placed at the bottom of ItemTemplate. The CommandName property of the Edit button is set to Edit. Setting CommandName property to Edit ensures that the FormView switches from ItemTemplate to EditItemTemplate when this button is clicked. Because ItemTemplate displays data in read-only mode, the Label controls are data bound using the Eval() data binding expression.

The EditItemTemplate displays EmployeeID using a Label control, LastName and FirstName columns using TextBox controls, a Country column using a DropDownList control, and a Notes column using a TextBox control with TextMode property set to Multiline. These controls are data bound with EmployeeID, LastName, FirstName, Country, and Notes columns, respectively. While performing the databinding, the Bind() method is used because EditItemTemplate allows the users to edit data. The DropDownList control is bound with the other SQL Data Source so it displays the unique countries from the Employees table. Notice the Update and Cancel buttons placed at the end of EditItemTemplate. These buttons have their CommandName property set to Update and Cancel, respectively. Due to these CommandName values, clicking the Update button saves the data to the database, and clicking the Cancel button takes the FormView from edit mode to read-only mode.

Next, add a script reference to jQuery and add a `<script>` block in the head section of the Web Form. The `<script>`block contains the ready() method handler. Inside the ready() method handler, event handlers are attached for focus, blur, change, click, and submit events. Listing 4-14 shows the focus and blur event handlers.

Listing 4 14. Using the focus() and blur() Methods

```
$("input:text,textarea").focus(function (evt) {
  $(evt.target).addClass("Highlight");
});
$("input:text,textarea").blur(function (evt) {
  $(evt.target).removeClass("Highlight");
});
```

The code in Listing 4-14 is responsible for adding a highlight to the text boxes when they get focus and removing the highlight when they lose focus. The :text form selector and `<textarea>` element selector are used to select `<input>` elements of type text as well as `<textarea>` elements. Notice that these two selectors are separated by a comma, indicating that multiple selectors are to be used while matching the elements.

To handle focus and blur, the JavaScript events focus() and blur() methods are used. These methods accept an event handler function as their parameter. Inside the focus() method handler, the function Highlight CSS class is added to the target element using the addClass() method. The target element is obtained as the evt.target property. Inside the blur() method handler, the function Highlight CSS class is removed from an element using removeClass() method.

Changing the country in the DropDownList should prompt the user to confirm the change. This is accomplished by handling the change event of the `<select>` element (the ASP.NET DropDownList control is rendered as the `<select>` element in the browser). Listing 4-15 shows how the change event is handled.

Listing 4-15. Using the change()method

```
$("select").change(function (evt) {
  if (!confirm("You are changing country of an employee. Are you sure?")) {
    evt.preventDefault();
  }
});
```

The select element selector matches the DropDownList from the form. The change() method is then used to wire an event handler to the change event of the matched element. Inside the handler function, a confirm() dialog is displayed to the user, asking whether the country is really to be changed or not. If the user selects Cancel, the preventDefault() method of the event object is called. Calling preventDefault() will cancel the country change in the `<select>` element.

Now, let's discuss the code that performs the validation that all the text boxes contain some value. This validation is performed using the submit() method. Listing 4-16 shows the relevant code.

Listing 4-16. Using the submit() Method

```
var cancel = false;
$("#Button2").click(function () {
  cancel = true;
});

$("#form1").submit(function (evt) {
  if (!cancel) {
    $("input:text,textarea").each(function () {
```

```
    if ($(this).val() == "") {
      $("#Label1").text("All fields must be filled before submitting the form!");
      $(this).focus();
      evt.preventDefault();
      return;
    }
  });
  cancel = false;
 }
});
```

The code from Listing 4-16 begins by declaring a global variable: cancel. This variable is intended to store a Boolean value that indicates whether the Cancel button was clicked (true) or not (false). The cancel variable is set inside the click event handler of the Cancel button (Button2). The ID selector matches Button2. By using the click() method, it wires an event handler function to the click event of the button. The event handler simply sets the cancel variable to true.

Next, the ID selector is used to match form1; the submit() method is then used on the matched element to wire an event handler function to the submit event of the form. The event handler checks whether the Cancel button was clicked by checking the value of the cancel variable. If so, the :text selector and <textarea> element selectors are used to match <input> elements with the type text as well as <textarea> element.

The each() method iterates through all the matched elements. The function supplied as a parameter to the each() method checks the value of the element under consideration. Inside the each() method handler function, the keyword this points to the current element from the matched set that is being iterated at a given point in time. So the val() method returns the text entered in a text box. If the text box is empty an error message is displayed in the Label using the text() method.

To highlight the element causing this error, that element is given the current focus by using the focus() method. Recall from the earlier discussion that any event method called without any parameters triggers that event. Calling preventDefault() on the event object ensures that the form submission is canceled. After the iteration, the cancel variable is set to false so a new attempt to save the data can be made.

That's it! Run the Web Form and test all the event methods discussed here.

■ **Note**   Although performing validations using client-side script provides a better user experience, you should also consider a situation in which a client script is disabled in a browser or a malicious user is submitting a form through some automated tool. To take care of such situations, it is recommended that you also perform server-side validations on the data being submitted.

Advanced Event Handling Concepts

By now, you have a good understanding of jQuery event handling. Although the knowledge you gained so far is most commonly needed in web applications, there are a few advanced techniques that you need to master to tap into the full power of jQuery event handling. For example, jQuery offers built-in event methods for commonly used events such as click and keypress. However, there are events such as play that do not have corresponding jQuery event methods.

How are these events handled? To deal with them and a few other situations, this section introduces you to some advanced techniques. Specifically you will learn the following:

- How to cancel the default action of an event

- How to cancel event bubbling

- How to pass custom data to event handler functions

- How to wire event handlers for events that do not have corresponding jQuery event methods

You may not need these techniques in each and every application, but it is worthwhile to know them so that you can apply these techniques as and when required.

Stopping Default Event Behavior

Many HTML elements have some default behavior associated with them. Consider a submit button, for example. When you click a submit button, it submits the form. So, submitting a form to the server is the default behavior for the submit button. Similarly, navigating to a page specified in the href attribute is the default action for an anchor element.

Although default actions are usually fine, sometimes you may want to prevent a default behavior from taking place. For example, if a form contains invalid data, you may not want to submit it even if a submit button is clicked. Another example is an anchor element that acts like a button rather than a link (the LinkButton control is actually that). In these cases, the default behavior needs to be canceled. Luckily, jQuery provides easy ways to deal with such situations. The two methods of event objects—preventDefault() and stopPropagation()—are used to prevent the default action from taking place and to cancel the event bubbling, respectively. Although you are already familiar with the preventDefault() method, for the sake of completeness let's develop an example that makes use of both methods.

Have a look at Figure 4-7, which shows a Web Form using these two methods.

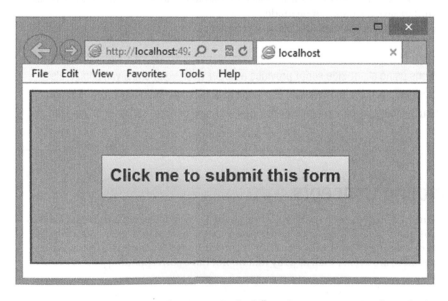

Figure 4-7. *Web Form using the preventDefault() and stopPropagation() methods*

The Web Form consists of a Button server control placed inside a Panel server control. The Button server control is rendered as an <input> element with the type submit, and the Panel server control is rendered as a <div> element. When a user clicks the button, a confirmation is sought for submitting the form. If the user proceeds with the form submission, a message displays to inform the user that the form is being submitted; otherwise, no message displays. The jQuery code responsible for the functionality just described is shown in Listing 4-17.

Listing 4-17. Using preventDefault() and stopPropagation()

```
$(document).ready(function () {
  $("#Button1").click(function (evt) {
    if (!confirm("Do you want to submit this form?")) {
      evt.preventDefault();
      evt.stopPropagation();
    }
  });

  $("#Panel1").click(function (evt) {
    if (evt.isDefaultPrevented()) {
      alert("You cancelled the form submission!");
    }
    else {
      alert("You are submitting this form!");
    }
  });
});
```

The click() method is called on Button1 and Panel1 to wire a click event handler to the respective elements. When a user clicks the button, the click event of the button is raised. The event is bubbled to the parent element (the Panel1 <div> element in this case). So clicking the button raises the click event handler of Button1 as well as Panel1 unless you cancel the event bubbling.

The click event handler of Button1 prompts the user with a confirm() dialog asking whether the form is to be submitted. If the user decides to cancel the form submission, the preventDefault() and stopPropagation() methods are called on the event object. For a submit button, submitting a form is the default action, but calling preventDefault() cancels that operation. Similarly, by default, the click event of a button gets bubbled up to its parent element, but calling stopPropagation() stops the event bubbling. Because the event bubbling is canceled, Panel1 doesn't get a chance to handle its click event.

The control reaches the click event handler of Panel1 only if the user decides to submit the form. Although not necessary in this example, the click event handler of Panel1 checks whether the default action is prevented by using the isDefaultPrevented() method. This method returns true if the default action has been prevented previously; it returns false otherwise. Accordingly, a message is displayed to the user in an alert dialog.

■ **Note** Just like isDefaultPrevented(), there is another method, isPropagationStopped(), which returns true if event bubbling has been canceled previously.

Passing Event Data

So far, all the event handlers you wrote were self-contained in that they could grab all the data they needed on their own. That may not always be the case, however. At times, you may want to pass some custom data to the event handlers so that they can use it in some way.

You can see this by revising the character counter example you developed earlier. In Listing 4-10, you see three global variables declared as follows:

```
var maxLength = 20;
var allowOverflow = true;
var counterType = 'Remaining';
```

These variables supply the settings for the character counter displayed on a web page. The character counter also often uses CSS class names. Although this configuration works well in simple scenarios, there are other situations in which it doesn't work so well.

What if the counter settings are to be fetched from the server? What if these settings are being returned from another function or library? Rather than making event handlers such as OnKeyUp() dependent on these variables or fixed values, wouldn't it be nice if you can pass the counter settings to the OnKeyUp() event handler function? That way, the event handler need not look here or there to figure out these settings; they will be readily available to the event handler function. That's where needing to pass custom data to an event handler comes into the picture.

All the jQuery event methods—such as click(), keyup(), and keydown()—allow you to pass a custom JavaScript object as the first parameter, followed by the event handler function. This custom object consists of one or more key-value pairs. Consider Listing 4-18, which illustrates how such a custom object can be created.

Listing 4-18. Creating a Custom Object to Pass to Event Handlers

```
var options = {};
options.MaxLength = 20;
options.AllowOverflow = true;
options.CounterType = "Remaining";
options.NormalCssClass = "NormalCounter";
options.WarningCssClass = "WarningCounter";
options.SpecialKeysOnCssClass = "SpecialKeysOn";
options.SpecialKeysOffCssClass = "SpecialKeysOff";
```

A variable named options is declared at the top. (Notice the {} syntax, which indicates that the variable holds an object.) Next, you assign values to various properties of the options variable. These properties are developer defined and you are free to name them per your requirements. Notice that all the settings, such as maximum length and CSS classes, are now stored in the options object. Once the options object is ready, you can pass it in the event methods, as shown in Listing 4-19.

Listing 4-19. Passing Custom Data to Event Methods

```
$(document).ready(function () {
  $("#TextBox1").keydown(options,OnKeyDown);
  $("#TextBox1").keyup(options,OnKeyUp);
})
```

The event methods such as keydown() and keyup() now pass options object as the first parameter. The options object passed in these methods can be accessed inside the event handler functions by using the data property of the event object. Listing 4-20 makes this clear.

Listing 4-20. Accessing Custom Data Inside Event Handlers

```
function OnKeyUp(evt) {
  var text = $("#TextBox1").val();
  if (text.length > evt.data.MaxLength) {
    if (!evt.data.AllowOverflow) {
        $("#TextBox1").val(text.substring(0, evt.data.MaxLength));
    }
  }
...
...
}
```

Notice that the `if` conditions use the `evt.data` property to access the `options` object properties such as `MaxLength` and `AllowOverflow`.

Using on(), off, and trigger()

So far in this chapter you wired event handlers to events using jQuery event methods. However, not every event is covered by these event methods. For example, events such as `play` and `pause` or events related to drag-and-drop don't have any equivalent jQuery event methods.

How to wire event handlers for these events? jQuery offers three methods that come in handy in such situations: `on()`, `off()`, and `trigger()`. These methods are described in Table 4-7.

Table 4-7. *Event Wiring Methods*

Method	Description
`on(event, handler)`	Used to bind an event handler to one or more events of selected elements. You can also pass custom data (optional) while performing the binding.
`off(event)`	Unbinds an event handler from one or more events of selected elements.
`trigger(event)`	Triggers an event handler attached with an event programmatically.

To understand how `on()`, `off()`, and `trigger()` are used, let's develop the application shown in Figure 4-8.

Figure 4-8. *Application using on(), off(), and trigger()*

The application consists of a Web Form that houses an <audio> element and a Label control below it. Whenever the audio file is played, paused, or completed, an appropriate message is displayed in the Label. The application also traps F7, F8, and F9 key presses. Pressing F7 and F8 plays and pauses the audio player, respectively. Pressing F9 removes event handlers attached with the events of the audio player. The markup of the audio element and Label is as follows:

```
<form id="form1" runat="server">
  <audio src="media/audio1.mp3" controls="controls"></audio>
  <br />
  <asp:Label ID="spanMsg" runat="server" Font-Bold="True" ForeColor="Red"></asp:Label>
</form>
```

The <audio> element has its src attribute set to the media/audio1.mp3 file. The jQuery code responsible for attaching event handlers to various events of the <audio> element is shown in Listing 4-21.

Listing 4-21. Handling play, pause, and ended Events

```
$(document).ready(function () {
  $("audio").on("play pause ended", function (evt) {
    switch (evt.type) {
      case "play":
        $("#spanMsg").text("Audio is playing.");
        break;
      case "pause":
        $("#spanMsg").text("Audio has been paused.");
        break;
      case "ended":
        $("#spanMsg").text("Audio has completed.");
        break;
    }
  });
});
```

The code from Listing 4-21 uses an element selector to match the <audio> element. Then it uses the on() method to attach an event handler function to three events: play, pause, and ended. Notice that multiple event names are separated by a white space. The play event is raised when a file is played in the audio player. The pause event is raised when a file is paused, and the ended event is raised when a file has played completely in the player. All three events are wired to a common event handler function. Inside the event handler function, the code checks the type property of the event object. The type property returns the type of an event such as play or pause. Based on the type of an event, a message is displayed in the spanMsg Label control.

To program the function keys F7, F8, and F9, you need to handle the keydown event of the whole document. Listing 4-22 shows how this is done.

Listing 4-22. Handling the Document keydown Event

```
$(document).keydown(function (evt) {
  switch (evt.which) {
    case 118:
      $("audio").trigger("play");
      break;
```

```
      case 119:
        $("audio").trigger("pause");
        break;
      case 120:
        $("audio").off("play pause ended");
        $("#spanMsg").text("Event handlers are removed.");
    break;
        default:
        alert('F7 - Play, F8 - Pause, F9 - Off');
        break;
    }
});
```

The keydown event handler checks the which property of the event object to determine which key was pressed. If F7 (118) was pressed, the <audio> element is selected, and the trigger() method is called on it. Because pressing F7 is supposed to play the audio file, the parameter of the trigger() method is passed as play. This way, pressing F7 triggers the play event of the audio player.

Along the same lines, the pause event is triggered when F8 (119) is pressed. If a user presses F9 (120), the off() method is called on the <audio> element to remove the event handlers of play, pause, and ended events. A message is displayed in the Label informing the user that the event handlers have been removed. If any key other than F7, F8, or F9 is pressed, an alert dialog is displayed with a list of valid function keys and their operation.

That's it! Run the application and first test the play, pause, and ended events by playing/pausing the player. Then use the F7 and F8 function keys to see whether the play and pause events are triggered programmatically.

You will find that pressing these keys also displays the correct message in the Label, indicating that the event handler is correctly invoked. Press F9 to remove the event attachment and then play and pause the player again. This time the Label won't reflect the messages because the event handlers have been removed.

Summary

Client-side event handling is an important and frequently necessary operation in ASP.NET applications. Things such as validations, fancy mouseover effects, keyboard shortcuts, and more call for handling various events of DOM elements. jQuery offers a rich set of event methods that allow you to attach event handlers to JavaScript events. Event methods such as click(), keypress(), and focus() allow you to easily handle corresponding JavaScript events. The event handlers can be passed a custom object that encapsulates the data needed by the event handler.

I hope that this chapter gave you a thorough understanding of mouse, keyboard, and form events. Additionally you learn advanced techniques such as stopping the default action of an element, canceling event bubbling, and using on(), off(), and trigger() methods to attach, remove, and trigger event handlers via code.

Although event handling allows you to respond to user actions, you also have to frequently manipulate the values of DOM elements or DOM elements. Changing DOM object properties, dynamically adding or removing DOM elements, and changing page content on the fly are some of such tasks. These tasks and more are the subjects of the next chapter.

■ ■ ■

CHAPTER 5

DOM Manipulation and Dynamic Content

Although HTML pages are static by nature, jQuery can be used to make them dynamic in many ways. Using jQuery you can not only change the content of Document Object Model (DOM) elements but also add, remove, or replace DOM elements on the fly. This makes your web page dynamic in terms of its content and DOM structure. Consider a situation in which you are fetching data residing in SQL Server using the Ajax technique and then want to display this data to the end user in a table. Because you don't know how many rows will be returned by the server, you have to add rows and columns to the table dynamically. The DOM manipulation techniques discussed in this chapter are handy in such situations.

This chapter discusses all these techniques in detail. Specifically you will learn the following:

- How to work with CSS classes and CSS style properties

- How to manipulate the content of a DOM element

- How to add, remove, and replace DOM elements in a web page

You used some of these techniques in earlier chapters (especially those dealing with CSS), but this chapter focuses on them in more detail.

CSS Classes and Styles

Working with CSS classes and CSS properties is a common need in web applications, especially when CSS classes and properties are to be accessed from client-side script.

So far in this book, you used methods such as addClass(), removeClass(), and css() to deal with CSS styles. In addition to these methods, there a few more that jQuery has to offer. Using these methods, you can perform three main operations:

- Add, remove, or check the existence of a CSS class on a DOM element.

- Set or retrieve CSS properties on one or more DOM elements.

- Set or retrieve height and width CSS properties for DOM elements.

Note that although the second and third operations seem to overlap somewhat, there is a difference. The jQuery methods involved in the third operation are mainly used when height and width are needed for a mathematical calculation. These methods return their values as a number without any unit, such as px (pixels). The second operation changes the style of an element in some way. The jQuery methods involved in the first operation are listed in Table 5-1.

Table 5-1. Methods that Deal with CSS Classes

Method	Description
addClass()	Adds one or more CSS classes to a set of selected elements. Class names to be added are specified as a parameter. Multiple class names are separated by a white space.
removeClass()	Removes one or more classes from a set of selected elements. The class name to be removed can be specified as a parameter. Multiple class names are separated by a white space. If no class name is supplied as a parameter, all the CSS classes are removed.
hasClass()	Returns true if a specified CSS class is assigned to any of the selected elements; false otherwise.
toggleClass()	Adds or removes one or more classes from a set of selected elements, depending on whether the CSS class is present. Alternatively, you can also specify whether the class is to be added or removed.

Out of all the methods listed in Table 5-1, addClass() and removeClass() are most commonly used. Moreover, you will often use them in combination. For example, to add a fancy mouseover effect to a button, you may add a CSS class to it when the mouse is on the button element and you may remove the previously added class as the mouse pointer leaves the element. Let's quickly see an example of using each of these methods.

Suppose that you have a <div> element with an ID of div1 and you want to add a CSS class named MyClass to it. To accomplish this task, use the addClass() method as follows:

```
$("#div1").addClass("MyClass");
```

If you want to add more than one class (say MyClass1 and MyClass2) to div1, write this:

```
$("#div1").addClass("MyClass1 MyClass2");
```

If you want to remove MyClass from the div1 element, the following line of code does the job:

```
$("#div1").removeClass("MyClass");
```

If you want to add the CSS class MyClass2 only if MyClass1 has already been applied to it, write this:

```
if($("#div1").hasClass("MyClass1")){
  $("#div1").addClass("MyClass2");
}
```

If you want to add MyClass to div1 if it isn't added already and you want to remove MyClass from div1 if it is added already, toggleClass() does the trick:

```
$("#div1").toggleClass("MyClass");
```

The methods listed in Table 5-1 are quite handy when you have CSS classes defined for various elements and want to add or remove them via jQuery code. However, sometimes you may want to manipulate only a specific CSS property (or a set of a few). In such cases, you need to resort to other methods that jQuery offers. These methods are summarized in Table 5-2.

Table 5-2. *Methods to Deal with CSS Properties*

Method	Description
css()	Gets or sets a value of a CSS style property for the selected elements.
height()	Gets or sets the CSS height property of an element. The height returned by the height() method is the content height that excludes things such as the border and padding.
innerHeight()	Returns the height of an element excluding the border, but including padding.
outerHeight()	Returns the height of an element including the border, padding, and optionally the margin.
width()	Gets or sets the CSS height property of an element. The width returned by the width() method is content width, and excludes things such as the border and padding.
innerWidth()	Returns the width of an element, excluding the border but including padding.
outerWidth()	Returns the width of an element, including the border, padding, and optionally the margin.
scrollLeft()	Gets or sets the horizontal scroll position, which is the number of pixels that are hidden from view to the left of the scrollable area. If an element is not scrollable, or if the scrollbar thumb is toward the extreme left, scrollLeft() will return 0.
scrollTop()	Gets or sets the vertical scroll position, which is the number of pixels that are hidden from view from the top of the scrollable area. If an element is not scrollable, or if the scrollbar thumb is toward the extreme top, scrollTop() will return 0.
position()	Returns an object that gives information about the x and y coordinates of an element. The returned object has two properties: left and top. The coordinates are returned relative to the offset parent, which is the one that is a closed container to the target element.
offset()	Gets or sets x and y coordinates of an element relative to the document. The coordinates are specified as an object with two properties: left and top.

Figure 5-1 gives a visual representation of the height- and width-related methods from Table 5-2.

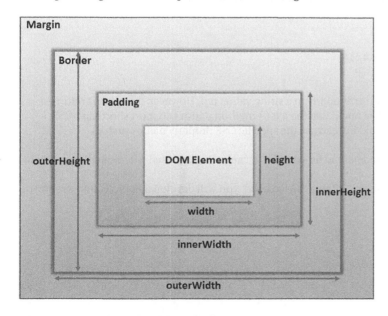

Figure 5-1. *Height and width methods*

In the center of Figure 5-1 is a DOM element. The padding of the DOM element is shown around it, and its border is shown outside that. The margin from the surrounding is the final layer in the picture. Notice how the values returned by height(), innerHeight(), outerHeight(), width(), innerWidth(), and outerWidth()are shown. The outerHeight() and outerWidth() methods accept an optional Boolean parameter that controls whether the margin is included in the returned value. If the Boolean parameter is omitted or passed as false, only padding and border are included while calculating the resultant height and width, respectively. Otherwise, the margin is also included in the calculated height and width.

You have used the css() method before. Let's see some of its variations. Have a look at the code that sets background-color CSS property for a <div> element div1 to red:

```
$("div1").css("background-color","red");
```

If you want to add multiple CSS style properties at one go, you can call the css() method in a chain like this:

```
$("div1").css("background-color","red").css("border","2px solid blue");
```

There is, however, an alternative way to accomplish the same in just one call to the css() method. Have a look at the following code:

```
$("div1").css({"background-color" : "red", "border-top" : "2px solid blue"});
```

In this case, multiple CSS properties are passed to the css() method as a JavaScript object. A JavaScript object is a collection of key-value pairs in which the key (background-color and border-top, in this example) is referred as a property of the object. A property and its value are separated by a colon (:) character. Multiple property-value pairs are separated by commas (,).

If you want to remove a CSS style property, set its value to an empty string ("") like this:

```
$("div1").css("background-color","");
```

The css() method is not limited to setting the values. You can also retrieve CSS style values using the css() method. The following code shows how this is done:

```
$("div1").css("background-color","red");
var style = $("div1").css("background-color");
alert(style) // returns rgb(255,0,0)
```

Notice that the code sets the background-color property to a string value: red. However, the value is returned in the form of the CSS rgb() function. It should be noted that the css() method doesn't support shorthand CSS properties such as border and padding. You should instead use the specific CSS property names such as border-top-width and padding-top.

The other properties of Table 5-2 are best understood by example because they are used when calculating height and width programmatically.

To understand how many of the methods listed in Table 5-2 are used, you will develop an application as shown in Figure 5-2.

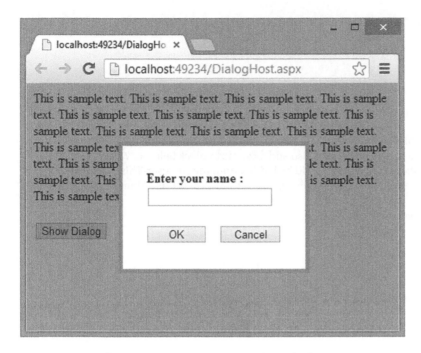

Figure 5-2. *Application using CSS class and style methods*

The application consists of a Web Form that has a button called Show Dialog. Clicking the Show Dialog button displays a modal dialog that collects the name from the end user. Clicking the OK button of the modal dialog closes the dialog, submits the form, and displays the name in another Label. Clicking the Cancel button closes the modal dialog and cancels the form submission.

Although this functionality is simple and straightforward, what is more important is that the modal dialog is actually a Panel server control and is displayed at the center of the browser window using the methods listed in Table 5-2. The modal dialog is centered even if the browser window is resized.

To begin developing the application, create an empty ASP.NET Web Forms project and add a Web Form to it. Design the Web Form as shown in Figure 5-2.

The markup for the Web Form is shown in Listing 5-1.

Listing 5-1. Web Form Markup

```
<form id="form1" runat="server">
  This is sample text
  ...
  <asp:Button ID="Button1" runat="server" Text="Show Dialog" />
  <asp:Label ID="Label2" runat="server" Font-Bold="True"
   ForeColor="Red"></asp:Label>
  <div id="backgroundDiv"></div>
  <asp:Panel ID="Panel1" runat="server">
    <asp:Label ID="Label1" runat="server" Text="Enter your name :">
    </asp:Label>
    <br />
    <asp:TextBox ID="TextBox1" runat="server"></asp:TextBox>
    <br /><br />
```

```
    <asp:Button ID="Button2" runat="server" Text="OK" Width="75px"
     OnClick="Button2_Click" />
    <asp:Button ID="Button3" runat="server" Text="Cancel" Width="75px" />
  </asp:Panel>
</form>
```

Notice that in addition to server controls such as Label, TextBox, Button, and Panel, the markup also contains a <div> with an ID of backgroundDiv. This <div> is displayed in the background to the user when the modal dialog is visible. It adds the semitransparent gray background effect.

Now add a <script> reference to the jQuery library and also add a <script> block below it. When the Web Form is loaded, initially the Panel that makes the modal dialog should be hidden from the end user. This is achieved by applying a certain CSS class to it in the ready() method handler. Listing 5-2 shows how this is done.

Listing 5-2. Hiding the Modal Dialog when the Page Loads

```
$(document).ready(function () {
  $("#Panel1").addClass("dialogHidden");
});
```

The ready() method handler function assigns the dialogHidden CSS class to Panel1 using the addClass() method. The ready() method handler also contains a few event handlers. The most important event handler from the point of application functionality is the click event handler of the Show Dialog button. This event handler is shown in Listing 5-3.

Listing 5-3. Displaying the Modal Dialog in the click Event Handler

```
$("#Button1").click(function (evt) {
  var top = 0;
  var left = 0;
  if ($("#Panel1").hasClass("dialogHidden")) {
    $("#Panel1").removeClass("dialogHidden");
  }
  $("#Panel1").addClass("dialogVisible");
  var windowHeight = $(window).height();
  var windowWidth = $(window).width();
  var dialogHeight = $("#Panel1").outerHeight();
  var dialogWidth = $("#Panel1").outerWidth();
  top = ((windowHeight - dialogHeight) / 2 +
        $(window).scrollTop()) + "px";
  left = ((windowWidth - dialogWidth) / 2 +
        $(window).scrollLeft()) + "px";
  $("#Panel1").css("top", top);
  $("#Panel1").css("left", left);
  $("#backgroundDiv").addClass("dialogBackground")
                     .height(windowHeight)
                     .width(windowWidth)
                     .css("display", "block");
  evt.preventDefault();
});
```

The click event handler function declares two variables—top and left—to hold the top and left coordinates of the modal dialog. These coordinates are calculated dynamically based on the current window height and width.

The code then checks whether Panel1 already has the dialogHidden CSS class applied to it by using the hasClass() method. The dialogHidden class hides the modal dialog. If this class is already applied, the removeClass() method is used to remove the dialogHidden class so that the modal dialog can now be displayed. The look and feel of the modal dialog when it is displayed is controlled by the dialogVisible CSS class. This class is added to Panel1 using addClass() method.

The next six lines of code determine the top and left coordinates where the modal dialog is to be displayed. The windowHeight and windowWidth variables store the window height and width, respectively. The window height and width is obtained by using the height() and width() methods. Because the modal dialog is to be displayed at the center of the screen for calculations, its coordinates outerHeight() and outerWidth() are used to retrieve its total height (including borders and padding) and total width. The total height and total width are stored in the dialogHeight and dialogWidth variables.

The top coordinate of the modal dialog is calculated by subtracting dialogHeight from windowHeight and dividing the result by 2. A value equal to scrollTop() is then added to the result to account for a scrollable region, if any. The left coordinate of the modal dialog is calculated by subtracting dialogWidth from windowWidth and then dividing the result by 2. This time, a value of scrollLeft() is added to the result. Notice that all the methods used in the calculation return numbers and "px" is appended to the final result.

Once the top and left coordinates are calculated, the css() method is called on Panel1 to set the top and left CSS properties. When the modal dialog is displayed the background should appear grayed-out. This is accomplished by adding the dialogBackground CSS class to backgroundDiv with the help of the addClass() method. The backgroundDiv should cover the entire window, so its height and width are set to the window height and width, respectively. This time, the height() and width() methods are used to set the height and width of backgroundDiv. The css() method is used to set the display mode of backgroundDiv to block. This way, backgroundDiv becomes visible. Finally, preventDefault() is called to cancel the form submission (Show Dialog is a Button control and causes a postback).

The code discussed so far takes care of showing the modal dialog at the center of the window when the Show Dialog button is clicked. But what if the dialog is already being displayed, and the browser window is resized? In this case, the resize event of the window object needs to be handled. Listing 5-4 shows how this is done.

Listing 5-4. Centering the Modal Dialog when the Window is Resized

```
$(window).resize(function () {
  if ($("#Panel1").hasClass("dialogVisible")) {
    $("#Button1").click();
  }
});
```

The resize() method wires an event handler function for the resize event of the window. Inside the event handler, the hasClass() method checks whether the modal dialog is already visible. This is done by hasClass(), which checks for the existence of the dialogVisible CSS class on Panel1. The presence of this class indicates that the modal dialog is displayed; the click() method is called on Button1 to simulate its click event. This process invokes the code from the click event handler again, and the left and top coordinates of the modal dialog will be recalculated.

The final piece of code deals with the scenario in which a user clicks the Cancel button of the modal dialog. In this case, the form submission is to be canceled and the modal dialog is to be made invisible. Listing 5-5 shows how this is done.

Listing 5-5. Handling the click Event of Cancel Button

```
$("#Panel1 input:submit[value='Cancel'] ").click(function (evt) {
  if ($("#backgroundDiv").hasClass("dialogBackground")) {
    $("#backgroundDiv").removeClass("dialogBackground")
                       .css("display",  "none");
  }
```

```
  if ($("#Panel1").hasClass("dialogVisible")) {
    $("#Panel1").removeClass("dialogVisible");
  }
  $("#Panel1").addClass("dialogHidden");
  evt.preventDefault();
});
```

The code from Listing 5-5 selects the Cancel submit button using a combination of :submit form selector and an attribute equals selector. The click event handler is wired using the click() method. The click event handler checks whether dialogBackground CSS class is applied to backgroundDiv element. This is done using the hasClass() method. If dialogBackground class is applied it is removed from backgroundDiv using the removeClass() method. The css() method call ensures that the backgroundDiv is now hidden because the modal dialog is to be closed. The code then checks whether the dialogVisible CSS class is added to Panel1 and if so the dialogVisible CSS class is removed from Panel1 using the removeClass() method. Then the dialogHidden CSS classes is added to Panel1 using the addClass() method so that Panel1 is now hidden from the end user. Finally, the form submission is canceled by calling preventDefault() on the event object.

The CSS classes discussed in the preceding example are shown here for your quick reference:

```
.dialogBackground {
    background-color:rgba(0, 0, 0,0.7);
    opacity:0.5;
    position:fixed;
    left:0;
    top:0;
}

.dialogVisible {
    opacity:1;
    position:fixed;
    border:5px solid #ff6a00;
    background-color:white;
    font-weight:bold;
    padding:30px;
}

.dialogHidden {
    display:none;
}
```

Before you run this example, write the server-side click event handler for the OK button (Button2) as shown below:

```
protected void Button2_Click(object sender, EventArgs e)
{
  Label2.Text = TextBox1.Text;
}
```

As you can see, the click event handler simply sets the Text property of Label2 to the value entered in the text box.

Working with Attributes and Properties

Most HTML elements have one or more attributes that can be used to define either the look and feel or behavior of the element under consideration. For example, the <input> element has the type attribute, which governs the type of control rendered in the browser. Similarly, <table> has the border attribute, which can draw a border for the table and its cells. Although attributes are assigned some value at design time, sometimes it becomes necessary to change their values at runtime.

Suppose that you are building a custom HTML media player that allows the user to select a media file from a list and then plays the selected file. Further assume that you are using HTML5 <audio> and <video> elements to build the media player. In this case, you need to change the src attribute of the <audio> and <video> elements on the fly, depending on the selection made.

To manipulate HTML attributes and properties, jQuery offers a set of methods. Before discussing these methods, it is important to understand the difference between an attribute and a property. An *attribute* is always associated with some HTML markup element; a *property* is always associated with a DOM element. Because the DOM tree is built based on HTML elements, many attributes have the corresponding DOM property. For example, the type attribute of the <input> element is represented by the type property of the input DOM element. Not all DOM properties have equivalent attributes, however. For example, the select DOM element has the selectedIndex property, which returns the index of the item selected in the element. However, the <select> HTML element doesn't have any equivalent attribute. Another example is the defaultSelected property of an option DOM element. This property reflects the selected attribute of the <option> element.

Now that you have an idea about what attributes and properties are, let's see what jQuery has to offer to manipulate them. Table 5-3 shows a list of jQuery methods that allow you to retrieve or assign attribute and property values.

Table 5-3. *Methods to Manipulate Attributes and Properties*

Method	Description
attr()	Allows you to get or set the value of an attribute for the selected element. If the attribute is not specified on an element, undefined is returned.
removeAttr()	Removes an attribute from a selected element.
prop()	Allows you to get or set the value of a DOM property for the selected element. If the property is not assigned for the DOM element, undefined is returned.
removeProp()	Removes a property from a selected element.
val()	Used to get or set values of input, select, and textarea elements.

The attr(), prop(), and val() methods allow you to retrieve as well as assign values depending on the usage syntax. For example, the following code snippet shows how the src attribute of an img element is first assigned and then retrieved using attr() method.

```
$("#img1").attr("src","images/flower.png");
var imgSrc = $("#img1").attr("src");
```

Here, the ID selector selects an <img> element whose ID is img1 and then uses the attr() method to set its src attribute. The first parameter is the name of the attribute to set, and the second parameter is its value. The next line retrieves the value of the same attribute and stores it in the imgSrc variable. In this version, the attr() method accepts just one parameter that indicates the attribute whose value is to be retrieved. The usage syntax for prop() is quite similar. The only difference is that the prop() method deals with a property instead of an attribute.

The `val()` method is used to assign or retrieve the value of an `input`, `select`, or `textarea` element. The following code shows how it can be used to set and get values:

```
$("#text1").val("Hello World!");
var value = $("#text1").val();
```

The first line of code grabs a text box with the ID `text1` using an ID selector. The `val()` method is then called to assign a value of `"Hello World!"` to the text box. The second line retrieves the value of the same text box using the `val()` method without any parameters.

Now let's develop a simple application that illustrates how many of the methods listed in Table 5-3 can be used. The main Web Form of the application is shown in Figure 5-3.

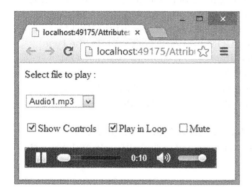

Figure 5-3. *Application that uses attribute and property manipulation methods*

The Web Form consists of a `DropDownList` at the top that lists available audio files. Upon selecting a file from the list, that file is played using the `<audio>` element. The three check boxes Show Controls, Play in Loop, and Mute control the behavior of the player. The Show Controls check box toggles the display of the `<audio>` element controls such as the play/pause button and volume slider. The Play in Loop check box controls whether the audio file is played over and over again. The Mute check box controls whether sound is played. Four elements (a `DropDownList` and three check boxes) manipulate various attributes of the `<audio>` element to obtain the desired behavior.

To begin developing the application, create an empty ASP.NET Web Forms application and add a new Web Form to it. Design the Web Form as shown in Figure 5-3. The relevant HTML markup of the Web Form is shown in Listing 5-6.

Listing 5-6. Markup of the Web Form

```
<form id="form1" runat="server">
  <asp:Label ID="Label1" runat="server" Text="Select file to play :">
  </asp:Label>
  ...
  <asp:DropDownList ID="DropDownList1" runat="server">
    <asp:ListItem>Please Select</asp:ListItem>
    <asp:ListItem>Audio1.mp3</asp:ListItem>
    <asp:ListItem>Audio2.mp3</asp:ListItem>
    <asp:ListItem>Audio3.mp3</asp:ListItem>
  </asp:DropDownList>
  ...
```

```
   <asp:CheckBox ID="CheckBox1" runat="server" Text="Show Controls" />
   ...
   <asp:CheckBox ID="CheckBox2" runat="server" Text="Play in loop" />
   ...
   <asp:CheckBox ID="CheckBox3" runat="server" Text="Mute" />
   ...
   <audio id="audio1"></audio>
</form>
```

The Web Form markup is straightforward and needs no explanation. Notice that there is an <audio> element at the end of the form for playing the selected audio file.

Add a <script> reference and a <script> block to the jQuery library. The ready() event handler function attaches four event handlers: one for the change event of DropDownList1 and three for the click event of the three check boxes. The change event handler function is shown in Listing 5-7.

Listing 5-7. DropDownList change Event Handler

```
$("#DropDownList1").change(function () {
  var selectedIndex = $("#DropDownList1").prop("selectedIndex");
  if (selectedIndex > 0) {
    $("#audio1").attr("src", "media/" + $("#DropDownList1").val());
    $("#audio1").get(0).play();
  }
});
```

The change event handler function begins by retrieving the index of the selected option from the drop-down list with the help of the prop() method. The selectedIndex property of the selected DOM element returns a zero-based index of the option that has been selected. The selected index is stored in the selectedIndex variable.

The first option in the drop-down list is Please Select, which is not associated with any audio file. An if block checks whether the selectedIndex is greater than zero. If it is, the audio1 element's src attribute is set to the path of the file selected in the drop-down list. (Note that the code assumes that files are located inside the media folder.)

Change this path per your folder structure. To get the value selected in the drop-down list, the val() method is used. Once the file selection changes, the newly selected file is played using the <audio> element's play() method. Notice the use of the jQuery get() method to retrieve the first element from the selection. This is necessary because jQuery selectors return zero or more matched elements as a collection.

The click event handlers of the three check boxes add or remove controls and loop and muted attributes from the <audio> element. These event handlers are shown in Listing 5-8.

Listing 5-8. Manipulating Controls and Loop and Muted Attributes

```
$("#CheckBox1").click(function () {
  if ($("#CheckBox1").prop("checked")) {
    $("#audio1").attr("controls", "controls");
  }
  else {
    $("#audio1").removeAttr("controls");
  }
});
```

```
$("#CheckBox2").click(function () {
  if ($("#CheckBox2").prop("checked")) {
    $("#audio1").attr("loop", "loop");
  }
  else {
    $("#audio1").removeAttr("loop");
  }
});

$("#CheckBox3").click(function () {
  if ($("#CheckBox3").prop("checked")) {
    $("#audio1").attr("muted", "muted");
  }
  else {
    $("#audio1").removeAttr("muted");
  }
});
```

All the click event handlers are quite similar, so I'll discuss just the first one. The click event handler of CheckBox1 (Show Controls) checks the checked property of CheckBox1 using the prop() method. The prop() method returns a true if the check box is checked; false otherwise. If the check box is checked, the attr() method is used to add the controls attribute to the <audio> element. Setting the controls attribute to controls displays the play/pause controls of the audio player. If the check box is unchecked, the removeAttr() method is used to remove the controls attribute from the <audio> element. The other two click event handlers add or remove <audio> element loop and muted attributes.

Changing the Contents of DOM Elements

When it comes to manipulating DOM elements, jQuery offers a plethora of methods. This section discusses jQuery methods that allow you to change the whole content of a DOM element. This content can be HTML markup or plain text. Methods discussed in this section come in handy to get or set contents of an element. (You already used some of them in earlier chapters.)

Table 5-4 lists these methods for your reference.

Table 5-4. *Methods to Change Contents of a DOM Element*

Method	Description
text()	Gets or sets text content of an element. While returning the text content, it returns the summation of text content of all the descendent elements. While setting the content, the text is HTML encoded.
html()	Gets or sets HTML content of an element. While returning the HTML content, the entire HTML markup making the selection is returned. While setting the HTML content, all the existing content of the selected element is replaced with the supplied HTML markup.
empty()	Empties an element by removing all its content.

The text() method is intended to deal with the text content of an element. Consider the following markup:

```
<div id="container">
  <strong>Hello</strong> <em>World!</em>
</div>
```

The markup consists of a <div> element with an ID of container. It further contains some HTML markup consisting of <strong> and <em> elements. Now, look at the following jQuery code that uses the text() method to manipulate the previous markup:

```
alert($("#container").text());
$("#container").text("Hello Universe!")
alert($("#container").text());
$("#container").text("<strong>Hello Universe!</strong>")
alert($("#container").text());
```

The first line of code retrieves the text content of the container <div> element and outputs Hello World! in the alert dialog. The second line of code uses the text() method and passes a "Hello Universe!" string as its parameter. This sets the text content of the container <div> to Hello Universe! as confirmed by the alert dialog. The fourth line of code uses the text() method and passes a string with some HTML markup as the parameter. Because the text() method HTML-encodes the strings, the alert dialog displays the text as is (i.e., the text won't appear bold, but the literal tags <strong> and </strong> are displayed).

Now, let's use the html() method instead of text() in the preceding code. Here is the modified version of the code:

```
alert($("#container").html());
$("#container").text("Hello Universe!")
alert($("#container").html());
$("#container").html("<strong>Hello Universe!</strong>")
alert($("#container").html());
```

In this case, the first line of code uses the html() method to retrieve the HTML content of the container, and the alert dialog displays <strong>Hello</strong> <em>World!</em>. The second line uses the html() method to set the content of the container <div> to Hello Universe!, and this is confirmed by the alert dialog that follows. The fourth line of code again uses the html() method, but this time passes an HTML fragment as the parameter. Because the html() method sets the HTML content of the container <div>, the string is displayed in bold letters. The final alert() simply outputs the new HTML content of the <div> element.

The empty() method is quite straightforward. It takes no parameters and empties an element by removing all its child elements—element nodes as well as text nodes. The following line shows how it can be used:

```
$("#container").empty();
```

Here the container <div> is emptied.

Adding and Removing DOM Elements

Although the text() and html() methods work with the whole content of selected elements, at times you need to add, remove, or replace elements inside another element. jQuery offers many ways to add and remove elements as outlined in Table 5-5.

Table 5-5. Adding, Removing, and Replacing DOM Elements

Method	Description
append()	Adds the specified content at the end of the selected element.
appendTo()	Adds the selected elements at the end of the specified target.
prepend()	Adds the specified content at the beginning of the selected element.
prependTo()	Adds the selected elements at the beginning of the specified target.
after()	Adds the specified content after the selected element.
insertAfter()	Adds the selected elements after the specified target.
before()	Adds the specified content before the selected element.
insertBefore()	Adds the selected elements before the specified target.
replaceWith()	Replaces selected elements with the specified content.
replaceAll()	Replaces the target with the content from the selected elements.
remove()	Removes the selected elements from the DOM tree.

Most of the methods listed in Table 5-5 are pairs that do the same task with their source and target interchanged. Consider, for example, the append() and appendTo() methods. Suppose you have a table with an ID of table1, and you want to append a row to this table. This task can be accomplished by using the append() method like this:

```
$("#table1").append("<tr><td>Hello World!</td></tr>");
```

The ID selector selects table1, and then append() is called on the result. The append() method accepts the HTML markup for a table row and adds that row as the last child of the table. The same task can be performed by using the appendTo() method as follows:

```
$("<tr><td>Hello World!</td></tr>").appendTo("#table1");
```

Here the markup of the new row to be added is the selector, and this markup is appended to the target. The target is retrieved using the ID selector.

The same pattern of usage can be seen in the prepend(), prependTo, after(), insertAfter(), before(), and insertBefore() methods.

Copying DOM Elements

Sometimes you need to create a copy of selected DOM elements. For example, let's say you want to display multiple previews of certain content on the page. In such cases, you may need to copy the DOM elements. Such a copy can be created using the clone() method. The following code shows how the clone() method can be used:

```
var clonedElement = $("div.class1").clone();
$("#divTarget").append(clonedElement);
```

The first line of code uses the class selector to select the <div> element with the class1 CSS class applied. It then calls the clone() method on it to create a deep copy of the element. *Deep copy* means that all the child elements (including text) will be cloned. The cloned elements are appended to the divTarget element using the append() method.

The clone() method without any parameters copies the elements, but not the event handlers attached with the elements. You can pass a Boolean parameter to indicate whether event handlers are also to be copied (true) or not (false). Note that using clone() on elements that have ID attributes specified causes duplicate elements with the same ID and can create problems for further processing. So it is recommended to avoid such cloning operations or use some other selection criteria that will guarantee the unique selection of an element.

Creating an RSS Reader Widget

Now that you have a reasonable understanding of the various DOM manipulation methods offered by jQuery, let's develop a web application that puts many of them to use. In this section, you will develop a web application that reads an RSS feed and outputs the feed content in a <div> element. We will refer to this application as an RSS widget. The RSS widget renders the feed content based on several configurable parameters such as title, text, background color, and number of feed items. Figure 5-4 shows the part of the Web Form that accepts these configuration settings.

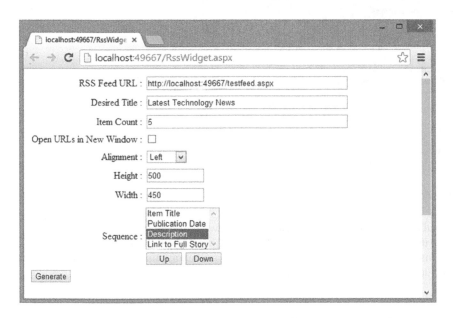

Figure 5-4. *Web Form that accepts RSS Widget settings*

As shown in Figure 5-4, the Web Form consists of a series of text boxes, drop-down lists, and a list box. The RSS Feed URL text box accepts the URL of an RSS feed. You can either enter some test feed URL or enter some live feed URL. The Desired Title text box allows you to specify a title for the RSS feed items. You can also specify how many feed items are to be displayed in the widget by using the Item Count text box. Whether to open the individual feed items in the same browser window or open a new window is governed by the Open URLs in New Window check box. The text alignment for the feed items is controlled by the Alignment drop-down list. The Height and Width text boxes specify the height and width of the <div>. The Sequence list box allows you to specify how the feed items are displayed. Using this list box and the Up and Down buttons placed below it, you can arrange the sequence of Item Title, Description, Publication Date, and URL. Clicking the Generate button fetches the RSS feed items and displays them in a <div>, as shown in Figure 5-5.

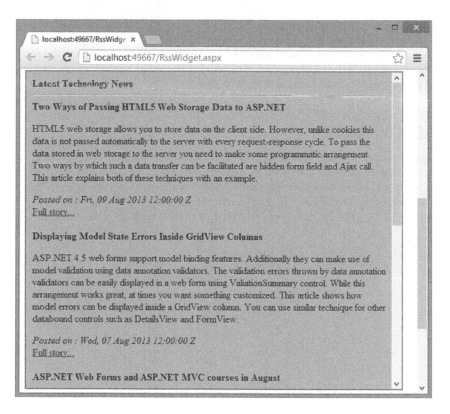

Figure 5-5. *RSS feed displayed in a <div>*

Below the data entry controls and the <div> element is a text area (not shown in the figure) that outputs the raw HTML markup of the <div>. Because the Web Form shown in Figure 5-4 and Figure 5-5 contains lengthy markup, the entire markup is not given here. Instead, Table 5-6 lists the various controls and elements that are used on the Web Form and that are important for the functioning of the application.

Table 5-6. *Controls and Elements from the RSS Widget Web Form*

Control / Element ID	Type	Description
txtURL	TextBox	Allows the user to enter a URL to any RSS feed.
txtTitle	TextBox	Allows the user to specify the title for the feed items.
txtItemCount	TextBox	Specifies the number of feed items to be displayed.
chkTarget	Checkbox	Controls whether feed items will be displayed in the same browser window (unchecked) or opened in a new browser window (checked).
ddlAlign	DropDownList	Contains three values—Left, Right, and Center—that control the alignment of the feed items.
txtHeight	TextBox	Specifies the height of the <div> element.
txtWidth	TextBox	Specifies the width of the <div> element.

(continued)

Table 5-6. (*continued*)

Control / Element ID	Type	Description
lstSequence	ListBox	Contains four values—Item Title, Description, Publication Date, and Link to Full Store—that are part of a feed item.
btnUp	Button	A button to move the items from lstSequence up.
btnDown	Button	A button to move the items from lstSequence down.
btnGenerate	Button	A button to trigger the RSS fetching operation.
RssBox	<div>	Once RSS feed items are retrieved, they are displayed inside this <div> element.
HtmlSource	<textarea>	This text area displays the raw HTML markup contained in RssBox.

Now let's get going. Begin by creating an empty ASP.NET Web Forms application and add a new Web Form to it: RssWidget.aspx. Design the Web Form as shown in Figure 5-4 and Figure 5-5. You can refer to Table 5-6 to assign IDs to various controls and HTML elements. Add the Scripts folder to the project and place the jQuery library into it.

Now add a <script> reference to the jQuery library and also add a <script> block in the head section. The ready() method handler binds event handler function to three buttons (btnUp, btnDown, and btnGenerate), shown in Listing 5-9.

Listing 5-9. ready() Method Handler

```
$(document).ready(function () {
  $("#btnUp").click(OnUp);
  $("#btnDown").click(OnDown);
  $("#btnGenerate").click(OnGenerate);
});
```

The code shown in Listing 5-9 uses the click() method on the three btnUp, btnDown, and btnGenerate buttons to wire the event handler functions OnUp, OnDown, and OnGenerate, respectively. For the sake of simplicity and readability, these three event handlers are created as separate functions instead of anonymous functions.

The OnUp() function performs the task of moving the selected item from lstSequence up in the list when the Up button is clicked. This function is shown in Listing 5-10.

Listing 5-10. Using insertBefore() to Move an Item Up

```
function OnUp(evt) {
  $('#lstSequence option:selected').each(function () {
    $(this).insertBefore($(this).prev());
  });
  evt.preventDefault();
}
```

The code picks up an <option> from the lstSequence drop-down list that is currently selected by the user. This is done using a combination of the ID selector and :selected selector. The each() method iterates through all the matched elements (in this case, only one element is selected). Inside the each() method function, the insertBefore() method is called to insert the current <option> before its previous item. Notice the use of the prev() method called on this to retrieve the previous sibling <option> element. Inside the function, this refers to the current item being iterated (the selected <option> in this case). To prevent the form submission, the preventDefault() method of the evt object is called.

The counterpart of the OnUp() function is the OnDown() function that is responsible for moving the selected item down in the list. The OnDown() function is shown in Listing 5-11.

Listing 5-11. Using insertAfter() to Move an Item Down

```
function OnDown(evt) {
  $('#lstSequence option:selected').each(function () {
    $(this).insertAfter($(this).next());
  });
  evt.preventDefault();
}
```

The OnDown() function is quite similar to the OnUp() function, except that it uses the insertAfter() method, so the selected <option> is inserted after the next option. Notice the use of the next() method to obtain the next sibling of the selected <option>.

After the Generate button is clicked, you must fetch the RSS feed items at the specified URL. This is done in the click event handler function OnGenerate(), as shown in Listing 5-12.

Listing 5-12. Fetching RSS Feed Items

```
function OnGenerate(evt) {
  var SourceUrl = "RssReader.aspx?feedUrl=" + $("#txtURL").val();
  $.get(SourceUrl, OnSuccess);
  evt.preventDefault();
}
```

The OnGenerate() function retrieves the URL entered by the user in the txtURL text box using the val() method. This URL is appended as a querystring parameter to RssReader.aspx, and the resultant URL is stored in the SourceUrl variable. RssReader.aspx will retrieve the RSS feed and return it to RssWidget.aspx. The RSS feed is an XML markup, so the response from RssReader.aspx will be in XML form. You will develop RssReader.aspx shortly. Just for your understanding, the structure of XML elements that make a feed item is given here:

```
<item>
  <title>title goes here</title>
  <link>URL goes here</link>
  <description>description goes here</description>
  <pubDate>publication date goes here</pubDate>
</item>
```

The $.get() method of jQuery is used to make an Ajax GET request to RssReader.aspx. The $.get() method takes two parameters: the URL that is to be accessed and a callback function that is invoked upon the successful completion of the request. The OnSuccess() function is shown in Listing 5-13.

Listing 5-13. OnSuccess() Function

```
function OnSuccess(feedData) {
  $("#RssBox").empty();
  $("#RssBox").append("<div><strong>" +
                      $("#txtTitle").val() +
                      "</strong></div>")
           .append("<hr />")
           .css("width", $("#txtWidth").val())
```

```
                .css("height", $("#txtHeight").val())
                .css("overflow", "auto")
                .css("text-align", $("#ddlAlign").val())
                .css("padding", "10px");
        $(feedData).find("item").each(ProcessFeedItem);
    }
}
```

The `OnSuccess()` function receives a parameter (`feedData`) that holds all the feed data. This data will be sent by `RssReader.aspx`. The `OnSuccess()` function begins by emptying the `RssBox` `<div>` element by using the `empty()` method and ensures that the widget works correctly even if the `Generate` operation is triggered multiple times. The title is retrieved from `txtTitle` and added to `RssBox` using the `append()` method. A series of `css()` calls is used to add CSS style attributes for height, width, text alignment, and so on. Notice that the `overflow` CSS attribute is also set so that scrollbars are displayed to the `RssBox` `<div>` element whenever necessary.

Once the look and feel of `RssBox` is configured, the code proceeds to read the `feedData` returned by `RssReader.aspx`. RSS feeds contain XML data, and each feed item is represented by an `<item>` element. The `find()` method is used on `feedData` to search for all the `<item>` elements. The search results are iterated upon by using the `each()` method. The `each()` method takes the `ProcessItem()` function as its parameter. The `ProcessItem()` function is discussed next (see Listing 5-14).

Listing 5-14. ProcessItem() Function

```
function ProcessFeedItem(index) {
    if (index >= $("#txtItemCount").val()) {
        return;
    }
    var item = $(this);
    var title = item.find("title").text();
    var link = item.find("link").text();
    var description = item.find("description").text();
    var pubDate = item.find("pubDate").text();
    var newDiv = $("<div></div>");
    for (var i = 1; i <= $("#lstSequence option").length; i++) {
        switch ($("#lstSequence option:nth-child(" + i + ")").val()) {
            case "title":
                $("<strong>" + title + "</strong><br />").appendTo(newDiv);
                break;
            case "date":
                $("<em>Posted on : " + pubDate + "</em><br />").appendTo(newDiv);
                break;
            case "desc":
                $("<p>" + description + "</p>").appendTo(newDiv);
                break;
            case "link":
                $("<a href='" + link + "' target='" +
                ($("#chkTarget").is(":checked") ? '_blank' : '_self') + "'>
                Full story...</a><br /><br />").appendTo(newDiv);
                break;
        }
    }
}
```

```
    $("#RssBox").append(newDiv);
    var clonedRssBox = $("#RssBox").clone();
    $("#HtmlSource").val($(clonedRssBox).html());
}
```

The ProcessItem() function accepts an index of the element being iterated. Inside, it checks whether this index is greater than or equal to the feed item count specified in txtItemCount. If so, the control is returned without performing any further processing. Otherwise, the code grabs values from the <title>, <description>, <pubDate>, and <link> elements. Notice that these elements are found by calling the find() method on the current <item> element (in this context, it refers to the current <item>). To extract the values of these elements, the text() method is used.

Each feed item is added to the RssBox as a child <div> element. This child <div> is formed dynamically like this: $("<div></div>"). A for loop then iterates through all the options of lstSequence. With every iteration, a switch statement checks the value of the <option> element using the nth-child() selector and val() method. Based on the option element, title, description, pubDate, and link values are appended to the newDiv using the appendTo() method. Compare the usage of append() and appendTo() to see how source and target switch their positions.

If the Open URL In New Window check box is checked, the hyperlink should open in a new window. To accomplish this, the behavior target attribute is added to the <a> element. Notice the use of the is() method to determine whether the check box is checked. The is() method accepts a selector (:checked in this case) and returns true if at least one of the source elements (in this case, the source element is chkTarget) matches the selector; it returns false otherwise. Accordingly, the target attribute is added to the anchor element with a value of _blank or _self.

The dynamically formed <div> element (newDiv) is added to the RssBox using the append() method. This way, all the feed items are added to RssBox and are displayed on the Web Form.

Finally, the code creates a clone of RssBox by calling the clone() method on it. The html() method called on the clonedRssBox returns the HTML content of the element. The HTML content thus returned is assigned to the <textarea> using the val() method.

This completes RssWidget.aspx. The small task that still remains is to create the RssReader.aspx file that does the job of pulling the RSS feed items from the specified URL. This form is quite straightforward and contains the code shown in Listing 5-15 in its Page_Load event handler.

Listing 5-15. Generating RSS Feed and Sending it to the Client

```
protected void Page_Load(object sender, EventArgs e)
{
    string url = Request.QueryString["feedUrl"];
    XmlReader reader = XmlReader.Create(url);
    Rss20FeedFormatter formatter = new Rss20FeedFormatter();
    formatter.ReadFrom(reader);
    reader.Close();
    Response.ContentEncoding = System.Text.Encoding.UTF8;
    Response.ContentType = "text/xml";
    XmlWriter rssWriter = XmlWriter.Create(Response.Output);
    formatter.WriteTo(rssWriter);
    rssWriter.Close();
    Response.End();
}
```

The code from Listing 5-15 uses classes from the System.Xml and System.ServiceModel.Syndication classes. The code retrieves the URL entered in the txtURL using the querystring parameter. Although not shown in the code, you should consider validating this URL before processing it further for security reasons. Recall that this query string parameter is passed from the OnGenerate() function while making a $.get() call to RssReader.aspx. Although detailed discussions of these classes are out of the scope of this book, suffice it to say that these classes essentially read an RSS feed and write it back on the response stream.

You might be wondering why the RSS feed is to be read on the server end instead of accessing the feed URL directly from the client script. It is necessary because browsers prohibit cross-domain Ajax calls. On the server side, you can easily create an `XmlReader` that reads a specified URL. The `Rss20FeedFormatter` is used to extract the feed data. Finally, the `XmlWriter` is used to write the feedback to the response stream.

That's it! Run the `RssWidget.aspx` and test it by entering a feed URL and configuration information.

Summary

Manipulating DOM is often required in web pages that change the content dynamically. jQuery offers a plethora of methods to add, remove, and replace DOM elements, attributes, and CSS styles. Methods such as `attr()` and `prop()` allow you to read and write attributes and properties, respectively. The methods such as `css()`, `addClass()`, and `removeClass()` allow you to manipulate CSS styling properties. Methods such as `text()` and `html()` allow you to deal with the contents of an element. Finally, methods such as `append()`, `remove()`, `insertAfter()`, and `insertBefore()` allow you to add or remove DOM elements.

The next chapter covers a few miscellaneous jQuery techniques such as data storage and collection manipulation.

CHAPTER 6

■ ■ ■

Traversal and Other Useful Methods

While working with DOM using jQuery, you often need to travel through a set of elements. There are different types of traversals, including traversing various child nodes of a given parent element and iterating though a set of DOM elements. jQuery offers a rich set of methods to accomplish this task. To that end, this chapter covers these methods in detail. Additionally, this chapter covers some miscellaneous techniques such as data storage, searching, and filtering DOM elements. Finally, this chapter also discusses some handy utility methods that simplify your coding. Specifically, the chapter covers the following topics:

- How to traverse through a DOM tree
- How to filter, search, and iterate through DOM elements
- How to work with HTML5 custom data attributes
- Using utility methods offered by jQuery

Tree Traversal

DOM arranges various elements in the form of a tree. You may need to access these elements based on their relationship or hierarchy (for example, parent, child, or siblings). jQuery tree traversal methods allow you to do just that. You typically use these methods to traverse the DOM tree or a branch of it. Table 6-1 lists the jQuery methods in this category.

Table 6-1. *jQuery Tree Traversal Methods*

Method	Description
children()	Returns immediate child elements of one or more selected elements.
parent()	Returns the immediate parent element of one or more matched elements.
parents()	Returns all the elements in the hierarchy that are parent for the matched elements.
closest()	Returns an element that is the closest ancestor of the matched element.
siblings()	Returns all the elements that are siblings of the matched elements.
next()	Returns the next sibling element of the matched elements.
nextAll()	Returns all the sibling elements that follow the matched elements.
prev()	Returns the element immediately preceding the matched elements.
prevAll()	Returns all the preceding elements of the matched elements.

Let's see how some of the methods outlined in Table 6-1 can be used. Suppose that you have a bulleted list placed in a Web Form:

```
<ul id="root">
  <li>C#</li>
  <li>Windows Forms</li>
  <li id="level1">ASP.NET
    <ul id="level2">
      <li id="level3">Web Forms</li>
      <li>MVC</li>
      <li>Configuration</li>
    </ul>
  </li>
  <li>.NET Framework</li>
  <li>Security</li>
</ul>
```

The markup consists of an outer `<ul>` element with the root ID. It has five direct child elements. The `<li>` element with the level1 ID contains another `<ul>` element with the level2 ID. The level2 `<ul>` element contains three child elements.

If you want to get all the direct child elements of the root `<ul>` element, this code will do the job:

```
var children = $("#root").children();
```

This line of code uses the ID selector to match the root `<ul>` element and then calls the `children()` method on it. This returns five `<li>` child elements: C#, Windows Forms, ASP.NET, .NET Framework, and Security.

If you want to get the parent elements of the level2 `<li>` element, you could write this:

```
var parent = $("#level2").parent();
var parents = $("#level2").parents();
```

The first line of code returns the immediate parent element of level2: the `<li>` element containing 'ASP.NET'. The second line of code, however, returns all the parent elements of level2 in the hierarchy (i.e., level1, root, `<form>`, `<body>`, and `<html>`.

If you want to work with siblings of the level1 `<li>` element, you can access them using any of these methods:

```
var siblings = $("#level1").siblings();
var nextSiblings = $("#level1").next();
var nextAllSiblings = $("#level1").nextAll();
var prevSiblings = $("#level1").prev();
var prevAllSiblings = $("#level1").prevAll();
```

The first line of code returns four sibling elements of level1: the `<li>` elements containing C#, Windows Forms, .NET Framework, and Security. The second line returns the immediate next sibling element of level1 (i.e., the `<li>` containing .NET Framework. The third line of code returns all siblings of level1 that follow it (i.e., `<li>` elements containing .NET Framework and Security. The fourth and fifth lines of code return the sibling immediately preceding level1 (the `<li>` element containing Windows Forms) and all the siblings that precede level1 (the `<li>` elements containing Windows Forms and C#), respectively.

Finally, to get the closest `<ul>` element of level3, write this:

```
var closest = $("#level3").closest("ul");
```

Here, the `closest()` method called on `level3` specifies a `<ul>` element selector and hence returns the closest `<ul>` element (the `level2` element).

Using Tree Traversal Methods

Now that you know the basics of jQuery tree traversal methods, let's develop a more realistic example based on the knowledge you've gained so far. Figure 6-1 shows the Web Form that makes this example.

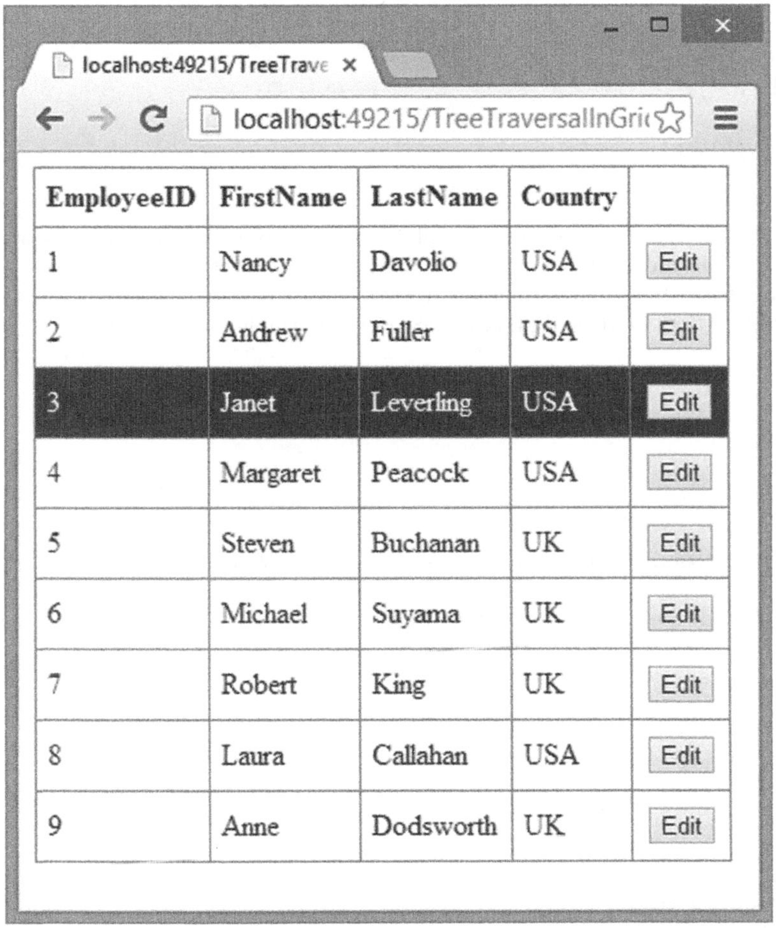

EmployeeID	FirstName	LastName	Country	
1	Nancy	Davolio	USA	Edit
2	Andrew	Fuller	USA	Edit
3	Janet	Leverling	USA	Edit
4	Margaret	Peacock	USA	Edit
5	Steven	Buchanan	UK	Edit
6	Michael	Suyama	UK	Edit
7	Robert	King	UK	Edit
8	Laura	Callahan	USA	Edit
9	Anne	Dodsworth	UK	Edit

Figure 6-1. *Application that uses tree traversal methods*

Although the application may seem like the one you developed in the earlier chapters, this time you will use the tree traversal methods to accomplish several things. First, whenever you hover your mouse pointer over any `GridView` row, that row gets highlighted. Taking the mouse away from that row removes the highlight. When the `GridView` enters edit mode, all the table cells being edited are shown with a different CSS styling to indicate the editable row. If you try to update a row with empty values in any of the text boxes, that text box gets a red border and that table cell is also highlighted. Although one row is being edited, the remaining rows of the `GridView` are dimmed to focus user attention to the editable row.

To begin developing this application, create an empty ASP.NET Web Forms application. Add a new Web Form in it and drag-and-drop a SQL Data Source control. Configure the SQL Data Source control to select the EmployeeID, FirstName, LastName, and Country columns from the Employees table of the Northwind database. Make sure to select the Generate INSERT, UPDATE, and DELETE statements option from the Configuration Wizard. Now place a GridView control on the Web Form and from its smart tag set its data source to the SQL Data Source control you just configured.

Next, add the Scripts folder to the project and place the jQuery library in it. Then add a <script> reference and a <script> block to the jQuery library. Add an empty ready() handler function and write the code shown in Listing 6-1.

Listing 6-1. Adding Hover Functionality

```
$("#GridView1 td").hover(function () {
    $(this).parent().addClass("Highlight");
  }, function () {
  $(this).parent().removeClass("Highlight");
});
```

The code selects all the table cells from GridView1 and wires event handler functions using the hover() method. When the mouse pointer is moved over a table cell, the first function is called; when the mouse pointer is moved out, the second function is called. The first function uses the parent() method on this selector to return the parent row of the current table cell. The addClass() method is used to add a Highlight CSS class to the table row. The Highlight CSS class looks like this:

```
.Highlight {
    background-color:navy;
    color:white;
}
```

The removeClass() method is used in the second function to remove the Highlight CSS class from the parent table row.

Now, add the code shown in Listing 6-2 inside the ready() function handler.

Listing 6-2. Validating Data Before Updating a Row

```
$("#GridView1 input:submit[value='Update']").click(function (evt) {
  var row = $(evt.target).parent().parent();
  var children = $(row).children();
  $(children).each(function () {
    if ($("input:text", this).val() == "") {
      $("input:text", this).addClass("Error");
      $(this).closest("td").removeClass("EditCell");
      $(this).closest("td").addClass("ErrorCell");
      evt.preventDefault();
    }
    else {
      $("input:text", this).removeClass("Error");
      $(this).closest("td").removeClass("ErrorCell");
    }
  });
});
```

The code selects the Update button using a combination of the ID selector, :submit selector, and attribute equals selector. Then a click event handler function is wired to handle the client-side click event of the Update button. Inside the click event handler, a reference to the table row is obtained using the parent() method. The Update button is placed inside a table cell so the first call to parent() will return this table cell. Calling parent() on this table cell will return the table row. Then all the table cells of the row are retrieved using the children() method.

In this example, the children() method returns five table cells. The each() method is used to iterate through all the table cells. With each iteration, the value of the text box inside a table cell is checked. Notice how the value of the text boxes is obtained. The input:text selector selects the text box within the context of this. In this case, this refers to a table cell being iterated. So, matching for input:text happens only within that table cell.

If the text box value is empty, the Error CSS class is added to the text box. The closest() method is used to get a reference to the table cell that houses the text box, and the EditCell CSS class is removed from it. (Notice that td is specified as the parameter to the closest() method to retrieve the closest table cell.) The ErrorCell CSS class is added to the table cell. Because empty text boxes indicate validation errors, the form submission is halted by using the preventDefault() method. If the text boxes contain some value, the else block gets executed, and the Error and ErrorCell CSS classes are removed from the respective elements.

The Error and ErrorCell CSS classes are shown here:

```
.Error {
    border:2px solid red;
}
.ErrorCell {
    background-color:#cec5c5;
}
```

Next, add the code shown in Listing 6-3 inside the ready() handler.

Listing 6-3. Highlighting the Editable Row

```
if ($("#GridView1 input:submit[value='Update']").length > 0) {
  var cell = $("#GridView1 input:submit[value='Update']").parent();
  var siblings = $(cell).siblings();
  $(siblings).each(function () {
    $(this).addClass("EditCell");
  });
  var row = $(cell).parent();
  $(row).nextAll("tr").addClass("NonEditableRow");
  $(row).prevAll("tr").addClass("NonEditableRow");
}
```

The code shown in Listing 6-3 gets executed every time the Web Form is loaded (either during the first request or as a result of postback). It checks whether the GridView is in update mode by seeing if the Update button can be selected successfully (length > 0). If so, a table cell reference that houses the Update button is obtained using the parent() method. Then the siblings() method is used on this table cell to retrieve all the other cells from the same row. The each() method loops through all the sibling table cells, and the EditCell CSS class is added to the respective table cell. Then a reference to the parent table row is obtained using the parent() method on the cell containing the Update button. All the next table rows of the row being edited are obtained using the nextAll() method, and the NonEditableRow CSS class is added to them. Similarly, all the preceding table rows of the row being edited are obtained using the prevAll() method and NonEditableRow CSS class is added to them. The EditCell and NonEditableRow CSS classes look like this:

```
.EditCell {
    background-color:#ffd800;
}
.NonEditableRow {
    background-color:rgba(0, 0, 0,0.5);
    opacity:0.5;
}
```

Notice how the rgba() function and opacity CSS property are used to specify the opacity of the target elements.

This completes the application. Figure 6-2 shows how the application behaves when the update operation is attempted while the Country text box is empty.

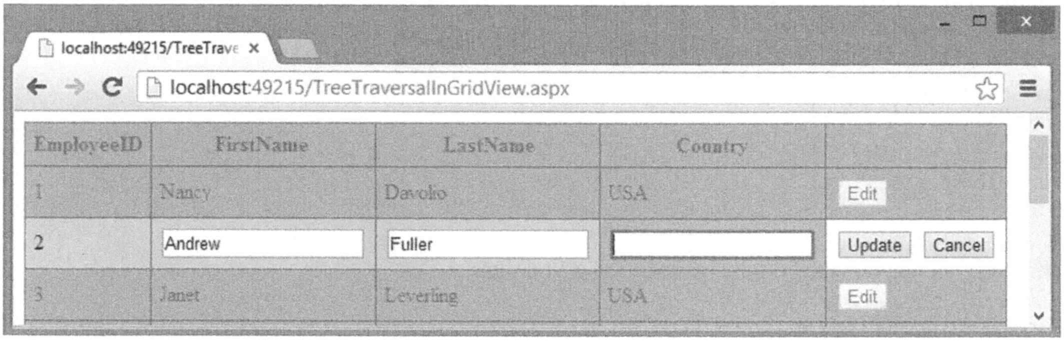

Figure 6-2. *GridView with some errors*

The editable row is highlighted, and the remaining rows are dimmed. The Country text box has a red border because it is empty.

■ **Note**   Some of the tasks from the previous example could have been accomplished by using selectors alone. However, because the example aimed at illustrating the use of the jQuery tree traversal methods, methods were used instead of selectors.

Tree traversal methods can be useful when you want to access and manipulate tree structures such as a TreeView or an organizational chart. Consider, for example, that you are building a web page that displays organizational hierarchies in the form of a TreeView or chart. In such cases, you can access the individual hierarchy level or nodes using the tree traversal methods discussed in this section. Another example is when XML files are loaded and displayed in some tree structure (for example, a web-based XML editor), and you want to access and manipulate various nodes of that tree.

Filtering

Although selectors allow you to pick elements matching a condition, sometimes you need more. You may want to select a set of elements and then work with a subset from those elements. For example, you may use an element selector to match all the table rows from a table and then access only a few rows from the result to perform some processing. jQuery filtering methods allow you to filter matched elements to return a subset that can be accessed for further processing. Table 6-2 lists the filtering methods offered by jQuery.

Table 6-2. *jQuery Filtering Methods*

Method	Description
first()	Returns the first element from the selected DOM elements.
last()	Returns the last element from the selected DOM elements.
eq()	Returns an element at specified index (zero-based) from the selected DOM elements.
has()	Returns all the elements from a set of DOM elements that have a given element as their descendant.
is()	Returns true if at least one element matches the criteria specified in the parameter; returns false otherwise.
not()	Returns all the elements that do not match the criteria specified in the parameter.
slice()	Returns all the elements between a zero-based start index and an end index (or until the end if the end index is not specified).
filter()	Returns all the elements from the selected DOM elements that match the specified condition.
map()	Used to pass each element from the selected DOM elements though a function and get the return values of the function calls.

To understand the usage syntax of these methods, consider the following markup that represents a bulleted list:

```
<ul>
  <li>C#</li>
  <li>Windows Forms</li>
  <li>ASP.NET
    <ul>
      <li class="sublist">Web Forms</li>
      <li class="sublist">MVC</li>
      <li class="sublist">Configuration</li>
    </ul>
  </li>
  <li>.NET Framework</li>
  <li>Security</li>
</ul>
```

The markup is quite similar to what you used in the preceding section, except all the sublist items have the sublist CSS class attached with them. Assuming that you have selected all <li> elements and now want to work with the first element from the matched elements, this is how to use the first() method:

```
var first = $("li").first();
```

This line of code selects all the <li> elements using the element selector and then retrieves the first element using the first() method. This first variable contains an element indicated by C#. You can retrieve the last element using the last() method like this:

```
var last - $("li").last();
```

To retrieve an element at a specific index, you can use the eq() method as shown here:

```
var fourth = $("li").eq(3);
```

This line of code returns a second <li> element (the index is zero-based) using the eq() method and stores it in a variable. This fourth variable will hold a reference to the Web Forms element.

If you want to filter the selection so that only first-level elements are returned, write the following code:

```
var sublist = $("li").not(".sublist");
```

The above code uses the not() method to filter all the <li> elements that do not have the sublist CSS class attached to them. Notice that the CSS class selector is specified as a parameter to the not() method. After executing this statement, the sublist variable will contain elements representing Web Forms, MVC, and Configuration.

The is() method is commonly used with check boxes to figure out whether a check box is checked. Of course, you can also use it for other purposes. For example, if you want to determine whether any of the matched elements have the sublist CSS class attached to them, you can write the following:

```
var flag = $("li").is(".sublist");
```

In this case, flag contains a Boolean value of true because there are elements with the sublist CSS class. Note that unlike most of the other filter methods, is() returns a Boolean value, not a jQuery object.

To slice the matched elements so that only the first two elements are returned, the following code can be used:

```
var sliced = $("li").slice(0,2);
```

The slice() method takes two parameters: the first parameter specifies the start index of an element at which slicing should begin; the second parameter indicates the end index of an element before which the slicing should stop. Both the indices are zero-based. In the preceding example, the sliced variable contains elements representing C# and Windows Forms. If you omit the end index, all the elements starting from the start index until the end of the selection are returned.

To run a custom filter on the selected elements so that only those having the sublist CSS class attached to them are returned, the following code can be used:

```
var sublist = $("li").filter(".sublist");
```

Here, the filter() method specifies a CSS class selector as its parameter, and hence the results of the first selector are filtered to retrieve only the elements having the sublist CSS class attached.

Suppose that you want to retrieve all the leaf-level list items as a comma-separated list, the following code does the trick:

```
var result = $("li").map(function () {
  if ($(this).children().length == 0) {
    return $(this).text();
  }
});
var finalResult = result.get().join(",");
```

This code uses the map() method and specifies a function as its parameter. Inside the function, this represents the current element being passed to the function. The function checks whether the element being passed has any child elements by using the children() method. If the element doesn't have a child element, the text of that element is retrieved using the text() method and returned. When all the elements are passed through the map() method, the collective result of all the function invocations is stored in the result variable as the jQuery object. The get() method is used to retrieve the result as an array, and then the join() method is called on it to get a comma-separated string of values. The previous code will store C#, Windows Forms, Web Forms, MVC, Configuration, .NET Framework, and Security in the resultant string.

Using Filtering Methods

In this section, you develop a Web Form that illustrates a more meaningful example of using filter methods. Figure 6-3 shows the Web Form that you will develop in this example.

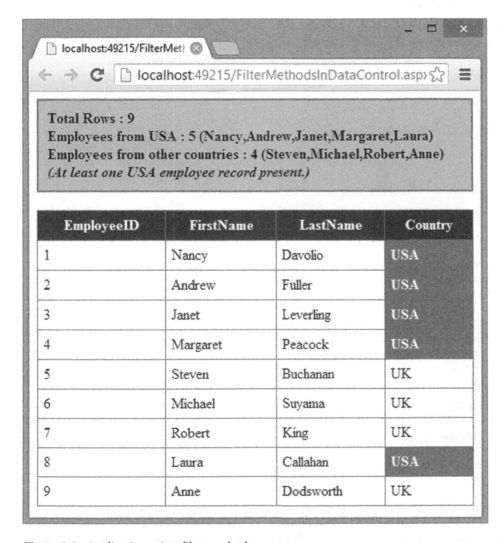

Figure 6-3. *Application using filter methods*

The Web Form consists of a <div> element at the top that shows some statistics about the records being shown in the GridView below it. The GridView displays records from the Employees table of the Northwind database. The <div> element shows information such as total number of rows in the grid, total number of employees from the USA and their names, and the total number of employees living outside the USA and their names. It also tells whether there is at least one employee from USA or not. A quick glance at the GridView will tell you that the Country table cells for USA employees are highlighted.

To begin developing this Web Form, create an empty ASP.NET Web Forms application and add a Web Form to it. Add the jQuery library to the Scripts folder and add a <script> reference to it in the head section of the Web Form. Then place a SQL Data Source control and a GridView on the Web Form. Configure the SQL Data Source control to pick EmployeeID, FirstName, LastName, and Country from the Employees table of the Northwind database. From the <smart> tag of the GridView, set its data source to the SQL Data Source control you just configured. Also add a <div> element and set its CSS class to InfoPanel. To highlight the Country cells for USA employees, handle the RowDataBound event of the GridView control, as shown in Listing 6-4.

Listing 6-4. RowDataBound Event Handler

```
protected void GridView1_RowDataBound(object sender,
            GridViewRowEventArgs e)
{
  if (e.Row.RowType == DataControlRowType.DataRow)
  {
    if (e.Row.Cells[3].Text == "USA")
    {
      e.Row.Cells[3].CssClass = "HighlightCountry";
    }
    else
    {
      e.Row.Cells[3].CssClass = "OtherCountry";
    }
  }
}
```

The RowDataBound event is raised for each and every row of a GridView, including header and footer, when the row is data bound. That is why a check is performed to see whether a row is a DataRow. This is done with the RowType property and DataControlRowType enumeration. If a row is a DataRow, another if condition checks whether the third cell of the row (the Country column) contains USA. If so, the HighlightCountry CSS class is attached to that cell by using its CssClass property. Otherwise, the OtherCountry CSS class is attached to that cell.

Now add a <script> block in the header section and an empty ready() handler function as before. Add the code shown in Listing 6-5 in the ready() handler function.

Listing 6-5. Total Table Rows

```
$(document).ready(function () {
  var infoHtml = "";
  var totalRows = $("#GridView1 tr");
  var dataRows=$(totalRows).slice(1);
  infoHtml += "Total Rows : " + $(dataRows).length + "<br/>";
});
```

The code begins by declaring the infoHtml variable for storing the HTML markup that will go inside the <div> element. Then all the table rows are selected from GridView1 and stored in the totalRows variable. This matched set becomes the basis for further processing. The totalRows variable will contain all the table rows, including the header row. To get only the data rows, the slice() method is used. The index value of 1 means that slicing will begin from second row and will continue until the end. The total number of data rows is then found using the length property of the dataRows variable.

Now add the code shown in Listing 6-6 inside the ready() handler.

Listing 6-6. Finding USA Employees

```
var usa = $(totalRows).has(".HighlightCountry");
infoHtml += "Employees from USA : " + $(usa).length;
infoHtml += " (";
var usaEmp = $(usa).map(function () {
  var children = $(this).children();
  return $(children).eq(1).text();
});
infoHtml += $(usaEmp).get().join(",");
infoHtml += ") <br/>";
```

The code shown in Listing 6-6 uses the has() method to filter all the rows from totalRows that have the HighlightCountry CSS class attached to them. Remember that only those cells that contain USA have this CSS class. So the usa variable will contain only those rows that have the Country cell with the HighlightCountry CSS class.

The total number of employees residing in the USA is then found by using the length property. The map() method is used on usa to obtain the FirstName column values of all the employees residing in the USA. Inside the map() callback function, the children() method is used to get all the table cells of the row under consideration (here it points to that row). To retrieve the FirstName value, the eq() method is called on the children with an index of 1 (FirstName is the second column in the GridView).

The text() method returns the FirstName value for an employee. Next, the get() method is used on usaEmp to convert the return value of map() into an array; then the join() method is called on the array to generate a comma-delimited string of FirstName values. To get the number of employees not residing in the USA and to output their names, a similar process is used. The only exception is that instead of the has() method checking for HighlightCountry, it checks for OtherCountry like this:

```
var others = $(totalRows).has(".OtherCountry");
```

Now add the code shown in Listing 6-7 below the code just discussed.

Listing 6-7. Checking for at Least One USA Employee

```
if ($("#GridView1 td").is(".HighlightCountry")) {
  infoHtml += "<em>(At least one USA employee record present.)</em>";
}
$(totalRows).first().addClass("HeaderRow");
$(".InfoPanel").html(infoHtml);
```

The code selects all the table cells and then uses the is() method to determine whether at least one of the cells has the HighlightCountry CSS class attached with it. If the is() method returns true, there is at least one employee residing in the USA. Accordingly, a string is added to the infoHtml variable.

To display the header row in a different way, the HeaderRow CSS class is added to it. To get a reference to the header row, the first() method is called on totalRows and then the addClass() method is used to attach the HeaderRow CSS class to it. Finally, the HTML markup stored in the infoHtml variable is assigned as the content of the <div> element using the html() method. The HighlightCountry, InfoPanel, and HeaderRow CSS classes are shown in Listing 6-8.

Listing 6-8. CSS Classes in the Application

```
.HighlightCountry {
    background-color:red;
    color:white;
    font-weight:bold;
}
.InfoPanel {
    border:2px solid rgb(128, 128, 128);
    background-color:#cec5c5;
    font-weight:bold;
    padding:10px;
}
.HeaderRow {
    background-color:navy;
    color:white;
    font-weight:bold;
}
```

You can add these classes to a style sheet and then link that style sheet from the head section of the Web Form using the <link> tag.

Filtering methods can be useful whenever you want to filter the selected elements and work with that subset. Suppose that you are building a Web Form that allows a user to generate custom reports. The page might display a whole set of data, but the user can filter it based on some conditions and then generate an onscreen report based on the filtered data.

Iterating and Searching

You often need to iterate through a set of DOM elements and may also want to search for certain elements. The jQuery each() and find() methods are used for these very purposes, respectively. Although you have used each() and find() before, this section examines them in more detail, along with an example.

Let's discuss the each() method first. It allows you to iterate through a set of DOM elements and execute a custom callback function on each object being iterated upon. The function receives a zero-based index of the element being iterated and the DOM element as the parameters. Inside the callback function, the keyword this represents the element being iterated. If you want to explicitly break the looping operation for some reason, you should return false from the callback function. Listing 6-9 shows how the each() method can be used to iterate through all <li> elements and perform processing on each of them.

Listing 6-9. Using the each() Method

```
$(document).ready(function () {
  $("li").each(function (index) {
    $(this).css("font-weight", "bold");
    if (index > 3) {
     return false;
    }
  });
});
```

The code shown in Listing 6-9 selects all <li> elements from a web page and iterates through them using the each() method. The callback function passed to the each() method takes index as its parameter. Inside, the function constructs a jQuery object using the this keyword and calls the css() method on it to set the font-weight CSS property to bold. Here, this points to the <li> element being iterated. An if condition checks whether the index of the element is greater than 3; if so, it breaks the each() operation. Thus running this code will cause the first <li> elements to be shown with font-weight of bold and the remaining will be unaffected.

The find() method allows you to search for and retrieve elements within a set of matched elements. Thus, find() searches all the descendant elements for a matching condition. For example, suppose that you have selected a set of table rows and want to find only those table cells that have certain CSS class attached. You can accomplish this task by using the find() method, as shown in Listing 6-10.

Listing 6-10. Using the find() Method

```
var results = $("tr").find(".class1");
  $(results).each(function () {
  $(this).addClass("class2");
});
```

The code uses the find() method on a set of matched <tr> elements and searches for all the descendant elements with the class1 CSS class attached with them. In this case, all the table cells and their contents will be searched, and the elements matching the search criteria are stored in results variable. The each() method is used to iterate through the search results, and the class2 CSS class is added to each found element using the addClass() method.

Using each() and find()

Now that you understand the each() and find() methods, you can develop a Web Form that illustrates how they can be used. The Web Form that makes this example is shown in Figure 6-4.

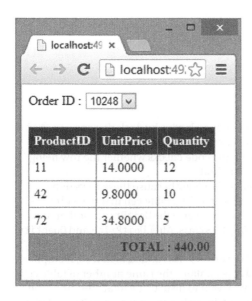

Figure 6-4. *Application using each() and find()*

The application consists of a Web Form that has a DropDownList at the top and a GridView below it. The DropDownList displays all the OrderIDs from the Order Details table of Northwind database. The GridView below shows ProductID, UnitPrice and Quantity for the selected OrderID. What is more important is the footer of GridView that renders the total order amount by multiplying UnitPrice with Quantity. This total amount is calculated using the each() and find() methods as discussed shortly.

Begin by creating an empty ASP.NET Web Forms application and add a new Web Form to it. Drag and drop a SQL Data Source control and a DropDownList on the form. Configure the SQL Data Source control to select the OrderID column from the Orders table of the Northwind database. Data bind the DropDownList with the SQL Data Source you just configured so that it displays the OrderID column. Drag and drop another SQL Data Source control and a GridView on the Web Form.

Configure this SQL Data Source control to select rows from the Order Details table for the OrderID selected in the DropDownList. You can do so by adding a control parameter in the Add WHERE clause dialog of the second SQL Data Source control. Data bind the GridView with the second SQL Data Source control. Configure the ItemTemplate for the UnitPrice and Quantity columns to set the CssClass property to Price and Qty, respectively. Set the CssClass property of the header and footer to Header and Footer, respectively (these classes are quite straightforward, so are not discussed here to save some space).

Next, add a <script> reference to the jQuery library and also add an empty <script> block. Add the code shown in Listing 6-11 inside the <script> block.

Listing 6-11. Calculating the Order Total with each() and find()

```
$(document).ready(function () {
  var totalAmount = 0;
  $("tr").each(function () {
    if (!$(this).hasClass("Header") && !$(this).hasClass("Footer")) {
      var price = $(this).find(".Price").text();
      var qty = $(this).find(".Qty").text();
      totalAmount += (price * qty);
    }
    if ($(this).hasClass("Footer")) {
      $(this).empty();
      $(this).append("<td colspan='3' align='right'>TOTAL : "
                  + totalAmount.toFixed(2) + "</td>");
    }
  });
});
```

The code in Listing 6-9 consists of the ready() handler function. The function begins by declaring the totalAmount variable intended to store the total order amount. Then an element selector is used to select all table rows. The each() method iterates through all the rows. With every iteration, the code checks whether the row being iterated has Header or Footer CSS classes added by using the hasClass() method.

The header and footer row needs to be skipped from the amount calculation logic because these rows don't contain any order details. Inside the if block, the find() method is used to search for a table cell that has Price CSS class attached with it. Calling the text() method on the return value of find() will give the UnitPrice for that row. Similarly, Quantity is found out using the find() method to look for the Qty CSS class. After UnitPrice and Quantity are known, they are multiplied and added to the totalAmount value.

The second if block checks whether the row being iterated has the Footer CSS class added to it. If so, it empties that row using the empty() method. By default, the footer row of the GridView contains the same number of table cells as the columns shown in the GridView (three cells in this case). Because you want to display the total amount in the footer, these three cells are removed by using the empty() method. Finally, a table cell with a colspan of 3 is added to the footer row using the append() method. Notice the use of the toFixed() method to display totalAmount with only two decimals.

The methods discussed in this section are useful whenever you want to do some custom processing for each element from the matched set. Suppose, for example, that you select a set of customers and want to display order details for certain customers from that set. You can use find() to retrieve the customers for which order information is needed and then use each() to iterate through each customer. Inside the each() callback, you can make an Ajax request to the server and retrieve order information for that customer. The retrieved order details can then be displayed onscreen or used for further processing.

Accessing Custom Data Attributes

HTML markup elements use attributes to specify configuration information. For example, the height and width attributes of the <div> element govern the height and width of the <div> when displayed in the browser. Most of the attributes of HTML elements affect the user interface or visual display of the element under consideration.

When developing web applications, developers may need to emit metadata about an element to the client browser. Such metadata doesn't affect the display of the element directly. Nevertheless, the metadata holds pieces of information relating to that element.

Consider an example in which an HTML form is to be validated using jQuery code. When the jQuery code validates the form fields, it is supposed to display validation errors if any of the fields hold invalid values. Often, the error message text is directly embedded in the JavaScript code. But what if the error message text is to be changed after the deployment?

Embedding the error message text directly in the script calls for editing the script. This in turn amounts to changing the application's code-base. In such situations, it's helpful if the error message text is stored separately from the web pages (in a database table, for example). At runtime, the error messages can be retrieved from the database and emitted to the client. These emitted messages form the metadata of the HTML elements. If any change is required in the error messages, you change the database entries, and the application begins using the new values from the next run.

Prior to HTML5, there wasn't a standard to deal with such metadata information. HTML5 introduces custom data attributes that can be used to define metadata about elements. The HTML5 custom data attributes are special attributes that take the following form:

```
data-<name>="value"
```

Custom data attributes always begin with data- followed by a developer-defined name. For example, for the custom validation scenario discussed earlier, you can create a custom data attribute named data-errormessage.

The developer-defined name can contain a hyphen (-). For example, data-customer-id and data-customer-name are valid custom data attributes.

■ **Note**   Custom data attributes are also referred as data-* attributes due to the naming convention they follow.

A custom data attribute can be assigned a value just like any other HTML attribute. Unlike standard HTML attributes, custom data attributes don't affect the visual look and feel of the element. You need to programmatically access them and execute the intended logic on them. An HTML element can have any number of custom data attributes defined on it. Listing 6-12 shows some sample HTML markup that uses custom data attributes.

Listing 6-12. Using Custom Data Attributes

```
<table border="1" cellpadding="3">
  <tr id='emp1' data-employeeid='1' data-title='Sales Representative'>
    <td>Nancy</td>
    <td>Davolio</td>
  </tr>
```

```
  <tr id='emp2' data-employeeid='2' data-title='Vice President, Sales'>
    <td>Andrew</td>
    <td>Fuller</td>
  </tr>
  ...
</table>
```

This listing shows an HTML table containing employee data. Each table row contains the name of the employee and has two custom data attributes: data-employeeid and data-title. The data-employeeid attribute stores the employee's EmployeeID, and the data-title attribute stores the employee's job title.

jQuery provides the data() method for accessing custom data attributes. Listing 6-13 shows how you can use jQuery to get and set custom data attributes.

Listing 6-13. Using jQuery to Access Custom Data Attributes

```
alert('Employee ID : ' + $("#emp1").data('employeeid'));
alert('Title : ' + $("#emp1").data('title'));

$("#emp1").data('employeeid', '100');
$("#emp1").data('title', 'Senior Manager');

alert('Employee ID : ' + $("#emp1").data('employeeid'));
alert('Title : ' + $("#emp1").data('title'));
```

The jQuery library provides the data() method to access custom data attributes. To retrieve a custom data attribute, call data() on the underlying DOM element and pass the attribute name without data-. For example, Listing 6-13 uses data('employeeid') to retrieve the value of the data-employeeid attribute. To assign a value to a custom data attribute, call the data() method and supply an attribute name without data- and its new value. In the previous example, data-employeeid is set to 100, and data-title is set to Senior Manager.

If the custom data attribute contains a hyphen (-) in the name (data-employee-birthdate, for example), you can access it using camel-casing syntax, as shown here:

```
alert('Title : ' + $("#emp1").data('employeeBirthdate'));
```

If you call data() without any parameters, it returns an object of key-value pairs containing all the custom data attributes of that element and their values. Listing 6-14 shows how to use this variation of the data() method.

Listing 6-14. Using the data() Method to Obtain Custom Data Attributes as an Object

```
var obj = $("#emp1").data();
alert('Employee ID : ' + obj.employeeid);
alert('Title : ' + obj.title);
alert('Birth Date : ' + obj.employeeBirthdate);
```

As you can see, the data() method is called without any parameters. Doing so returns an object with key-value pairs. To read a particular custom data attribute, you can use its name without data- against the object returned.

Using data() Method

Now that you know how to use custom data attributes, let's develop a Web Forms application that illustrates how you can implement the validation scenario discussed at the beginning of this section. You will develop a Web Form as shown in Figure 6-5.

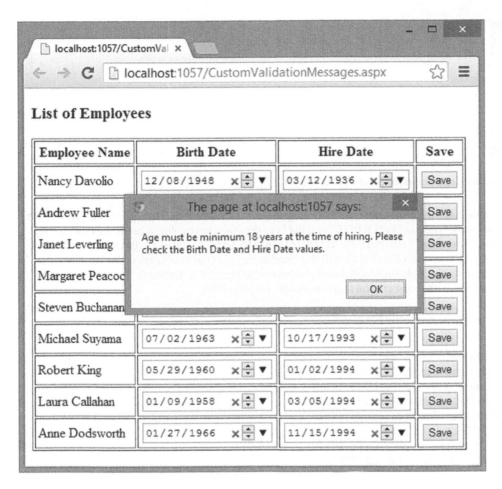

Figure 6-5. *Application using custom data attributes for validation*

The Web Form shows employee names from the Employees table of the Northwind database along with their BirthDate and HireDate values. The user can select the respective dates and click the Save button. Clicking Save triggers validation logic that checks whether the employee is at least 18 years old at the time of hiring. If not, an error message is displayed in an alert box. The validation message isn't embedded anywhere in the code; it is stored in a database table named ErrorMessages.

To begin developing this application, create an empty ASP.NET Web Forms project and add a new Web Form to it. Then add a local SQL Server database (you can either use SQL Express or LocalDB) and create a table named ErrorMessages. You also need to create an Entity Framework data model for this table. The ErrorMessages table has a simple structure, as shown in its Entity Framework data model (see Figure 6-6).

173

Figure 6-6. *Entity Framework data model for ErrorMessages table*

The ErrorMessages table contains three columns: Id, ErrorCode, and ErrorMessageText. The ErrorCode column contains a short code for an error (such as INVALIDDATE), and the ErrorMessageText column holds the descriptive error message (for example, "The Hire Date must be later than Birth Date"). Add a SQL Data Source control on the Web Form and configure it to select the EmployeeID, BirthDate, and HireDate columns of the Employees table. Next, place a Repeater control on the Web Form and design it to resemble Figure 6-5. Listing 6-15 shows the markup for the ItemTemplate of the Repeater server control that renders the employee list.

Listing 6-15. Web Form Markup Showing the Employee List

```
<ItemTemplate>
  <tr id='<%# Eval("EmployeeID","emp{0}") %>'
                    data-employeeid='<%# Eval("EmployeeID") %>'>
    <td><%# Eval("FirstName") %> <%# Eval("LastName") %></td>
    <td><asp:TextBox ID="txtBirthDate" runat="server"
        CssClass="birthdate" TextMode="Date"
        Text='<%# Eval("BirthDate") %>'
        data-error-invaliddate=
        '<%# GetValidationMessage("INVALIDDATE") %>'>
        </asp:TextBox>
    </td>
    <td><asp:TextBox ID="txtHireDate" runat="server" CssClass="hiredate"
        TextMode="Date"
        Text='<%# Eval("HireDate") %>'
        data-error-invaliddate=
        '<%# GetValidationMessage("INVALIDDATE") %>'>
        </asp:TextBox>
    </td>
    <td><input type="button" value="Save"/></td>
  </tr>
</ItemTemplate>
```

This markup consists of two TextBox server controls that display the BirthDate and HireDate column values, respectively. The TextMode property of these text boxes is set to Date, so the browsers supporting the HTML5 date input type can display a date-picker to select the dates. Each text box has a custom data attribute named data-error-invaliddate. The value of this attribute comes from the GetValidationMessage() method, which picks up the ErrorMessageText from the ErrorMessages table based on the ErrorCode passed:

```
public string GetValidationMessage(string errorCode)
{
  ValidationDbEntities db = new ValidationDbEntities();
  var data = from item in db.ErrorMessages
             where item.ErrorCode == errorCode
             select item.ErrorMessageText;
  return data.SingleOrDefault();
}
```

The jQuery code that performs the validation and displays the validation error, if any, resides in the Save button's click event handler. This code is shown in Listing 6-16.

Listing 6-16. Validating Employee's Age

```
$("input[value='Save']").click(function () {
  var birthDateTxtbox = $(this).closest('tr').find(".birthdate");
  var hireDateTxtbox = $(this).closest('tr').find("hiredate");
  var birthDate = ToDate($(birthDateTxtbox).val());
  var hireDate = ToDate($(hireDateTxtbox).val());
  birthDate.setFullYear(birthDate.getFullYear() + 18);
  if ((hireDate.getTime() - birthDate.getTime()) < 0) {
    alert($(birthDateTxtbox).data('errorInvaliddate'));
    return;
  }
  //make Ajax request to update the database
  alert('Data saved!');
});
```

The Save button's click event handler begins by grabbing a reference to the BirthDate and HireDate input fields. The closest() method returns the row that holds the input fields and the Save button. The find() method then searches for elements with the birthdate and hiredate CSS classes attached.

The input fields hold the date value in *yyyy-MM-dd* format. These dates are converted into JavaScript Date objects using the ToDate()custom function. The ToDate() function looks like this:

```
function ToDate(input) {
  var parts = input.match(/(\d+)/g);
  return new Date(parts[0], parts[1] - 1, parts[2]);
}
```

The ToDate() function parses the supplied input value using the JavaScript match() method and returns a JavaScript Date object that represents that value. The match() method called on a string accepts a regular expression as its parameter. It then matches the string against that pattern and returns an array containing the matched parts from the string. In this case, the first array element contains year, the second element contains month and the third element contains day. Based on these elements, a Date object is created and returned to the caller.

Next, the code checks the difference between the HireDate and BirthDate to determine whether the employee is at least 18 years old at the time of hiring. If not, an error message, as specified in the data-error-invaliddate custom data attribute, is displayed to the user in an alert dialog. The data() method is used to retrieve the value of the data-error-invaliddate attribute. Although the code doesn't actually save the changed data to the server, you can add that functionality if the age validation succeeds. In Listing 6-16, a success message is displayed after the age check is successful.

Other Useful Methods

Most of the methods discussed so far in this chapter participate in the processing of the DOM elements in some way or another. They allow you to read, write, or reach a particular set of DOM elements. The methods (and a property) discussed in this section are types of helper methods. These methods perform tasks such as obtaining the total number of elements in a matched set, obtaining DOM elements from a matched set, and so on. Table 6-3 lists these methods for your quick reference.

Table 6-3. *Miscellaneous jQuery Methods*

Method / Property	Description
get()	Returns the DOM element(s) matched by the jQuery object under consideration. It can take a zero-based index to retrieve just an object at that index.
index()	Returns a zero-based index of a DOM element with respect to its siblings. It can also take a selector or element as its parameter and return the index of the matching element.
toArray()	Returns a JavaScript array from a matched set of elements.
length	Returns the number of elements in a matched set.

The get() method comes in handy when you need to access the DOM elements from a set of matched elements. Suppose, for example, that you are working with an <audio> element and want to call the play() method of the element. You can use the get() method to do so:

```
var audio = $("#audio1").get(0);
audio.play();
```

This code uses the ID selector to select an <audio> element with an ID of audio1. It then calls the get() method and passes an index value of 0. Thus, the audio variable contains a reference to the audio1 DOM element. You can then call the play() method on the audio object to play the audio file. If you don't specify an index while calling the get() method, all the matched elements are returned as an array. The following code shows how this is done:

```
var audioList = $("audio").get();
for (var i = 0; i < audioList.length; i++) {
  audioList[i].play();
}
```

This code retrieves all the <audio> elements from the page by using the element selector. The get() method is called on the matched set to return the elements as an array. A for loop iterates through the array and calls the play() method on each audio DOM element.

The get() method accepts an index and returns a DOM element. The index() method does the opposite. It returns an index of a DOM element. Suppose that you have a series of <li> elements as part of a bulleted list like this:

```
<ul id="root">
  <li>C#</li>
  <li>Windows Forms</li>
  <li id="level1">ASP.NET</li>
  <li>.NET Framework</li>
  <li>Security</li>
</ul>
```

If you want to know the index of an element with the ID of level1, you can write this:

```
var idx = $("#level1").index();
```

This line of code uses the ID selector to select the level1 element. Calling the index() method on the matched set returns the index of the element with respect to its siblings. In this case, because the level1 element is third in the list, the index() method will return 2. If you have a reference to the element whose index is to be determined, you can also write this:

```
var item = $("#level1");
var idx = $("li").index(item);
```

In this case, the item variable holds a reference to level1. The second line of code selects all the <li> elements and then calls the index() method on the matched set by passing the item as a parameter. This will return the index of the supplied object with respect to the matched set (2 in this case).

The toArray() method doesn't accept any parameters and returns an array of the matched elements:

```
var arr = $("li").toArray();
```

This line of code gets an array from the matched set and stores it in a variable. Thus, the arr variable is an array with five elements.

The length property is quite straightforward, and you have used it before. It simply returns the number of elements in a matched set:

```
var count = $("li").length;
```

This line selects all the <li> elements and uses the length property to retrieve the number of elements in the matched set. In this case, the count is five.

Summary

This chapter covered tree traversal methods and several methods that allow you to access DOM elements. The tree traversal methods such as children(), parents(), and siblings() allow you to navigate and access through a hierarchy of DOM elements. The jQuery filter methods allow you to filter a matched set based on some condition. Methods such as first(), last(), eq(), has(), and not() fall in this category. A common task while working with jQuery is iterating through a set of elements, and the each() method does that for you. The find() method comes in handy when it comes to searching a matched set for a certain condition. The HTML5 custom data attributes (data-*) allow you to attach metadata information to DOM elements. These attributes can be accessed by using the data() method. Finally, you learned some handy helper methods such as get() and index(), and the length property.

To grab users' attention and keep them interested while they surf web sites, developers often resort to fancy effects, including sliding, fading, and animations. jQuery offers many ways to add such jazz to your web pages. To that end, the next chapter teaches you to develop great-looking pages using jQuery effects and animations.

CHAPTER 7

■ ■ ■

Effects and Animations

Modern web applications are a lot more than a bunch of static HTML pages. Web designers and developers always look for innovative ways to keep visitors glued to their web sites. There are many aspects to keeping a visitor interested and engaged in web sites, including interactive design, user interface elements, and content usefulness. One area that is quite popular in this regard is addition of fancy effects and animations to web pages. And jQuery has a nice set of methods to offer. Although mouseover effects developed using plain JavaScript are not at all uncommon, what makes jQuery special is its capability to add fancy effects and animations with ease. In many situations, just a few lines of code are sufficient to produce an eye-catching effect. To that end, this chapter dissects jQuery effects and animation techniques. Specifically, you'll learn the following:

- How to hide and show elements
- How to add sliding and fading effects
- How to add custom animations to web pages
- How to terminate animations being played

Showing and Hiding Elements

One of the simplest forms of animation effect is hiding and showing DOM elements. Although you can always hide or show a DOM element using CSS properties such as `display` and `visibility`, jQuery offers readymade methods that make your job easy. Table 7-1 lists jQuery methods that deal with the element visibility.

Table 7-1. *Methods that Show and Hide Elements*

Method	Description
hide()	Hides selected elements.
show()	Shows selected elements.
toggle()	Hides selected elements if they are visible and shows them if they are hidden.

All three methods—hide(), show(), and toggle()—mentioned in Table 7-1 allow you to configure the duration of the effect under consideration, the easing function, and the completion callback function.

The hide() method hides the selected elements. If you call hide() without any parameters, the element is hidden immediately. The hide() method can also take three optional parameters: duration, easing, and complete.

The duration parameter specifies the number of milliseconds for which the hiding effect should be played. This means that instead of an element being hidden immediately, it will be progressively hidden over a certain period specified by the duration parameter, by progressive reduction in its height, width, and opacity. Instead of specifying the duration as a number, you can also specify it using built-in string constants: fast (200 milliseconds) and slow (600 milliseconds).

The easing parameter specifies the name of an easing function to be used while the animation effect plays. An easing function controls the speed of an animation effect at different stages within the animation being played. The values of the easing parameter are swing (default) and linear. The linear easing function progresses at a constant speed throughout the duration of an animation effect; the swing easing function increases the speed of an animation at the beginning and at the end. In addition to these two built-in easing functions, you can also write custom easing functions or use easing functions that are part of the JQuery UI. Discussion of custom easing functions is beyond the scope of this book. Refer to the jQuery documentation for more information about the easing functions.

The complete parameter is a callback function that gets invoked when the element is hidden. Inside the callback, the keyword this refers to the element being hidden. The following code samples show how hide() can be used:

```
$("#div1").hide();
$("#div1").hide(3000);
$("#div1").hide("slow",function(){ alert('Done!'}; );
```

The first line of code hides a DOM element with the ID of div1. Because no parameters are supplied to hide(), the element is hidden immediately. The second line of code specifies the duration parameter to be 3000 milliseconds, which hides the element in 3 seconds rather than immediately. Finally, the third line of code specifies the animation duration as slow and also passes a callback function. The callback function simply displays a message using an alert dialog.

The show() method shows a set of matched elements. The show() method takes the same three parameters (duration, easing, and complete) that the hide() method takes. The following code illustrates how show() can be used:

```
$("#div1").show();
$("#div1").show(3000);
$("#div1").show("slow",function(){ alert('Done!'}; );
```

The first call to show() shows the div1 element immediately. The second call shows it progressively after 3000 milliseconds. In the case of the show() height, width, and opacity are progressively increased during the time span specified by the duration parameter. The third call to show() shows the element using slow duration and also supplies a callback function.

The toggle() method hides an element if the element is visible and shows the element if it is hidden. The toggle() method takes the same three optional parameters that hide() and show() take.

Now let's build a Web Form that illustrates a more meaningful use of the hide() and show() methods. Figure 7-1 shows this Web Form.

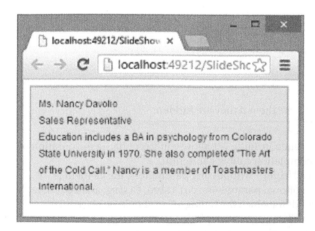

Figure 7-1. *Application using hide() and show()*

The Web Form consists of a Repeater control that displays records from the Employees table of the Northwind database. What is interesting about this Repeater is that unlike its normal behavior, it doesn't display all the records at once; instead, only one employee record is displayed at a time and the next record is displayed like a slide show. The slide show loops continuously as long as the Web Form is displayed in the browser. Converting the Repeater items into a slide show is accomplished by using the jQuery hide() and show() methods.

To begin developing this form, create an empty ASP.NET Web Forms application and add a new Web Form to it. Then drag and drop an SQL Data Source control on the Web Form and configure it to select the FirstName, LastName, Title, TitleOfCourtesy, and Notes columns from the Employees table. Then place a Repeater control on the Web Form and set its data source to the SQL Data Source control you just configured. Then design the <ItemTemplate> of the Repeater, as shown in Listing 7-1.

Listing 7-1. Repeater <ItemTemplate>

```
<asp:Repeater ID="Repeater1" runat="server" DataSourceID="SqlDataSource1">
  <ItemTemplate>
    <div class="Panel">
    <span><%# Eval("TitleOfCourtesy") %></span>
    <span><%# Eval("FirstName") %></span>
    <span><%# Eval("LastName") %></span>
    <br />
    <span><%# Eval("Title") %></span>
    <br />
    <span><%# Eval("Notes") %></span>
    </div>
  </ItemTemplate>
</asp:Repeater>
```

As you can see, each Employee record is placed in a <div> element that has the CSS Panel class attached to it. ASP.NET databinding expression syntax (<%# ... %>) is used to display various column values inside <span> elements.

Add a reference to the jQuery library and add a <script> block in the head section. Immediately inside the <script> block, declare four global variables as shown here:

```
var index = 0;
var panels = null;
var visibleTime = 2000;
var animationTime = 1000;
```

The index variable indicates an index of a <div> that is to be displayed at a given point in time. The panels variable holds reference to all the <div> elements that show the Employee records. The visibleTime and animationTime variables govern the amount of time for which the employee record is displayed to the user and the duration of the hide/show animation effect. Now add the ready() handler as shown in Listing 7-2.

Listing 7-2. Retrieving <div> Elements

```
$(document).ready(function () {
  panels = $(".Panel").get();
  $(".Panel").hide();
  $(panels[0]).show();
  setTimeout(ShowSlide, visibleTime);
});
```

The code shown in Listing 7-2 retrieves all the <div> elements using the CSS class selector. The get() method returns them as an array of DOM elements. All the <div> elements are then hidden using the hide() method. The first Employee record is then displayed to the user by calling the show() method on the first element of the panels array. The setTimeout() method is called to invoke the ShowSlide() function after a duration, as indicated by visibleTime. The ShowSlide() function is shown in Listing 7-3.

Listing 7-3. ShowSlide() Function

```
function ShowSlide() {
  $(panels[index]).hide(animationTime, function () {
    index++;
    if (index >= panels.length) {
      index = 0;
    }
    $(panels[index]).show(animationTime, function () {
      setTimeout(ShowSlide, visibleTime);
    });
  });
}
```

The ShowSlide() function hides the <div> element per the index value using the hide() method. The animationTime variable is passed as the duration parameter. The completion callback function increments the index by 1 with each run of ShowSlide(). To loop the slide show once the last Employee is displayed, the value of index is checked with the total number of panels. If index is greater than or equal to the total number of panels, it is reset to 0. The show() method is called on the next panel by passing animationTime as its duration. The completion callback function uses setTimeout() to recursively call the ShowSlide() function.

Adding Sliding Effects

The slideUp(), slideDown(), and slideToggle() jQuery methods allow you to add a sliding motion effect to DOM elements. During the sliding-up operation, an element's height is progressively reduced to give the desired effect. As soon as the height becomes zero, the element is hidden. During sliding-down operations, the element's height is progressively increased from zero to the height of the element. Table 7-2 describes these three methods.

Table 7-2. *Methods that add Sliding Effects*

Method	Description
slideUp()	Hides selected elements with a sliding motion.
slideDown()	Shows selected elements with a sliding motion.
slideToggle()	Displays selected elements if they are hidden and hides the selected elements if they are visible. The sliding motion is applied during both of the operations.

The slideUp(), slideDown(), and slideToggle() methods accept three optional parameters: duration, easing, and complete. The significance of these three parameters is the same, as discussed in the preceding section.

Assuming that you have a <div> element on the page and you want to animate it with the slideUp() method, you can use any of the following variations:

```
$("#div1").slideUp();
$("#div1").slideUp(3000);
$("#div1").slideUp("slow", function () { alert('done'); });
```

The first line of code selects div1 and calls the slideUp() method on it. Because no duration is mentioned, a default of 400 milliseconds is assumed, and the sliding motion effect is applied to the element for that long. The second and third lines of code specify the duration as 3000 milliseconds and slow respectively. .

To display a <div> element using the slideDown() method, you can write this:

```
$("#div1").slideDown();
$("#div1").slideDown (3000);
$("#div1").slideDown ("slow", function () { alert('done'); });
```

The slideDown() method is quite similar to slideUp(), except that it applies a sliding-down effect and shows the element at the end of the animation. The slideToggle() method is also similar in terms of signature to slideUp() and slideDown(). However, it toggles between slide-up and slide-down effects. depending on whether an element is visible or hidden.

Now that you understand how a sliding effect can be applied to elements, let's create an application that puts this knowledge to use. The Web Form that you develop is shown in Figure 7-2.

Figure 7-2. *Accordion menu with sliding effects*

Figure 7-2 displays an accordion menu rendered in a Web Form. A peculiar feature of an accordion menu is that only one of the menus will be fully expanded at a time. For example, if you click ASP.NET menu, it will expand to reveal its menu items and previously expanded menu (if any) will be collapsed. As the menus are expanding and collapsing, you can add sliding effects to them to make them more appealing and fancier.

To develop this Web Form, begin by creating an empty ASP.NET Web Forms application. Then place a Repeater control on the Web Form and design its ItemTemplate as shown here:

```
<asp:Repeater ID="Repeater1" runat="server" ClientIDMode="AutoID"  OnItemDataBound="Repeater1_
ItemDataBound">
  <ItemTemplate>
    <asp:Panel ID="Panel1" runat="server" CssClass="Menu">
      <asp:Label ID="lblText" runat="server" Text='<%# Eval("Text") %>'>
      </asp:Label>
      <asp:Panel ID="menuItemGroup" runat="server" CssClass="MenuItem">
      </asp:Panel>
    </asp:Panel>
  </ItemTemplate>
</asp:Repeater>
```

The Repeater has its ClientIDMode set to AutoID so that the IDs of the constituent controls, such as Panel, consist of three parts: the ID of the Repeater, an incrementing value, and the ID of the constituent control. For example, the client-side ID of the first menuItemGroup will be Repeater1_ctl00_menuItemGroup. The ItemTemplate consists of an outer Panel control that houses a Label and a Panel. The Label is used to display menu text such as ASP.NET. The Panel menuItemGroup acts as a container to all the menu items (hyperlinks) belonging to that menu. The outer Panel has the Menu CSS class attached to it, and the inner Panel has the MenuItem CSS class attached to it. You need to handle the ItemDataBound event of Repeater to add menu items for each menu. Listing 7-4 shows the ItemDataBound event handler.

Listing 7-4. ItemDataBound Event Handler

```
protected void Repeater1_ItemDataBound(object sender,
RepeaterItemEventArgs e)
{
  if (e.Item.ItemType == ListItemType.Item ||
      e.Item.ItemType==ListItemType.AlternatingItem)
  {
    Label l = (Label)e.Item.FindControl("lblText");
    Panel p = (Panel)e.Item.FindControl("menuItemGroup");
    HyperLink l1 = new HyperLink();
    HyperLink l2 = new HyperLink();
    HyperLink l3 = new HyperLink();
    switch (l.Text)
    {
      case "ASP.NET":
        l1.Text="Web Forms";
        l1.NavigateUrl = "~/webform.aspx";
        l2.Text="MVC";
        l2.NavigateUrl = "~/mvc.aspx";
        l3.Text="Security";
        l3.NavigateUrl = "~/security.aspx";
        break;
      case "Windows Forms":
        ...
        break;
      case "C# Language":
        ...
        break;
    }
    p.Controls.Add(l1);
    p.Controls.Add(new LiteralControl("<br/>"));
    p.Controls.Add(l2);
    p.Controls.Add(new LiteralControl("<br/>"));
    p.Controls.Add(l3);
  }
 }
}
```

The ItemDataBound event handler first checks whether the item being rendered is an Item or AlternatingItem. This is necessary because menu items are to be added only if the item type is Item or AlternatingItem. Then a reference to lblText and menuItemGroup is obtained by using the FindControl() method, which accepts the name of the control to be searched inside the item and returns its reference. A set of HyperLink controls is then created.

A switch statement checks the Text property of lblText to determine which menu is being rendered. Accordingly, the Text and NavigateUrl properties of the HyperLink controls are set. Finally, all the HyperLink controls are added to the Controls collection of the menuItemGroup Panel using the Add() method. Notice that in addition to HyperLink controls, the LiteralControls are also being added for the line break (<br />) element.

The Repeater is bound with a generic List of Menu objects. Each Menu object supplies the Text of the menu. The Menu class and the Page_Load event handler are shown in Listing 7-5.

Listing 7-5. Menu Class and Page_Load Event Handler

```
public class Menu
{
  public Menu(string text)
  {
    this.Text = text;
  }
  public string Text { get; set; }
}

protected void Page_Load(object sender, EventArgs e)
{
  List<Menu> list = new List<Menu>();
  list.Add(new Menu("ASP.NET"));
  list.Add(new Menu("Windows Forms"));
  list.Add(new Menu("C# Language"));
  Repeater1.DataSource = list;
  Repeater1.DataBind();
}
```

The Menu class consists of a single property (Text) that represents the menu text. The Page_Load event handler creates a generic List of Menu objects and adds three Menu instances to it: ASP.NET, Windows Forms, and C# Language. The generic List is then bound with the Repeater by using its DataSource property and the DataBind() method.

Although the server-side code fills up the Repeater with all the menus and menu options, on the client side you need to display the Repeater as an accordion menu. This is done by adding sliding effects to menuItemGroup panels. So, add a <script> reference to the jQuery library and also add a <script> block. Then write the code shown in Listing 7-6 inside the <script> block.

Listing 7-6. Converting the Repeater into an Accordion Menu

```
$(document).ready(function () {
  $("div[id $= 'menuItemGroup']").hide();
  $(".Menu").click(function (evt) {
    $("div[id $= 'menuItemGroup']").slideUp(1000);
    if (evt.target.tagName == "DIV") {
      var child = $(evt.target).children("div[id $=
                  'menuItemGroup']").eq(0);
    }
    else {
      var child = $(evt.target).parent().children("div[id $=
                  'menuItemGroup']").eq(0);
    }
    $(child).slideDown(1000);
  });
});
```

The code shown in Listing 7-6 consists of the ready() handler that hides all the <div> elements whose IDs end with menuItemGroup. You need to use the attribute ends with selector here because Repeater automatically generates unique IDs for the controls it houses. The hide() method is used to hide the selected <div> elements. Then a CSS class selector is used to select all the elements with the Menu CSS class added (remember that the outer Panel from the Repeater's ItemTemplate has this CSS class).

The click() method is used to wire a click event handler to the click event of the selected elements. When a user clicks the menu before expanding it, all the other menus need to be collapsed. The slideUp() method is used to apply a slide-up effect to all the menus. A user can click the outer <div> element or the <span> displaying the menu text (Label is rendered as a <span> tag). So the evt.target property can be either a <div> or a <span>. The if block checks the evt.target.tagName property to figure out whether a <div> or a <span> was clicked. If it was a <div>, a reference to the menuItemGroup child element is obtained using the children() and eq() methods. If a <span> was clicked, a reference to the menuItemGroup child element is obtained through the parent of the <span> element. The slideDown() method is used to apply a sliding-down effect to the menuItemGroup.

■ **Note** Although the preceding example deals with a fixed set of menu items, you can easily transform it into a database-driven accordion.

Adding Fading Effects

Fading involves progressively decreasing or increasing an element's opacity. The opacity value varies between 0 and 1, where 0 means fully transparent and 1 means fully opaque. Decreasing the opacity from 1 to 0 gives a fade-out effect, whereas increasing the opacity from 0 to 1 gives a fade-in effect. jQuery offers four methods that add fading effects to DOM elements: fadeIn(), fadeOut(), fadeToggle(), and fadeTo(). These methods are described in Table 7-3.

Table 7-3. *Methods that Add Fading Effects*

Method	Description
fadeIn()	Gradually increases the opacity of the selected elements from the current value to 1 so that those elements are displayed with a final opacity value of 1.
fadeOut()	Gradually decreases the opacity of the selected elements from the current value to 0 so that those elements are hidden with a final opacity value of 0.
fadeToggle()	Toggles between fade-in and fade-out effects, depending on whether an element is hidden or visible.
fadeTo()	Increases or decreases the opacity of the selected elements to a specified value.

The fadeIn(), fadeOut(), and fadeToggle() methods accept the same three parameters (duration, easing, and completion callback) as the methods discussed in earlier sections.

Suppose that you want to apply a fade-in effect to a hidden <div> element whose ID is div1. You can use the following code:

```
$("#div1").fadeIn();
$("#div1").fadeIn(3000);
$("#div1").fadeIn("slow", function () { alert('done'); });
```

The three calls to the fadeIn() method use a default duration of 400 milliseconds, 3000 milliseconds, and slow, respectively.

The fadeOut() and fadeToggle() methods are quite similar to fadeIn() in terms of method parameters. The fadeTo() method is slightly different in that it allows you to explicitly specify the final opacity of the selected elements. For example, if you want to set the opacity of a fully opaque <div> element to 0.7, you can write this:

```
$("#div1").fadeTo(3000, 0.7,function () { alert('done'); });
```

This line of code calls the fadeTo() method on div1 and specifies that the effect is to be applied in 3000 milliseconds. The final opacity is specified as 0.7.

Now let's develop a simple application that illustrates a more realistic use of fading effects. Figure 7-3 shows a Web Form that makes use of the fading effects to display a progress indicator to the end user.

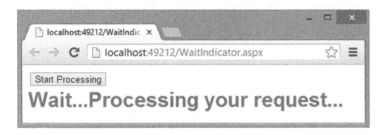

Figure 7-3. *Displaying a progress indicator using fading effects*

The Web Form consists of a button and a panel that houses a Label control. Clicking the Start Processing button invokes an ASP.NET generic handler. The generic handler is supposed to be doing some lengthy processing and then returns a success message to the Web Form. As soon as the user clicks the button, the button is disabled and a wait message starts flashing on the page. The blinking of the wait message stops and the button is enabled again once the generic handler returns successfully.

To develop this application, begin by creating an empty ASP.NET Web Forms application and add a new Web Form to it. Place a Button and a Panel control on it. Place a Label inside the panel. Set the Text property of the Label to some progress message. Add a <script> reference to the jQuery library and add a <script> block. Then add the code shown in Listing 7-7 inside the <script> block.

Listing 7-7. *Flashing Wait Message Using fadeToggle().*

```
var handle;
$(document).ready(function () {
  $("#Panel1").hide();
  $("#Button1").click(function (evt) {
    $("input:submit").prop("disabled", true);
    handle=setTimeout(Wait, 1000);
    var xhr = new XMLHttpRequest();
    xhr.open("POST", "ProcessingHandler.ashx");
    $(xhr).on("load", function (evt) {
      clearTimeout(handle);
      $("#Panel1").hide();
      $("input:submit").prop("disabled", false);
      alert(evt.target.responseText);
    });
```

```
    xhr.send();
    evt.preventDefault();
  });
});

function Wait() {
  $("#Panel1").fadeToggle("slow");
  handle=setTimeout(Wait, 1000);
}
```

The ready() handler first uses the hide() method to hide Panel1 so that no wait message is displayed to the user when the page loads. Then the code uses the .click() method to wire an event handler to the click event of the Start Processing button. The click event handler disables the Start Processing button so that users can't click it multiple times when the processing is already in progress. This is done with the :submit selector and the prop() method. The prop() method .sets the disabled property to true.

The code then uses the JavaScript setTimeout() method .to invoke the Wait() function after a delay of 1000 milliseconds. The setTimeout() method returns a numeric handle that is saved in the handle variable for later use. It them proceeds to create a new instance of the XMLHttpRequest object, which is used to make asynchronous requests to server-side resources. In this case, XMLHttpRequest makes a POST request to ProcessingHandler.ashx using the open() method. The load event of the XMLHttpRequest is raised when the request completes.

A load event handler is wired using the jQuery on() method. The load event handler calls the clearTimeout() method to clear the timeout previously set by the code. The handle of the previous setTimeout() method is passed as a parameter to the clearTimeout() method. .

Because the request has been successfully completed, Panel1 is hidden using the hide() method. The Start Processing button is enabled, again by using the prop() method. .This time, the prop() method sets the disabled property to false. The response from the generic handler is displayed to the user in an alert dialog. The request is initiated using the XMLHttpRequest send() method.

■ **Note**   jQuery Ajax techniques use the XMLHttpRequest object internally for their functioning. You will learn about jQuery Ajax techniques in Chapter 8.

The Wait() function is where fading effects are added to the contents of Panel1. This is done using the fadeToggle() method on Panel1. At the end of the toggle operation, Wait() is called recursively using the setTimeout() method. .This way, the Label appears to be flashing in the browser.

Now add a generic handler to the project and name it **ProcessingHandler.ashx**. ProcessingHandler.ashx is supposed to contain some lengthy processing. For the sake of this example, add Thread.Sleep() to substitute the processing time. Listing 7-8 shows the code that goes inside ProcessingHandler.ashx.

Listing 7-8. Code Inside ProcessingHandler.ashx

```
public void ProcessRequest(HttpContext context)
{
  //add your processing here and remove the Sleep() call
  System.Threading.Thread.Sleep(10000);
  context.Response.ContentType = "text/plain";
  context.Response.Write("Processing is over!");
}
```

The ProcessRequest() method of the generic handler calls the Thread.Sleep() method and specifies the sleep duration of 10000 milliseconds, so the execution will halt for 10 seconds. The ProcessRequest() method then simply returns a success message using the Response.Write() method.

Performing Custom Animations

So far, you have used jQuery methods that readily add animation effects such as slide-up, slide-down, fade-in, and fade-out. However, there is more to the story. jQuery also allows you to play custom animations by changing the CSS properties of DOM elements. In situations where other effects prove to be inadequate, you can write your own logic of animating CSS properties. To that end, the animate() method comes to your rescue.

The animate() method allows you to specify one or more CSS properties to animate along with their expected final values. Those CSS properties are then progressively adjusted from their current values to their final values, producing an animation effect. For example, let's say you have a <div> element whose height is 200px. You can call the animate() method in the click event handler of the <div> and specify that its height be changed to 20px. The animate() method will gradually reduce the height of the <div> from 200px to 20px to produce an animation effect. Of course, just like other animation effects learned so far, you can also specify a duration in which the transition should take place.

The animate() method takes four optional parameters: a set of CSS properties to animate, duration, easing, and completion callback. A set of CSS properties is passed as a JavaScript object. For example, to pass height and width CSS properties to the animate() method, you would write:

```
$("#div1").animate({height:"20px",width:"20px"});
```

This line of code adds an animation effect to div1 by gradually changing its height and width to 20px. Because no duration is specified, a default of 400 milliseconds is used. You can specify the duration either as a number or string constants—fast and slow. The following line of code shows how:

```
$("#div1").animate({height:"20px",width:"20px"},"slow");
```

Note that not all properties can be animated; the numeric properties are the primary candidates for adding animation effects. The significance of easing and completion callback parameters is the same as in the case of methods such as slideUp(), slideDown(), and fadeIn().

Now let's put your knowledge about the animate() method to use by developing a Web Form (see Figure 7-4).

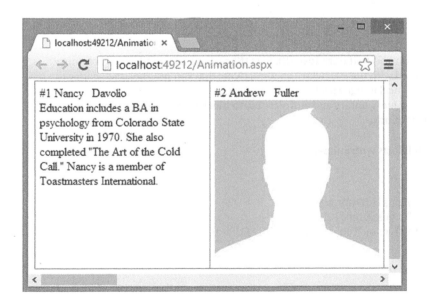

Figure 7-4. *A Web Form using the animate() method*

Figure 7-4 shows a DataList control that displays records from the Employees table. What is special about the display is the employee photo. When the page is loaded in the browser, only EmployeeID, FirstName, and LastName are displayed, along with a photo as indicated by the PhotoPath column. If you move your mouse onto an employee photo, the photo shrinks to the left-bottom corner of that table cell, revealing Notes for that employee. When you move the mouse pointer away from the record, the photo again grows back to its original size and position, thus hiding the note. This shrinking and growing effect is added by using the animate() method. In Figure 7-4, the first record shows how the Note column is revealed after shrinking of the photo; the second record shows the photo covering the Note column.

To begin developing this Web Form, create an empty ASP.NET Web Forms application; then drag and drop a SQL Data Source control and a DataList on the Web Form. Configure the SQL Data Source control to select data from the Employees table and design the ItemTemplate of the DataList control as shown in Listing 7-9.

Listing 7-9. ItemTemplate DataList Control

```
<asp:DataList ID="DataList1" runat="server" CellPadding="6" DataKeyField="EmployeeID"
DataSourceID="SqlDataSource1" GridLines="Both" RepeatDirection="Horizontal">
  <ItemStyle Width="225px" />
  <ItemTemplate>
    <asp:Label ID="lblEmployeeID" runat="server" Text='<%#
    Eval("EmployeeID","#{0}") %>' />
    <asp:Label ID="lblFirstName" runat="server" Text='<%#
    Eval("FirstName") %>' />  
    <asp:Label ID="lblLastName" runat="server"
    Text='<%# Eval("LastName") %>' />
    <br />
    <div class="Notes" style="height:225px;width:225px;overflow:auto">
      <asp:Label ID="lblNotes" runat="server"
      Text='<%# Eval("Notes") %>' />
    </div>
    <asp:Image ID="Image1" runat="server"
    ImageUrl='<%# Eval("PhotoPath")%>' />
  </ItemTemplate>
</asp:DataList>
```

The ItemTemplate binds four Label controls to the EmployeeID, FirstName, LastName, and Notes columns, respectively. Then an Image control is bound with the PhotoPath column. (Note that you may need to change the PhotoPath values from the database to use local image files.)

Then add a <script> reference to the jQuery library and add a <script> block in the head section. Write the code shown in Listing 7-10 in the <script> block.

Listing 7-10. Adding Custom Animation Effects with animate()

```
$(document).ready(function () {
  $("img").each(function () {
    var top = $(this).prev(".Notes").position().top;
    var left = $(this).prev(".Notes").position().left;
    $(this).css("position","absolute").css("top", top).css("left", left);
  });
```

```
$("img").hover(function () {
    var top = $(this).prev(".Notes").position().top;
    $(this).animate({ top: (top + 225) + 'px', height: '0px' }, 500);
}, function () {
    var top = $(this).prev(".Notes").position().top;
    $(this).animate({ top: top + 'px',height:'225px' }, 500);
});
});
```

The ready() handler selects all the <img> elements using the element selector and then iterates through all of them using the each() method. For every <img> element, the top and left coordinates of the <div> showing Notes are determined. A reference to the Notes <div> is obtained using the prev() method and the .Notes CSS selector is supplied to it. The position() method is then used to retrieve the top and left coordinates of the <div> element.

The css() method calls are used to set the position, left, and right CSS properties of the <img> element being iterated. This way, the image covers the employee notes.

The hover() method is used to attach the mouseenter and mouseleave event handlers to the <img> element. The mouseenter handler uses the animate() method to animate the top and height CSS properties of the image. Because the image is to be shrunk to the left-bottom area of the cell, the final top coordinate is set to (top + 225), where 225 is the height of the images, and the height is set to 0 pixels. The duration of the animation is set to 500 milliseconds.

The mouseleave handler is similar to the mouseenter handler, except that the animate() method sets the final top and height to the original values.

■ **Note**   To produce advanced and highly customized animations, jQuery also offers methods such as queue() and dequeue(). Coverage of these advanced techniques is beyond the scope of this book, but you can refer to the official jQuery documentation at http://api.jquery.com for more details about these techniques.

Stopping the Animation

Sometimes you may need to stop currently running animations. jQuery offers two methods that allow you to do this: stop() and finish().

When you call the stop() method on a set of matched elements, the currently running animation, if any, is immediately stopped. If more animation effects are waiting to be applied to the element (suppose that you have called the animate() method multiple times on an element), the next animation begins after stopping the current animation. The following code shows how stop() can be used:

```
$("#div1").stop();
```

This line of code calls the stop() method on div1 to stop any currently running animation and proceed to the next animation in the sequence.

The finish() method is quite similar to stop() in that it stops the animations. The difference between stop() and finish() is that finish() stops current as well as all pending animations. Additionally, the CSS properties of the target element are set to their final values, as indicated by all the animations involved. Thus all the animations are immediately *finished*. The following code shows how finish() can be used.

```
$("#div1").finish();
```

This line of code calls the finish() method on div1 and finishes all the animations being applied on it.

Summary

jQuery allows you to add fancy effects to your web pages using various animation effects. The `slideUp()` and `slideDown()` methods animate elements by gradually changing their height. Similarly, the `fadeIn()` and `fadeOut()` methods animate elements by changing their opacity.

If you need custom animations, you can use the `animate()` method, which animates a set of CSS properties of elements. All the jQuery animation effects can be fine-tuned by specifying an effect duration and a completion callback.

So far in this book you used jQuery to perform client-side operations. However, you can also use jQuery to access server-side resources through Ajax. The next chapter discusses several Ajax techniques and how to use them in ASP.NET Web Forms as well as ASP.NET MVC applications.

CHAPTER 8

■ ■ ■

Ajax Techniques

So far in this book, most of the examples involved only the client browser. The jQuery code you wrote executed inside the browser window and was totally disconnected from the server-side resources such as a SQL server database. Although this behavior works for things such as mouseover effects and animations, it is far from adequate for modern web applications. Modern web applications often need to access some server-side resources from the client script. That's where Asynchronous JavaScript and XML (Ajax) steps in. With Ajax you can communicate between the client browser and the server. To that end, jQuery offers several methods that help you to accomplish this goal. This chapter discusses them in detail.

Specifically, you will learn the following:

- What Ajax is and its benefits

- How jQuery allows you to make Ajax calls

- The role of JSON and Json.NET in Ajax communication

- How to call Web Services, Windows Communication Foundation (WCF) services, controller actions, and the Web API using jQuery Ajax methods

Ajax Overview

Ajax was originally meant to be an acronym for Asynchronous JavaScript and XML. However, over the years, its meaning and use has evolved to a new level. Ajax is not a new invention; it's a way of communication that harnesses the power of existing technologies such as HTML, XML, and JavaScript.

To understand Ajax, you need to understand what an asynchronous communication is. Suppose that you have a data entry page that allows you to enter some data and then submit that data to the server. The server processes the submitted data and sends the result of the processing back to the client. Assuming that this form doesn't use any Ajax techniques, its function can be represented by Figure 8-1.

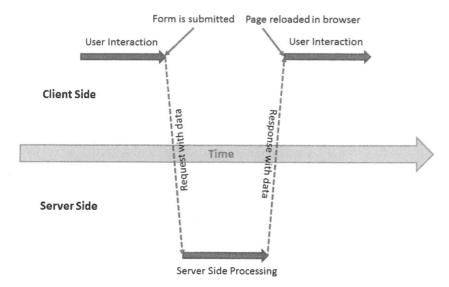

Figure 8-1. *Synchronous processing*

Figure 8-1 shows how a request-response cycle works for a Web Form. When a user initially requests the Web Form, the server serves the form to the user, and it is loaded in the client browser. The user can now interact with the form and fill it up with necessary data. When the form is filled, the user clicks the Submit button to submit the data to the server.

At this point, a POST request is made to the server, and the data entered by the user is also sent along with the request. Once the POST request is made, the user can no longer interact with the form because the browser is waiting for the response to arrive from the server. The server then processes the submitted data and sends the result of the processing back to the browser. When the response is received and the form is reloaded in the browser, the user can interact with the form again. The user interaction is interrupted during the postback, which is a synchronous operation because data entry and processing activities happen serially, one after the other.

Now assume that the same form is built using an asynchronous processing technique. Figure 8-2 shows the new way in which the form is processed.

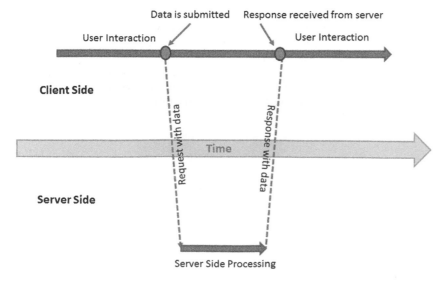

Figure 8-2. *Ansynchronous processing*

As shown in Figure 8-2, when the user initially requests the data entry form, the form is loaded in the browser. The user can now interact with the form and fill it up with necessary data. Once the data is entered, the user can submit the data to the server.

This time, however, the POST request is made in an asynchronous fashion. That means the user can interact with the form even after making the request to the server. Of course, at this point the result of the processing isn't available to the client. The asynchronous request is triggered by some client-side event (such as a button click).

The server processes the data as before and sends the processing result back to the client. Once the response from the server is received by the client browser, it notifies the user that the operation is complete. In asynchronous processing, user interaction remains uninterrupted between request-response cycles because user interaction and server processing occur in parallel.

In Figure 8-1 the data is sent from the client to the server as a part of POST request body. You need not worry about how the browser packs this data and which format is being used while sending it to the server. However, in Figure 8-2 since you are making the request programmatically you need to decide upon the format in which the data is packed and sent to the server.

At the heart of Ajax is the XMLHttpRequest object implemented by all the modern browsers. This object is responsible for establishing communication between the client and the server. It allows you to make Ajax requests to server-side resources such as Web Services, WCF services, controller actions, and the Web API.

Under Ajax, the asynchronous request is made using JavaScript and the XMLHttpRequest object. The format for data transfer can be XML or JSON. An Ajax request can be initiated as a result of user interaction (such as a button click) or some developer-defined process that doesn't depend on user interaction (such as periodically polling a server resource).

Although Ajax originally meant to use XML as the format for data transfer between the client and the server, most of the modern web applications using Ajax rely on JSON as the data format. You will learn more about JSON later in this chapter.

Benefits of Using Ajax

Now that you have a basic understanding of Ajax, let's see some of its core benefits. Although these benefits are interdependent, understanding them individually is essential to understanding how Ajax enriches your web applications.

Performance

When you make a GET or POST request using traditional form submission techniques, all the data from the web page is submitted to the server. And when a response is sent by the server, the entire web page is sent to the client browser.

Consider a case in which a user can open a web site account by filling in a registration page. Let's say that as a step of the validation process, you need to check whether the user ID requested by the user has been taken by somebody else. Under traditional form submission, the entire registration page needs to be submitted to the server, only to return the error of a duplicate user ID. Using Ajax, you can send only the data needed for the server-side processing at a given point in time (user ID, in this case). This process greatly reduces the amount of data transferred between the client and the server. Because fewer bytes of data travel over the wire, the performance of the Ajax–based web pages is better than that of pages using traditional form-submission techniques.

Interactive User Interface

In traditional client-to-server communication techniques, there is often a period for which the user interface is unavailable to the user. When the user clicks the submit button, the page refresh begins in the browser. From this point until the response from the server is reloaded, the user interface is unavailable to the user, which can be annoying, especially on slower Internet connections. Under Ajax, the full page doesn't need any refresh because Ajax requests are being made programmatically, thus enabling the user to keep interacting with the user interface even after submitting the data for processing.

User Experience

Ajax often enhances the end user's experience with your web application. Think of a situation in which a huge table will be displayed on the page. With the traditional approach, the process might take several seconds, and the user can't do anything with your page in the meantime. With Ajax, you can load the data in the background, and the user is free to interact with the page while the data is being populated in the table.

Creative developers have endless opportunities to use Ajax to improve the user experience. If you look at web applications such as Gmail, Twitter, and Facebook, you'll see Ajax being used in variety of ways to provide better user experience.

Understanding the JSON Format

As mentioned in the preceding section, the two commonly used formats for transferring data during Ajax communication are XML and JSON. As an ASP.NET developer, you are already aware of XML because ASP.NET uses XML extensively in the web.config file, and ASP.NET server control markup also closely resembles XML. The JSON format needs special attention because most modern web applications prefer to use JSON over XML.

JSON, which stands for *JavaScript Object Notation*, is a lightweight text-based format for data interchange. By using the JSON format, you can pack the data that needs to be transferred between the client and the server. JSON supports strings, numbers, Booleans, objects, and arrays. (If you want to represent any other data type, you must represent it in a supported format.)

■ **Note**   A frequently used data type that's not supported by JSON is DateTime. You can use a string representation of DateTime during the serialization and deserialization process. Although you can use any date format when dealing with dates in JSON, I recommend that you stick with the ISO date format (*YYYY-MM-DD* for date and *hh:mm:ss* for time).

Although the recommended way to represent dates is the ISO date format, you should be aware of the date format used by older frameworks such as ASP.NET AJAX. It represents a date as \/Date(ticks)\/, where *ticks* is the number of milliseconds since 1 January 1970. The Json.NET component, discussed later, uses the ISO date format.

An object in JSON format typically consists of one or more name-value pairs. The object begins with { and ends with }. The name-value pairs are placed in-between. A property name and its value (if `string` type) are enclosed in double quotes ("..."). A property and its value are separated by a colon (:). Multiple name-value pairs are delimited by commas (,). The following code shows an object represented in JSON format:

```
var employee={
            "EmployeeID":1,
            "FirstName":"Nancy",
            "LastName":"Davolio",
            "IsContract":false;
        };
```

After a JSON object is created, you can use it like a JavaScript object. For example, the following code retrieves the FirstName and LastName properties of the employee object and displays them in an alert dialog:

```
alert(employee.FirstName + employee.LastName);
```

The first line of code displays the FirstName and LastName properties of the employee object, and the alert displays Nancy Davolio. If you want to create an array of employee objects, you can write the following:

```
var employeeArray =[
                    {
                     "EmployeeID":1,
                     "FirstName":"Nancy",
                     "LastName":"Davolio",
                     "IsContract":false;
                    },
                    {
                     "EmployeeID":2,
                     "FirstName":"Andrew",
                     "LastName":"Fuller",
                     "IsContract":true;
                    }
                   ];
```

This code creates an array with two employee objects as its elements. Just like a JavaScript array, a JSON array also begins with [and ends with]. Multiple JSON objects that make the array elements are separated by commas (,).

Using the JSON format, you represent objects. In that respect, JSON objects are quite similar to JavaScript objects. However, it is important to remember that although JavaScript objects and JSON objects look quite similar, the two formats are not exactly the same. For example, JavaScript object properties can be enclosed in single quotes ('...') or double quotes ("..."), or you can omit using quotes altogether. The JSON format, on the other hand, requires you to enclose property names in double quotes.

Sometimes JavaScript objects from your jQuery code need to be transferred to the server during an Ajax communication. Considering the inconsistency between JavaScript object syntax and the JSON format, you should ensure that JavaScript objects are encoded in JSON format before you send them to the server. To accomplish this task, all the modern browsers provide a JSON object, which has two methods: stringify() and parse(). The stringify() method accepts a JavaScript object and returns its JSON representation as a string. The parse() method does exactly the opposite; it accepts a JSON string and parses into a JavaScript object. The following code shows how both of these methods are used:

```
var obj = {Name:'Andrew',Age:45};
var strObj = JSON.stringify(obj);
alert(strObj);
var obj2 = JSON.parse(strObj);
alert(obj2.Name);
```

The first line of code creates a JavaScript object with two properties: Name and Age. Notice that property names are not enclosed at all. Then JSON.stringify() is used to encode obj into its JSON representation. This strObj variable contains '{"Name":"Andrew","Age":45}'. The alert dialog confirms that this is the case. JSON.parse() is used to parse strObj into a JavaScript object. Another alert dialog correctly shows the value of the Name property as Andrew.

■ **Note** Keep in mind that when I use the phrase "JSON object" in the context of the stringify() and parse() methods, I am reffering to the JSON object provided by the browser. At other times "JSON object" means an object represented in JSON format.

Understanding Json.NET

Although the JSON.stringify() and JSON.parse() methods come in handy inside your client-side script, you might also have to deal with JSON format inside your server-side code. For example, you might be receiving data from some service in JSON format and want to process that JSON data in your server-side code. Or you might want to send data in JSON format to the client browser so that it can be processed in the client script. Luckily, there is a popular library—Json.NET—that comes to your rescue. Using Json.NET, you can easily serialize and deserialize JSON data from .NET applications. Json.NET is also used in the latest versions of ASP.NET MVC and the Web API, which underline its popularity.

To use Json.NET, you need to install it in your project. Json.NET is available as a NuGet package and can be installed using the Manage NuGet Packages menu option from the PROJECT menu. Figure 8-3 shows Json.NET listed in the NuGet Package Manager dialog.

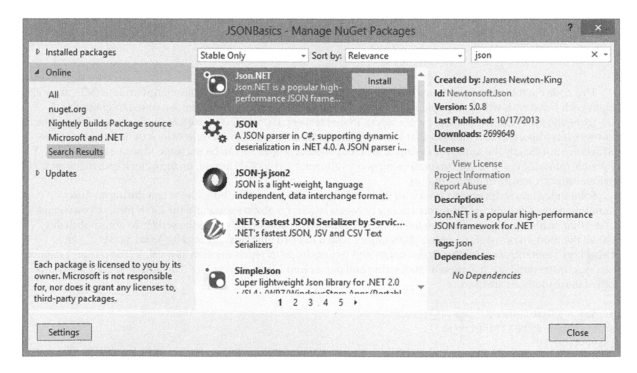

Figure 8-3. *Json.NET listed in the NuGet Package Manager*

Once Json.NET is installed, you can use its classes to serialize and deserialize JSON data. The following code shows how JSON data can be deserialized into a .NET object:

```
string strJson = "{\"Name\":\"Andrew\",\"Age\":45}";
Employee emp= JsonConvert.DeserializeObject<Employee>(strJson);
```

This code stores a JSON object with two properties—Name and Age—in a string variable. The DeserializeObject() method of the JsonConvert class accepts a JSON string and parses it into a .NET object of generic type argument (Employee in this case). The JsonConvert class is provided by the Json.NET framework and resides in the Newtonsoft.Json namespace. The preceding example assumes that the Employee class is already defined in your server-side code and has two public properties: Name and Age.

The preceding example deserializes a JSON string into a .NET object. The reverse can also be done by using the SerializeObject() method of JsonConvert. The following code shows how:

```
Employee emp = new Employee();
emp.Name = "Nancy";
emp.Age = 35;
string strJson = JsonConvert.SerializeObject(emp);
```

This code creates an Employee object and assigns its Name and Age properties. It then calls the SerializeObject() method of JsonConvert to convert the .NET object emp to its equivalent JSON representation.

jQuery Ajax Methods

At the heart of Ajax communication is the XMLHttpRequest object, which enables you to programmatically make HTTP requests—such as GET, POST, PUT, and DELETE—to the web server. The XMLHttpRequest object was first introduced by Internet Explorer, but it was soon absorbed in all the other browsers. Today, XMLHttpRequest is supported by all the leading browsers. Although XMLHttpRequest can be used in synchronous as well as asynchronous mode, asynchronous mode is more commonly used.

jQuery wraps the XMLHttpRequest object into a set of easy-to-use methods. These methods are intended to serve different purposes, although they all use Ajax. These methods are listed in Table 8-1.

***Table 8-1.** jQuery Ajax Methods*

Technique	Request Method	Description
$.ajax()	GET/POST/other HTTP verbs also supported	Generic function that can be used to make AJAX calls to the server. All the other techniques listed here internally use $.ajax() to perform their operations.
$("...").load()	GET / POST	Fetches HTML markup or text from the server dynamically and then sets it to the contents of a selected DOM element.
$.get()	GET	Makes generic GET requests to the server. For example, by using the $.get() method, you can make a request to an MVC action method and fetch data from the database.
$.post()	POST	Makes generic POST requests to the server. For example, by using the $.post() method, you can submit a form to an action method for further processing.
$.getJSON()	GET	Makes GET requests to the server and fetches data in JSON format.
$.getScript()	GET	Loads remote scripts dynamically so you can execute them further in the code.

Notice that all methods in the table except load() use $. before the method name. This means that such methods are called on the jQuery object rather than on the matched elements. Thus, $.ajax() is the same as jQuery.ajax(). The load() method, however, is called on a matched set of DOM elements.

Your method selection for the purpose of making an Ajax request generally depends on the type of request (GET, POST, and so on) you want to make and how much control you need of the overall Ajax operation. For example, if you want to make an Ajax request to a web page that returns JSON data, $.getJSON() might do the job. However, if you want to make DELETE or PUT requests to a Web API and need to fine-tune the overall Ajax operation, $.ajax() would be more suitable. Note that $.ajax() is the mother of all the other Ajax methods; the rest of the methods internally use $.ajax() to get their job done.

At a minimum, all the jQuery Ajax methods expect a URL to the server-side resource that needs to be accessed. As far as ASP.NET applications are concerned, the most commonly used resources are these:

- A Web Form (.aspx)

- A web service (ASMX)

- A web method residing inside a Web Form (often called a page method)

- A Windows Communication Foundation (WCF) service

- A controller action in MVC applications

- A Web API

- A generic handler (.ashx)

Of course, these methods can also request plain HTML pages, XML files, and script files whenever needed.

All the Ajax methods except $.getScript() can send data along with the request. The data can be sent as a JavaScript object or a string. The data type of the response can also be specified; the possible formats are XML, JSON, HTML, or script. You can wire a success handler with all the Ajax methods that get executed when the request completes successfully.

Now that you know the basics of Ajax and jQuery support for Ajax, let's see all the methods listed in Table 8-1 in action by developing a few sample applications.

■ **Note**　A browser enforces the same origin policy on Ajax calls made by a web page. This is done for security reasons and ensures that an Ajax call is made only to resources belonging to the same origin as that of the page initiating the Ajax request. An origin consists of the combination of scheme, host, and port. Thus http://www.website1.com/page1.aspx and http://www.website2.com/page2.aspx belong to different origins.

Loading HTML Markup Using load()

In this section, you use the load() method to load HTML markup dynamically through a client-side script. The Web Form that loads the HTML markup is shown in Figure 8-4.

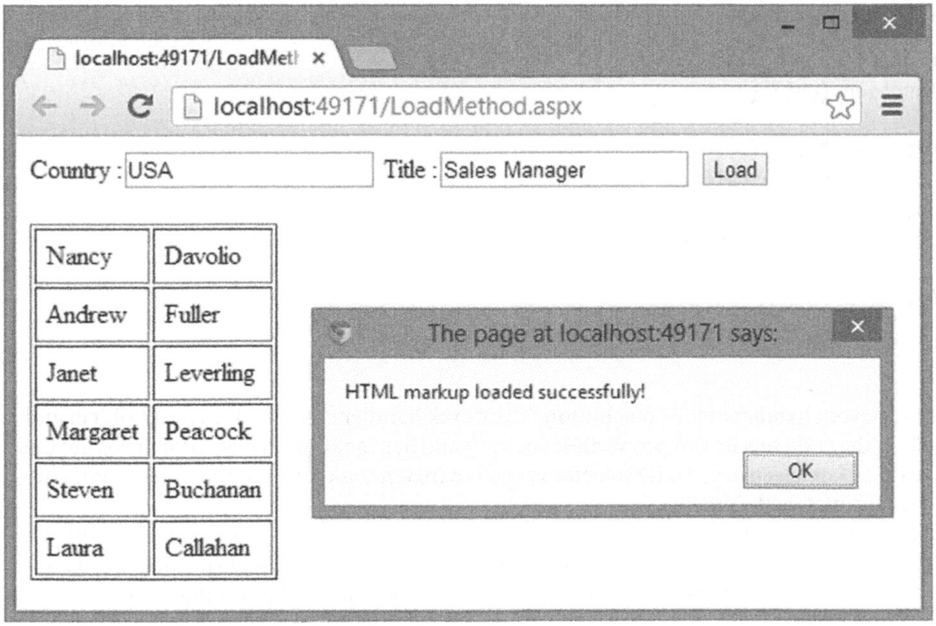

Figure 8-4. *Application using the load() method*

The Web Form consists of two text boxes that accept values for employee country, and title, respectively. Clicking the Load button makes an Ajax request to another Web Form and passes the country and title entered by the user as request data. The other Web Form retrieves the employees residing in the specified country or having the specified title. The HTML table is then generated dynamically based on these results. The HTML markup thus generated is then loaded inside a <div> element, and an alert notification is also displayed to the user.

To begin developing this application, create an empty ASP.NET Web Forms application and add a Web Form to it. Design the Web Form as shown in Figure 8-4. Listing 8-1 shows the markup of this Web Form.

Listing 8-1. LoadMethod.aspx Markup

```
<form id="form1" runat="server">
  <asp:Label ID="Label1" runat="server" Text="Country :"></asp:Label>
  <asp:TextBox ID="TextBox1" runat="server"></asp:TextBox>
  <asp:Label ID="Label2" runat="server" Text="Title :"></asp:Label>
  <asp:TextBox ID="TextBox2" runat="server"></asp:TextBox>
  <asp:Button ID="Button1" runat="server" Text="Load" />
  ...
  <div id="container"></div>
</form>
```

The markup consists of two Label controls, two TextBox controls, a Button control, and a <div> element. The HTML table containing the employee details will be rendered in the <div> container.

Now add a script reference to the jQuery library and add a script block. Then write the code shown in Listing 8-2 inside the script block.

Listing 8-2. Using load() to Load HTML Markup

```
$(document).ready(function () {
  $("#Button1").click(function (evt) {
    var data = {};
    data.Country = $("#TextBox1").val();
    data.Designation = $("#TextBox2").val();
    $("#container").load("LoadTarget.aspx", data, function () {
      alert("HTML markup loaded successfully!");
    });
    evt.preventDefault();
  });
});
```

Listing 8-2 shows the click event handler of the Load button. The click handler creates a JavaScript object and stores it in a data variable. Then the code sets its two properties: Country and Designation. These properties get their values from TextBox1 and TextBox2, respectively. An ID selector is used to match the <div> container element, and the load() method is called on the matched element.

The load() method takes three parameters. The first parameter is a URL to the remote resource that is to be accessed. In this example, LoadTarget.aspx is requested. The second parameter is optional and specifies the data accompanying the request. If the data parameter is an object, the load() method makes a POST request to the remote resource; otherwise, a GET request is made.

In this example, the data JavaScript object is passed in the second parameter. The third parameter is also optional and indicates a callback function that is invoked when the loading operation is complete. In this example, an alert dialog with a notification message is displayed by the completion function. The content of the container element is set to the HTML markup returned by LoadTarget.aspx.

Next, add an entity framework data model for the Employees table. Also, add another Web Form to the project and name it **LoadTarget.aspx**. The LoadTarget.aspx filters Employee objects that have Country or Title that matches the user-supplied values. The code that does this filtering goes in the Page_Load of the Web Form and is shown in Listing 8-3.

Listing 8-3. Generating HTML Markup Dynamically

```
protected void Page_Load(object sender, EventArgs e)
{
  string country=Request.Form["Country"];
  string title = Request.Form["Designation"];
  NorthwindEntities db = new NorthwindEntities();
  var data = from emp in db.Employees
             where emp.Country == country || emp.Title == title
             select emp;
  Response.Clear();
  Response.Write("<table border='1' cellpadding='6'>");
  foreach (var obj in data)
  {
    Response.Write("<tr><td>" + obj.FirstName +
                   "</td><td>" +    obj.LastName +
                   "</td></tr>");
  }
  Response.Write("</table>");
  Response.Flush();
  Response.End();
}
```

This code retrieves the Country and Designation values entered in the text boxes using the Request.Form collection. It then proceeds to select Employee records in which either Country is equal to the supplied country value or Title is equal to the supplied designation value. The response buffer is then cleared by using the Clear() method of the Response object.

An HTML table is written on the response stream by using the Response.Write() method. A foreach loop iterates through all the filtered records and emits the FirstName and LastName values of the Employee objects. Finally, the Flush() method flushes the response buffer to ensure that all markup is pushed to the client, and the End() method is called to flag the end of the response.

Loading and Executing a Script Using $.getScript()

While the load() method loads the HTML markup or text data from the server, the $.getScript() method loads and executes script files. You can use $.getScript() to dynamically load and execute scripts based on some logic. The $.getScript() method takes two parameters: a URL to a remote resource and a success callback function. Once the script returned by the URL is loaded, it is executed just like any other script. If the request succeeds, the callback function indicated by the second parameter is invoked. Specifying a callback function is optional.

To understand how $.getScript() can be used, let's develop a simple Web Form as shown in Figure 8-5.

Figure 8-5. *Web Form displaying an advertisement using getScript()*

The Web Form shown in Figure 8-5 displays an advertisement in all the elements that have the CSS adspace class attached to them. As soon as the page is loaded, a script file is requested using the $.getScript() method. The script included in the script file renders the advertisement. A callback function simply displays a notification to the user in an alert dialog.

To develop the Web Form, create an empty ASP.NET Web Form application. Add a Web Form to the project and add the following code in a `<script>` block:

```
$(document).ready(function () {
  $.getScript("Scripts/AdScript.js", function () {
    alert("Ad script executed successfully!");
  });
});
```

This code uses the `$.getScript()` method inside the ready() handler and requests the AdScript.js file. The callback function simply displays an alert dialog to the user. The AdScript.js file contains jQuery code, as shown here:

```
$(".adspace").html("<h1>Buy ONE get one FREE!!!</h1>")
           .css("background-color", "yellow")
           .css("border", "2px solid orange")
           .css("text-align", "center")
           .css("padding", "10px");
```

As you can see, the code selects all the elements that have the CSS adspace class attached to them. A typical candidate for displaying an advertisement can be a `<div>` or a `<span>`. It then sets the HTML content of the elements to some advertisement text (Buy ONE get one FREE!!!, in this case) by using the html() method. It also sets a few CSS styles (such as background-color, border, text-align, and padding to control the overall look and feel of the advertisement.

Before you run the Web Form, add one or two `<div>` elements in the Web Form and set their class attribute to adspace. When the Web Form is loaded, the AdScript.js file is loaded and also executed. As a result, all the `<div>` elements display the advertisement as expected.

Making GET Requests Using $.get()

In the preceding sections, you used load() and $.getScript() to request HTML markup and scripts, respectively. But sometimes you may want to make a generic GET request to a server-side resource. Suppose, for example, that you want to retrieve the latest news items from the server in HTML, XML, or JSON format. In this case, load() isn't be useful because you want the raw data of news items; you might not want to directly load it in a DOM element. Also, $.getScript() isn't useful because you aren't requesting a script file. In such cases, you can use the $.get() method.

The $.get() method takes four parameters and its general signature is shown here:

```
$.get(url, data, success_callback, data_type);
```

Except for url, all the parameters are optional. The significance of each of the parameters is outlined here:

- The first parameter is the URL of the resource you want to access using a GET request.

- The second (optional) parameter is data that needs to accompany the request. Because a GET request is being made, this data is passed in the query string.

- The third (optional) parameter is a success callback function that gets invoked upon successful completion of the request. The callback function receives the data returned from the server as its parameter.

- The fourth (optional) parameter is the type of data expected from the server. Possible values for this parameter are html, xml, json, and script. If no data type is specified, jQuery attempts to identify it through intelligent guessing.

Now, let's build a Web Form that illustrates the use of the $.get() method. Figure 8-6 shows the Web Form you'll develop in this example.

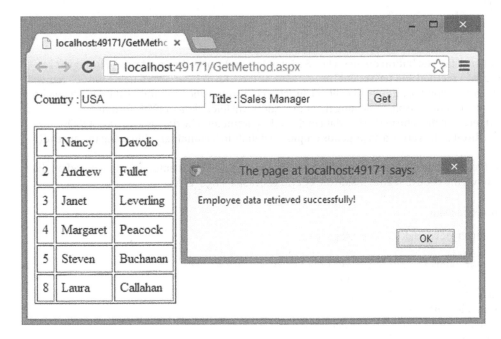

Figure 8-6. *Searching employees by using $.get()*

The Web Form shown in Figure 8-6 may seem similar to the one developed while illustrating the load() method. It performs the same task of searching the employees based on Country and Title values, but there are a few significant differences in the way it works. First, clicking the Get button causes a GET request to be sent to the server using the $.get() method. Second, the search results are not directly loaded in any element; they are received by a callback function. The callback function then iterates through them and adds them into a table. The search results are retrieved as JSON objects, not as HTML markup.

To begin developing this Web Form, create an empty ASP.NET Web Forms application and add a Web Form to it. Design the Web Form as shown in Figure 8-6. Then add a script reference to the jQuery library and a script block. Then add the code shown in Listing 8-4 to the script block.

Listing 8-4. Using $.get() to Make a GET Request

```
$(document).ready(function () {
  $("#Button1").click(function (evt) {
    var data = {};
    data.Country = $("#TextBox1").val();
    data.Designation = $("#TextBox2").val();
    $.get("GetTarget.aspx", data, function (data) {
      $("#container").empty();
      for (var i = 0; i < data.length; i++) {
        $("#container").append("<tr><td>" +
        data[i].EmployeeID + "</td><td>" +
        data[i].FirstName + "</td><td>" +
        data[i].LastName + "</td></tr>");
      }
```

```
      alert("Employee data retrieved successfully!");
    },"json");
    evt.preventDefault();
    });
});
```

The click event handler of the Get button creates a JavaScript object and stores the Country and Designation values. It then calls the $.get() method and passes GetTarget.aspx as the URL to be accessed using the GET request. The data object is passed as the second parameter. A callback function is also specified to process the search results. The fourth parameter is set to a value of json, indicating that the request will fetch data in JSON format.

The callback function receives the returned JSON data in the data parameter. The data is an array of JSON objects. A for loop iterates through this array and appends employee details to a container table using the append() method.

The GetTarget.aspx file reads the data accompanying the GET request and fetches employee data based on the filter criteria. Listing 8-5 shows the code that goes inside the GetTarget.aspx Page_Load.

Listing 8-5. Fetching Employee Data

```
protected void Page_Load(object sender, EventArgs e)
{
  string country = Request.QueryString["Country"];
  string title = Request.QueryString["Designation"];
  NorthwindEntities db = new NorthwindEntities();
  var data = from emp in db.Employees
             where emp.Country == country || emp.Title == title
             select new EmployeeSearchResult{
                EmployeeID=emp.EmployeeID,
                FirstName=emp.FirstName,
                LastName=emp.LastName};
  List<EmployeeSearchResult> list = data.ToList();
  Response.Clear();
  Response.Write(JsonConvert.SerializeObject(list));
  Response.Flush();
  Response.End();
}
```

This code is similar to the one you wrote in the example illustrating the load() method. In this case, the Country and Designation values are retrieved by using the Request.QueryString collection because the $.get() method makes a GET request to the server-side resource. Note that not all the properties of Employee are selected; only EmployeeID, FirstName, and LastName are selected as the EmployeeSearchResult object. The EmployeeSearchResult class looks like this:

```
public class EmployeeSearchResult
{
  public int EmployeeID { get; set; }
  public string FirstName { get; set; }
  public string LastName { get; set; }
}
```

The query results are converted into a generic list of EmployeeSearchResult objects. What's more interesting is that this time the data is sent to the client in JSON format. This is done using the SerializeObject() method of the JsonConvert class and passing the generic list as its parameter. This way, the generic list is serialized as a JSON array.

> ■ **Note** This example makes an Ajax request to a Web Form. Although you can make an Ajax request to any ASP.NET resource, it is recommended that you place your processing logic inside a service (ASMX/WCF/Web API) and then call that service from Ajax. The latter sections of this chapter discuss how services can be consumed using Ajax.

Making GET Requests Using $.getJSON()

When you use the $.get() method, you can retrieve data as html, xml, json, or script. When you want to retrieve data only in JSON format, the $.getJSON() method comes in handy. The $.getJSON() method is similar to $.get() in that it issues a GET request to a server-side resource. However, it expects that the response will be in JSON format only. The $.getJSON() method accepts the first three parameters that the $.get() method accepts. Because $.getJSON() exclusively uses JSON format, the fourth parameter (data type) doesn't apply.

In the preceding example employee data was returned in JSON format. You can rewrite the same jQuery code using $.getJSON(), as shown in Listing 8-6.

Listing 8-6. Using the getJSON() method

```
$(document).ready(function () {
  $("#Button1").click(function (evt) {
    var data = {};
    data.Country = $("#TextBox1").val();
    data.Designation = $("#TextBox2").val();
  $.getJSON("GetTarget.aspx", data, function (data) {
      $("#container").empty();
      for (var i = 0; i < data.length; i++) {
        $("#container").append("<tr><td>" +
          data[i].EmployeeID + "</td><td>" +
          data[i].FirstName + "</td><td>" +
          data[i].LastName + "</td></tr>");
      }
      alert("Employee data retrieved successfully!");
    });
    evt.preventDefault();
  });
});
```

Notice the line of code highlighted in bold. It uses the $.getJSON() method to call GetTarget.aspx. The rest of the code is the same as in the preceding example.

Making POST Requests Using $.post()

To make GET requests, you can use the $.get() method; to make POST requests, you can use the $.post() method. Apart from the difference in the method of making a request, $.post() is quite similar to $.get() in terms of parameters. It takes the same four parameters that the $.get() takes: URL, data, success callback, and data type. Normally, post() is preferred over $.get() when the amount of data to be sent along with the request is large.

Let's modify the preceding example to use the $.post() method. Listing 8-7 shows the modified code of the click handler.

Listing 8-7. Using the post() Method

```
$(document).ready(function () {
  $("#Button1").click(function (evt) {
    var data = {};
    data.Country = $("#TextBox1").val();
    data.Designation = $("#TextBox2").val();
    $.post("PostTarget.aspx", data, function (data) {
      $("#container").empty();
      for (var i = 0; i < data.length; i++) {
        $("#container").append("<tr><td>" +
          data[i].EmployeeID + "</td><td>" +
          data[i].FirstName + "</td><td>" +
          data[i].LastName + "</td></tr>");
      }
      alert("Employee data retrieved successfully!");
    });
    evt.preventDefault();
  });
});
```

The code uses the $.post() method to post some data to PostTarget.aspx. The PostTarget.aspx Web Form is quite similar to GetTarget.aspx, developed earlier. The only difference is that it uses Request.Form collection to retrieve Country and Designation values, as shown here:

```
protected void Page_Load(object sender, EventArgs e)
{
  string country = Request.Form["Country"];
  string title = Request.Form["Designation"];
  ...
  ...
}
```

PostTarget.aspx uses the Request.Form collection because $.post() issues a POST request. It then forms a generic list of EmployeeSearchResult objects and returns it after converting it into a JSON array.

Using the $.ajax() Method

As mentioned earlier, $.ajax() is the mother of all Ajax methods. Methods such as $.get() and $.post() internally use $.ajax() to get their job done. Although the $.get(), $.post(), $.getJSON(), and $.getScript() methods provide an easy way to make Ajax requests, they lack some advanced features. For example, none of these methods allows you to take action when a request fails for some reason. This configuration option and many others are available when you use the $.ajax() method. In its most common form, $.ajax() looks like the following:

```
$.ajax({property1:value,property2:value})
```

As shown in the preceding syntax, the $.ajax() method accepts a JavaScript object as its parameter. The JavaScript object contains various configuration settings (the names property1 and property2 are merely used for the sake of showing the syntax) to be used while making an Ajax request.

Table 8-2 lists some of the frequently used $.ajax() configuration settings.

Table 8-2. *ajax() Configuration Settings*

Setting	Description
async	Governs whether Ajax requests are made asynchronously or synchronously. By default, ajax() requests are asynchronous, and async is true. If you set it to false, a request is made in a synchronous fashion.
contentType	Sets the MIME content type of the data that accompanies a request.
data	Holds the data accompanying a request. If a GET request is being made, the data is sent as a query string; otherwise, data is sent as a part of the request body.
dataType	Allows you to specify the type of data expected from the server as a response. Possible values are html, xml, json, or script. If you don't specify this parameter, jQuery attempts to detect the data type using intelligent guessing.
error	Allows you to wire a function that gets called if a request fails. Error details are passed as the parameters of the function.
username	Allows you to specify a username in case the request needs authentication.
password	Allows you to specify a password in case a request needs authentication.
success	Allows you to wire a function that gets called when a request is successful. It receives the data returned from the server as its parameter.
timeout	Specifies the timeout duration in milliseconds. If a request takes more time than this value, it is cancelled.
type	Allows you to specify the type of request: GET, POST, PUT, or DELETE. If you don't specify this option, GET is assumed.
url	Points to a resource on the server to which the request is to be made. Typically this is a Web Form, controller action, service, or generic handler.

In the preceding section, you issued a POST request to PostTarget.aspx. The same task can be accomplished using $.ajax(), as shown here:

```
$.ajax({
  url: "PostTarget.aspx",
  type: "POST",
  data: data,
  contentType:"application/x-www-form-urlencoded;charset=UTF-8",
  dataType: "json",
  success: function (result,status,jqXHR) {
    $("#container").empty();
    for (var i = 0; i < result.length; i++) {
      $("#container").append("<tr><td>" +
      result[i].EmployeeID + "</td><td>" +
      result[i].FirstName + "</td><td>" +
      result[i].LastName + "</td></tr>");
    }
    alert("Employee data retrieved successfully!");
  },
  error: function (jqXHR,status,err) {
    alert("ERROR : " + status);
  }
});
```

Notice that various configuration options are specified as a JavaScript object and that contentType is specified as application/x-www-form-urlencoded for the data object being sent. Also observe the success and error functions; they both receive the jQuery XMLHttpRequest (jqXHR) object, along with other parameters. The jqXHR object is a wrapper over the underlying XMLHttpRequest object and provides access to its features if needed.

The jqXHR Object

Before you move on to using $.ajax() to develop more complete examples, I'll quickly discuss an object that was silently working behind the scenes for all the Ajax methods: the jQuery XMLHttpRequest or jqXHR object. As mentioned earlier, jqXHR is a wrapper over the browser's XMLHttpRequest object. Additionally it implements the Promise interface. JavaScript promises are objects that represent a pending result of an Ajax operation. You can use Promises to wire callback functions when the Ajax call completes. Most of the methods discussed in this chapter—$.get(), $.getJSON(), $.getScript(), $.post(), and $.ajax()–return a jqXHR object that can be used to wire success, error, and completion callbacks.

Consider the following code:

```
var jqXHR = $.ajax({...})
.done(function() {...})
.fail(function() {...})
.always(function() {...});
```

This code shows the $.ajax() method being used. The return value of $.ajax() is a jqXHR object and is stored in a variable. Three callback functions are wired to the jqXHR object using done(), fail(), and always(). The done() function is invoked when an Ajax request completes successfully; the fail() function is invoked when an Ajax request fails; and the always() function is invoked after completion of an Ajax request, whether it succeeded or not.

Although you can usually live without using the jqXHR object because the methods allow you to wire these functions as a part of their signature, you can use it if you need to. In some of the examples discussed later, you will use jqXHR to wire success, failure, and completion callbacks.

Making Ajax Call to an ASMX Web Service

In this section, you create an ASMX web service and call it by using $.ajax(). The web service does a simple job of converting temperature values from Celsius to Fahrenheit and vice versa. Figure 8-7 shows the Web Form that calls the web service.

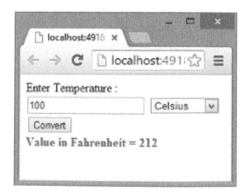

Figure 8-7. *Web Form calling a temperature conversion web service*

The Web Form consists of a `TextBox` to enter temperature value to convert and a `DropDownList` to select the scale of the temperature value. Clicking Convert button converts the value into the other scale. The result of the conversion is displayed below the Convert button.

To begin developing this application, create an empty ASP.NET Web Forms project and add a new ASMX web service using the Add New Item dialog (see Figure 8-8).

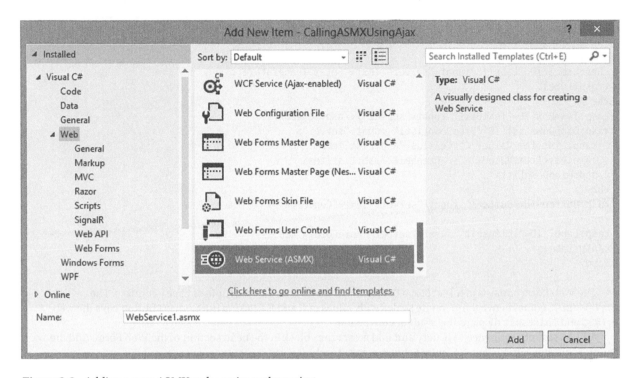

Figure 8-8. *Adding a new ASMX web service to the project*

Give the web service the name of **TemperatureService.asmx** and add a web method to the web service named `Convert`. The `Convert()` web method is shown in Listing 8-8.

Listing 8-8. Convert() Web Method

```
[WebMethod]
public decimal Convert(decimal t, char scale)
{
  switch (scale)
  {
    case 'C':
      t = (t * 1.8m) + 32;
      break;
    case 'F':
      t = (t - 32) / 1.8m;
      break;
  }
  return t;
}
```

211

Notice that the Convert() method is decorated with the [WebMethod] attribute and accepts two parameters: the first parameter represents a temperature value, and the second parameter indicates its scale (C for Celsius and F for Fahrenheit). Inside, it checks the scale of the temperature and accordingly calculates its value in the other scale. The converted value is returned to the caller.

Add a Web Form in the project and design it as shown in Figure 8-7. Listing 8-9 shows the essential markup from the Web Form.

Listing 8-9. Temperature Conversion Web Form Markup

```
<form id="form1" runat="server">
  <asp:Label ID="Label1" runat="server" Text="Enter Temperature :">
  </asp:Label>
  <br />
  <asp:TextBox ID="TextBox1" runat="server"></asp:TextBox>
  <asp:DropDownList ID="DropDownList1" runat="server">
    <asp:ListItem Value="C">Celsius</asp:ListItem>
    <asp:ListItem Value="F">Fehrenheit</asp:ListItem>
  </asp:DropDownList>
  <br />
  <asp:Button ID="Button1" runat="server" Text="Convert" />
  <br />
  <asp:Label ID="lblResult" runat="server" ForeColor="Red">
  </asp:Label>
</form>
```

The Web Form consists of a TextBox, a DropDownList, a Button, and a couple of Label controls. The DropDownList contains two temperature scales with values of C and F. Clicking the Convert button calls the web service, and lblResult displays the result of conversion.

Add a <script> reference to jQuery and add a <script> block in the head section of the Web Form. Add the jQuery code shown in Listing 8-10 inside the <script> block.

Listing 8-10. Calling TemperatureService.asmx Using $.ajax()

```
$(document).ready(function () {
  $("#Button1").click(function (evt) {
    var options = {};
    options.url = "TemperatureService.asmx/ConvertSimpleType";
    options.type = "POST";
    options.data = JSON.stringify(
    { t: $("#TextBox1").val(),
      scale: $("#DropDownList1").val() });
    options.contentType = "application/json";
    options.dataType = "json";
    options.success = function (data) {
    if ($("#DropDownList1").val() == "C") {
      $("#lblResult").html("Value in Fahrenheit = " + data.d);
    }
    else {
      $("#lblResult").html("Value in Celsius = " + data.d);
    }
  };
```

```
  options.error = function (jqXHR, status, err) { alert(status); };
  $.ajax(options);
  evt.preventDefault();
 });
});
```

The code in Listing 8-10 shows the click event handler of Button1. The code creates an options JavaScript object and assigns its various properties. The url property points to TemperatureService.asmx/Convert. This way, an Ajax call is made to the Convert() web method from TemperatureService.asmx. The type property indicates that a POST request is being made. The Convert() web method accepts two parameters, t and scale, which are passed as a JSON object through the data property.

Notice the use of JSON.stringify() to convert a JavaScript object into a JSON string. Also notice that the code uses the same parameter names (t and scale) as those of the web method while constructing the JSON object. This is necessary for proper mapping of parameter values while invoking the web method. The values of t and scale are obtained from TextBox1 and DropDownList1, respectively. Because the data property holds data in JSON format, the contentType property is set to application/json. The web method returns its value in JSON format, so dataType property is set to json.

The success function receives the return value of the web method. Inside the function a message is formed based on the scale selected in the DropDownList. Notice how the actual return value is accessed: data.d. The actual return value is wrapped in a data object and can be accessed using its d property. The result is then displayed in lblResult. The error function is called if an error occurs while calling the web service and displays the status returned from the server in an alert dialog.

Once the options object is configured, the $.ajax() method is called, and the options object is passed to it. The postback is prevented by calling preventDefault() on the evt object.

Making an Ajax Call to a Page Method

In the preceding example, you created an ASMX web service that contained the Convert() method. Creating a web service is useful when the service is consumed by many Web Forms. If you want to consume a web method from only a single Web Form, you can create it as a page method rather than an ASMX web service. (A page method is a web method that is housed inside a Web Form.) You can then call this page method using $.ajax(). Consider the code shown in Listing 8-11.

Listing 8-11. Convert( ) Page Method

```
[WebMethod]
public static TemperatureData Convert(TemperatureData data)
{
  TemperatureData resultData = new TemperatureData();
  switch (data.Scale)
  {
    case 'C':
      resultData.Value = (data.Value * 1.8m) + 32;
      resultData.Scale = 'F';
      break;
    case 'F':
      resultData.Value = (data.Value - 32) / 1.8m;
      resultData.Scale = 'C';
      break;
  }
  return resultData;
}
```

213

The Convert() method shown in Listing 8-11 is a static method that is also decorated with the [WebMethod] attribute. This makes it a page method that can be called from jQuery code. This time, the temperature value and its scale is passed as a TemperatureData object rather than a simple type. The Convert() method returns the TemperatureData object with the converted value instead of a decimal value. The TemperatureData class contains only two properties: Value and Scale (see the following code):

```
public class TemperatureData
{
  public decimal Value { get; set; }
  public char Scale { get; set; }
}
```

To call the Convert() method from the Web Form, write the code shown in Listing 8-12.

Listing 8-12. Calling a Page Method Using $.ajax()

```
$("#Button1").click(function (evt) {
  var options = {};
  options.url = "PageMethodClient.aspx/Convert";
  options.type = "POST";
  options.data = JSON.stringify(
 { data: { Value: $("#TextBox1").val(),
 Scale: $("#DropDownList1").val() } });
  options.contentType = "application/json";
  options.dataType = "json";
  options.success = function (data) {
    if ($("#DropDownList1").val() == "C") {
      $("#lblResult").html("Value in Fahrenheit = " + data.d.Value);
    }
    else {
      $("#lblResult").html("Value in Celsius = " + data.d.Value);
    }
  };
  options.error = function (jqXHR, status, err) { alert(status); };
  $.ajax(options);
  evt.preventDefault();
});
```

Most of the code involved in calling the Convert() page method remains the same as in the preceding example. Notice the code marked in bold letters. The url property of the options object is pointing to PageMethodClient.aspx/Convert. This time, you are passing the value for a complex type (TemperatureData) from the client side. This value is encapsulated in a JavaScript object with two properties: Value and Scale. This object is to be passed as a value of the data parameter. Hence, the data object is constructed as shown by the second bold line of code.

The return value of the Convert() page method is the TemperatureData object. This object is sent to the client in JSON format, and its Value and Scale properties can be accessed as data.d.Value and data.d.Scale, respectively.

Making an Ajax Call to a WCF Service

Although calling a WCF service is quite similar to calling an ASMX service, you need to create a WCF service (.svc) and write the Convert() method as an [OperationContract]. To add a new WCF service to your project, you can use the Add New Item dialog and select WCF Service (Ajax-enabled) from the list (see Figure 8-9).

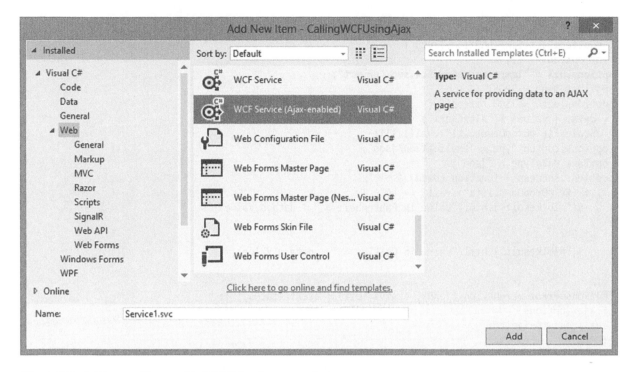

Figure 8-9. *Adding an Ajax-enabled WCF Service to a project*

Name the service **TemperatureService.svc** and add the Convert() method to it, as shown in Listing 8-13.

Listing 8-13. Convert( ) Method of a WCF Service

```
[OperationContract]
public TemperatureData Convert(TemperatureData data)
{
  TemperatureData resultData = new TemperatureData();
  switch (data.Scale)
  {
    case 'C':
      resultData.Value = (data.Value * 1.8m) + 32;
      resultData.Scale = 'F';
      break;
    case 'F':
      resultData.Value = (data.Value - 32) / 1.8m;
      resultData.Scale = 'C';
      break;
    }
  return resultData;
}
```

As you can see, the Convert() method is quite similar to the one you used previously. This time, however, it is decorated with the [OperationContract] attribute. To call the Convert() method from the jQuery code, write the code shown in Listing 8-14.

Listing 8-14. Calling a WCF Service Using $.ajax()

```
$("#Button1").click(function (evt) {
  var options = {};
 options.url = "TemperatureService.svc/Convert";
  options.type = "POST";
  options.data = JSON.stringify(
  { data: { Value: $("#TextBox1").val(),
    Scale: $("#DropDownList1").val() }});
  options.contentType = "application/json";
  options.dataType = "json";
  options.success = function (data) {
    if ($("#DropDownList1").val() == "C") {
      $("#lblResult").html("Value in Fahrenheit = " + data.d.Value);
    }
    else {
      $("#lblResult").html("Value in Celsius = " + data.d.Value);
    }
  };
  options.error = function (jqXHR, status, err) { alert(status); };
  $.ajax(options);
  evt.preventDefault();
});
```

The only change needed this time is in the url property of the options object. As shown by bold highlighting, the url property now points to TemperatureService.svc/Convert.

Making an Ajax Call to a Controller Action

So far, you used $.ajax() to call ASMX and WCF services that were part of a Web Forms project. You can also use jQuery Ajax methods to call ASP.NET MVC action methods. This section discusses how. The overall process of making an Ajax call remains the same, but there are a few differences that you should be aware of.

Begin by creating an empty ASP.NET MVC application. Right-click the Controllers folder and choose the Add ➤ Controller option to add an empty controller (see Figure 8-10).

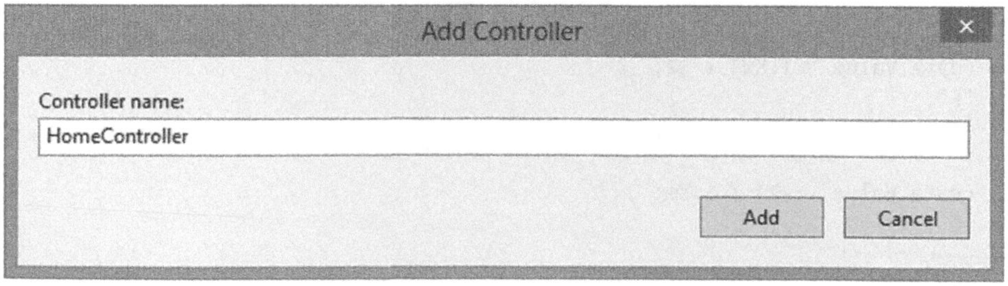

Figure 8-10. *Adding the HomeController*

Name the controller **HomeController** and click the Add button to add it to the project. The HomeController class has the Index() action method by default. Add the Convert() method inside the home controller, as shown in Listing 8-15.

Listing 8-15. Adding Convert() Inside the Home Controller

```
public JsonResult Convert (decimal t, char scale)
{
  switch (scale)
  {
    case 'C':
      t = (t * 1.8m) + 32;
      break;
    case 'F':
      t = (t - 32) / 1.8m;
      break;
    }
  return Json(t);
}
```

The Convert() method shown in Listing 8-15 is quite similar to the one you developed in the ASMX web service example earlier in this chapter. The only difference is that Convert() is an action method. Because you want to pass the result of the temperature conversion in JSON format, the return type of the Convert() method is specified as JsonResult (usually an action method returns ActionResult). The calculation result is t, which is then returned to the caller using the Json() method. The Json() method accepts any .NET object and returns its JSON representation, which is then sent back to the client.

To call the Convert() action method, you need to add the Index view by right-clicking the Index() action method and then choosing the Add View option. In the View name field, add **Index** (see Figure 8-11).

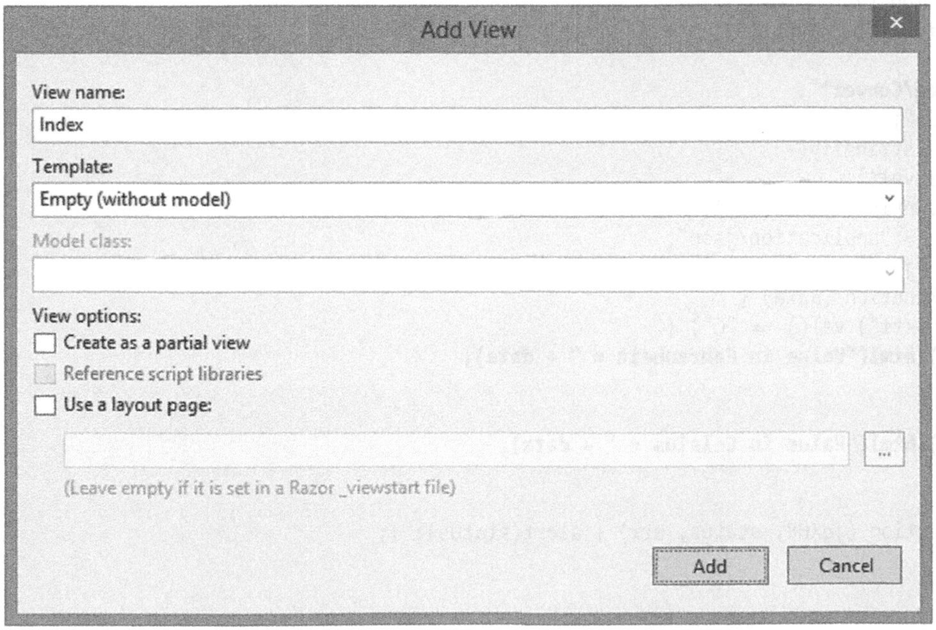

Figure 8-11. Adding the Index view

The Index view contains HTML markup that renders the same user interface as you used earlier. Listing 8-16 shows this markup.

Listing 8-16. Index View Markup

```
<form id="form1">
  <span id="Label1" runat="server">Enter Iemperature : </span>
  <br />
  <input type="text" id="TextBox1" />
  <select id="DropDownList1">
    <option value="C">Celsius</option>
    <option value="F">Fehrenheit</option>
  </select>
  <br />
  <input id="Button1" type="button" value="Convert" />
  <br />
  <span id="lblResult"></span>
</form>
```

The markup is straightforward and consists of a text box, a drop-down list, a button, and a couple of span elements. Now add a jQuery `<script>` reference in the head section of the view. Also add a `<script>` block and key in the code shown in Listing 8-17.

Listing 8-17. Calling an Action Method Using $.ajax()

```
$(document).ready(function () {
  $("#Button1").click(function (evt) {
    var options = {};
    options.url = "/Home/Convert";
    options.type = "POST";
    options.data = JSON.stringify(
    { t: $("#TextBox1").val(),
      scale: $("#DropDownList1").val() });
    options.contentType = "application/json";
    options.dataType = "json";
    options.success = function (data) {
      if ($("#DropDownList1").val() == "C") {
        $("#lblResult").html("Value in Fahrenheit = " + data);
      }
      else {
        $("#lblResult").html("Value in Celsius = " + data);
      }
    };
    options.error = function (jqXHR, status, err) { alert(status); };
    $.ajax(options);
  });
});
```

Most of the code shown in Listing 8-17 should look familiar to you. Notice the code marked in bold highlighting. This time, the url property points to the Convert() action as Home/Convert. The return value of the Convert() method can be directly accessed using the data parameter of the success function.

In the example just discussed, the Convert() method accepts parameters of simple types. You can also pass (and return) object data to the Convert() method as shown in Listing 8-18.

Listing 8-18. Passing Object Data to Convert()

```
public JsonResult Convert(TemperatureData data)
{
  TemperatureData resultData = new TemperatureData();
  switch (data.Scale)
  {
    case 'C':
      resultData.Value = (data.Value * 1.8m) + 32;
      resultData.Scale = 'F';
      break;
    case 'F':
      resultData.Value = (data.Value - 32) / 1.8m;
      resultData.Scale = 'C';
      break;
  }
  return Json(resultData);
}
```

The Convert() action method now accepts the TemperatureData object and returns a TemperatureData object containing the converted value. The Json() method is used as before to convert the resultData object into its JSON form. To call the modified Convert() method from the client script, modify the jQuery code, as shown in Listing 8-19.

Listing 8-19. Calling Convert(), which Returns a TemperatureData Object

```
$("#Button1").click(function (evt) {
  var options = {};
  options.url = "/Home/Convert";
  options.type = "POST";
  options.data = JSON.stringify(
  { Value: $("#TextBox1").val(),
  Scale: $("#DropDownList1").val() });
  options.contentType = "application/json";
  options.dataType = "json";
  options.success = function (data) {
    if ($("#DropDownList1").val() == "C") {
      $("#lblResult").html("Value in Fahrenheit = " + data.Value);
    }
    else {
      $("#lblResult").html("Value in Celsius = " + data.Value);
    }
  };
  options.error = function (jqXHR, status, err) { alert(status); };
  $.ajax(options);
});
```

Notice the code marked in bold highlighting. This time, the data property of the options object is set to a JavaScript object with two properties: Value and Scale. The TemperatureData object is returned in its JSON equivalent form and the resulting object is received as the data parameter of the success function. Then the data.Value and data.Scale properties give the value and scale of the returned object.

Making an Ajax call to a Web API

Modern applications often rely on RESTful services for the purpose of consuming the services exposed by them. Commonly a web application invokes these RESTful services using Ajax. Although this chapter is not about REST, a brief discussion REST is worthwhile.

REST stands for REpresentational State Transfer. REST is not a standard; it's a way of architecting your services. Unlike ASMX web services that use complex mechanisms such as Simple Object Access Protocol (SOAP) and Web Services Description Language (WSDL), RESTful services harness the simplicity and power of HTTP.

Here are some fundamental characteristics of RESTful services:

- REST services use the HTTP protocol.

- REST services make HTTP requests (using meaningful HTTP verbs such as GET, POST, PUT, and DELETE) to fetch and submit data.

- REST services are stateless in nature.

- REST exposes services as resources-accessible and discoverable through URLs.

- REST services typically transfer data in XML or JSON format.

The ASP.NET Web API is a .NET way of developing RESTful services. To invoke a Web API from the client-side script, developers commonly use an Ajax technique such as $.ajax().

■ **Note** The HTTP verbs such as GET, POST, PUT, and DELETE indicate the desired action to be performed on a resource. If a service performs create, read, update, and delete (CRUD) operations on a database, you could use POST to indicate an INSERT operation, GET to indicate a SELECT operation, PUT to indicate an UPDATE operation and DELETE to indicate a DELETE operation. However, merely using a specific verb won't enforce the principle that only a particular type of operation is allowed. It's up to you to implement these verbs in a service depending on application's requirements.

Now let's develop an application that demonstrates how a Web API can be consumed using $.ajax(). Figure 8-12 shows the main view of the application.

Figure 8-12. *Application consuming a Web API*

The view represents a data entry page for the Employees table. At the top is a drop-down list with existing EmployeeID values. After an EmployeeID is selected, its details are displayed in the other text boxes. You can then modify and update the data with the Update button.

To add a new Employee, you need to enter a new EmployeeID in the text box placed beside the drop-down list and fill in the other text boxes. Clicking the Insert button adds that Employee to the database. Selecting an EmployeeID from the drop-down list and clicking the Delete button deletes that Employee. A success or error message is displayed at the bottom of the table, depending on the outcome of the operation. Although the data entry page is rendered by an ASP.NET MVC view, the CRUD operations on the Employees table are performed through a Web API.

To develop this application, begin by creating a new ASP.NET Web Application based on the Web API project template (see Figure 8-13).

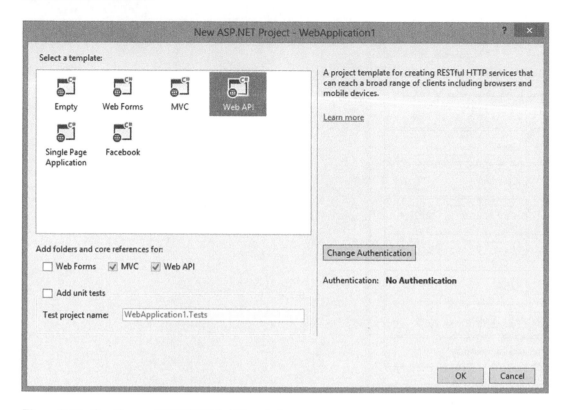

Figure 8-13. *Creating an ASP.NET Web API project*

Once the project is created, right-click the Models folder and add an ADO.NET Entity Data Model to the project. Let the wizard generate a model for the Employees table residing in the Northwind database. Figure 8-14 shows the Employee model class.

Figure 8-14. *Employee model class*

The Employee class has properties representing all the columns from the Employees table. However, for the sake of this example, you need only six of them: EmployeeID, FirstName, LastName, BirthDate, HireDate, and Country. To avoid transferring the data of unused columns, you can create the EmployeeData class that has just six properties. Although the Employee class is used in LINQ to Entities queries, the EmployeeData class is used to transfer the data between the client and the server.

The EmployeeData class is shown here:

```
public class EmployeeData
{
  public int EmployeeID { get; set; }
  public string FirstName { get; set; }
  public string LastName { get; set; }
  public DateTime? BirthDate { get; set; }
  public DateTime? HireDate { get; set; }
  public string Country { get; set; }
}
```

The EmployeeData class has six properties for holding the pieces of information you need as part of a data transfer. By default, a newly created Web API project has two controllers: HomeController and ValuesController. The HomeController is a normal MVC controller, whereas ValuesController is an ApiController and represents the Web API. Rename the ValuesController to **EmployeesController** and add the skeleton code shown in Listing 8-20 to the EmployeesController.

Listing 8-20. Skeleton of EmployeesController

```
public class EmployeesController : ApiController
{
  NorthwindEntities db = new NorthwindEntities();
  public List<EmployeeData> GetEmployees() {}
  public EmployeeData GetEmployeeByID(int id) {}
  public string PostEmployee(EmployeeData empData) {}
  public string PutEmployee(int id, EmployeeData empData) {}
  public string DeleteEmployee(int id) {}
}
```

The Employees Web API consists of five methods: GetEmployees(), GetEmployeeByID(), PostEmployee(), PutEmployee(), and DeleteEmployee().

■ **Note**   If you are not familiar with ASP.NET Web API consider visiting http://www.asp.net/web-api for more details.

Notice the nomenclature of these methods. Each method starts with an HTTP verb: Get, Post, Put, or Delete. The Web API framework automatically maps a request to an appropriate Web API method based on the HTTP verb used in the request. For example, a GET request with no data accompanying it is handled by the GetEmployees() method, and a POST request is handled by PostEmployees() method.

The GetEmployees() method returns a generic List of EmployeeData objects and handles GET requests that do not carry any data with them. The GetEmployeeByID() method accepts id as its parameter and returns an EmployeeData for the specified EmployeeID. GET requests that carry EmployeeID information are handled by the GetEmployeeByID() method.

The PostEmployee() method handles POST requests and is indented to add a new Employee in the database. It accepts the EmployeeData object and returns a string indicating a success message.

The PutEmployee() method handles PUT requests and is intended to update an existing Employee from the database. It accepts id and the EmployeeData object as its parameters and returns a string indicating a success message.

The DeleteEmployee() method handles DELETE requests and is intended to delete an Employee from the database. It accepts id as a parameter and returns a string indicating a success message. The EmployeesController class also declares a database context variable (db) at the top that is used by all the methods to perform their respective operations.

All the EmployeesController methods aren't discussed here for the want of space. It suffices to see and discuss a couple of methods for the sake of better understanding. Listing 8-21 shows the GetEmployees() method.

Listing 8-21. GetEmployees( ) Method

```
public List<EmployeeData> GetEmployees()
{
  var data = from e in db.Employees
             orderby e.EmployeeID
             select new EmployeeData {
             EmployeeID=e.EmployeeID,
             FirstName=e.FirstName,
             LastName=e.LastName,
             BirthDate=e.BirthDate,
```

```
            HireDate=e.HireDate,
            Country=e.Country };
  List<EmployeeData> list = data.ToList();
  return list;
}
```

The GetEmployees() method creates a LINQ to Entities query that fetches all the Employee objects from the Employees DbSet. The query also shapes the results into the EmployeeData object using projection. This way, the query returns a collection of EmployeeData objects. The query results are transformed into a generic List of EmployeeData objects and then returned to the caller.

The PutEmployee() method updates an existing Employee and is shown in Listing 8-22.

Listing 8-22. PutEmployee() Method

```
public string PutEmployee(int id, EmployeeData empData)
{
  Employee emp = db.Employees.Find(id);
  emp.FirstName = empData.FirstName;
  emp.LastName = empData.LastName;
  emp.BirthDate = empData.BirthDate;
  emp.HireDate = empData.HireDate;
  emp.Country = empData.Country;
  db.SaveChanges();
  return "Employee updated successfully!";
}
```

The PutEmployee() method finds an Employee object from the Employees DbSet using the Find() method. The Find() method returns an existing Employee whose EmployeeID is same as id. The code assigns the FirstName, LastName, BirthDate, HireDate and Country properties of the Employee object with the respective properties of the EmployeeData object. The changes are saved to the database by calling the SaveChanges() method of the context. A success message is then returned to the caller.

You can also complete the GetEmployeeByID(), PostEmployee(), and DeleteEmployee() methods. Once the methods are created, open the HomeController class, right-click its Index() action method, and select the Add View menu option to add the Index view to the project. The Index view should resemble Figure 8-12 and can be designed using HTML helpers. Listing 8-23 shows the Index view markup.

Listing 8-23. Index View Markup

```
<form method="post">
  <table border="1" cellpadding="6">
    <tr>
      <td>@Html.Label("EmployeeID","EmployeeID :")</td>
      <td>
        <select id="ddlEmployeeID"></select>
        OR
        @Html.TextBox("EmployeeID","", new { size="5" })
      </td>
    </tr>
    <tr>
      <td>@Html.Label("FirstName","First Name :")</td>
      <td>@Html.TextBox("FirstName")</td>
    </tr>
```

```
    <tr>
      <td>@Html.Label("LastName","Last Name :")</td>
      <td>@Html.TextBox("LastName")</td>
    </tr>
    <tr>
      <td>@Html.Label("BirthDate","Birth Date :")</td>
      <td>@Html.TextBox("BirthDate", "", new { type="date" })</td>
    </tr>
    <tr>
      <td>@Html.Label("HireDate","Hire Date :")</td>
      <td>@Html.TextBox("HireDate", "", new { type="Date" })</td>
    </tr>
    <tr>
      <td>@Html.Label("Country","Country :")</td>
      <td>@Html.TextBox("Country")</td>
    </tr>
    <tr>
      <td colspan="2">
        <input id="btnInsert" type="button" value="Insert" />
        <input id="btnUpdate" type="button" value="Update" />
        <input id="btnDelete" type="button" value="Delete" />
      </td>
    </tr>
    <tr>
      <td colspan="2">
        <span id="lblMessage"></span>
      </td>
    </tr>
  </table>
</form>
```

The markup is quite straightforward and uses the Label() and TextBox() Html helpers to render field labels and text boxes, respectively. Notice that names used as the first parameter of the TextBox() helper are identical to the property names of the EmployeeData class, so MVC can automatically map text box values to the EmployeeData properties.

The BirthDate and HireDate text boxes use the HTML5 Date input type so that a browser capable of displaying a date-picker (Chrome, for example) can display the respective fields as date-pickers. Since the application uses Ajax to insert, update and delete an employee, the type of btnInsert, btnUpdate, and btnDelete is set to button. You will call the Employees Web API through $.ajax().

Once the Index view is designed, add a <script> reference to jQuery library and also add a <script> block in the head section. When the view loads in the browser, you have to fill in the EmployeeIDs in the drop-down list, which is done using the code shown in Listing 8-24.

Listing 8-24. Filling in EmployeeIDs in the Drop-down List

```
$(document).ready(function () {
  var options = {
    url: "/api/Employees",
    type: "GET",
    contentType:"application/json",
    dataType: "json"
  };
```

```
$.ajax(options).done(function (employees) {
  for (var i = 0; i < employees.length; i++) {
    $("#ddlEmployeeID").append("<option>" +
      employees[i].EmployeeID + "</option>");
  }
}).fail(function (jqXHR, status, err) {
  $("#lblMessage").html(err);
});
});
```

This code creates JavaScript options object inside the ready() handler and sets its various properties.

■ **Note** The url property is set to /api/Employees. This is the URL at which the Employees Web API is accessible. Unlike ASMX and WCF service URLs, this URL doesn't include the method names anywhere. This is because the HTTP verb (GET, POST, and so on) decides the method to be called. Because you want to invoke the GetEmployees() method, you set the type to GET. The other event handlers also use the same options object while making Ajax calls.

The options object is passed to the $.ajax() call. This time, the success and error functions are wired to the jqXHR object returned by $.ajax(). Notice that these functions are wired immediately after the $.ajax() call so that they are immediately available to handle the respective conditions.

The function supplied to the done() method receives the EmployeeData objects returned by GetEmployees() as the employees parameter. The employees parameter is a JSON array that holds JSON objects that mimic the original EmployeeData object. Thus, all the properties such as EmployeeID are also available for these employee objects. A for loop iterates through the employees array, and EmployeeID values are added to the drop-down list using the append() method.

The function supplied to the fail() method is called if the Web API call fails and displays an error message in the lblMessage <span> element.

When an EmployeeID is selected in the drop-down list, its details are displayed in the other text boxes by invoking the GetEmployeeByID() Web API method in the change event handler of the drop-down list. The change event handler is shown in Listing 8-25.

Listing 8-25. Calling the GetEmployeeByID() Web API Method

```
$("#ddlEmployeeID").change(function () {
  options.url = "/api/Employees/" + $("#ddlEmployeeID").val();
  options.type = "GET";
  $.ajax(options).done(function (employee) {
    $("#FirstName").val(employee.FirstName);
    $("#LastName").val(employee.LastName);
    $("#BirthDate").val(employee.BirthDate.substring(0, 10));
    $("#HireDate").val(employee.HireDate.substring(0, 10));
    $("#Country").val(employee.Country);
  }).fail(function (jqXHR, status, err) {
    $("#lblMessage").html(err);
  });
});
```

The change event handler function sets the url property to /api/Employees/<emp_id> where emp_id is the EmployeeID selected in the drop-down list. The type of request is still GET, but because of the URL pattern (the GET request accompanying the EmployeeID data), the Web API invokes the GetEmployeeByID() method.

The options object is passed to $.ajax() to invoke the Web API. The done() handler function receives a single employee object mimicking the EmployeeData object. The values of various text boxes are then set to the respective properties of the employee object.

Notice how the values of the BirthDate and HireDate text boxes are being set. The BirthDate and HireDate properties are DateTime properties on the server. When these values are sent to the client, they are converted to ISO date format (*YYYY-MM-DDThh:mm:ss*). The input fields of the date type expect their value in *YYYY-MM-DD* format, so the BirthDate and HireDate values are trimmed up to ten characters from the beginning. The fail() handler simply displays an error message in the lblMessage <span> element.

The click event handlers of btnInsert, btnUpdate, and btnDelete call the Employees Web API after setting the request type to POST, PUT, and DELETE, respectively. (These event handlers are not discussed here for the want of space.) The click event handler for btnUpdate is shown in Listing 8-26.

Listing 8-26. Click Event Handler for btnUpdate

```
$("#btnUpdate").click(function () {
  var employee = {};
  employee.FirstName = $("#FirstName").val();
  employee.LastName = $("#LastName").val();
  employee.BirthDate = $("#BirthDate").val();
  employee.HireDate = $("#HireDate").val();
  employee.Country = $("#Country").val();

  options.url = "/api/Employees/" + $("#ddlEmployeeID").val();
  options.type = "PUT";
  options.data = JSON.stringify(employee);

  $.ajax(options).done(function (result) {
    $("#lblMessage").html(result);
  }).fail(function (jqXHR, status, err) {
    $("#lblMessage").html(err);
  });
});
```

The click event handler of btnUpdate invokes the PutEmployee() method of the Web API. The code creates a JavaScript object to hold the employee data. This object mimics the EmployeeData object on the server. The FirstName, LastName, BirthDate, HireDate, and Country properties of this employee object are set to the values entered in the respective text boxes. The url property of the options object is in the form/api/Employees/<emp_id> where emp_id is the EmployeeID selected in the drop-down list. This time, the type of request is set to PUT.

The employee JavaScript object is converted into its JSON representation using the JSON.stringify() method and then assigned to the data property of the options object. Remember that the PutEmployee() method has two parameters: id and EmployeeData. The id parameter is supplied through the url property of the options object, whereas the EmployeeData parameter is supplied by the data property of the options object.

An Ajax call is then made to the Web API by passing the options object to $.ajax(). The done() handler function receives a success message from the PutEmployee() method, which is then displayed in lblMessage.

You can complete the click event handlers for btnInsert and btnDelete on similar lines. Once they are completed, you can run the application and test whether the CRUD operations are being performed as expected.

Summary

Ajax is increasingly being used in modern web applications. Ajax applications make asynchronous requests to server-side resources and can update parts of a web page without causing a full page postback. This also makes Ajax applications faster compared with the ones using the full page postback model.

jQuery offers many methods to make Ajax requests to server-side resources. These methods include `load()`, `$.get()`, `$.getJSON()`, `$.getScript()`, `$.post()`, and `$.ajax()`.

The `$.ajax()` method is the mother of all Ajax methods because the other methods internally use `$.ajax()` to get their job done. Using jQuery Ajax techniques, you can consume ASMX web services, page methods, WCF services, controller actions, and the Web API.

So far in this book, you have written a lot of jQuery code that used built-in jQuery methods. However, there is more to the story. You can also extend the jQuery functionality by creating your own plugins. Once created, a plugin can be used across multiple pages of an application or across multiple web applications. The next chapter looks into this aspect of jQuery.

CHAPTER 9

■ ■ ■

Creating and Using Plugins

So far in this book, you have learned about features that are integral to the jQuery library. However, the story doesn't end there. jQuery also allows you to extend its core functionality through plugins. A plugin is an extension that adds some custom functionality to jQuery. For example, you may want to add fancy tooltips to a web page or display masked text boxes that accept input in a specific format. This functionality isn't available in the core jQuery library, but you can create a plugin that encapsulates the code required to display such fancy tooltips and then use that plugin on any web page.

This chapter discusses what plugins are and how to create your own plugin. Specifically you learn the following:

- How to use existing plugins

- How to create a plugin

- Guidelines to follow while building plugins

Understanding jQuery Plugins

Simply put, a plugin is an extension to the core jQuery library. Most of the time, a plugin is developed to offer some functionality that's not available as a part of the jQuery library. A plugin can also do the job of enhancing an existing piece of functionality. Suppose, for example, that you want to display a slideshow in your ASP.NET Web Forms or MVC views. The slide images and associated data, such as title and description, are stored in a SQL server database. The slideshow also needs to have configurable settings such as delay between two slides, transition effect, playing slides in loopback mode, and so on.

A straightforward way of developing such a slideshow is to write the necessary code in the web page. This approach, although workable, suffers from drawbacks that the code you write is specific to that web page. If you ever need to use the slideshow on multiple pages of the same application or across different applications, you can't reuse the code easily. You can overcome this problem by placing the code in a separate JavaScript file. This approach, although better than the previous one, suffers from the drawback that the resultant code is merely a collection of functions and lacks the structure of a framework. Selecting target DOM elements to participate in the slideshow and configuration information (delay and transition effect, for example) are totally developer defined and dependent on how a developer decides to wrote them.

A plugin need not restrict itself merely to adding jazzy effects to a web page. What can go as a plugin is governed by a web application under consideration and a developer's choice. Consider the following extensions to jQuery code that can go as plugins (and they are just a few!):

- Commonly used form validations

- Uploading files to server

- Customizable date, time, font, and color pickers

- Zooming in and out of images and DOM elements

- Masked text boxes that restrict input to a specified format

A plugin follows a structure and usage pattern that is familiar to any developer working with jQuery. You may bundle all the functionality of the slideshow into a plugin named SlideShow, for example. You can then use that plugin in any web page. You may find the concept of plugins somewhat analogous to ASP.NET custom server controls and components.

A jQuery plugin exhibits the following features:

- A plugin promotes a structured way of extending and enhancing the core jQuery library. So your code follows the same coding and usage patterns as that of the core jQuery framework.

- A plugin provides a reasonable set of default configuration options and allows you to override them by supplying the configuration from the code external to the plugin.

- A plugin allows you to provide the designated functionality to one or more DOM elements. These DOM elements are selected using any of the jQuery selectors. Thus the target DOM elements are supplied by the code external to the plugin.

- A plugin resides in a JavaScript (.js) file and is referenced in ASP.NET Web Forms and views along with the jQuery library.

Now that you have some idea of what jQuery plugins are, let's see how to use an existing plugin in your ASP.NET web application.

Using the PowerTip Plugin

In order to use a jQuery plugin, you need to have its JavaScript (.js) file and associated files such as style sheets and images. Of course, all the plugins might not have CSS and image files. You can get a plugin either from a known plugin developer or from a plugin repository. The jQuery Plugin Registry (plugins.jquery.com) is a huge registry in which hundreds of plugins can be found categorized based on the kind of functionality they offer. Figure 9-1 shows the main page of this web site.

Figure 9-1. *The jQuery Plugin Registry*

On the left side, various categories of plugins can be found based on their tags. You can also search the registry for a particular plugin.

To learn how a plugin can be used, let's use a plugin called PowerTip. The PowerTip plugin displays fancy tooltips when the mouse pointer is moved over the target DOM elements. It can be used to display help text or provide additional information about an application-specific feature or functionality. You can easily customize PowerTip to control its placement and appearance. To get PowerTip plugin files, search `plugins.jquery.com` for **PowerTip** and locate its page from the plugin registry (see Figure 9-2).

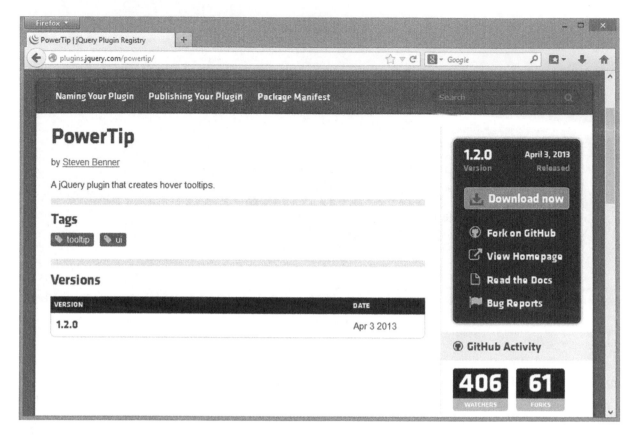

Figure 9-2. *PowerTip plugin page from the plugin registry*

On the right side are various links, such as Download now, View Homepage, and Read the Docs. Download the PowerTip plugin files by clicking the Download link and unzip them in a folder. Figure 9-3 shows the files that are obtained after extracting the zip file into a folder.

Name	Date modified	Type	Size
css	9/10/2013 12:01 PM	File folder	
examples	9/10/2013 12:01 PM	File folder	
jquery.powertip.js	4/3/2013 8:04 PM	JS File	34 KB
jquery.powertip.min.js	4/3/2013 8:04 PM	JS File	10 KB
LICENSE.txt	4/3/2013 8:04 PM	Text Document	2 KB

Figure 9-3. *PowerTip plugin files*

The jquery.powertip.js and jquery.powertip.min.js files are the core JavaScript files of the plugin. The css folder contains style sheets that you may need to include in your project to control the appearance of the tooltips. The LICENSE.txt file also details the licensing terms of the PowerTip plugin.

Figure 9-4 shows a sample ASP.NET Web Form that shows the PowerTip plugin in action.

Figure 9-4. *PowerTip plugin being used on a Web Form*

The Web Form consists of a GridView control that displays records from the Employees table of the Northwind database. The FirstName and LastName columns are rendered as hyperlinks. Moving your mouse pointer over these links displays a PowerTip tooltip showing the Title and Country of the employee under consideration.

To begin developing this Web Form, create an empty ASP.NET Web Forms application and add a Web Form to it. Then create a Scripts folder in the project and place the jQuery library and jquery.powertip.js file inside the Scripts folder. Place the jquery.powertip.css file inside the root folder of the project.

■ **Note** Although you can add references to jQuery using alternate techniques such as the Content Delivery Network (CDN), this example assumes that you have a local copy of the jQuery library.

Then add <script> references to the jQuery library and PowerTip plugin, as shown here:

```
<script src="Scripts/jquery-2.0.3.js"></script>
<script src="Scripts/jquery.powertip.js"></script>
```

Although it is obvious, note that the reference to the jQuery library appears prior to the reference to jquery.powertip.js. This is necessary because PowerTip is dependent on core jQuery for its functionality. Also, add a link to a CSS file that ships with the download of PowerTip, as follows:

```
<link href="jquery.powertip.css" rel="stylesheet" />
```

The jquery.powertip.css file supplies various CSS classes that control the look and feel of the resultant tooltips. You can even change the CSS rules defined in this style sheet to customize the appearance of the tooltips.

Drag and drop a SQL Data Source control on the Web Form and configure it to select the EmployeeID, FirstName, LastName, Title, and Country columns from the Employees table. Then place a GridView on the Web Form and add a BoundField column and two TemplateField columns to it. Design the GridView as shown in Listing 9-1.

Listing 9-1. GridView markup

```
<asp:GridView ID="GridView1" runat="server" AutoGenerateColumns="False" CellPadding="10"
DataKeyNames="EmployeeID" DataSourceID="SqlDataSource1">
<Columns>
  <asp:BoundField DataField="EmployeeID" HeaderText="EmployeeID"
  InsertVisible="False" ReadOnly="True" SortExpression="EmployeeID" />
  <asp:TemplateField HeaderText="FirstName">
    <ItemTemplate>
      <asp:HyperLink ID="HyperLink1" runat="server"
      NavigateUrl='#'
      Text='<%# Eval("FirstName") %>'
      data-powertip='<%# Eval("Title") + " (" + Eval("Country") + ")" %>'>
      </asp:HyperLink>
    </ItemTemplate>
  </asp:TemplateField>
  <asp:TemplateField HeaderText="LastName">
    <ItemTemplate>
      <asp:HyperLink ID="HyperLink2" runat="server"
      NavigateUrl='#'
      Text='<%# Eval("LastName") %>'
      data-powertip='<%# Eval("Title") + " (" + Eval("Country") + ")" %>'>
      </asp:HyperLink>
    </ItemTemplate>
    </asp:TemplateField>
  </Columns>
</asp:GridView>
```

The BoundField is bound to the EmployeeID column, whereas the two TemplateField columns display FirstName and LastName respectively. The templates contain a HyperLink control whose Text property is bound with the FirstName and LastName columns using the Eval() databinding expression. Notice that the NavigateUrl property points to # because you don't want to navigate away as such. More importantly, notice that both HyperLink controls have the data-powertip attribute added to them. The data-powertip attribute is a custom data attribute, and its value comes from Title and Country columns. The data-powertip attribute supplies the content of the PowerTip tooltip.

Once you finish designing the GridView, add a <script> block below the <script> references added earlier and key in the code shown in Listing 9-2.

Listing 9-2. Showing PowerTip Tooltips

```
$(document).ready(function () {
  $("a").powerTip();
});
```

The code in Listing 9-2 selects all the hyperlinks from the page (which means all the FirstName and LastName hyperlinks, in this case) and initializes the powerTip() plugin on them. This is all it takes to make the PowerTip tooltips functional.

Customizing PowerTip Tooltips

In the preceding section, you used PowerTip plugin with its default configuration. You can customize many aspects of PowerTip plugin by doing the following:

- Specifying options while initializing the plugin
- Modifying the CSS style sheet

The first way to customize the plugin is important because it reflects a standard way of supplying configuration settings to any jQuery plugin. The PowerTip documentation describes various settings of the plugin that can be changed. Although you won't use all of them, a few are used, as listed here:

- placement: This option controls the placement of the tooltip. Some of the possible values are e (east), w (west), n (north), and s (south).

- offset: This option controls the gap between the DOM element being hovered and the tooltip.

- fadeInTime: This option controls the duration of the fade-in effect applied while displaying a tooltip.

- fadeOutTime: This option controls the duration of the fade-out effect applied while hiding a tooltip.

These configuration options can be passed to the plugin as a JavaScript object:

```
$(document).ready(function () {
  $("a").powerTip({
    placement: 'e',
    offset:20,
    fadeInTime: 300,
    fadeOutTime:300
  });
});
```

As shown here, a JavaScript object encapsulates placement, offset, fadeInTime, and fadeOutTime settings. The placement of the tooltip is set to e (east), and its offset from the FirstName and LastName hyperlinks is set to 20 pixels. The fadeInTime and fadeOutTime settings are set to 300 milliseconds.

The second form of customization changes the appearance of the PowerTip tooltips using CSS. To change the tooltip appearance, open the jquery.powertip.css file and locate the CSS rule shown here:

```
#powerTip {
  cursor: default;
  background-color: #333;
  background-color: rgba(0, 0, 0, 0.8);
```

```
border-radius: 6px;
color: #fff;
display: none;
padding: 10px;
position: absolute;
white-space: nowrap;
z-index: 2147483647;
}
```

This CSS rule governs the look and feel of the tooltip. There are many other CSS rules defined by the style sheet that contribute to the appearance of the tooltip, but the preceding code is the main CSS rule for changing tooltip background color and text color. For the sake of testing, change the background-color and color CSS properties to different values.

Figure 9-5 shows what the tooltips look like after the customization.

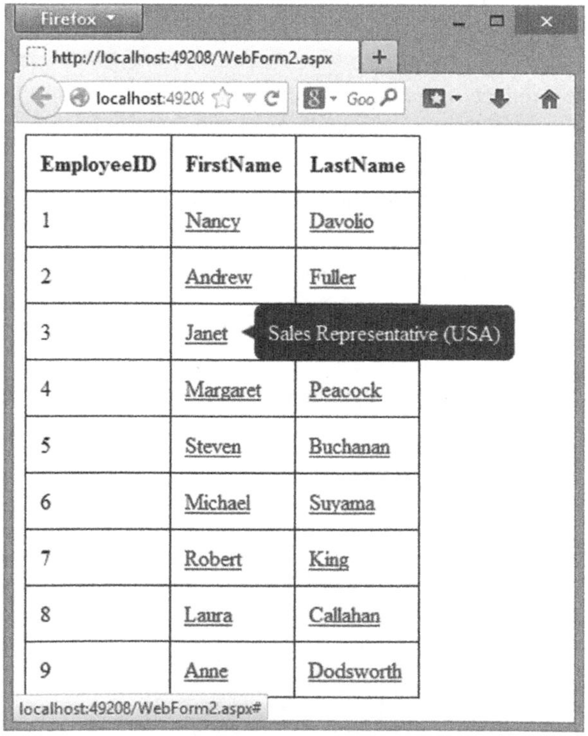

Figure 9-5. *PowerTip tooltips after customization*

As you can see from Figure 9-5, the background color of the tooltips is now changed to dark blue, and the text color is white. The tooltips are displayed toward the east of the hyperlinks, and their fade-in and fade-out duration is now 300 milliseconds.

Overview of JavaScript Function Prototypes

Before you learn how to create your own jQuery plugins, it is worthwhile to take a quick look at JavaScript function prototypes that form the basis of plugin development.

■ **Note**   This section is not intended to give you a thorough understanding of JavaScript prototypes. It discusses only the minimum information necessary to carry on the plugin development discussed in the later sections.

It may sound bit confusing, but a JavaScript function is actually an object (a function object, to be specific) and it gets a few prebuilt properties. One of these properties is the prototype property. The prototype property—often referred to as a function prototype—allows you to add properties and methods to the function under consideration. (Remember what was just mentioned: functions are objects and hence can have properties and methods!) Here's an example. Consider the piece of code shown here:

```
function Employee() {
  this.employeeID = 0;
  this.firstName = '';
  this.lastName = '';
};
```

The code declares a function named Employee. The Employee function declares three members—employeeID, firstName, and lastName–intended to store employee ID, first name, and last name, respectively. Once created, you can instantiate and use Employee like this:

```
var objEmp1 = new Employee();
objEmp1.employeeID = 1;
objEmp1.firstName = 'Nancy';
objEmp1.lastName = 'Davolio';
alert('#' + objEmp1.employeeID + ' ' + objEmp1.firstName +
      ' ' + objEmp1.lastName);
```

This code creates an instance of Employee and stores it in an objEmp1 variable. When you instantiate an Employee, its members assume the values as assigned in the Employee() function. This is analogous to a constructor in C#. The code then assigns employeeID, firstName, and lastName members of Employee to 1, Nancy, and Davolio, respectively. Finally, values of the members are displayed using an alert dialog. You can add more members to Employee by using its prototype property as illustrated here:

```
Employee.prototype.hireDate = null;
Employee.prototype.getEmploymentPeriod = function () {
  var currentDate=new Date();
  var timePeriod = Math.abs(currentDate.getTime() - this.hireDate.getTime());
  var dayPeriod = Math.ceil(timePeriod / (1000 * 60 * 60 * 24));
  return dayPeriod;
};
```

The code accesses the prototype property of the Employee object and adds a hireDate member to store the hire date of an employee. Then the code defines the getEmploymentPeriod() method on the Employee object. The getEmploymentPeriod() method is intended to calculate the period of employment in days for a given employee. The getEmploymentPeriod() method calculates the period of employment by subtracting the hire date from the current

239

date. The getTime() function returns the number of milliseconds since 1 January 1970. The Math.abs() function returns the absolute value after the subtraction. This value is in milliseconds; to convert it into days, timePeriod is divided by (1000 * 60 * 60 * 24). The Math.ceil() function returns the smallest integer greater than or equal to the supplied value. Finally, the number of days thus calculated is returned from getEmploymentPeriod() method.

Once you add the properties and methods to the function prototype, you can instantiate and use the Employee object as follows:

```
var objEmp2 = new Employee();
objEmp2.employeeID = 2;
objEmp2.firstName = 'Andrew';
objEmp2.lastName = 'Fuller';
objEmp2.hireDate = new Date(1992, 8, 14);
var daysEmp2 = objEmp2.getEmploymentPeriod();
alert(objEmp2.firstName + ' ' + objEmp2.lastName + ' is employed for ' +
      daysEmp2 + ' days.');
```

This code created an object named objEmp2 that is of type Employee. The code then sets the employeeID, firstName, lastName, and hireDate properties of the object and calls its getEmploymentPeriod() method. The firstName, lastName, and employment period are displayed in an alert dialog.

You can also use the newly defined properties and methods with the instances of Employee created earlier. The following code shows how:

```
objEmp1.hireDate = new Date(1992, 5, 1);
var daysEmp1 = objEmp1.getEmploymentPeriod();
alert(objEmp1.firstName + ' ' + objEmp1.lastName + ' is employed for ' +
      daysEmp1 + ' days.');
```

This code uses the same objEmp1 that you declared earlier and sets its hireDate property. It then calls the getEmploymentPeriod() method on objEmp1. The alert correctly shows the employment period for the employee represented by objEmp1.

Now let's see how this whole prototype thing is related to jQuery plugin development. Suppose that the initial Employee object is supplied to you by some third party. You find the Employee object inadequate and want to extend it to have more properties and methods. How can you do that? You can add your own code that adds properties and methods to the function prototype of the Employee object.

Thus the code that adds properties and methods will be written by you. The exact same analogy holds true for jQuery plugin development. jQuery offers you certain built-in functionality that is accessible through a jQuery object (or jQuery function), and you can extend it by adding more methods to the function prototype of the core jQuery object. These additional methods you create are plugins!

Creating Your Own Plugin

Now that you have a fair idea about jQuery plugins, let's develop one that illustrates the overall process of creating plugins. In this section you develop a plugin called myPlugin that does an easy task: it applies a CSS class to the selected DOM elements. Although the functionality accomplished by myPlugin isn't rocket science, this simple plugin makes you aware of several recommended guidelines you should follow while developing any jQuery plugin. You will also use what you learn from this example to create a more interesting plugin (popupAd) in the sections that follow.

Figure 9-6 shows a Web Form that uses myPlugin.

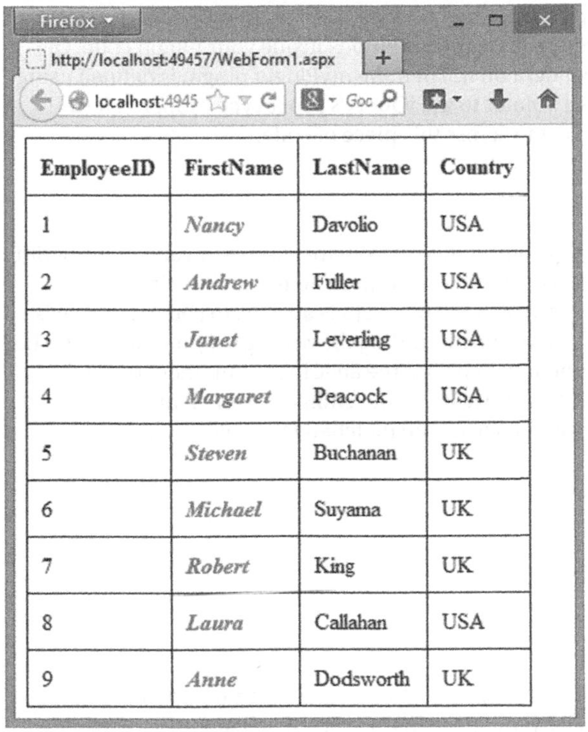

EmployeeID	FirstName	LastName	Country
1	*Nancy*	Davolio	USA
2	*Andrew*	Fuller	USA
3	*Janet*	Leverling	USA
4	*Margaret*	Peacock	USA
5	*Steven*	Buchanan	UK
6	*Michael*	Suyama	UK
7	*Robert*	King	UK
8	*Laura*	Callahan	USA
9	*Anne*	Dodsworth	UK

Figure 9-6. *myPlugin used in a Web Form*

The Web Form consists of a `GridView` control displaying records from the Employees table. Notice that the `FirstName` column is displayed with different styling. This styling is applied by myPlugin. Let's get going!

Defining a Basic Plugin

Begin by creating an empty ASP.NET Web Forms application. Add a Scripts folder to the project and place the jQuery library into it. Add a new JavaScript file to the folder and name it `jquery.myplugin.js`. This file will contain the plugin code and later will be referenced in a Web Form. Then add the code shown in Listing 9-3 inside the `jquery.myplugin.js` file.

Listing 9-3. Basic myPlugin Code

```
///<reference path="jquery-2.0.3.js" />

$.fn.myPlugin = function () {
  this.addClass("myplugin");
}
```

You might be surprised, but the code from Listing 9-3 represents a functional jQuery plugin! The code begins by a <reference> to the jQuery library. This way, you get IntelliSense for jQuery methods inside your plugin code. Of course, this line is optional, and the plugin is not directly dependent on it. Then the myPlugin plugin is defined using $.fn.myPlugin syntax. What is this strange looking $.fn? It is a pointer to the jQuery's prototype property. If you open the jQuery library in any text editor, somewhere you will come across this piece of code:

```
jQuery.fn = jQuery.prototype = {...}
```

This code means that fn is pointing to the jQuery.prototype object. Recall from the discussion about JavaScript function prototypes that you can add properties and methods to the prototype object. So the second line from Listing 9-3 adds a new method called myPlugin() to the jQuery's prototype object ($ is an alias to jQuery, and fn is an alias to prototype). In other words, you are extending the jQuery core by adding the myPlugin() method to it. The myPlugin() method is referred to as a plugin. The myPlugin function then uses the addClass() method to add the myplugin CSS class to this. What is this here? Here, "this" points to the jQuery collection of DOM elements matched using some selector. So this.addClass() adds the specified CSS class to all the matched DOM elements. A sample myplugin CSS class is shown here:

```
.myplugin {
    font-weight: bold;
    color: red;
    font-style: italic;
}
```

The myplugin CSS class simply sets font-weight to bold, font-style to italic, and color to red. Add a style sheet (jquery.myplugin.css) to the project root folder and place the myplugin CSS class inside it.

Now add a new Web Form to the project and place a SQL Data Source control on it. Configure the SQL Data Source to select the EmployeeID, FirstName, LastName, and Country columns from the Employees table. Then place a GridView on the Web Form and design it as per the markup given in Listing 9-4.

Listing 9-4. GridView Markup

```
<asp:GridView ID="GridView1" runat="server" DataKeyNames="EmployeeID" DataSourceID="SqlDataSource1" >
  <Columns>
    <asp:BoundField DataField="EmployeeID" HeaderText="EmployeeID" />
    <asp:TemplateField HeaderText="FirstName">
      <ItemTemplate>
        <asp:Label ID="lblFirstName" runat="server" CssClass="firstname"
                   Text='<%# Bind("FirstName") %>'>
                   </asp:Label>
      </ItemTemplate>
    </asp:TemplateField>
    <asp:BoundField DataField="LastName" HeaderText="LastName" />
    <asp:BoundField DataField="Country" HeaderText="Country" />
  </Columns>
</asp:GridView>
```

Most of the markup shown in Listing 9-4 is straightforward. Notice the line marked in bold letters. The FirstName is a TemplateField and its ItemTemplate consists of a Label control bound with the FirstName column. The Label has CssClass property set to firstname. You will use this class name later in a jQuery selector to match DOM elements.

Next, add references to script and CSS files:

```
<link href="jquery.myplugin.css" rel="stylesheet" />
<script src="Scripts/jquery-2.0.3.js"></script>
<script src="Scripts/jquery.myplugin.js"></script>
```

The first line references the jquery.myplugin.css style sheet. The jQuery library is referenced, and finally the jquery.myplugin.js is referenced. Now add a `<script>` block in the head section of the Web Form and key in the code shown in Listing 9-5.

Listing 9-5. Using myPlugin on a Web Form

```
$(document).ready(function () {
  $(".firstname").myPlugin();
});
```

The code selects all the DOM elements that have the `firstname` CSS class attached with them. In this case, all the `FirstName` `<span>` elements get selected. `myPlugin()` is then called on the matched elements. For all the selected `<span>` elements, `myPlugin()` is called and the `myplugin` CSS class gets applied to them. You can load the Web Form in a browser and confirm that myPlugin is indeed working as expected. In the preceding example, you used the jQuery CSS class selector to match certain elements. You could have used any other selector to match elements, and myPlugin would have added the `myplugin` CSS class to them.

Supporting Chaining

Although myPlugin developed in the preceding section works as expected, there is a flaw: you can't use jQuery method chaining with the current implementation of myPlugin. For example, suppose that you write the following line of code:

```
$(".firstname").myPlugin().css("text-decoration", "underline");
```

This code uses the method chaining syntax to call the `css()` method on the matched elements. The `css()` method sets the `text-decoration` CSS style property to underline the `FirstName` values. Such method chaining works with most of the built-in jQuery methods. However, the previous line fails because myPlugin doesn't participate in the method chaining yet.

To support method chaining in your plugin, you should return the matched set from the plugin. You can modify the `myPlugin()` method as shown in Listing 9-6.

Listing 9-6. Supporting Method Chaining in a Plugin

```
$.fn.myPlugin = function () {
  this.addClass("myplugin");
  return this;
}
```

The `myPlugin()` method now returns the matched DOM elements back to the caller. This way, the same DOM elements are available to the next method in the chaining (the `css()` method, for example). Once you add chaining support to myPlugin, the `css()` method works as expected (see Figure 9-7).

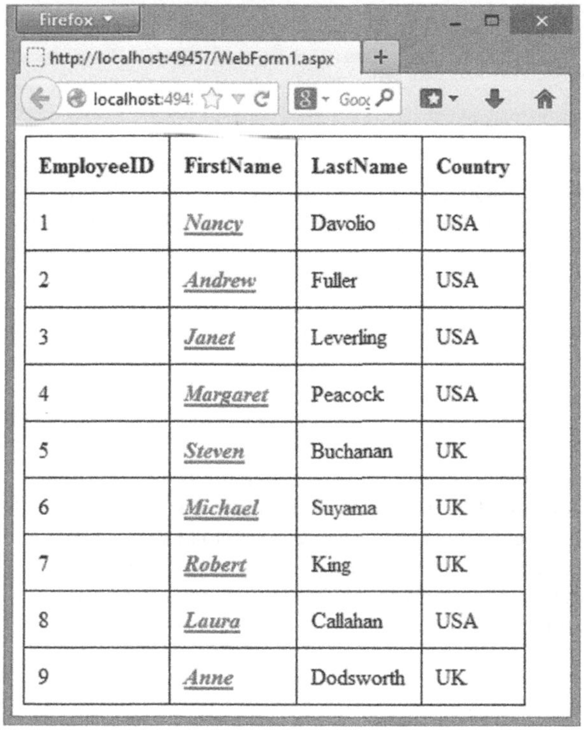

EmployeeID	FirstName	LastName	Country
1	Nancy	Davolio	USA
2	Andrew	Fuller	USA
3	Janet	Leverling	USA
4	Margaret	Peacock	USA
5	Steven	Buchanan	UK
6	Michael	Suyama	UK
7	Robert	King	UK
8	Laura	Callahan	USA
9	Anne	Dodsworth	UK

Figure 9-7. *myPlugin after adding chaining support*

The `FirstName` column values are now underlined due to the successful call to the `css()` method.

Preserving the Meaning of $

So far, so good. Although myPlugin is meeting its expectations, if you are serious about plugin development, you should also think about the real-world scenarios in which your plugin might be used. In the myPlugin code, so far you have assumed that $ is an alias to jQuery, but it might not be true in all cases. There are many JavaScript libraries out there, and some use $ for their own functionality. If your web application is using such a library in addition to jQuery, myPlugin may fail because $ is being redefined by some other library and is no longer pointing to jQuery. As a precaution, ensure that your plugin code explicitly points $ to jQuery. Listing 9-7 shows how this can be done.

Listing 9-7. Preserving the Meaning of $

```
(function ($) {
  $.fn.myPlugin = function () {
    this.addClass("myplugin");
    return this;
  }
})(jQuery);
```

Listing 9-7 uses the same myPlugin code, but this time it is wrapped inside an anonymous function call. The anonymous function accepts a single parameter ($). Remember that in JavaScript, $ is a valid parameter name. The whole function definition is enclosed in round brackets (), and immediately the `jQuery` object is passed as the parameter to the function. This way, the function is invoked as soon as it is encountered during the script loading process. So you pass jQuery object to an anonymous function. The anonymous function receives it as a $ parameter. The myPlugin() method is placed inside this anonymous function. Thus anywhere inside myPlugin, $ always points to the jQuery object, and $.fn holds the same meaning as before.

Adding Actions to Plugins

If your plugin is doing something complex, chances are it may need to expose additional methods to the external world. An immediate solution that may cross your mind is to create additional methods similar to myPlugin() and then call them from the Web Form. Although this approach may work, it makes your code messy, and the overall footprint of your plugin becomes larger. The recommended approach is to pass actions you want to perform to the core plugin method and let the plugin method invoke appropriate logic based on the action specified. For example, in its current form, myPlugin always adds the myplugin CSS class to the selected DOM elements.

What if you want to remove myplugin class so that the elements are reset to their initial state? This can be accomplished by making myPlugin() accept a parameter that tells the plugin whether to add myplugin class or remove it. Listing 9-8 shows the modified myPlugin code.

Listing 9-8. myPlugin with actions

```
(function ($) {
  $.fn.myPlugin = function (action) {
    if (action == "reset") {
      this.removeClass("myplugin");
    }
    else {
      this.addClass("myplugin");
    }
    return this;
  }
})(jQuery);
```

The code shown in Listing 9-8 shows that myPlugin() accepts a parameter: action. Inside the function, an if block checks whether the action is reset; if so, the removeClass() method is called on the selected elements. For any other action, the addClass() method is called. In this case, myPlugin() has only two actions: adding a CSS class or removing it. If you want to have more actions, you can add a series of if blocks or a switch statement to check for an action. In the preceding example, if you don't pass any parameter to myPlugin(), the else block will get executed, and the myplugin CSS class will be added to the elements.

To test the reset action, place a button on the Web Form and handle its click event handler as shown here:

```
$("#button1").click(function () {
  $(".firstname").myPlugin("reset");
});
```

This code assumes the presence of a button whose ID is button1 on the Web Form. The click() method wires a click event handler to the click event of the button. Inside the click handler, myPlugin() is called on all the DOM elements having the firstname CSS class. Notice that this time, the action parameter is supplied as reset. This will cause the plugin to remove the myplugin CSS class from the selected elements. Figure 9-8 shows a sample run of the Web Form when button1 is clicked.

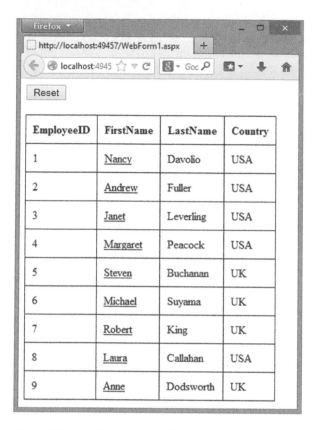

Figure 9-8. *Invoking a reset action*

The FirstName column no longer has the myplugin CSS class applied. The FirstName values are still underlined due to the call made to the css() method while the page was displayed initially.

Iterating Through the Selected DOM Elements

In the examples discussed so far, you added or removed the myplugin CSS class to a whole set of selected elements. What if you want to add or remove a CSS class conditionally? This calls for examining each element from the selection and processing it to obtain the desired effect. If you need such a functionality, you can resort to the each() method.

Suppose that you want to add the myplugin CSS class only to employees residing in the USA (or want to apply different CSS classes based on their country of residence). To identify the employees residing in the USA, you can add a custom data attribute, data-country, to the FirstName Label control. This is done by handling the RowDataBound event of the GridView (see Listing 9-9).

Listing 9-9. RowDataBound event handler of GridView

```
protected void GridView1_RowDataBound(object sender,
             GridViewRowEventArgs e)
{
  if (e.Row.RowType == DataControlRowType.DataRow)
  {
    Label l = (Label)e.Row.FindControl("lblFirstName");
        l.Attributes.Add("data-country", e.Row.Cells[3].Text);
  }
}
```

The code looks for lblFirstName in all the data rows. This is the Label control that displays FirstName (refer to the GridView markup discussed at the beginning of this example). The code then adds the data-country attribute to the Label using its Attributes collection. Now you can modify the plugin code as shown in Listing 9-10.

Listing 9-10. Using each() to iterate through the selected elements

```
(function ($) {
  $.fn.myPlugin = function (action) {
    if (action == "reset") {
      return this.removeClass("myplugin");
    }
    else {
      return this.each(function () {
        var country = $(this).data("country");
        if (country == "USA") {
          $(this).addClass("myplugin");
        }
      });
    }
  }
})(jQuery);
```

Have a look at the else block. It uses the each() method to iterate through the selected DOM elements one by one. With each iteration, the data-country attribute is retrieved using the data() method. Notice that inside the each() method function, this points to the DOM element being iterated upon. Hence it is used as $(this) before calling any jQuery methods on it. Then the country of an employee, as returned by the data-country attribute, is checked. If the country is USA only, the myplugin CSS is added using the addClass() method. If you run the Web Form with the modified version of myPlugin, it should resemble Figure 9-9.

247

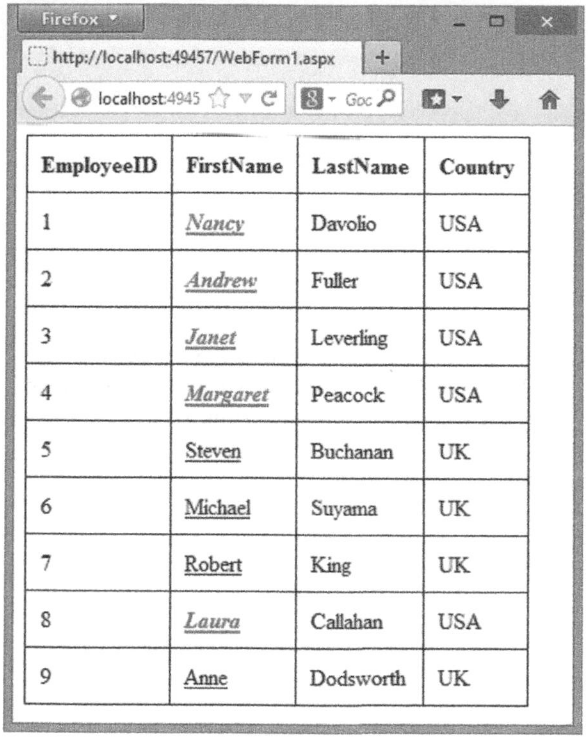
Firefox
http://localhost:49457/WebForm1.aspx
localhost:4945
EmployeeID FirstName LastName Country
1 Nancy Davolio USA
2 Andrew Fuller USA
3 Janet Leverling USA
4 Margaret Peacock USA
5 Steven Buchanan UK
6 Michael Suyama UK
7 Robert King UK
8 Laura Callahan USA
9 Anne Dodsworth UK

Figure 9-9. *Only employees from the USA have the myplugin CSS class applied*

As you can see, the `FirstName` values of the employees residing in the USA are applied `myplugin` CSS class.

Making a Plugin Configurable

In the myPlugin code, you see the country name (USA) and CSS class name (`myplugin`) hardcoded. But what if you need to run the plugin for employees residing in other countries? What if you want to apply a different CSS class?

To take care of such requirements, your plugin should be configurable. And to make a plugin configurable there has to be a provision to pass configuration settings from the external world. This is done by making your plugin accept an `options` parameter (in addition to the `action` parameter you added earlier). The `options` parameter accepts a `JavaScript` object. Inside the plugin, use the settings supplied by this object. As a recommended practice, you should provide a default configuration so that if the consumer of the plugin supplies an `options` object, those values are used; otherwise, the default configuration is used. Listing 9-11 shows the modified version of myPlugin that accepts the `options` parameter.

Listing 9-11. myPlugin now accepts the options parameter

```
(function ($) {
  $.fn.myPlugin = function (action,options) {
      var defaultOptions = {"className":"myplugin","country":"USA"};
      var settings = $.extend({},defaultOptions, options);
      if (action == "reset") {
        return this.removeClass("myplugin");
      }
      else {
        return this.each(function () {
          var country = $(this).data("country");
          if (country == settings.country) {
            $(this).addClass(settings.className);
          }
        });
      }
    }
})(jQuery);
```

The myPlugin() method now accepts the options parameter in addition to action. Inside, it declares the defaultOptions object with two properties: className and country. The defaultOptions object holds the default settings for the plugin. It is possible that the object passed as the options parameter may specify values for only a few configuration settings. In all the configuration settings for which no values are supplied by the options parameter, you should use the default values. To arrive at the resultant set of configuration settings, the $.extend() method is used. The $.extend() method accepts two or more objects and merges their content into the first object. The $.extend() method also returns the resultant object as its return value. In this example, the first parameter is an empty object ({}), the second parameter is defaultOptions, and the third parameter is options. Thus, the settings object contains the resultant configuration settings. The else block no longer uses the hardcoded country name and CSS class name. Instead, it uses the settings.country and settings.className properties. Listing 9-12 shows how options can be passed to the plugin from the Web Form.

Listing 9-12. Passing options to the plugin

```
$(document).ready(function () {
  var options= { className: "myplugin2", country: "UK" };
  $(".firstname").myPlugin("set",options)
                .css("text-decoration", "underline");
});
```

The code creates an options object and specifies className and country properties as myplugin2 and UK, respectively. Then myPlugin is invoked by passing the action "set" and the options parameter. Figure 9-10 shows what the GridView looks like.

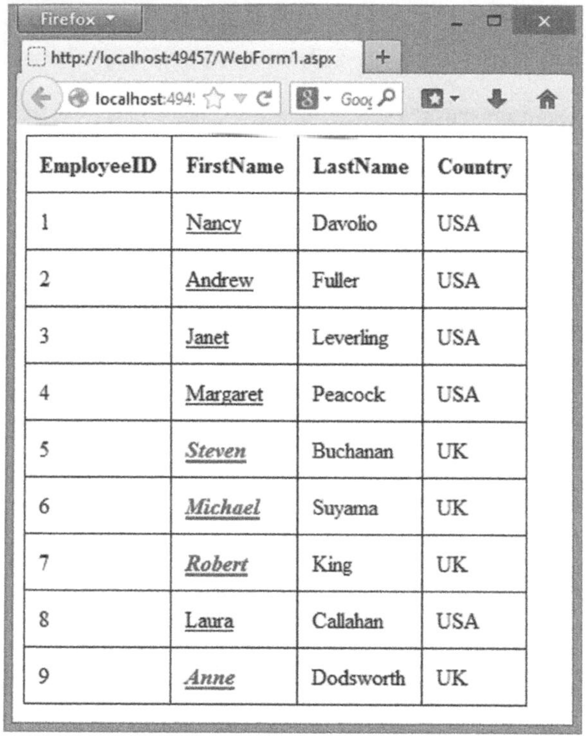

EmployeeID	FirstName	LastName	Country
1	Nancy	Davolio	USA
2	Andrew	Fuller	USA
3	Janet	Leverling	USA
4	Margaret	Peacock	USA
5	*Steven*	Buchanan	UK
6	*Michael*	Suyama	UK
7	*Robert*	King	UK
8	Laura	Callahan	USA
9	*Anne*	Dodsworth	UK

Figure 9-10. *myPlugin being invoked with options parameter*

This time, employees residing in the UK are highlighted with the myplugin2 CSS class.

Developing a popupAd Plugin

In the initial part of this chapter, you used the PowerTip plugin, and you might have wondered how it works. You might have even opened the JavaScript source code file of the plugin to see its internal workings. How about concluding this chapter by developing your own plugin that does something similar?

In this section, you will develop a popupAd plugin that displays a pop-up advertisement when the mouse is hovered over DOM elements. The purpose of this plugin is to show an advertisement when a user hovers the mouse pointer over a selected DOM element. The user can read the advertisement and may decide to navigate to the link provided in the advertisement. Of course, the popupAd plugin won't be as feature rich and complete as a professionally written plugin, but developing such an example will help you understand the process. Figure 9-11 shows what the popupAd plugin looks like in the browser.

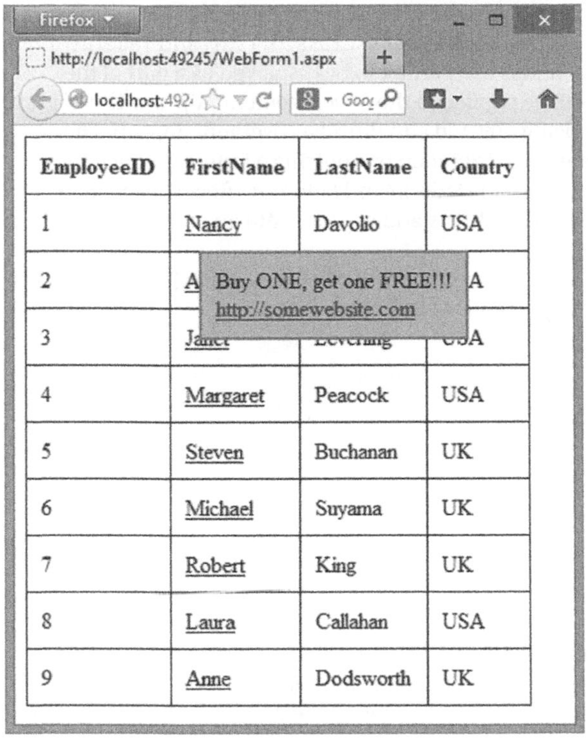

Figure 9-11. *popupAd plugin in action*

As you can see, the Web Form consists of the same GridView that you used in the preceding example. This time, however, moving your mouse pointer on the FirstName values displays a pop-up advertisement. The pop-up advertisement is displayed using the popupAd plugin mentioned earlier. Various aspects of the advertisement, such as the CSS class being applied, advertisement text, advertisement link, and fade effect duration are configurable.

Begin by creating an empty ASP.NET Web Forms application. Add a new Web Form and design it in exactly the same way as in the preceding example. Then add the Scripts folder to the project and place the jQuery library into it. Add the jquery.popupad.js JavaScript file to the Scripts folder. Then add the basic skeleton of the popupAd plugin, as shown in Listing 9-13.

Listing 9-13. Skeleton of popupAd plugin

```
(function ($) {
    $.fn.popupAd = function (options) {
        var defaultOptions = {
            adText: "This is ad text",
            adLink: "http://www.website.com",
            adCssClass: "ad",
            offset: 5,
            fadeInterval:200
        };
        var settings = $.extend({}, defaultOptions, options);
    }
})(jQuery);
```

251

The code from Listing 9-13 defines the popupAd plugin that accepts the options parameter. The defaultOptions object holds the default values for five configuration settings: adText, adLink, adCssClass, offset, and fadeInterval. The adText setting holds the advertisement text. The adLink contains a hyperlink to be displayed as a part of the advertisement. The adCssClass setting specifies the CSS class to be applied to the advertisement pop-up. The offset value indicates the top and left padding between the element being hovered and the advertisement pop-up. The advertisement pop-up is made visible by applying a fade-in effect and is hidden by applying a fade-out effect. The fadeInterval setting controls the duration in milliseconds for which the fade-in and fade-out effect is applied to the advertisement pop-up. The $.extend() method merges defaultOptions and options into an empty object. The resultant object is stored in the settings variable.

The advertisement pop-up is created dynamically by adding a <div> tag to the document at runtime (see Listing 9-14). You need to place this code after the line that creates the settings object.

Listing 9-14. Creating an advertisement pop-up dynamically

```
var adMarkup = $("<div class='" + settings.adCssClass + "'>" +
                    settings.adText +
                    "<br>" +
                    "<a href='" + settings.adLink + "'>" +
                    settings.adLink + "</a>" +
                    "</div>");
$(document.body).append(adMarkup);
```

The adMarkup variable contains a jQuery object for the <div> markup. Notice that various settings are added to the <div> definition. The <div> contains the adText and a hyperlink pointing to the adLink. Also, the adCssClass is applied to the <div> to control its appearance. Once the <div> is created, it is added to the document body by using the append() method.

When an advertisement pop-up is displayed, a user might move the mouse pointer away from a target element. If so, the advertisement pop-up should be made invisible. However, if a user moves the mouse pointer onto the advertisement pop-up, the advertisement should be kept visible. This is accomplished by supplying handlers to the hover() method, as shown in Listing 9-15. You need to place this code below the line that appends adMarkup to the body.

Listing 9-15. Supplying handlers to the hover() method

```
var flag = false;
adMarkup.hover(function () {
  flag = true;
  $("." + settings.adCssClass).show();
  }, function () {
  flag = false;
  $("." + settings.adCssClass).hide();
});
```

The code declares a flag variable that indicates whether the mouse pointer is over the advertisement pop-up. The flag variable is set to true in the first function supplied to the hover() method. Additionally, the first function displays the advertisement pop-up by calling the show() method on a <div> that has adCssClass attached with it. Similarly, the second function supplied to the hover() method sets flag to false and hides the advertisement pop-up by calling the hide() method. The flag variable assigned inside the hover() functions is used later in the code while fading out a pop-up ad (as discussed shortly).

When a user hovers the mouse pointer over the selected DOM elements, the advertisement pop-up will be displayed. This is accomplished as shown in Listing 9-16. You need to place this code after the line that calls hover() on adMarkup.

Listing 9-16. Displaying or hiding the advertisement pop-up

```
this.hover(function (evt) {
    $("." + settings.adCssClass).css("top", $(this).position().top +
                                       $(this).height()+
                                       settings.offset);
    $("." + settings.adCssClass).css("left", $(this).position().left +
                                       settings.offset);
    $("." + settings.adCssClass).fadeIn(settings.fadeInterval);
}, function (evt) {
    window.setTimeout(function () {
        if (!flag) {
            $("." + settings.adCssClass).fadeOut(settings.fadeInterval);
        }
    }, 1000)
});
return this;
```

The code from Listing 9-16 supplies mouse-in and mouse-out functions to the hover() method. Notice that hover() is called directly on this because you want to handle these events for all the selected elements.

The mouse-in function supplied to the hover() method sets the top CSS property of the advertisement pop-up. Notice that inside the function, this refers to the current DOM object, so it is used as $(this) to call any jQuery methods on it. The top coordinate is calculated by finding the top coordinate of the element being hovered and then adding height() and the offset value to it. Similarly, the left coordinate is determined by finding the left coordinate of the element being hovered and then adding the offset value to it. Then the advertisement pop-up is made visible by calling the fadeIn() method. The fadeInterval setting is supplied to the fadeIn() method to control the duration of the fade-in effect.

The mouse-out function hides the advertisement pop-up by calling the fadeOut() method. Notice that window.setTimeout() is used to delay the fadeOut() for 1,000 milliseconds. If this is not done, the pop-up will be made invisible even if the mouse pointer is on the pop-up. Adding the delay gives the mouse-in function of the advertisement pop-up a chance to set the flag variable. The pop-up is made invisible only if flag is false (that is, the mouse pointer is not on the pop-up). Finally, this is returned from the popupAd() method so that it supports chaining.

This completes the popupAd plugin. Now add a style sheet (jquery.popupad.css) and add the ad CSS class to it as shown here:

```
.ad {
    position:absolute;
    background-color:silver;
    border:2px solid gray;
    display:none;
    padding:10px;
}
```

The ad CSS class is simple to understand and sets the style properties such as position, display, padding, and background-color. Next, add the references to the CSS file and script files in the Web Form you developed earlier:

```
<link href="jquery.popupad.css" rel="stylesheet" />
<script src="Scripts/jquery-2.0.3.js"></script>
<script src="Scripts/jquery.popupad.js"></script>
```

As before, the jQuery library is referenced first, followed by the jquery.popupad.js file. Finally, add a <script> to invoke the plugin, as shown in Listing 9-17.

Listing 9-17. Using the popupAd Plugin

```
$(document).ready(function () {
  var options = {
      adText: "Buy ONE, get one FREE!!!",
      adLink: "http://somewebsite.com",
      offset:10
  };
  $(".firstname").popupAd(options);
});
```

The code creates the `options` object and specifies custom values for the `adText`, `adLink`, and `offset` settings. Then the CSS class selector is used to match all the DOM elements that have the `.firstname` CSS class attached to them. Finally, `popupAd()` is called by supplying the `options` object as its parameter.

That's it! You can now run the Web Form and test whether the pop-up advertisements are displayed as expected.

Summary

jQuery not only offers rich built-in functionality but also allows you to extend the library through plugins. jQuery plugins are methods that you add to the prototype of jQuery to extend its core functionality. Before you decide to create a jQuery plugin yourself, make sure to search the jQuery plugins registry because somebody might have already developed what you are looking for. While authoring a plugin, you should follow the recommended guidelines to make it fall in line with thousands of other plugins and make it structured. If you feel so inclined, you can also submit your plugin to the jQuery plugin registry (see `plugins.jquery.com` for more details).

So far in this book, you learned about the core jQuery library. There are a couple of other projects that are developed on top of the jQuery library and are worth exploring: jQuery Mobile and jQuery UI. To that end, the next chapter gives you an overview of these popular libraries.

CHAPTER 10

jQuery UI and jQuery Mobile

So far, you have used the jQuery library to accomplish various tasks. Although this book primarily focuses on the jQuery core, there are two popular libraries built on top of the jQuery core that are worth noting: jQuery UI and jQuery Mobile. *jQuery UI* is a JavaScript library that provides themeable widgets and effects that can be used in your web pages. *jQuery Mobile* is a JavaScript library intended for web applications targeting mobile phones and tablets. This chapter will give you an overview of these two libraries. Specifically you will learn the following:

- How to add jQuery UI widgets such as Accordion, Autocomplete, Menu, Datepicker, and Tabs to ASP.NET Web Forms and MVC views

- How to use jQuery Mobile in ASP.NET to build mobile-friendly web applications

- How to detect a request coming from mobile device in Web Forms and MVC applications

A thorough coverage of jQuery UI and jQuery Mobile is beyond the scope of this book, however. In this chapter, you will become familiar with these two libraries so that you can code basic scenarios with them. The official jQuery UI and jQuery Mobile web sites provide good documentation, so for a deeper understanding of these libraries, consider reading their documentation.

Overview of jQuery UI

When developing real–world web applications, you often need professional-looking user interface (UI) elements such as menus, tabs, progress bars, sliders, dialog boxes, and more. You can develop these UI elements from the ground up, but that would be a time-consuming and tedious process. How about utilizing UI elements that were created by experts and are being used by thousands of fellow developers? That's what jQuery UI is about. The official jQuery UI web site (http://jqueryui.com) defines jQuery UI like this:

> *jQuery UI is a curated set of user interface interactions, effects, widgets, and themes built on top of the jQuery JavaScript Library.*

As is clear from the definition, jQuery UI is a selected set of UI elements. Although jQuery UI includes a bunch of things including interactions, effects, widgets, and themes, the primary piece of jQuery UI is widgets. As of this writing, the following widgets are available as a part of jQuery UI:

- **Accordion**: Displays collapsible panels of content. It comes in handy when you need to present lot of information in a limited screen space.

- **Autocomplete**: Typically associated with a text box; allows users to quickly find and select from a list of values as they key in the text.

- **Button**: Enhances the appearance of button elements and allows you to build pushbuttons, toolbars, split buttons, and more.

- **Datepicker**: Presents a pop-up or inline datepicker.

- **Dialog**: Shows content in a dialog box that is displayed on top of other content.

- **Menu**: Shows a menu that can be operated with a mouse or keyboard.

- **Progressbar**: Shows the progress of a process. The process can have a definite or indefinite end value.

- **Slider**: Allows you to pick a value from a range of values. The slider can be displayed horizontally or vertically.

- **Spinner**: Allows you to display a text box with up or down arrows to increment or decrement numbers.

- **Tabs**: Displays a tabbed user interface that has one or more tabbed panels showing content to the user.

- **Tooltip**: Shows a tooltip that replaces the default tooltip of an element.

The jQuery UI not only provides these widgets but also comes with a theming framework. You can easily customize the look and feel of these widgets using built-in or custom themes. You can even develop your own widgets.

■ **Note**   At this point, you might be tempted to compare widgets with plugins. Although they are similar in that they extend the core jQuery library, they are not the same. A plugin may or may not occupy screen space, but a widget does. You can think of a widget as a special case of plugin that occupies some screen real estate. An analogy from .NET world is the difference between a component and a control. All controls are components in a way, but the term *control* implies that they have some visual existence.

Although jQuery UI also offers interactions, effects, and utilities, this chapter focuses on jQuery widgets. Visit http://jqueryui.com for more details and documentation.

Downloading and Referencing jQuery UI

Before you use any of the jQuery UI features, you have to download the jQuery UI library. You can grab jQuery UI using any of the following three options (for more information on these methods, refer to Chapter 2):

- Download the jQuery UI library in a local folder and use that local copy.

- Refer jQuery UI from a Content Delivery Network (CDN).

- Install jQuery UI as a NuGet package.

When you include the whole jQuery UI library in your project, you are incorporating everything that jQuery UI has to offer. However, you might be using only a few widgets or features of jQuery UI, which is why the jQuery UI web site enables you to create a custom download that includes just the features you need in an application. Figure 10-1 shows the Download Builder section of the jQuery UI web site.

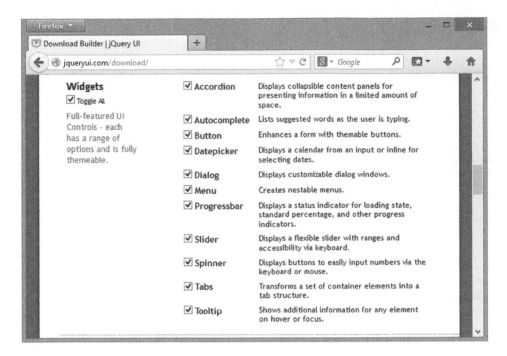

Figure 10-1. *jQuery UI Download Builder*

As you can see, the Download Builder allows you to pick only the widgets and features you want to include in a web application.

When the download is complete, you can add a reference to the jQuery UI library as you did for the jQuery core. For example, the following markup shows the jQuery UI files referenced using the static `<script>` tag:

```
<link href="jquery-ui.css" rel="stylesheet" />
<script src="Scripts/jquery-2.0.3.js"></script>
<script src="Scripts/jquery-ui.js"></script>
```

This markup references the `jquery-ui.css` file because that file supplies the default CSS styling rules. The jQuery library is referenced first because jQuery UI requires the jQuery core. Finally, `jquery-ui.js` is referenced. The default theme also uses certain images that you need to place in the Images folder. These images are available as a part of the jQuery UI download. Figure 10-2 shows the folder structure and a typical placement of these files.

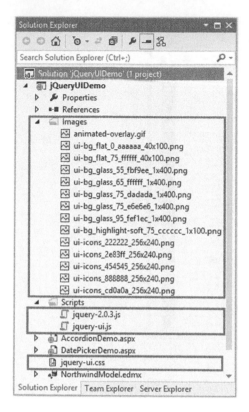

Figure 10-2. *Placement of jQuery UI files*

Once you reference jQuery UI, you can use any of its features. For example, with the preceding markup in place, you can use the datepicker widget like this:

```
<head runat="server">
  ...
  <script>
    $(document).ready(function () {
      $("#datepicker").datepicker();
    });

  </script>
</head>
<body>
    <form id="form1" runat="server">
        <span>Select Date : </span><input type="text" id="datepicker" />
    </form>
</body>
</html>
```

This markup contains a text box whose ID is datepicker. The ready() handler selects this text box using the ID selector and initializes the datepicker widget on it. If you move the keyboard focus to the text box, you will see a datepicker popping out of the text box (see Figure 10-3).

Figure 10-3. *Using the jQuery UI datepicker widget*

The datepicker assumes a default coloring and uses images for navigating the months because of the CSS file and images you included.

Using the Accordion Widget

Now that you know the basics of jQuery UI, let's build an ASP.NET Web Forms application that uses the accordion widget. Figure 10-4 shows what the Web Form looks like.

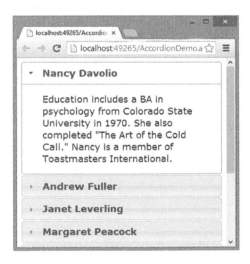

Figure 10-4. *Accordion displaying employee data*

The Web Form consists of the jQuery accordion widget. The header of each accordion panel displays the Employee FirstName and LastName values. Click an accordion header; the accordion panel expands and reveals the Notes for the employee under consideration. The accordion panels are generated on the fly using a Repeater control.

What is more interesting is that the Notes of an employee record are loaded in "lazy" fashion, which means that the Notes for all the employees are not fetched and loaded at once. When a user clicks an accordion header, an Ajax call is made to the server and the Notes for that employee are fetched and loaded in the associated accordion panel. Although the Employee table doesn't contain too many records, such a lazy loading is quite helpful when the accordion needs to display a lot of information. Rather than loading all the content of all the accordion panels, loading it only as and when required will boost the initial load time of the Web Form.

■ **Note**   The official jQuery UI web site provides detailed API documentation that covers the options, methods, events, and theming of each widget. Only the options actually used in the example are discussed here. (You can refer to the documentation at http://api.jqueryui.com to learn more.)

To begin developing this Web Form, create an empty ASP.NET Web Forms application and add a new Web Form to it. Then create a Scripts folder under the project root folder and place the jQuery library and jQuery UI library inside it. Place the jQuery UI default style sheet file in the project root folder. Create an Images folder inside the project root folder and place all the image files needed by jQuery UI into it. Next, add references to the jQuery library, jQuery UI library, and jQuery UI style sheet in the head section as shown here:

```
<link href="jquery-ui.css" rel="stylesheet" />
<script src="Scripts/jquery-2.0.3.js"></script>
<script src="Scripts/jquery-ui.js"></script>
```

Add an ADO.NET Entity Data Model into the project and configure it to create the model class for the Employees table of the Northwind database. Then place a Repeater control on the Web Form and design its templates as shown in Listing 10-1.

Listing 10-1. Repeater with HeaderTemplate, FooterTemplate, and ItemTemplate

```
<asp:Repeater ID="Repeater1" runat="server"
    SelectMethod="Repeater1_GetData">
  <HeaderTemplate>
    <div id="accordion">
  </HeaderTemplate>
  <ItemTemplate>
    <h3><%# Eval("FirstName") %> <%# Eval("LastName") %></h3>
    <div>
      <input type="hidden" class="hidden"
      value="<%# Eval("EmployeeID") %>" />
    </div>
  </ItemTemplate>
  <FooterTemplate>
    </div>
  </FooterTemplate>
</asp:Repeater>
```

To display the accordion correctly, you need to arrange its content in a specific way. The general arrangement of the accordion is like this:

```
<div id="accordion">
  <h3>Panel1 Heading</h3>
  <div>Panel1 content</div>
  <h3>Panel2 Heading</h3>
  <div>Panel2 content</div>
  ...
</div>
```

The outermost `<div>` element acts as the container for all the accordion panels. Each accordion panel has an associated heading represented with a `<h3>` tag by default (you can deviate from this default, as you will learn later). The contents of an accordion panel are wrapped inside another `<div>` that immediately follows the heading. To render such a markup, the Repeater control is useful.

The `<HeaderTemplate>` of the Repeater control contains the start `<div>` tag of the accordion container, and the `<FooterTemplate>` contains the corresponding `</div>` tag. The `<ItemTemplate>` consists of an `<h3>` element that displays FirstName and LastName values using the Eval() databinding expression. The `<div>` that follows contains a hidden element for storing the EmployeeID belonging to that accordion panel. This EmployeeID is used later while making an Ajax call to retrieve the Notes. To quickly select this hidden field from jQuery code, a CSS class (hidden) is attached with it. The Repeater can be data bound with the Employee records by setting its SelectMethod to Repeater1_GetData.

The Repeater1_GetData method looks like this:

```
public IQueryable Repeater1_GetData()
{
  NorthwindEntities db = new NorthwindEntities();
  var data = from e in db.Employees
             select new { e.EmployeeID,e.FirstName,e.LastName };
  return data;
}
```

The Repeater1_GetData() method selects all the Employee objects from the Employees DbSet and returns an IQueryable. Because you need only the EmployeeID, FirstName, and LastName values for databinding purposes, only those properties are selected in the query.

Now add a `<script>` block in the head section of the Web Form and key in the code shown in Listing 10-2.

Listing 10-2. Configuring the Accordion Widget

```
$(document).ready(function () {
  var options = {};
  options.heightStyle = "content";
  options.collapsible = true;
  options.header = "h3";
  options.active = 0;
  options.beforeActivate = function (evt, ui) {...};
  options.create = function (evt, ui) {...};
  $("#accordion").accordion(options);
});
```

The ready() handler creates an object for storing various accordion widget configuration options. The heightStyle setting controls the height of the accordion and its panels. A value of content indicates that the accordion panels will have height sufficient to accommodate their contents. By default, an accordion shows at least one expanded, and the collapsible option controls whether all the panels are allowed to be collapsed. Setting its value to true means that all the panels can be collapsed. The header option specifies a selector matching the header elements. Setting it to h3 means that <h3> elements are selected as accordion panel headers. The active option indicates an index of the panel that is initially expanded. Setting it to 0 (default) means than the first panel will be visible.

Handling beforeActive and create Events

beforeActive and create are accordion widget events. The beforeActive event is raised just before activating an accordion panel. An active panel is the one that's being expanded or collapsed. In this example, you use the beforeActive event to make an Ajax call to the server and fetch the Notes for an Employee under consideration.

The create event is raised when the accordion is created; it takes place when an accordion comes into existence on a web page. In this example, you use the create event to fetch and display the Notes of the first Employee as soon as the accordion is displayed.

The beforeActive and create event handler functions receive two parameters: event object and ui object. The ui object provides information specific to the widget, such as the new header and the panel being expanded.

Finally, the accordion container is selected using the jQuery ID selector, and the accordion widget is initialized on it. While initializing the accordion widget, the options object is passed as the parameter.

Complete the beforeActive event handler function as shown in Listing 10-3.

Listing 10-3. beforeActive Event Handler

```
options.beforeActivate = function (evt, ui) {
  if ($(ui.newPanel).find(".hidden").val()) {
    $.ajax({
      url: "AccordionDemo.aspx/GetNotes",
      type: "POST",
      data: JSON.stringify({
              employeeid: $(ui.newPanel).find(".hidden").val()
            }),
      dataType: "json",
      contentType: "application/json",
      success: function (result) {
        $(ui.newPanel).find(".notes").remove();
        $(ui.newPanel).append("<div class='notes'>" +
                              result.d + "</div>");
      },
    error: function (xhr, status, err) { alert('Error' + err); }
  });
  }
};
```

The beforeActive event handler first checks whether a panel has EmployeeID in a hidden field. This is done by selecting the panel being activated by using the ui.newPanel property and then finding an element with a hidden CSS class attached with it by using find() method. If the hidden field is found and has a value assigned to it, an Ajax call is made to a page method using $.ajax().

Various configuration options needed by $.ajax() are passed as an object while making the call. Notice that the url points to AccordionDemo.aspx/GetNotes, where GetNotes() is a page method with a single parameter: employeeid. (You will create GetNotes() shortly.) The data property passes the employeeid value needed by the GetNotes() method. This value is obtained from the hidden field as before.

The success function receives the Notes returned by the GetNotes() method. To display the notes, you dynamically create a <div> element that has its content set to the result.d value (i.e., Notes). The newly created <div> is appended to the newPanel object by using the append() method.

Notice that an accordion panel can be activated multiple times, so it is necessary to first remove the <div> element displaying the notes (if any). This is accomplished by finding the element that has the notes CSS class attached with it and then removing it with the remove() method. The error handler simply displays the error message in an alert dialog.

The GetNotes() page method used by the beforeActive event handler is shown in Listing 10-4.

Listing 10-4. GetNotes() Page Method

```
[WebMethod]
public static string GetNotes(int employeeid)
{
  NorthwindEntities db = new NorthwindEntities();
  var data = from e in db.Employees
             where e.EmployeeID == employeeid
             select e.Notes;
  return data.SingleOrDefault();
}
```

The GetNotes() method is a static method and is decorated with the [WebMethod] attribute so it can be called from the jQuery code using the $.ajax() method. The GetNotes() method accepts an EmployeeID whose Notes are to be retrieved. Inside, the method selects the Notes of an Employee whose EmployeeID matches the supplied employeeid parameter.

Because EmployeeID is the primary key, the LINQ to Entities query will return just a single value, so the SingleOrDefault() method is used to retrieve and return that value to the caller. The create event handler is quite similar to beforeActive event handler in that it makes an Ajax call to GetNotes() and retrieves Notes for the first EmployeeID. Listing 10-5 shows the create event handler.

Listing 10-5. create Event Handler

```
options.create = function (evt,ui) {
  $.ajax({
    url: "AccordionDemo.aspx/GetNotes",
    type: "POST",
    data: JSON.stringify(
           { employeeid: $(ui.panel).find(".hidden").val() }),
    dataType: "json",
    contentType: "application/json",
    success: function (result) {
      $(ui.panel).find(".notes").remove();
      $(ui.panel).append("<div class='notes'>" +
        result.d + "</div>");
    },
    error: function (xhr, status, err) { alert('Error' + err); }
  });
};
```

The code inside the create event handler is almost identical to the beforeActive event handler, except that the ui parameter of the event handler has a panel property that gives a reference to the active panel.

Changing the Default Theme

You can alter the default theming of the accordion widget by modifying the default style sheet. The CSS classes related to the accordion widget are as follows:

- ui-accordion: This style is applied to the outer accordion container.

- ui-accordion-header: This style is applied to the headers of the individual accordion panels.

- ui-accordion-content: This style is applied to the content panels of an accordion.

Although a detailed discussion of jQuery UI theming is beyond the scope of this book, let's quickly alter some basic UI attributes of the accordion. Open the jquery-ui.css file and modify the CSS classes as shown here:

```
.ui-accordion .ui-accordion-header {
        display: block;
        cursor: pointer;
        position: relative;
        margin-top: 2px;
        padding: .5em .5em .5em .7em;
        min-height: 0; /* support: IE7 */
        background-color:#cd0a0a;
        color:white;
}
.ui-accordion .ui-accordion-content {
        padding: 1em 2.2em;
        border-top: 0;
        overflow: auto;
        background-color:yellow;
}
```

In this CSS markup, the lines shown in bold letters indicate the additions to the default style rules. Figure 10-5 shows the accordion after making the changes.

Figure 10-5. *Theming the accordion widget*

Now the accordion header and accordion content panels assume the background color and text color per the theming rules specified in the modified CSS classes.

JUICE UI

Although ASP.NET developers have been using jQuery UI in their web sites, one downside of the jQuery UI from an ASP.NET perspective is that it is purely a client-side library. ASP.NET Web Forms often rely on server-side processing, and configuring. The script-based jQuery UI widgets don't have any server-side counterparts, so it can become tedious to use them in certain cases. Juice UI components address this deficiency by wrapping jQuery UI widgets into ASP.NET server controls to be accessed in server-side code just like any other ASP.NET server controls. The following excerpts from the Juice UI web site (http://juiceui.com) summarize what it has to offer to ASP.NET developers:

Juice UI is an open-source collection of WebForms components that brings jQuery UI Widgets to your project with ease. Start leveraging the power of the world's most popular JavaScript UI library while working with familiar code in your ASP.NET projects.

Juice UI allows you to create flexible, interactive web applications quickly. Entice your users with behaviors such as drag & drop, resizing, sorting and selecting. Build first class apps with accordions, autocompletes, datepickers, sliders, and more. Juice UI provides the simplicity needed for prototyping and the robustness needed for enterprise class production applications.

Juice UI is an open source library and can be installed by using the NuGet package manager.

Overview of jQuery Mobile

Because the use of mobile devices such as smartphones and tablets is increasing rapidly, keep in mind that a web application might be used from traditional desktops or mobile devices. Developing a mobile-friendly web application is challenging due to two primary reasons:

- Device screen dimensions
- Browser feature support

Mobile devices offer small screen real estate to display web page content as compared with a desktop computer. The size makes it difficult to design a user interface that can be accessed with ease from mobile devices. Moreover, mobile browsers may not support all the features of the desktop browsers. So a web page that works in a desktop browser may not work exactly in the same fashion in a mobile browser.

Developing Mobile Web Applications

To cope with these challenges, developers resort to one of the following approaches when building mobile-friendly web applications:

- **Version dedicated to mobile devices**: In this approach, a separate web site or module is developed to be accessed from mobile devices. Two versions of a web application are created: one to be accessed from desktop computers and one to be used from mobile devices.

- **Same version, dealing with desktops and mobiles**: In this approach, the web pages detect whether the requesting device is a desktop computer or a mobile device and then change the layout, navigation, and UI elements accordingly.

The former approach is often called an *m-dot* approach because the mobile version is often made available at a URL matching this form:

```
m.some_domain.com
```

The desktop version of the web application is available at some_domain.com and mobile version is made available at m.some_domain.com.

Although this approach works, you need to maintain two different versions. When features get added or changed in the main web application, you have to also change the mobile version of the application. This process can be tedious and prone to error.

Therefore, the modern trend is to use the second option listed, which is known as responsive web design (RWD). It offers an advantage that the same codebase serves multiple target devices such as mobile phones, tablets, and desktop computers. So maintaining the web site codebase is easy when compared with the former approach.

Now that you have background information, let's see where jQuery Mobile fits in. The official jQuery Mobile web site (http://jquerymobile.com) says the following:

> *jQuery Mobile is a touch-optimized Web Framework for Smartphones & Tablets. A unified, HTML5-based user interface system for all popular mobile device platforms, built on the rock-solid jQuery and jQuery UI foundation. Its lightweight code is built with progressive enhancement, and has a flexible, easily themeable design.*

This description highlights the fact that jQuery Mobile uses jQuery core to get its job done. jQuery Mobile offers touch-friendly UI elements, making it easy to navigate and use web applications on smartphones and tablets. jQuery Mobile follows progressive enhancement and responsive web design principles. Moreover, jQuery Mobile uses themeable design, making it easy for developers to customize the default look and feel of various UI elements.

■ **Note** Progressive enhancement uses web technologies such as HTML5, CSS, and JavaScript in a layered fashion. All users can access the basic functionality of a web application, regardless of the richness of browser features and network connectivity. Users who have feature-rich browsers and fast Internet connections are served an enhanced version of a web page.

A typical web application using jQuery Mobile consists of the following elements:

- Pages and dialogs
- Ajax navigation and transitions
- UI widgets and form elements
- Themes

Unlike traditional web development, in which one page refers to one .htm or .aspx file, a jQuery Mobile page refers to a <div> element that houses some content or UI elements and occupies the browser window. A single .htm or .aspx page can contain more than one jQuery Mobile page. A page can be displayed in a modal fashion, in which case it is referred to as a *dialog*.

jQuery Mobile uses Ajax-based navigation and form submission, which helps to avoid frequent window refreshes when a user navigates between pages or submits a form. Between the navigation transitions, effects can also be applied to the window.

A jQuery Mobile page can contain any standard HTML markup and form elements; and also UI widgets such as buttons, accordions, pop-ups, and dialogs.

jQuery Mobile has a rich theme framework that supports up to 26 sets of toolbar, content, and button colors. Each individual set is referred to as a *swatch*. The default theme comes with five swatches, named "a" to "e".

■ **Note** This chapter only briefly introduces you to jQuery Mobile because a detailed coverage of jQuery Mobile is beyond the scope of this book. For more information, see the official documentation for jQuery Mobile at `http://api.jquerymobile.com`.

Downloading and Installing jQuery Mobile

Just like jQuery core and jQuery UI, jQuery Mobile can be downloaded from the jQuery Mobile official web site, a CDN, or a NuGet package. Figure 10-6 shows the files installed by the jQuery Mobile NuGet package in an ASP.NET MVC project.

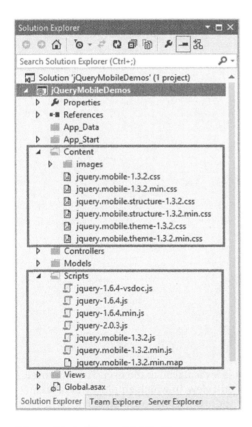

Figure 10-6. *jQuery Mobile files*

Figure 10-6 shows script, style sheet, and images for jQuery Mobile 1.3.2. The Scripts folder contains the compressed and uncompressed versions of the jQuery Mobile library (`jquery.mobile-1.3.2.min.js` and `jquery.mobile-1-3-2.js`). The style sheet files needed for proper theming of various UI elements are stored in the Content folder. The Images subfolder of the Content folder contains the images referenced by the style sheets.

Using jQuery Mobile

Now you can develop a web application that puts jQuery Mobile to use. Although you can use jQuery Mobile in both Web Forms and MVC projects, here you will develop an ASP.NET MVC project. ASP.NET MVC is a popular choice for developing mobile web applications because of the lightweight nature of the views and display modes support (more information on display modes can be found at the end of this chapter).

Figure 10-7 shows the Index view of the application displayed in the Opera Mobile Emulator.

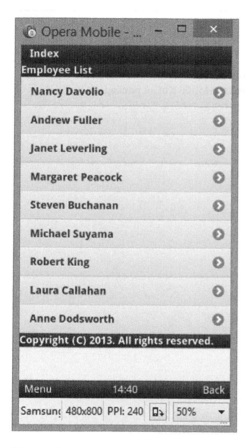

Figure 10-7. *Index view using jQuery Mobile*

As shown in the Index view, a list of employees from the Employees table is displayed to the user. The employee names are clickable links, and clicking an employee name takes the user to Edit view, in which employee details can be edited. The Edit view is divided into three logical "pages": Basic Details, Address Details, and Notes. The Basic Details page of the Edit view is shown in Figure 10-8.

Figure 10-8. *Basic Details page of Edit view*

The three pages present typical wizard navigation to a user, and the final page allows a user to save the data. The final step also validates that none of the fields is left empty.

■ **Note** Throughout this section, the term *page* refers to a jQuery Mobile page, whereas the term *view* refers to a physical MVC view file that is being rendered in the browser.

To begin developing this application, create an empty ASP.NET MVC application. Place the jQuery library and jQuery Mobile library files in the Scripts folder. Also place the style sheet file and image files for jQuery Mobile in the Content folder (refer to the earlier discussion for detailed folder structure).

Creating the Home Controller

The application uses the Entity Framework data model for the Employees table of the Northwind database. Add an ADO.NET Entity Data Model for the Employees table inside the Models folder. Next, add HomeController to the Controllers folder and add three action methods to it, as shown in Listing 10-6.

Listing 10-6. HomeController Action Methods

```
public class HomeController : Controller
{
  NorthwindFntities db = new NorthwindEntities();
  public ActionResult Index()
  {
    var data = from e in db.Employees
               select e;
    return View(data.ToList());
  }
  public ActionResult Edit(int id)
  {
    var data = from e in db.Employees
               where e.EmployeeID == id
               select e;
    return View(data.SingleOrDefault());
  }
  [HttpPost]
  public ActionResult Update(Employee emp)
  {
    Employee existing = db.Employees.Find(emp.EmployeeID);
    existing.FirstName = emp.FirstName;
    existing.LastName = emp.LastName;
    existing.Address = emp.Address;
    existing.Country = emp.Country;
    existing.Notes = emp.Notes;
    db.SaveChanges();
    return View();
  }
}
```

The code consists of three action methods: Index(), Edit(), and Update(). The Index() action method executes a LINQ to Entities query that selects all the Employee objects from the Employees DbSet. The Employee objects are obtained as a generic List using the ToList() method of the data variable and passed to the Index view as its model.

The Edit() method accepts an EmployeeID as its parameter. It then selects an Employee whose EmployeeID matches the supplied id. The Employee object is obtained by using the SingleOrDefault() method and is passed to Edit view as its model.

The Edit view is submitted to the Update() action method, so the Update() method is marked with the [HttpPost] attribute. The Update() method accepts the Employee object as its parameter and returns the Update view. Inside, it retrieves an existing Employee based on the EmployeeID of the employee being updated. Various properties of the existing Employee (FirstName, LastName, Address, Country, and Notes) are updated with their respective values from the Employee object received as the parameter. Finally, the SaveChanges() method of the database context is called to save the changes back to the database. The Update view simply displays a success message.

Now that you have completed the HomeController class, you can create Index, Edit and Update views.

Developing the Index View

The Index view displays a list of employees, so a particular employee can be selected for editing its details. Add the Index view to the project, and add a `<script>` reference and a style sheet reference to its head section like this:

```
<link href="../../Content/jquery.mobile-1.3.2.css" rel="stylesheet" />
<script src="../../Scripts/jquery-2.0.3.js"></script>
<script src="../../Scripts/jquery.mobile-1.3.2.js"></script>
```

As you can see, the `<link>` tag points to `jquery.mobile-1.3.2.css`, which is the default style sheet that comes with the jQuery Mobile download. Then a `<script>` tag points to `jquery-2.0.3.js`. Another `<script>` tag points to `jquery.mobile-1.3.2.js`. Notice that the head section also contains this important markup line:

```
<meta name="viewport" content="width=device-width" />
```

Mobile browsers sometimes load a web page inside a virtual window called viewport. This way, a mobile browser doesn't need to reduce the dimensions of the web page being viewed. Instead, a user can zoom in and out of the web page as necessary. The `viewport` meta tag allows developers to control the viewport dimensions. The `width` property (see the `content` attribute of the meta tag) sets the viewport width. The width can be a fixed number such as 480 or a special value (`device-width`) that means full available width for the device.

Set the model for the Index view to a `List` of `Employee` objects like this:

```
@model List<jQueryMobileDemos.Models.Employee>
```

Notice that the model for the view is set to `List<jQueryMobileDemos.Models.Employee>`. Make sure to change the namespace name of the `Employee` model class according to your project setup.

Key in the markup shown in Listing 10-7 inside the `<body>` section of the view.

Listing 10-7. Displaying a List of Employees in the Index View

```
<div data-role="page" id="home" data-theme="e">
  <div data-role="header">Employee List</div>
  <div data-role="content">
    <ul data-role="listview">

      @foreach (var employee in Model)
      {
        <li>@Html.ActionLink(employee.FirstName +
            " " + employee.LastName, "Edit",
            new { id = employee.EmployeeID },
            new { rel = "external" })</li>
      }
    </ul>
  </div>
  <div data-role="footer">Copyright (C) 2013. All rights reserved.</div>
</div>
```

jQuery Mobile uses HTML5 custom data attributes (`data-*`) extensively to specify metadata information that is then used by the framework. Of course, you can also do most of the tasks through code, but a markup-based approach is a convenient way to initialize and configure various widgets.

The markup from Listing 10-7 creates a jQuery Mobile page. A page consists of a `<div>` element whose `data-role` attribute is set to page. The `data-role` attribute indicates the type of widget a `<div>` represents. The id attribute of the `<div>` is set to home. You can refer a page from the other markup using its id. The `data-theme` attribute specifies the theme to be used. By default, themes a to e are included in the style sheet. Setting `data-theme` to e sets the theme as shown in Figure 10-7 earlier.

A jQuery Mobile page can have a header, a footer, and content regions. A page header is represented by the `data-role` of header and typically includes the title and navigation buttons. In this case, the header `<div>` contains the title of the page: Employee List. A page footer is represented by the `data-role` of footer. In this example, the footer displays a copyright notice.

The page content is where you add HTML markup that makes up the primary part of the page. A content area is indicated by the `data-role` of content. Inside the content `<div>` is a `<ul>` element whose `data-role` is set to listview, which creates a Listview widget. The Listview widget displays a list of items and is often used to present a menu of options to the user. The individual items of the Listview (`<li>` elements) come from the model of the Index view. A foreach loop iterates through the List of Employee objects accessible through the Model property. With every iteration, a hyperlink is generated that points to the Edit action method and passes EmployeeID in the route. The hyperlink is generated using the ActionLink() Html helper.

The first parameter of the ActionLink() is the text to be displayed in the link; in this case, the FirstName and LastName values are displayed. The second parameter is the name of the action method and is set to Edit. The third parameter is used to pass route values. In this case, you need to pass EmployeeID to the Edit method (Home/Edit/1); an anonymous object with the id property set to an EmployeeID is passed. The fourth parameter is an anonymous object that passes additional HTML attributes to be added to the resultant hyperlink. In this case, the rel attribute with a value of external is passed, ensuring that the full page is refreshed in the browser.

The Index view is complete. If you run the application, you should get a list of employees displayed in the browser. Of course, clicking any link won't do anything meaningful because the Edit view is not yet created.

Creating the Edit View

The Edit view allows a user to edit details of an employee selected on the Index view. Add the Edit view to the project and also add script and style sheet references as with the Index view. The model of the Edit view is set to the Employee object, as shown here:

```
@model jQueryMobileDemos.Models.Employee
```

Notice that the model is set to jQueryMobileDemos.Models.Employee. Make sure to change the model namespace per your project setup. The Edit view displays its user interface like a wizard. The entire UI is divided into three logical pages: Basic Details, Address Details, and Notes. These pages have the IDs step1, step2 and step3, respectively. Because the Edit view is a data entry form, the three pages are placed inside a `<form>` rendered using the BeginForm() Html helper:

```
@using (Html.BeginForm("Update", "Home", FormMethod.Post)){
...
}
```

The first parameter of BeginForm() is the action method name (Update in this case), the second parameter is the controller name (Home in this case), and the third parameter is the form submission method (FormMethod.Post in this case). The markup of all three pages goes inside this form.

Let's see the markup that makes the Basic Details page (step1). This markup is shown in Listing 10-8.

Listing 10-8. Basic Details Page

```
<div data-role="page" id="step1" data-theme="b">
  <div data-role="header">Basic Details</div>
  <div data-role="content">
    <div>@Html.LabelFor(e => e.EmployeeID)</div>
    <div>@Html.TextBoxFor(e => e.EmployeeID,
          new { @readonly = "readonly" })</div>
    <div>@Html.LabelFor(e => e.FirstName)</div>
    <div>@Html.TextBoxFor(e => e.FirstName)</div>
    <div>@Html.LabelFor(e => e.LastName)</div>
    <div>@Html.TextBoxFor(e => e.LastName)</div>
    <a href="/home/index" data-role="button" data-inline="true">List</a>
    <a href="#step2" data-role="button" data-inline="true">Next</a>
  </div>
</div>
```

The Basic Details page consists of a <div> whose data-role attribute is set to page and its id to step1. Notice that data-theme is set to b. The page contains header and content sections. The header section displays the page heading: Basic Details. The content section displays the values of EmployeeID, FirstName, and LastName. It uses a series of LabelFor() and TextBoxFor() Html helper calls to display text boxes and their associated labels. The LabelFor() Html helper displays the field label, whereas the TextBoxFor() Html helper displays text boxes for entering the corresponding fields. Because EmployeeID is a primary key, the corresponding text box is made readonly.

Notice the hyperlinks at the bottom of the page. The first hyperlink points to /home/index and allows the user to navigate to the launching page of the application. Its data-role is set to button, indicating that it will be rendered like a button rather than a plain hyperlink (see Figure 10-8 again). The second hyperlink points to #step2, the Address Details page. The data-inline attribute added to both hyperlinks indicates that the buttons will be placed side by side instead of on new line.

Now add the markup of Address Details page, as shown in Listing 10-9.

Listing 10-9. Address Details Page

```
<div data-role="page" id="step2" data-theme="b">
  <div data-role="header">Address Details</div>
    <div data-role="content">
      <div>@Html.LabelFor(e => e.Address)</div>
      <div>@Html.TextBoxFor(e => e.Address)</div>
      <div>@Html.LabelFor(e => e.Country)</div>
      <div>@Html.TextBoxFor(e => e.Country)</div>
      <a href="#step1" data-role="button" data-inline="true">Previous</a>
      <a href="#step3" data-role="button" data-inline="true">Next</a>
    </div>
</div>
```

The Address Details page is similar to the Basic Details page in terms of its overall setup. However, it displays Address and Country fields for editing. The two hyperlinks at the bottom point to #step1 and #step3, respectively.

The Notes field is displayed on the final page (step3). The markup of the Notes page is shown in Listing 10-10.

Listing 10-10. Notes Page

```
<div data-role="page" id="step3" data-theme="b">
  <div data-role="header">Notes</div>
  <div data-role="content">
    <div>@Html.LabelFor(e => e.Notes)</div>
    <div>@Html.TextAreaFor(e => e.Notes, new { rows = "5", cols = "30" })</div>
    <a href="#step2" data-role="button" data-inline="true">Previous</a>
    <input type="submit" value="Save Changes" data-inline="true" />
    <div data-role="popup" id="errpopup" class="ui-content"></div>
  </div>
</div>
```

The Notes page uses the TextAreaFor() Html helper to display a <textarea> with 5 rows and 30 columns. It also has a submit button that posts the form to the Update() action method. Notice the last <div> element: its data-role is set to popup. This <div> is meant to be used as a Popup widget and will display validation errors. The pop-up is displayed through jQuery code placed in a <script> block inside the head section. Listing 10-11 shows how this is done.

Listing 10-11. Displaying Validation Errors in a Pop-up

```
$(document).ready(function () {
  $("form").submit(function (evt) {
    var html="";
    $("input:text").each(function () {
      if ($(this).val() == "") {
        html += "Must enter value for " + this.name + "<br />";
      }
    });
    if (html != "") {
      $("#errpopup").html(html);
      $("#errpopup").popup("open");
      evt.preventDefault();
    }
  });
});
```

The code wires an event handler for the submit event of the form. Inside, the :text selector is used to select all the text boxes. The each() method iterates through the text boxes to see whether they are empty. Note that this jQuery code will select all the text boxes from all three pages. If the value of a text box is empty, an error message is appended to the html variable.

Once all the text boxes are checked, an if block checks to see whether the html variable contains any error messages. If so, the <div> popup is selected using the ID selector, and the popup() widget is initialized on it. The value of open passed to the popup widget indicates that the pop-up is to be displayed. evt.preventDefault() cancels the form submission if there are any validation errors.

Figure 10-9 shows a sample run of the Edit view displaying a pop-up with validation errors.

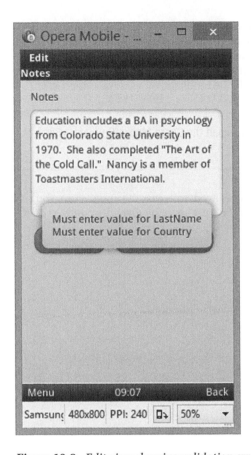

Figure 10-9. *Edit view showing validation errors in pop-up*

The pop-up informs a user that values for the LastName and Country fields must be supplied. Clicking anywhere on the page discards the pop-up.

Creating the Update View and Testing the Application

In this section, you'll finish the application by adding the Update view. You will also test the application in two mobile emulators, as discussed shortly.

Creating the Update view is quite straightforward. Simply add the Update view to the project and add script and style sheet references as before. Then add the HTML markup to the body section, as shown in Listing 10-12.

Listing 10-12. Update View

```
<div data-role="page" data-theme="b">
  <div data-role="header">Success</div>
  <div data-role="content">
    <div>Data saved successfully!</div>
    <a href="/home/index" data-role="button">Back To List</a>
  </div>
</div>
```

The markup should be familiar: it contains a page that displays a success message to the user. A hyperlink at the bottom displays the Back To List button, so the user can navigate back to the landing page after updating an employee.

This completes the application. Although you can run this application in any desktop browser, it is better to use some mobile emulator (or actual mobile device if you make the web site live!). Fortunately, two such emulators can be quickly used to test your web application: the Safari browser and Opera Mobile Emulator.

■ **Note**   To download Safari, visit `http://www.apple.com/safari/`. To download the Opera Mobile Emulator visit `http://www.opera.com/developer/mobile-emulator`.

If you run the web application in Safari, by default it uses the default user agent to access the application. You can change the user agent using the Develop ➤ User Agent menu option. Figure 10-10 shows the menu that allows you to select a user agent.

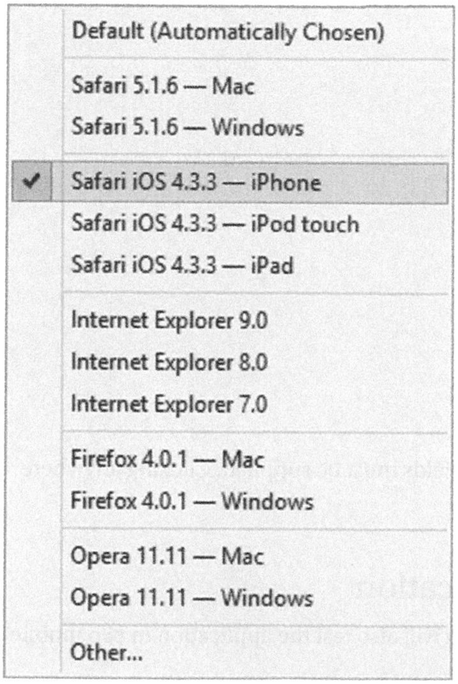

Default (Automatically Chosen)
Safari 5.1.6 — Mac
Safari 5.1.6 — Windows
✓ Safari iOS 4.3.3 — iPhone
Safari iOS 4.3.3 — iPod touch
Safari iOS 4.3.3 — iPad
Internet Explorer 9.0
Internet Explorer 8.0
Internet Explorer 7.0
Firefox 4.0.1 — Mac
Firefox 4.0.1 — Windows
Opera 11.11 — Mac
Opera 11.11 — Windows
Other...

Figure 10-10. *Selecting a user agent in Safari*

■ **Note**   If the Develop menu is not visible in your installation of Safari, go to Edit ➤ Preferences. Then switch to Advanced options and check the Show Develop Menu in Menu Bar check box.

Notice that the user agent is set to iPhone. This causes Safari desktop browser to send a user agent string for iPhone to the server, and your web application will respond as if iPhone is making a request. You can also specify a custom user agent string using the Others menu option.

You can use the Opera Mobile Emulator to test your web application for mobile devices that support the Opera browser. Figure 10-11 shows the main window of the emulator, in which you can select a target device.

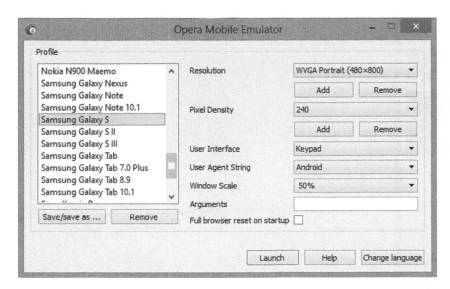

Figure 10-11. *Opera Mobile Emulator main window*

You can choose a profile depending on the target device of your choice and click the Launch button to open its window. Figure 10-12 shows what a sample emulator window looks like.

Figure 10-12. *Opera Mobile Emulator window*

Once the window is open, you can enter the web application URL in the address bar at the top; click Enter to load the web page. Test the web application by changing the data-theme value to a different theme.

■ **Note**   You can use IE10's Developer Tools to test the mobile version. Although you can easily set Windows Phone as the user agent, other user agents need to be specified manually.

Detecting Mobile Device in ASP.NET

In the initial sections of the chapter, you learned about the two approaches for developing a mobile web application: m-dot and responsive web design (RWD). Each of these approaches has its own advantages and disadvantages. Luckily, ASP.NET allows you to combine the good features of each while building a web site.

From the m-dot approach, you can choose to build different UIs for different devices, and from the RWD approach you can choose to have a common code base. So while developing ASP.NET web applications, you can have the same codebase (or at least as identical as possible) as far as server-side code is concerned. However, you develop different UIs when targeting different devices (that means .aspx markup for Web Forms and views for MVC).

In the preceding sections, you developed a "mobile only" web application, which means that you use the same jQuery Mobile–powered version of the web site regardless of whether the web application is accessed from desktop browsers or mobile browsers. However, sometimes you may want to present different layout and UI elements for different devices.

For example, if a Web Form is being accessed from a desktop computer, you may want to attach a master page that displays a three-column layout to the user. If it is being accessed from a smartphone, you may want to attach a master page that displays a single-column layout. Moreover, you may want to use jQuery Mobile only if a web page is being accessed by a mobile device. This calls for device detection in your server-side code so that you can respond differently depending on the requesting device. Although this book doesn't develop an example that uses device-detection techniques, the next couple of sections discuss these techniques so that you can use them if the situation arises.

Detecting a Mobile Device in Web Forms

If you are developing an ASP.NET Web Forms application, you can easily see whether the requesting device is a mobile device by using the `Request.Browser` object. The `Request.Browser` object, which is an instance of the `HttpBrowserCapabilities` class, gives you a lot of information about the capabilities of the requesting browser. In particular, the `IsMobileDevice` property of the `Request.Browser` object tells you whether the requesting device is a mobile device.

A few more properties of the `Request.Browser` object can also come in handy for developing mobile applications (see Table 10-1).

Table 10-1. *Properties of the Request.Browser Object*

Property	Description
IsMobileDevice	Returns true if the requesting browser is mobile device; false otherwise
MobileDeviceManufacturer	Returns the name of the mobile device manufacturer (if known)
MobileDeviceModel	Returns the model name of a mobile device (if it is known)
ScreenPixelsHeight	Returns the height of the display in pixels
ScreenPixelsWidth	Returns the width of the display in pixels

Figure 10-13 shows a sample Web Form that outputs the properties listed in Table 10-1 and is being accessed using the Safari desktop browser and an iPhone (via the Safari browser emulator).

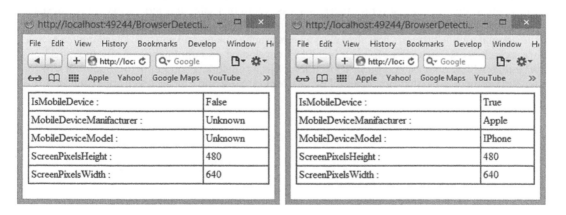

Figure 10-13. *Using Request.Browser to detect a mobile device*

A Web Form accessed using the Safari desktop browser returns IsMobileDevice as False, whereas the same Web Form when accessed from an iPhone returns True.

■ **Note**   Because this Web Form is quite straightforward, it's not discussed here. You can have a look at the source code of the Web Form from the source code download for this chapter.

Detecting a Mobile Device in MVC

Mobile device detection using Request.Browser also works with ASP.NET MVC applications. However, MVC4 has a more elegant mechanism for detecting requesting devices and rendering an appropriate user interface: display modes. Simply put, the display modes feature automatically picks up a view file that is appropriate for the requesting device.

Consider, for example, an MVC application that has the Index() action method inside the HomeController class:

```
public class HomeController : Controller
{
  public ActionResult Index()
  {
    return View();
  }
}
```

Assuming that you want to target desktop computers and mobile phones, you will need to create two views: Index.cshtml and Index.mobile.cshtml. Now if a user tries to access /home/index from a desktop computer, Index.cshtml will be served to the user. However, if a user tries to access /home/index over a mobile phone, Index.mobile.cshtml is served. This device detection and serving of content happens automatically based on display modes.

Summary

This chapter introduced you to two distinct libraries—jQuery UI and jQuery Mobile—that are built on the solid foundation of jQuery core. jQuery UI offers several widgets, such as accordions, tabs, and sliders, to help you develop jazzy web pages. You can also integrate these widgets with your server-side code. jQuery Mobile offers a unified interface for all the popular mobile browsers and also offers features such as pages and widgets. Developing a mobile application is always challenging, but jQuery Mobile is helpful for developing your applications easily and quickly.

You are now familiar with various aspects of the jQuery library. The concluding chapter of this book will take you through a few more interesting recipes that can be useful for developing real-world ASP.NET web applications.

■ ■ ■

CHAPTER 11

Useful jQuery Recipes for ASP.NET Applications

This book took you through the aspects and features of jQuery—from selectors to event handling to Ajax to plugins. You developed many examples that illustrated the topics at hand. This final chapter discusses six recipes that you will find useful while developing real—world web applications. These recipes also use multiple jQuery features together, giving you an opportunity to refresh the knowledge you've already acquired.

The recipes discussed in this chapter include the following:

- Converting GridView data to comma separated values (CSV)

- Implementing paging using Ajax

- Implementing client-side sorting for an HTML table

- Creating cascading drop-down lists

- Providing autocomplete for text boxes

- Using Ajax for file uploads

Recipe 1: Converting GridView Data to CSV

Sometimes you'll want to export data being displayed in an ASP.NET GridView control to comma separated values (CSV). This is needed when the data needs to be imported into another system or into software applications such as Microsoft Excel.

One approach to converting GridView data to CSV is to do it in the server-side code, but this approach calls for an additional postback. Using jQuery, you can convert GridView data into CSV format on the client side, thus avoiding additional postback.

To illustrate how this is done, you can develop a Web Form as shown in Figure 11-1.

Figure 11-1. *Exporting GridView data to CSV*

The Web Form consists of a `GridView` that displays `EmployeeID`, `FirstName`, `LastName`, `Title`, and `Country` columns. An Export To CSV button on the top allows you to convert `GridView` data into CSV format. The CSV data is then displayed in a multiline `TextBox` above the `GridView`. You can copy/paste this data directly to another application or save it to a disk file for later use.

To develop this application, create an empty ASP.NET Web Forms application and add a new Web Form to it. Then place a `Button`, a `TextBox`, and a `GridView` as shown in Figure 11-1. Set the `TextMode` property of the `TextBox` to `Multiline`, the `Rows` property to 10, and the `Columns` property to 50. Drag and drop a `SQL Data Source` control on the Web Form and configure it to select the `EmployeeID`, `FirstName`, `LastName`, `Title`, and `Country` columns from the Employees table of the Northwind database.

Listing 11-1 shows the Web Form markup of the resultant form.

Listing 11-1. Web Form Markup

```
<form id="form1" runat="server">
  <asp:Button ID="Button1" runat="server" Text="Export to CSV" />
  <asp:SqlDataSource ID="SqlDataSource1" runat="server"
  ConnectionString="<%$ ConnectionStrings:NorthwindConnectionString %>"
  SelectCommand="SELECT [EmployeeID], [FirstName], [LastName], [Title],
  [Country] FROM [Employees]"></asp:SqlDataSource>
  <asp:TextBox ID="TextBox1" runat="server" TextMode="MultiLine"
```

```
 Columns="50" Rows="10" Width="99%"></asp:TextBox>
 <br />
 <asp:GridView ID="GridView1" runat="server" AutoGenerateColumns="False"
  CellPadding="10" DataKeyNames="EmployeeID"
  DataSourceID="SqlDataSource1" Width="100%">
   <Columns>
     <asp:BoundField DataField="EmployeeID" HeaderText="EmployeeID"
      InsertVisible="False" ReadOnly="True" />
     <asp:BoundField DataField="FirstName" HeaderText="FirstName"
      SortExpression="FirstName" />
     <asp:BoundField DataField="LastName" HeaderText="LastName" />
     <asp:BoundField DataField="Title" HeaderText="Title" />
     <asp:BoundField DataField="Country" HeaderText="Country" />
   </Columns>
 </asp:GridView>
</form>
```

Add a `<script>` reference to the jQuery library and also add a `<script>` block in the head section. Key in the code shown in Listing 11-2.

Listing 11-2. Exporting GridView Data to CSV

```
$(document).ready(function () {
  $("#TextBox1").hide();
  $("#Button1").click(function (evt) {
    var rows = [];
    var str = '';
    $("#GridView1").find("tr").each(function () {
      if ($(this).find("th").length) {
        var headerArray = [];
        $(this).find("th").each(function () {
        str = $(this).text().replace(/"/g, '""');
        headerArray.push('"' + str + '"');
      });
      rows.push(headerArray.join(','));
      } else {
        var dataArray = [];
        $(this).find("td").each(function () {
        str = $(this).text().replace(/"/g, '""');
        dataArray.push('"' + str + '"');
      });
      rows.push(dataArray.join(','));
    }
  });
    var csv = rows.join('\n');
    $("#TextBox1").val(csv);
    $("#TextBox1").slideDown("slow");
    evt.preventDefault();
  });
});
```

The ready() handler function first hides TextBox1 using the hide() method. This way, initially, when there is no CSV data, the TextBox is kept hidden. The main code that converts GridView data to CSV goes inside the click event handler of Button1. The click handler function declares a rows array to hold the combined CSV data for the header and the item rows of the GridView. The str variable holds the CSV data for one row of the grid. Then the find() method is used to find all the <tr> elements from GridView1. The each() method then iterates through all the table rows. An if statement checks whether a row is a header row or an item row by checking for <th> elements in a row. The presence of the <th> element indicates that it is a header row; otherwise, it is an item row.

If a row is the header row, the headerArray variable is declared to store header row values. All the <th> elements of the header row are found using the find() method and are iterated over using the each() method. Remember that this points to the element being iterated. If a column value contains a double quote character, two double quote characters are substituted using the text() and replace() methods. The resultant column value is then pushed into headerArray using the push() method. Notice that while a value is pushed, it is enclosed inside double quotes.

Once all the column values are pushed inside headerArray, the values from headerArray are pushed into the rows array by calling the join() method on headerArray, passing a comma (,) as a delimiter, and then calling push() on the rows array to store CSV from a row.

The else block contains similar code, but it searches for <td> elements instead of <th> elements and uses the dataArray variable to store values. Just like the header row, the item rows are also pushed to the rows array.

After all the GridView rows are converted to CSV, the elements from the rows array are joined using the newline character (\n). This way, you get a string that contains CSV data for all the rows. The CSV data from each row is separated by a newline character, and the value of TextBox1 is set to this string variable using the val() method. The TextBox is shown by applying a slide-down effect to it using the slideDown() method. To prevent the form submission, the preventDefault() method of the evt object is called.

Recipe 2: Implementing Ajax Based Paging

ASP.NET Web Forms can use data-bound controls such as GridView and DetailsView that are capable of displaying data in one or more pages. This default paging mechanism is a server-side technique and requires an extra postback. ASP.NET MVC applications need to implement paging on their own.

Using jQuery $.ajax(), you can implement paging in an HTML table in Web Forms as well as MVC. This second recipe discusses how paging can be implemented in ASP.NET MVC using Ajax techniques. The view that you develop in this recipe is shown in Figure 11-2.

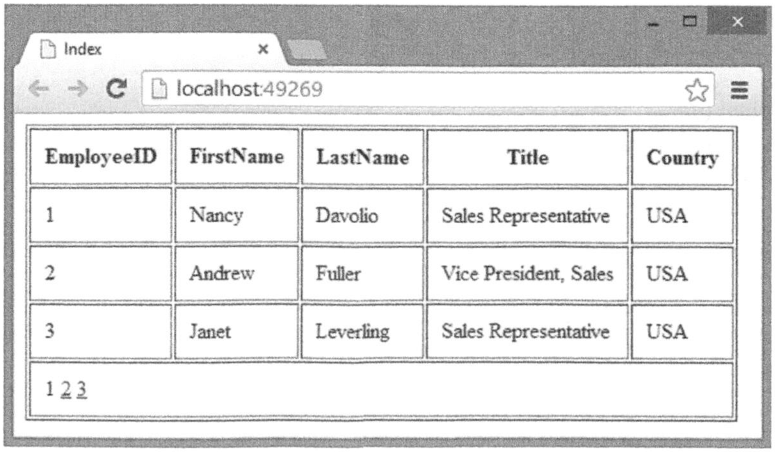

Figure 11-2. *Paging implemented for an HTML table*

As you can see, there is an HTML table that displays records from the Employees table. More importantly, the data is displayed in pages, with each page containing three records. At the bottom of the table is a pager that displays hyperlinks to navigate to different pages of data. The current page number is displayed as plain text, whereas other page numbers are displayed as hyperlinks.

To develop this application, create an empty ASP.NET MVC application and add an ADO.NET Entity Data Model for the Employees table in the Models folder. Then add the HomeController in the Controllers folder. The HomeController has the Index() action method by default. You need to add two more action methods: GetTotalRows() and GetPageData(). The former method returns the total number of rows in the Employees table, whereas the latter method returns Employee data belonging to a specified page. These methods are shown in Listing 11-3.

Listing 11-3. GetTotalRows() and GetPageData() Methods

```
[HttpPost]
public JsonResult GetTotalRows()
{
  NorthwindEntities db = new NorthwindEntities();
  return Json(db.Employees.Count());
}

[HttpPost]
public JsonResult GetPageData(int pageIndex, int pageSize)
{
  NorthwindEntities db = new NorthwindEntities();
  var data = (from e in db.Employees
              orderby e.EmployeeID
              select new {e.EmployeeID,
              e.FirstName, e.LastName,
              e.Title, e.Country })
              .Skip(pageIndex * pageSize)
              .Take(pageSize);
  return Json(data);
}
```

The GetTotalRows() action method is called from jQuery code, so it returns JsonResult to the caller. Inside, it instantiates the NorthwindEntities context and then calls the Count() method on its Employees DbSet. The returned count is converted into its JSON representation using the Json() method.

The GetPageData() action method also returns JsonResult and accepts two integer parameters: pageIndex and pageSize. The pageIndex parameter indicates a zero-based page number whose data is to be retrieved. The pageSize parameter indicates the number of records to be displayed per page. Inside, the method instantiates the NorthwindEntities context and executes a query against the Employees table.

Look at the query carefully: it selects the EmployeeID, FirstName, LastName, Title, and Country columns using projection and then uses the Skip() and Take() methods to retrieve only the records for a specified pageIndex. The Skip() method accepts a number indicating the number of elements to be skipped from the beginning of the results. In this case, (pageIndex * pageSize) is passed to Skip(). So if pageIndex is 1 (the second page) and pageSize is 3, Skip() will skip three elements. The Take() method then picks up the three elements, starting from the fourth element. Thus elements 4, 5, and 6 are selected. The selected data is returned to the caller in its JSON format by using the Json() method as before.

Now add the Index view to the project and place a table in it, as shown in Listing 11-4.

Listing 11-4. Index View Markup

```
<table id="tblGrid" border="1" cellpadding="10">
  <tr>
    <th>EmployeeID</th>
    <th>FirstName</th>
    <th>LastName</th>
    <th>Title</th>
    <th>Country</th>
  </tr>
  <tr>
    <td colspan="5"></td>
  </tr>
</table>
```

The tblGrid table consists of two rows: the first row contains the column headings, and the second row consists of a single cell spanning five columns. This cell is used to display the pager. At runtime, page data is retrieved using $.ajax(), and rows are inserted between the header and pager row.

Add a <script> reference to jQuery and a <script> block in the head section. The <script> block consists of a couple of variable declarations, two helper functions, and a ready() handler. The ready() handler and the variable declarations are shown in Listing 11-5.

Listing 11-5. Calling the GetTotalRows() Action Method

```
var pageSize = 3;
var pageCount = 0;

$(document).ready(function () {
  var options = {};
  options.url = "home/gettotalrows";
  options.type = "POST";
  options.dataType = "json";
  options.contentType = "application/json";
  options.success = function (count) {
    pageCount = count / pageSize;
    renderPager(0);
    getPageData(0);
  };
  options.error = function (xhr, status, err) { alert(err); };
  $.ajax(options);
});
```

The code from Listing 11-5 declares two variables—pageSize and pageCount—to store page size and total number of pages, respectively. The default value for pageSize is set to 3, and that for pageCount is set to 0. The pageSize variable is not changed further in the code, but pageCount is assigned a value returned from the GetTotalRows() method.

The ready() handler calls the GetTotalRows() action method using $.ajax(). It first creates an options object to store various settings to be used while making the Ajax request. The url property is set to /home/gettotalrows, and the type property is set to POST, indicating that a POST request will be made.

dataType and contentType are set to json and application/json, respectively. The success function receives the total number of records as the count parameter. The pageCount variable is then assigned value equal to (count / pageSize). Two helper functions, renderPager() and getPageData(), are then called. The renderPager()

function displays the pager row, whereas the getPageData() function retrieves the data needed to be displayed on a page. These functions accept the current page index as their parameter. Because the first page of data is to be initially displayed, 0 is passed to both of these functions (you will create these functions shortly). The error handler simply displays the error message, if any, to the user in an alert dialog. Finally, an Ajax call is made using the $.ajax() method by passing the options object as its parameter.

Next, add the renderPager() function to the <script> block, as shown in Listing 11-6.

Listing 11-6. renderPager() Function

```
function renderPager(currentPageIndex) {
  var html = '';
  for (var i = 0; i < pageCount; i++) {
    if (i == currentPageIndex) {
      html += "<span>" + (i + 1) + "</span> ";
    }
    else {
      html += "<a href='#' data-page-index='" + i + "'>" +
              (i + 1) + "</a> ";
    }
  }
  $("#tblGrid tr:last td").html(html);
  $("a").click(function (evt) {
    var pageIndex = $(this).data("pageIndex");
    getPageData(pageIndex);
    evt.preventDefault();
  });
}
```

The renderPager() function accepts the current page index as its parameter. Inside, a for loop is run from 0 to pageCount, and with each iteration, a page number is added to the html variable. If it matches the currentPageIndex, that page number is displayed using a <span> tag; otherwise, that page number is displayed as a hyperlink. Notice that the pager hyperlinks point to # because they don't actually take the user away from the page. Moreover, all the pager hyperlinks have the data-page-index attribute added.

The data-page-index attribute stores the zero-based index of a page, whereas the link text displays one-based page numbers. Once the html variable is ready with the pager markup, the last row of tblGrid is selected using the tr:last selector, and the generated pager markup is added to its cell using the html() method. Then a click event handler is wired to all the anchor elements (all the hyperlinks from the pager). The click event handler retrieves the value of the data-page-index attribute using the data() method and calls the getPageData() function by passing the value of data-page-index to it.

Now add the getPageData() method to the <script> block, as shown in Listing 11-7.

Listing 11-7. getPageData() method

```
function getPageData(index) {
  var options = {};
  options.url = "home/getpagedata";
  options.type = "POST";
  options.data = JSON.stringify(
                    { pageIndex: index, pageSize: this.pageSize }
                 );
  options.dataType = "json";
  options.contentType = "application/json";
```

```
  options.success = function (employees) {
    $("#tblGrid").find("tr:gt(0)").remove("tr:not(:last)");
    for (var i = 0; i < employees.length; i++) {
      var html = "<tr>";
      html += "<td>" + employees[i].EmployeeID + "</td>";
      html += "<td>" + employees[i].FirstName + "</td>";
      html += "<td>" + employees[i].LastName + "</td>";
      html += "<td>" + employees[i].Title + "</td>";
      html += "<td>" + employees[i].Country + "</td>";
      html += "</tr>";
      $("#tblGrid tr").eq(i).after(html);
    }
    renderPager(index);
  };
  options.error = function (xhr, status, err) { alert(err); };
  $.ajax(options);
}
```

The getPageData() function accepts the current page index as its parameter and displays data belonging to that page. The options object stores all the configuration settings needed while making an Ajax call to the GetPageData() action method. The url property points to /home/getpagedata, and the type is set to POST.

Remember that the GetPageData() action method accepts the current page index and page size as its parameters. Hence, the data property is set to an object in JSON format containing two properties: pageIndex and pageSize. The dataType and contentType properties are set to json and application/json, respectively.

The success function receives an array of JSON objects, and each element of that array represents an object with the EmployeeID, FirstName, LastName, Title, and Country properties. Inside, all the rows of the table except the header and pager row are removed by finding rows with the index greater than 0 (tr:gt(0)) and then removing all the rows that are not the last row (tr:not(:last)).

A for loop then iterates through the employee array, and each iteration generates an HTML markup for a table row. The resultant row is added to the tblGrid using the eq() and after() methods. The eq() method returns an element at a specified index, and the after() method inserts the supplied markup after that element. Thus rows are added one after the other between the header and pager rows. After the for loop, renderPager() is called to display the pager, considering the current page index. The error handler simply displays the error message, if any, to the user in an alert dialog. Finally, an Ajax call is made to the server using the $.ajax() method and passing the options object as its parameter.

Recipe 3: Client-Side Sorting in a Table

Sorting, as provided by data-bound controls such as a GridView, is a server-side feature. You can implement client-side sorting for an HTML table using the jQuery code. The client-side sorting doesn't need any postbacks because it sorts data on the client side. Figure 11-3 displays an MVC view that shows the client-side sorting in action.

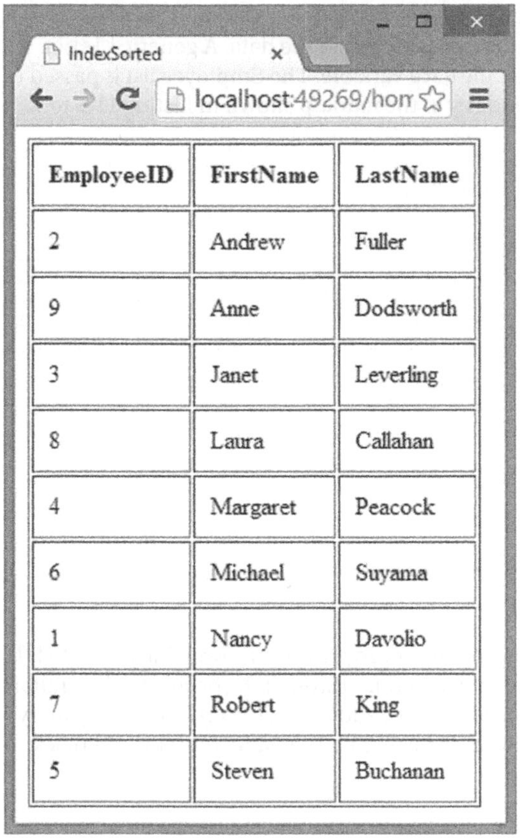

Figure 11-3. *Client-side sorting in action*

The table in Figure 11-3 shows the EmployeeID, FirstName, and LastName columns. You can click any of the column headings to sort the table on that column. For example, Figure 11-3 shows the table sorted on the FirstName column.

To begin developing this application, create an empty ASP.NET MVC application. Then add an ADO.NET Entity Data Model for Employees table in the Models folder as before. Also add HomeController to the Controllers folder. Modify the default Index() action method from the HomeController, as shown in Listing 11-8.

Listing 11-8. Index() Action Method

```
public ActionResult Index()
{
  NorthwindEntities db = new NorthwindEntities();
  var data = from e in db.Employees
                    orderby e.EmployeeID
                    select e;
  return View(data.ToList());
}
```

The Index() action method instantiates the NorthwindEntities context. A LINQ to Entities query is then constructed for retrieving Employees sorted on EmployeeID. This is the initial sorting of the data. A generic List of Employee objects is then obtained by calling the ToList() method on the data variable. The Employee list is passed to the Index view as its model. Now add the Index view to the project and key in the markup shown in Listing 11-9 to it.

Listing 11-9. Markup of Index View

```
<table id="tblGrid" border="1" cellpadding="10">
  <tr>
    <th>EmployeeID</th>
    <th>FirstName</th>
    <th>LastName</th>
  </tr>
  @foreach(var emp in Model){
    <tr>
      <td>@emp.EmployeeID</td>
      <td>@emp.FirstName</td>
      <td>@emp.LastName</td>
    </tr>
  }
</table>
```

As you can see, the tblGrid has one fixed header row. Depending on the Employee objects available in the Model, rows are dynamically added to the table with the help of a foreach loop that iterates through the Model. Each iteration generates a table row that displays EmployeeID, FirstName, and LastName. Next, add a <script> reference to jQuery and also add a <script> block in the head section. Write the code shown in Listing 11-10 inside the <script> block.

Listing 11-10. Sorting a Table

```
$(document).ready(function () {
  $("th").click(function () {
    var columnIndex = $(this).index();
    var tdArray = $(this).closest("table")
                          .find("tr td:nth-child(" + (columnIndex + 1) + ")");
    tdArray.sort(function (p, n) {
      var pData = $(p).text();
      var nData = $(n).text();
      return pData < nData ? -1 : 1;
    });
    tdArray.each(function () {
      var row = $(this).parent();
      $("#tblGrid").append(row);
    });
  });
});
```

The code shown in Listing 11-10 shows the ready() handler. Inside, the code wires a click event handler for all the table headings (<th>). The click event handler retrieves the zero-based index of the column whose heading is being clicked using the index() method. This index is stored in the columnIndex variable. Then all the <td> elements belonging to that column are retrieved. This is done by first retrieving the table reference using the closest() method on this and then using the find() method. The returned elements are stored in the tdArray variable.

The sort() method is called on tdArray, and a compare function is passed to the sort() method. The compare function receives array elements in pairs. If the compare function returns a value less than 0, p is sorted to a lower index than n. If the compare function returns 0, the position of p and n with respect to each other is kept unchanged. If the compare function returns a value greater than 0, p is sorted to a higher index than n. Inside the compare function, the text() method of the p and n elements are compared, and accordingly, 1 or -1 is returned. After calling the sort() method, tdArray holds the same elements but in a sorted manner.

The tdArray is then iterated upon by using the each() method. With each iteration, the parent row of the table cell under consideration is found by using the parent() method. Finally, the table row thus obtained is appended to tblGrid using the append() method.

Recipe 4: Creating Cascading Drop-Down Lists

Sometimes you need to display drop-down lists in your ASP.NET MVC views so that values in one drop-down list are dependent on the value selected in another drop-down list. The most common example of this is when countries and states drop-down lists are presented together, and, based on a selected country, you need to populate the states drop-down list. This recipe shows how such a cascading drop-down list can be developed using ASP.NET MVC and jQuery.

Figure 11-4 shows the view with two cascading drop-down lists.

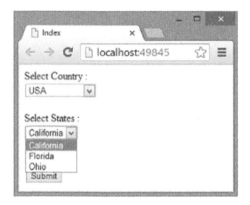

Figure 11-4. *Cascading drop-down lists showing countries and states*

As you can see, the view consists of two drop-down lists. The first drop-down list contains a list of countries along, with the first entry: Please Select. Initially, the states drop-down list is disabled because no country is selected. After a country is selected, the second drop-down list is populated with a list of states.

To begin developing this example, create an empty ASP.NET MVC application. Then add a new SQL Server database (SQL Express or LocalDB) to the App_Data folder and create two tables (Countries and States) in it. The Countries table has two columns, CountryId and CountryName; the States table has three columns: StateId, CountryId, and StateName.

Add some sample records in both tables for testing purpose. Then create an ADO.NET Entity Data Model for these two tables in the Models folder. Figure 11-5 shows this data model.

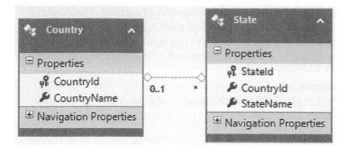

Figure 11-5. *Data model for Country and State tables*

Next, add HomeController to the Controllers folder and add the Index() method to it, as shown in Listing 11-11.

Listing 11-11. HomeController Index() Method

```
public ActionResult Index()
{

  CountryStateDbEntities db = new CountryStateDbEntities();
  var data = from c in db.Countries
                  orderby c.CountryName ascending
                  select c;
  List<Country> items = data.ToList();
  items.Insert(0, new Country() {CountryId=-1,CountryName="Please Select" });
  SelectList countries = new SelectList(items,"CountryId","CountryName");
  ViewData["countries"] = countries;
  return View();
}
```

This code instantiates the CountryStateDbEntities context and then constructs a query to fetch all the Country objects from the Countries DbSet. The Country objects are obtained as a generic List by calling the ToList() method on the data variable. An item is added at the beginning of the list that holds a CountryId of -1 and a CountryName of Please Select. This item doesn't come from the database and it doesn't represent a real country as such. You are adding it just for the sake of having the Please Select entry in the drop-down list.

You display the Country drop-down list using the DropDownList MVC HTML helper. To supply countries to the DropDownList helper, you create a SelectList object based on the country list you just created. The SelectList object is stored in the ViewData dictionary with the countries' key names.

The states will be fetched from the database using Ajax requests. Hence, you need an action method that returns JsonResult and that will be called from jQuery code. Listing 11-12 shows the GetStates() method that does just that.

Listing 11-12. GetStates() Action Method

```
public JsonResult GetStates(int countryid)
{
  CountryStateDbEntities db=new CountryStateDbEntities();
  var data = from s in db.States
                  where s.CountryId == countryid
                  orderby s.StateName
                  select new { s.StateId, s.StateName };
  return Json(data.ToList());
}
```

The GetStates() action method accepts a CountryId and returns a generic List of strings containing states for that country. Inside, it instantiates the CountryStateDbEntities context and prepares a query that fetches the StateName values from the States DbSet for a specified countryid. The data is selected as an anonymous object with two properties: StateId and StateName. The data is obtained as a generic List using the ToList() method. The Json() method is then used to convert this generic List to its JSON representation.

Now add the Index view to the project and key in the markup shown in Listing 11-13 in it.

Listing 11-13. Index View Markup

```
@using(Html.BeginForm()){
  <div>Select Country :</div>
  @Html.DropDownList("country", ViewData["countries"] as SelectList)
    <br /><br />
    <div>Select States :</div>
    <select id="state"></select>
}
```

The Index view uses the BeginForm() helper to define an HTML form. The DropDownList helper is used to render a <select> element for selecting a country. The first parameter of the DropDownList helper indicates the name of the resultant <select> element, whereas the second parameter indicates the SelectList that supplies data to the DropDownList. Notice that the countries ViewData variable needs type casting to SelectList because ViewData stores everything as an object. The DropDownList for states is rendered using the <select> element because items are added to this DropDownList on the fly.

Now, add a <script> reference to jQuery and also add a <script> block. Then add the code shown in Listing 11-14 to the <script> block.

Listing 11-14. Retrieving States Using $.ajax()

```
$(document).ready(function () {
  $("#state").prop("disabled", true);
  $("#country").change(function () {
    if ($("#country").val() != "-1") {
      var options = {};
      options.url = "/home/getstates";
      options.type = "POST";
      options.data = JSON.stringify({ countryid: $("#country").val() });
      options.dataType = "json";
      options.contentType = "application/json";
      options.success = function (states) {
        $("#state").empty();
        for (var i = 0; i < states.length; i++) {
          $("#state").append("<option value='" + states[i].StateId + "'>" +
                                      states[i].StateName + "</option>");

        }
        $("#state").prop("disabled", false);
      };
      options.error = function () { alert("Error retrieving states!"); };
      $.ajax(options);
    }
```

293

```
    else {
      $("#state").empty();
      $("#state").prop("disabled", true);
    }
  });
});
```

The code in Listing 11-14 shows the ready() handler function, which initially disables the state DropDownList by setting its disabled property to true with the prop() method. It then wires a change event handler to the country DropDownList. This event handler gets called whenever the selection in the country DropDownList changes. Inside, the change handler checks the value being selected in the country DropDownList. If the value is anything other than -1 (remember that -1 represents the Please Select item of the drop-down list), an Ajax call is made to the GetStates() method to retrieve the states.

The settings for making the Ajax request are stored in the options object. The url property points to /home/getstates. The type property is set to POST. The GetStates() method accepts countryid as a parameter. This parameter value is picked up from the country DropDownList using the val() method and then passed to the GetStates() action method in JSON format.

The dataType and contentType properties are set to json and application/json, respectively. The success function receives the return value of GetStates() as its parameter. Inside, it first empties the states DropDownList and then adds states from the array to the states DropDownList by iterating through the states array. The states are added as an <option> element.

The value of the <option> element being added is set to the StateId property; it displays StateName to the user. Once the states are filled in, the states DropDownList is enabled by setting its disabled property to false using the prop() method. The error handler simply displays an error message, if any, to the user in an alert dialog. Finally, an Ajax request is made to the server by using $.ajax() and by passing the options object as its parameter.

If the country DropDownList contains Please Select, the states DropDownList is emptied and disabled.

Recipe 5: Creating an Autocomplete Text Box

When you expect a user to specify a fixed value from a set of values (for example, one country from a set of countries), you normally use <select> to display a list of valid options to the user. However, sometimes you want the user to enter a value or select a value from a list. For example, you may want a user to enter a search phrase into a search box of your web site. Considering the diversity of the data being entered, you can't expect the user to pick a search phrase from a fixed set of values. Hence you can't use the <select> element in such cases because it element doesn't allow you to enter values.

An autocomplete text box can help. An autocomplete text box is an enhanced text box that allows you to enter data into it and pick a value from a set of values. As you start typing, a list of options is presented, based on the text you entered so far. You can then pick a value from the presented options or continue entering it.

In this recipe, you develop an autocomplete text box that resembles Figure 11-6.

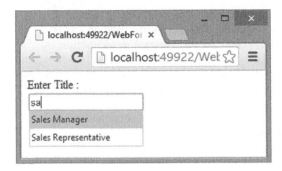

Figure 11-6. *Autocomplete text box in action*

The Web Form shown in Figure 11-6 consists of a Label and a TextBox. As you start typing in the text box, a list is displayed with options starting with the text you entered. You can then pick a value from the list or continue entering the value.

To develop this application, begin by creating an empty ASP.NET Web Forms project. Then add an ADO.NET Entity Data Model for the Employees table to the project. Place a Label control and a TextBox control on the Web Form so that it resembles Figure 11-6. Add a <datalist> element to the form, as shown in Listing 11-15.

Listing 11-15. Web Form Markup

```
<form id="form1" runat="server">
  <asp:Label ID="Label1" runat="server" Text="Enter Title :"></asp:Label>
  <br />
  <asp:TextBox ID="TextBox1" runat="server" list="titles"></asp:TextBox>
  <datalist id="titles"></datalist>
</form>
```

As you can see, the Web Form markup contains a <datalist> element in addition to Label and TextBox markup. The HTML5 <datalist> element allows you to associate a list of options with a TextBox. Notice that the TextBox1 list attribute is set to the ID of the <datalist> element (titles). You can specify values in the <datalist> by using <options> elements.

In this example, you populate the options dynamically by making Ajax requests to the server, so <datalist> is kept empty.

Switch to the code-behind file of the Web Form and add a web method, as shown in Listing 11-16.

Listing 11-16. Web Method Returning datalist Options

```
[WebMethod]
public static List<string> GetTitles(string title)
{
  NorthwindEntities db = new NorthwindEntities();
  var data = (from e in db.Employees
              where e.Title.StartsWith(title)
              orderby e.Title
              select e.Title).Distinct();
  return data.ToList();
}
```

The GetTitles() method accepts a string parameter (title) that indicates the text entered in a text box. It returns a List of strings that start with the specified title text. Notice that GetTitles() is a static method and is decorated with the [WebMethod] attribute. This enables you to call GetTitles() using jQuery Ajax techniques.

Inside, the code instantiates the NorthwindEntities context and prepares a query that fetches Title values from the Employees table that start with the supplied title. Notice the use of the StartsWith() method to filter the titles that begin with a specified text. Also notice the use of the Distinct() method to avoid any duplicate Title values. The ToList() method obtains the query results as a List of strings.

Add a <script> reference to the jQuery library and also add a <script> block in the head section of the Web Form. Then add the code shown in Listing 11-17 in the <script> block.

Listing 11-17. Calling GetTitles() Using $.ajax()

```
$(document).ready(function () {
  $("#TextBox1").on("input", function (evt) {
    var options = {};
    options.url = "WebForm1.aspx/gettitles";
    options.data = JSON.stringify({title:$(evt.target).val()});
    options.type = "POST";
    options.dataType = "json";
    options.contentType = "application/json";
    options.success = function (result) {
      $("#titles").empty();
      for (var i = 0; i < result.d.length; i++) {
        $("#titles").append("<option>" + result.d[i] + "</option>");
      }
    };
    options.error = function (xhr, status, err) { alert(err); };
    $.ajax(options);
  });
});
```

The code consists of a ready() handler that wires an input event handler to TextBox1. The input event is raised whenever text is entered into a TextBox. The on() method binds the input event handler to TextBox1. Inside, the options object stores various settings needed to make an Ajax request.

The url property points to WebForm1.aspx/gettitles. The type property is set to POST, indicating that a POST request will be made. The data property contains the value of the title parameter of GetTitles() in JSON format. Notice that the value entered in the text box is obtained using the val() method called on evt.target. The dataType and contentType properties are set to json and application/json, respectively.

The success handler function receives the matched titles as its parameter. It then empties the titles datalist using the empty() method. A for loop iterates through the titles returned by the GetTitles() method and adds <option> elements in the datalist using the append() method. Displaying the <datalist> when a user starts entering text in the TextBox is taken care of by the browser. The error handler simply displays an error message, if any, in an alert dialog. Finally, an Ajax call is made to the server by using the $.ajax() method and by passing the options object as its parameter.

Recipe 6: Uploading Files

One common task in web applications is allowing users to upload files from the client machine to the server. Usually files are uploaded along with a form submission. However, you can also accomplish that task using jQuery and Ajax. In such cases, you can allow a user to select files using the FileUpload server control of ASP.NET and then upload those files to the server through an Ajax request to a generic handler.

This recipe illustrates how to do this. The Web Form that you'll develop in this section is shown in Figure 11-7.

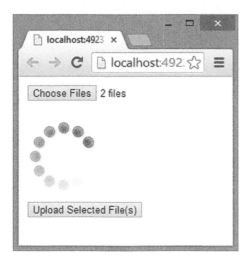

Figure 11-7. *Web Form for uploading files to the server*

The Web Form consists of a `FileUpload` server control. You can select one or more files using this control and then click the Upload Selected File(s) button. During the upload operation, which can be a long-running task, a progress indicator is displayed to the user with an animated GIF image. Once the upload operation completes, the progress indicator is hidden, and a success message is displayed to the user.

To develop this application, begin by creating an empty ASP.NET Web Forms application. Then add a new Web Form to the project and design it as shown in Figure 11-7. The markup of the Web Form is shown in Listing 11-18.

Listing 11-18. Web Form Markup

```
<form id="form1" runat="server">
  <asp:FileUpload ID="FileUpload1" runat="server" AllowMultiple="true" />
  <br /><br />
  <asp:Image ID="progress" runat="server"
   ImageUrl="~/images/progress.gif" />
  <asp:Button ID="Button1" runat="server"
   Text="Upload Selected File(s)" />
</form>
```

The Web Form consists of a `FileUpload` server control. The `AllowMultiple` property of the `FileUpload` control is set to `true` so that multiple files can be selected by the user. The `ImageUrl` property of the Image control is set to `~/images/progress.gif`–an animated GIF image. The `Button` control is used to initiate the file upload operation.

Now add a `<script>` reference to jQuery and also add a `<script>` block in the head section of the Web Form. Then write the code shown in Listing 11-19 to the `<script>` block.

Listing 11-19. Uploading Files Using jQuery

```
$(document).ready(function () {
  $("#progress").hide();
  $("#Button1").click(function (evt) {
    var fileUpload = $("#FileUpload1").get(0);
    var files = fileUpload.files;
    var data = new FormData();
    for (var i = 0; i < files.length; i++) {
```

```
        data.append(files[i].name, files[i]);
      }
      var options = {};
      options.url = "FileUploadHandler.ashx";
      options.type - "POST";
      options.data = data;
      options.contentType = false;
      options.processData = false;
      options.beforeSend = function () {
        $("#progress").show();
      };
      options.success = function (result) { alert(result); };
      options.error = function (err) { alert(err.statusText); };
      options.complete = function () {
        $("#progress").hide();
      }
      $.ajax(options);
      evt.preventDefault();
  });
});
```

As soon as the page is loaded in the browser, the ready() handler hides the progress indicator image using the hide() method. It then wires the click event handler of Button1. The code inside the click event handler gets the FileUpload control by using the ID selector. Calling the get() method returns the underlying DOM element. The files property of the fileUpload object returns a list of files selected by the user. Then a FormData object is created to store the form data for sending it to the server. The FormData object allows you to add arbitrary name-value pairs that can be sent to the server.

A for loop iterates through the files array; with each iteration, a file is added to the FormData object using append() method. The first parameter of append() is the name assigned to the value being added, and the second parameter is the value itself. In this case, file name is added as the name parameter, and the actual file contents are added as the second parameter.

Once the FormData object is ready with all the files added to it, the options object is created with various settings for making an Ajax request. The url property points to a generic handler: FileUploadHandler.ashx. (You'll develop FileUploadHandler.ashx shortly.)

The type of request is specified as POST using the type property. The data property is set to the data FormData object you created earlier. Note that this time you aren't sending data in JSON format. Files being uploaded can contain data in any form (text, binary, and so on), and that data must be submitted to the server as is. That's why the processData and contentType properties are set to false. Setting these properties to false ensures that these properties don't assume their default values of true and "application/x-www-form-urlencoded", respectively, during the form-submission process.

The beforeSend, success, error, and complete handler functions are wired. The beforeSend handler is called just before making the Ajax request. Inside the beforeSend handler, the progress indicator image is made visible by calling the show() method. This way, as soon as the Ajax request is made, the animated GIF starts showing the progress indicator.

The success handler simply displays the message returned by the generic handler in an alert dialog. The error handler displays an error message, if any, in an alert dialog. The complete handler is called when the Ajax request completes (with or without errors) and hides the progress indicator image using the hide() method. Finally, an Ajax request is made to the FileUploadHandler.ashx by using $.ajax() and by passing the options object as its parameter.

Now add a new generic handler to the project and name it FileUploadHandler.ashx. Then modify its ProcessRequest() method as shown in Listing 11-20.

Listing 11-20. Saving Uploaded File to the Server

```
public void ProcessRequest(HttpContext context)
{
  if (context.Request.Files.Count > 0)
  {
    HttpFileCollection files = context.Request.Files;
    for (int i = 0; i < files.Count;i++ )
    {
      HttpPostedFile file = files[i];
      string fname = context.Server.MapPath
                        ("~/uploads/" + file.FileName);
      file.SaveAs(fname);
    }
  }
  context.Response.ContentType = "text/plain";
  context.Response.Write("File(s) Uploaded Successfully!");
}
```

The code inside the ProcessHandler() method does the job of saving the files submitted by the client on the server. It first checks whether the incoming request contains any files by checking the Count property of the context. Request.Files collection. If the count is greater than 0, the files variable stores a reference to the Files collection. Notice that the files object is of type HttpFileCollection. Each element of HttpFileCollection is of type HttpPostedFile.

A for loop then iterates through the Files collection, and with each iteration the file under consideration is saved to the Uploads folder of the application. Although not incorporated in this example, in a real-world situation you should consider performing security checks (maximum size, permissible file types, virus scanning, and so on) on the files being uploaded. This is done using the SaveAs() method of the HttpPostedFile object.

Notice that the full physical path of a file is obtained by appending the FileName to the path returned by the Server.MapPath() method. Once all the files are saved on the server, a success message is sent to the client using the Response.Write() method.

Summary

This chapter covered several jQuery recipes that are very useful and tap the power of client-side and server-side processing. Although jQuery is a JavaScript library, it can be meshed with server-side code using Ajax techniques. A modern web application developed in ASP.NET needs to harness the power of client-side scripting as well as server-side processing. And jQuery allows you to do that easily. This book covered a wide spectrum of jQuery features, and this final chapter showed you how various features of jQuery can go hand in hand to handle a more complex task.

Learning any programming language or library involves understanding the language syntax and features and also the practical experience of using those features. This book showed you the jQuery library so that you get a good understanding of its features and constructs. It also presented many real-world examples to make the topic being discussed more relevant and practical. With this knowledge under your belt, you can leverage the full power and flexibility of this popular JavaScript library.

■ ■ ■

Learning Resources

Official jQuery Projects Websites
jQuery Learning center

http://learn.jquery.com

jQuery API Documentation

http://api.jquery.com

jQuery UI Documentation

http://api.jqueryui.com

jQuery Mobile Documentation

http://api.jquerymobile.com

jQuery Official Blog

http://blog.jquery.com

Author's Website
Articles on ASP.NET, HTML5 & jQuery

http://www.binaryintellect.net

Other Websites

JavaScript on the Mozilla Developer Network

`https://developer.mozilla.org/en-US/docs/Web/JavaScript`

Learning jQuery

`http://www.learningjquery.com`

jQuery For Designers

`http://jqueryfordesigners.com`

The jQuery Plugin Registry

`http://plugins.jquery.com`

Index

Get the eBook for only $10!

Now you can take the weightless companion with you anywhere, anytime. Your purchase of this book entitles you to 3 electronic versions for only $10.

This Apress title will prove so indispensible that you'll want to carry it with you everywhere, which is why we are offering the eBook in 3 formats for only $10 if you have already purchased the print book.

Convenient and fully searchable, the PDF version enables you to easily find and copy code—or perform examples by quickly toggling between instructions and applications. The MOBI format is ideal for your Kindle, while the ePUB can be utilized on a variety of mobile devices.

Go to www.apress.com/promo/tendollars to purchase your companion eBook.

CPSIA information can be obtained at www.ICGtesting.com
Printed in the USA
LVOW03s1650020514

384228LV00010B/422/P